# The Burdens of Empire

Throughout human history, empires have been far more constant and widespread, and the source of far more anguished political speculation, than nation states have ever been. But despite the long history of debate and the recent resurgence of interest in empires and imperialism, no one seems very clear as to what exactly an empire is. *The Burdens of Empire* strives to offer not only a definition but also a working description. This book examines how empires were conceived by those who ruled them and lived under them; it looks at the relations, real or imagined, between the imperial metropolis (when one existed) and its outlying provinces or colonies; and it asks how the laws that governed the various parts and ethnic groups, of which all empires were made, were conceived and interpreted. Anthony Pagden argues that the evolution of the modern concept of the relationship between states, and in particular the modern conception of international law, cannot be understood apart from the long history of European empire building.

Anthony Pagden is Distinguished Professor in the Departments of Political Science and History at the University of California, Los Angeles. He has been a Fellow of Merton College, Oxford; Senior Research Fellow of the Warburg Institute, London; Professor of History at the European University Institute, Florence; University Reader in Intellectual History and Fellow of King's College, Cambridge; and the Harry C. Black Professor of History at Johns Hopkins University. He is the author of more than a dozen books, many of which have been translated into a number of European and Asian languages. His most recent publications include *Worlds and War: The 2,500-Year Struggle between East and West* (2008) and *The Enlightenment: And Why It Still Matters* (2013). He has also written for the *New Republic*, the *National Interest*, the *New York Times*, the *Los Angeles Times*, *El País* (Spain), *Il Sole 24 Ore* (Italy), the *London Review of Books*, and the *Times Literary Supplement*.

# The Burdens of Empire

## 1539 to the Present

ANTHONY PAGDEN
*University of California, Los Angeles*

CAMBRIDGE
UNIVERSITY PRESS

# CAMBRIDGE
## UNIVERSITY PRESS

32 Avenue of the Americas, New York NY 10013-2473, USA

Cambridge University Press is part of the University of Cambridge.

It furthers the University's mission by disseminating knowledge in the pursuit of education, learning and research at the highest international levels of excellence.

www.cambridge.org
Information on this title: www.cambridge.org/9780521188289

First published 2015

*A catalogue record for this publication is available from the British Library*

*Library of Congress Cataloguing in Publication data*
Pagden, Anthony.
The burdens of empire : 1539 to the present / Anthony Pagden
(University of California, Los Angeles).
pages cm
ISBN 978-0-521-19827-1 (Hardback) – ISBN 978-0-521-18828-9 (Paperback)
1. Imperialism–History.   2. Europe–Territorial expansion–History.
3. Europe–Colonies–History.   4. Colonization–History.   5. Ethnic relations–History.
6. History, Modern.   7. Imperialism–Philosophy.   8. International relations–Philosophy.
9. International law–Philosophy.   I. Title.
JC359.P273 2015
325´.32094–dc23
2014035122

ISBN 978-0-521-18828-9 Paperback

*quae cum pulcherrima tota est For Giulia*

# Contents

# Preface

The essays in this book represent all that I wish to preserve of what I have written on the political and legal theory of empire over the past fourteen years. All have been extensively revised and rewritten to take account of recent scholarship and to give them an overall coherence as a single volume. Some now bear so little resemblance to their originals as to constitute new essays, and I have changed their titles accordingly. Chapter 6 appears here for the first time.

Some of the arguments presented in Chapter 1 were first used in "Conquest and the Just War: The 'School of Salamanca' and the 'Affair of the Indies'" in Sankar Muthu ed., *Empire and Modern Political Thought* (Cambridge: Cambridge University Press, 2012).

A shorter version of Chapter 2 was first published as "Gentili, Vitoria and the Fabrication of a 'Natural Law of Nations'" in Benedict Kingsbury and Benjamin Straumann eds., *The Roman Foundations of the Law of Nations: Alberico Gentili and the Justice of Empire* (Oxford: Oxford University Press, 2010), 340–61.

An earlier version of Chapter 3 first appeared as "Ethnos, Race and Empire: The Fabrication of Identity in the Early-Modern World" in Miriam Eliav-Feldon, Benjamin Isaac, and Joseph Ziegler eds., *The Origins of Racism in the West* (Cambridge: Cambridge University Press, 2009), 292–312.

Chapter 4 draws heavily on "Law, Colonization, Legitimation and the European Background" in *The Cambridge History of Law in America* (Cambridge University Press, 2008) and on "The Christian Tradition" in Allen Buchanan and Margaret Moore eds., *State, Nations and Borders: The Ethics of Making Boundaries* (Cambridge: Cambridge University Press, 2003), 103–26.

Chapter 5 relies in part on "Commerce and Conquest: Hugo Grotius and Serafim de Freitas on the Freedom of the Seas," *Mare liberum,* 20 (2000) 33–55.

Chapter 7 is a modified and revised version of "The Law of Continuity: Conquest and Settlement within the Limits of Kant's International Right" in Katrin Flikschuh and Lea Ypi eds., *Kant and Colonialism: Historical and Critical Perspectives* (Oxford: Oxford University Press, 2014).

Some of the ideas presented in Chapter 8 first appeared in "Il commercio, la conquista e la critica illuministica dell'impero" in Ruth Ben Ghiat ed., *Gli imperi: dall'antichita all'eta contemporanea* (Bologna: Il Mulino, 2009), 191–214.

An earlier version of Chapter 9 first appeared in *Political Theory*, 31 (2003), 171–99.

# Acknowledgements

I have incurred a great many debts in the course of writing and revising the essays in this volume. Above all I wish to thank David Armitage and Jennifer Pitts who were kind enough to read through the entire text at an early stage. Their characteristically perspicacious observations saved me from numerous errors, and their suggestions have contributed greatly to whatever overall coherence the volume might now possess. David Lupher has been very helpful in guiding me through a number of the Latin sources I have used and has saved me from a number of errors of interpretation. Clifford Ando, Benjamin Straumann, and Aldo Schiavone have been generous in answering my questions about the Roman law. I would also like to thank Sanjay Subrahmanyam, Theo Christov, Craig Yirush, Sankar Muthu, José Maria Hernandez, Fernando Cervantes, Kal Raustiala, Stuart Banner, Joshua Simon, Roberto Farneti, Anoush Terjanian, and Joan-Pau Rubies Rubiés Mirabet who, in their various, and sometimes unforeseen, ways, have contributed greatly to the development of these essays. Earlier versions of some were given as lectures or seminar papers to meetings in Santiago de Compostela; the École des Hautes EÉcoletudes en Sciences Sociales; Université Paris 7–Denis Diderot; Department of Political Science, McGill University; Department of Political Science, Yale University; Khan Liberal Arts Institute, Smith College; the European University Institute, Florence; Le Centre canadien d'études allemandes et européennes, Université de Montréal; and Blackfrairs Hall, Oxford. I would like to thank the various participants on these occasions for their often trenchant criticisms.

My thanks also to Robert Dreesen at Cambridge University Press for all his encouragement, to Elizabeth Janetschek and Paul Smolenski, also at the Press, for having steered this book so skilfully through the production process, and to my copy editor, Susan Kauffman at PETT Fox, Inc., for tidying up the final manuscript.

My most enduring debt is to Giulia Sissa, my wife, my friend, my colleague, who, in addition to always being there, has watched carefully over my often stumbling attempts at understanding the Ancients, and most of life itself. (She also chose the image for the cover.) To her, as always, this book is gratefully dedicated.

# Introduction

## *Anatomy of Empire from Rome to Washington*

I

*Le droit a ses époques*
"Pascal"

Of all the terms in the political lexicon, "empire" is one of the most elusive and among the most contentious. Achaemenid Persia, Ancient Macedonia, Rome, Parthia Byzantium, Ottoman Turkey, China, Vishanagar, Assyria, Elam, Urartu, Benin, Maori New Zealand, Peru and Mexico, Nazi Germany, the Soviet Union – even the United States, and the European Union (EU) – to name but a few, have all been described as "empires".[1] What all of these – other than either the United States or the EU – share in common with one another, apart from the obvious fact that they no longer exist, are four things: they were all (relatively) large; they were all believed to be, either actually or potentially, universal; they were all states in which one ethnic or tribal group, by one means or another, ruled over several others; and for the most part, most of them have been acquired by conquest.[2] The belief that a people has an inalienable right to be governed by one of its own own kind, whether real or imagined, – what the anthropologist Marshall Sahlins once called the "quaint Western concept that domination is a spontaneous expression of the nature of society" – is relatively recent and exclusively of European origin. "Eat-me" says the Fijian commoner in deference to his chief, because he knows that all rulership is a form of cannibalism and that the first rule of cannibalism is that no one eats his own kind.[3]

Empires are now no more. But they have always been a more frequent, more extensive, human experience than tribal territories or modern nations have ever been. Rome lasted for some 600 years in the west and for over a millennium longer in the East. The Ottoman Empire lasted for more than 600 years, and the Chinese, although governed by successive dynasties, for more than 2,000.[4] And endurance was not all. Empires also covered far

I

larger areas and included far larger populations than any previous or subsequent state forms. By the time he died in 323 BCE, Alexander the Great was the ruler of an empire – ramshackle and transitory though it was – which reached from the Adriatic to the Indus, from the Punjab to the Sudan. At its height in the second century CE the Roman Empire reached all the way from the Atlas Mountains in the south to Scotland in the north, and from the Indus valley in the east to the Atlantic in the west, a territory of about 5 million square miles (the continental United States is a little more than 3.5 million) with a population which has been estimated at about 55 million. In 1400, the empire of "Timur the Lame" – Christopher Marlowe's Tamburlaine – ran from the Black Sea to the gates of Kashgar. The lands of the Ottoman Sultanate, which in the thirteenth century had been a small Anatolian province of *ghazi* ("holy") warriors sandwiched between the Byzantine Empire and the Seljuk Turks, had by the beginning of the sixteenth century extended itself to more than 10,000 kilometers from Hungary to Central Asia. By the time the armies of Francisco Pizarro reached Peru in 1532, the domain of the Inka, which in the late fifteenth century had been limited to the region around Cuzco, stretched north though what are today Peru, Ecuador, and Columbia and south into Bolivia, northern Chile, and northwest Argentina. In 1923 the British Empire, territorially the most extensive ever, occupied some 21 million square miles.[5] By comparison most of the world's nation states are barely more than a century old and, with the exception of post-Soviet Russia and the United States, relatively small; most of them have also emerged out of the ruins of one kind of empire or another.

Yet, while large, multiethnic states may have been the common experience of much of mankind, the concept of an "empire", and of something which in the nineteenth century came to be called "imperialism", is largely confined to Europe and Asia. The word "empire" itself, and all its variants – "emperor", "imperialism", and so on – derive from the Latin word *imperium*, which originally described nothing more than the sphere of executive authority exercised by the Roman magistrates. *Imperator* "emperor" was originally a generic term for all Roman commanders, and it was not until the second century CE, and not consistently even then, that it became restricted to the supreme ruler of the Roman world – who also had other equally significant titles, *Augustus* "Revered One", *Princeps*, "Chief man of the state" *Pater Patriae*, "Father of the State", and *Caesar*, which was originally a family name and from which both the German Kaiser and the Russian Czar derive.

The conception of an "empire" in Western Europe, and all that that subsequently came to imply, was essentially Roman creation. As the English historian J. R. Seeley remarked in 1883, with characteristic nineteenth-century hyperbole, "this great phenomenon [the Roman Empire] stands out in the very centre of human history, and may be called the foundation of the present civilization of mankind".[6] Roman history offered a model (although in practice it was often very poorly understood) for all the later empires of Western Europe with which the essays in this volume are concerned. This is most obvious in the grandiose allusions to Roman imperial architecture with which the capital cities of Europe, London, Madrid, Vienna, Berlin, and, of course, Washington are filled; and in the adoption of romanticized Roman dress on the statutes of nineteenth-century imperial functionaries. However, it went far deeper than that. Above all the term empire designated an extended polity bound by a body of law. When in 1788, the great Indologist, linguist, and jurist Sir William Jones began the Herculean task of harmonizing the various legal systems which prevailed in India, he told the governor-general Lord Cornwallis that his new code would give to the people of the British Raj "security for the due administration of justice among them", and he compared this to the great codes of the Roman Law, which in the sixth century CE the Roman – Byzantine – Emperor Justinian "gave to his Greek and Roman subjects".[7] For Jones, and for most of its servants, the "British Empire" was, like its Roman antecedent, above all, a legal order.

The law was the central component of what the first–second century theologian Tertullian called *Romanitas*, "Romaness", something which was more or less coterminous with what, ever since the eighteenth century, has been called "civilization": the lure of a more desirable, more comfortable, more stable, as well as a more just, way of life than any which the "barbarians" who came under Roman rule could have enjoyed beyond the limits of the Roman world. To survive for long, all empires have had to win over their conquered populations. The Romans had learned this very early in their history.[8] "An empire", declared the Roman historian Livy at the end of the first century BCE, "remains powerful so long as its subjects rejoice in it."[9] And rejoice in it they very largely did. When the Western Empire fell, it was destroyed by recently arrived Gothic tribes from its northern and eastern borders. None of those who lived at the core of the Empire – the Gauls, the Dacians, the Iberians, and even the more distant Britons – chose rebellion as the Asians and Africans under later European rulers would do. And even the Goths did not wish to bring an end to Roman rule so much as to appropriate it for themselves. "An able Goth wants to be like a Roman", Theodoric king of the Ostrogoths once remarked. "only a poor Roman would want to be like a Goth."[10] Rome had had a lot to offer its conquered populations: architecture, baths, and the ability to bring fresh water from distant hills or to heat the rooms of marble-lined rooms in villas in the wilds of Northumberland. The most desirable of all, however, was citizenship – a concept which, in its recognizably modern form, the Romans had invented and which, ever since the early days of the Republic, had been the main ideological prop of Roman world. Not all of Rome's subject peoples wished for these things; but if a substantial number had not done so, the empire could not have survived as long as it did. The Romans, admitted the English liberal John Stuart Mill in 1859, "were not the most clean-handed of conquerors". Yet, he went on to ask, "Would it have been better for Gaul and Spain, Numidia and Dacia never to have formed part of the Roman Empire?"[11] For Mill, as for the generations of apologists for empire who preceded – and succeeded – him, the clear answer was no.

Rome was, as all successful empires have had to be, an essentially open society. She had, observed an admiring Niccolò Machiavelli, created a world empire precisely by "freely admitting strangers to her privileges and honours".[12] He was echoing a vision of the empire which the Romans themselves had carefully cultivated since the days of the late Republic. When in 212 CE the emperor Caracalla granted citizenship to all the free inhabitants of the empire, a common bond was created, at least in theory, which extended the Roman *civitas* to all the many peoples of which the empire was composed. "Those within the Roman World", declared the "Antonine Constitution" as it is known, "have become Roman citizens". This was, however, far from being an unmixed blessing. In his great treatise on the laws of war, *De iure belli ac pacis* of 1625, the seventeenth-century Dutch humanist Hugo Grotius (whom we shall meet again in Chapter 5) offered a rather less benign view of the ideal of Roman citizenship. There were, he argued, two forms of what he called "moderation in obtaining empire". The first – the Roman – was to attempt to make a "common county of all that were under its dominion". The second, "the method favoured by Cyrus and Alexander the Great" was "to leave the conquered, either kings or people, their own government".[13]

In Grotius' account, what Caracalla had intended was that all those males who "lived under the dominion of the Roman empire" should be "made capable of receiving the Honours and enjoying the privileges of real citizens of Rome". What, however, it had *not* meant was that the "spring and original of empire was in any other people except the people of Rome". Or, as the historian Edmund Gibbon later remarked, what he called sarcastically, "the prodigality of Caracalla" had created a situation in which "reluctant provincials were compelled to assume the vain title and the real obligations of Roman citizens".[14] Whereas Alexander and Cyrus had supposedly divided sovereignty, *imperium*, with the peoples they conquered, the Antonine Constitution had simply imposed citizenship without consent, thus transforming what, under the Republic had been the guarantor of individual freedoms, into the extension of the unquestioned imperium of the Caesars. From there it was but a brief step to declaring that Rome was the "common homeland" of the entire world. Citizenship, however, had also performed the miracle of transforming all those who came under its law into Romans while at the same time leaving them in full possession of their previous ethnic, religious, and cultural identities. Tertullian warned those Christians who might have been tempted to see their new faith as a reason for political dissent: "This empire of which you are servants is a lordship over citizens, not a tyranny."[15]

Modern law derives ultimately from Roman law, and Roman law was created, in large part, to serve the needs of a multiethnic empire. The very vocabulary of citizenship itself carried with it the idea of a society which was always ready to accept outsiders.[16] The Latin word *civis* ("citizen") derives from an Indo-European root connoting the idea of the family and, in particular, of an outsider admitted into the family – in other words, a guest. It is perhaps, therefore, best translated not as "citizen" but as "fellow citizen". A *civis* was a member of the *civitas*, and although this was also a term used to describe the whole Roman world, it was not so much a place as a body of rights and duties: a construct of law. It was in the formulation of the great Roman poet of the first century CE Virgil – Dante's "poet of Empire" – the place where the "wild races have been gathered together by Saturn and given laws".[17] As such it could only ever be available to the whole of mankind. "In all your empire all paths are open to all", the Greek orator Aelius Aristides told the people of Rome in CE 143 or 144. "No one worthy of rule or trust remains an alien, but a civil community of the World has been established as a Free Republic under one, the best, ruler and teacher of order; and all come together as into a common civic centre; in order to receive each man his due."[18] The emperor Antoninus Pius – whom Aristides may have been addressing – was not only "Lord of all the World", *Dominus totius orbis* – a title he was the first to adopt – he was also, as he said of himself, "guardian (*custos*) of the world".

All the later European empires did the best they could to follow at least part of the example Rome had set them. The French and even the Spanish – who for most Europeans had, by the late sixteenth century, emerged as the paradigm example of all that a true empire should *not* be – had attempted to create something resembling a single society governed by a single body of law.

Rome may have been exceptional, and Aelius himself was surely exaggerating. But although the Romans were the only ones to have developed a legal concept of citizenship as we understand it today, they were by no means unique in their inclusiveness. Most of the early empires were similarly multicultural. All made attempts to incorporate the various groups of which their empires were made into some larger cosmopolitan whole. The Achaemenid Persians governed through local rulers, called Satraps ("holders of power") – a system also adopted by Alexander – and they commanded armies made up of conscripts from all across Asia. The Ottomans, although there was never a Sultan who was not descended from Osman, the founder of the dynasty, relied heavily on non-Turcoman, and sometimes even non-Muslim, subjects; and although, in accordance with Islamic law, all those who refused to convert to Islam had to pay special taxes and wear distinctive clothing, they were generally free, under what was called the *millet* system, to live by their own laws and held responsible to their own religious communities.

Those empires, or would-be empires, which made no attempt to involve their subject peoples into some kind of larger political community, could not hope to last for long. The Third Reich – possibly the shortest-lived empire in history – is a case in point. Had Hitler been willing to involve the "collaborators" throughout Europe – of which there were many – into positions of power, had he chosen to rule through, rather than over, his conquered peoples, the outcome of the Second World War might have been very different.

Contrary to popular image, most empires were, in fact, for most of their histories, fragile structures, always dependent on their subject peoples for survival. Universal citizenship was not created out of generosity. It was created out of need. "What else proved fatal to Sparta and Athens in spite of their power in arms," the emperor Claudius asked the Roman Senate when it attempted to deny citizenship to the Gauls in Italy, "but their policy of holding the conquered aloof as alien-born?"[19] When Hernán Cortés besieged the Aztec capital Tenochtitlan in 1521, he did so at the head of a small ragtag army of Europeans and of a very large force of indigenous "allies", mostly Tlaxcalans, without whose assistance it is unlikely that he would have been successful. The British in India could never have been able to seize control of the former Mughal Empire without the active, and sometimes enthusiastic, assistance of the emperor's former subjects. Without Indian bureaucrats, Indian judges, and above all Indian soldiers, the British Raj would have remained a private trading company. At the battle of Plassey in 1757, which marked the beginning of the East-India Company's political ascendancy over the Mughals, twice as many Indians as Europeans fought on the British side.

This is not to diminish the very high level of violence which any form of imperial expansion has always necessarily involved. Nor is it meant to disguise the fact that, although the British, for instance, elevated a select number of Indians to positions of high administrative responsibility and even graciously bestowed titles on some of them, men like Satyendra Prasanno Sinha, who in 1919 became Baron Sinha of Raipur and went on to be the governor of Bihar and Odisha, were very much the exception rather than the rule. No Indian was ever given any position which might have conferred on him any degree of political authority within the metropolis itself. There was never any equivalent, nor could there be, of the first–second century Roman emperor Septimius Severus, a recently Romanized man of Punic origin from Leptis Magna (in what is now Libya) and who, on all accounts, spoke Latin with a strong regional accent, or of the great reforming emperor of the third century, Diocletian, the son of a freedman from Dalmatia, or of his successor, Galerius, who had begun life herding cattle in the Carpathians. And no African, Native American, Polynesian, or Australian Aboriginal was ever given any formal role in any European colonial government.

It remains the case, however, that the once commonplace portrayal of empire as an uncomplicated struggle between unbridled and unprincipled European exploiters and defenseless indigenes, although it certainly applied to some regions of the world (Australia, for instance, and parts of Africa) is, if only for simple logistical reasons, a vast and crude oversimplification. Even the Spanish Empire in America, which is frequently represented as bloody tyranny aimed at annihilating, or enslaving, the Amerindian populations, could not, in fact, have survived the first three decades after the initial conquest without the active participation of native rulers. In 1664, the French had followed Caracalla's example by decreeing that all the indigenous populations of New France who had converted to Christianity should "be registered and counted as denizens and French natives, and as such entitled for all rights of succession, goods, laws and other dispositions".[20] (No non-Europeans, however, were ever promoted into even the lowest ranks of the French aristocracy, nor did any of them choose to settle in metropolitan France.)

Claims to be providing the conquered peoples with an ordered law-governed society, which they lacked and should desire, inevitably involved an appeal to a set of universal values, and frequently an assertion of the right to universal rule. This, too, is by no means limited to Rome, or to Europe. Universalism, like the institution of monarchy with which it has always been closely associated, was probably first brought into Europe from Asia by Alexander the Great. The Roman, and subsequently European, conception of empire was unusual, however, in that the legal formulation of *imperium* was, from early on, merged with a late Stoic notion of a single human race – united, to use the phrase of the great Roman jurist Cicero – into "a single joint community of gods and men". On this account the Roman Empire became not merely a political authority; it became the embodiment of the Stoic notion of the *koinos nomous*, the universal law for all mankind.

Stoicism, and by implication cosmopolitanism, was therefore always closely, if uncomfortably, associated with the idea of empire. The founder of Stoicism, Zeno of Citium, in the third century BCE, is said to have told his followers: "We should all live not in cities and demes [tribal groups], each distinguished by separate rules of justice, but should regard all men as members of the same tribe and fellow citizens; and ... there should be one life and order (*koinos*) as of a single flock feeding together on a common pasture." Over the centuries this remark has been much quoted in defence of a cosmopolitan world. However, the context from which it comes is rarely mentioned. That is perhaps because Zeno's words have survived for us only because they were recorded by the first-century Graeco-Roman philosopher and biographer Plutarch, and Plutarch bothered to repeat them only because what he saw as embodying Zeno's "dream or, as it were shadowy picture, of a well-ordered and philosophical community" was the empire of Alexander the Great.[21] For Plutarch, cosmopolitanism did not so much mean making each man a citizen of the world as it meant making the world into a single body of citizens. If all humanity was to be one, then humanity should belong to one community, one city, one *polis*. For Zeno possibly, and for Plutarch certainly, that city had been Alexander's empire. For the Romans it could clearly only be Rome, or more precisely, the Roman *civitas*. The common law for all humanity, the *koinos nomos*, insofar as it had any content at all, was originally conceived as a Greek law, not the happy multicultural amalgam which has so often been made of it. Similarly, what Cicero and his successors understood by the "common law of humanity" was, in effect (as we shall see in Chapter 2), the law of the Roman *civitas* – the *ius civile* – extended to non-Romans.[22]

The reputation of Rome as the bearer of a new kind of universal order was greatly enhanced, in the minds of later generations at least, under the Antonines – the "Five Good Emperors" as they have come to be known – from Nerva (reigned 96–8 CE) to Marcus Aurelius (161–80), the last of whom was a self-declared Stoic cosmopolitan. They seemed to have erased the memory of their famously reprobate predecessors, Nero, Tiberius, and Caligula, and could indeed have been said to have brought peace, prosperity, order, and justice to what most of its citizens thought of as the "world". Centuries later, Edward Gibbon, looking back from well beyond the disasters which were soon to befall this Eden, declared: "If a man were called upon to fix the period in the history of the world, during which the condition of the human race was the most happy and prosperous, he would, without hesitation, name that which elapsed from the death of Domitian to the accession of Commodus." It was, he added, a time when "the Roman Empire comprehended the fairest part of the earth and the most civilized portion of mankind".[23]

The Christians, who embraced another type of cosmopolitanism, had similarly seen in the Roman Empire the embodiment of their own aspirations. God, it was said, had chosen Rome to unite the cosmos so that the birth of Christ might reach into – if not quite every part, then certainly most of – what the Greeks called the *oikoumene*, the "inhabited world". For the pagan Pliny it had been the *numen* of the gods which had been responsible for Rome's bid to "give humanity to man". For the Christians it had been the will, *voluntas*, of their God.

"God taught nations everywhere," wrote the fourth-century Christian panegyrist Aurelius Prudentius, "to bow their heads beneath the same laws and all to become Roman. ... A common law made then equals, bound them by a single name, and brought them, though conquered, into bonds of brotherhood. We live in every conceivable region scarcely different than if a single city and fatherland enclosed fellow citizens with a single wall."[24]

Such a state could, of course, only be a world one. Already by the end of the first century BCE, Cicero had spoken confidently of "our own people whose empire now holds the whole world".[25] This did not mean that the Romans ignored the actual existence of the rest of the globe. Indeed they possessed a lively and sophisticated ethnographical curiosity in the peoples who inhabited the lands beyond the frontiers of the empire. It was that these other worlds had no separate identity as communities – much less as political powers – and that, in the course of history, they would one day be absorbed into the *Imperium*, the world, itself. This is why Virgil makes Jupiter bestow on the new city of Rome an empire without limits in either space or time: "For these [Romans] I set neither bounds nor periods: *Imperium* without end I give."[26] By the time the Emperor Justinian drew up his codification of Roman law in the sixth century, the world (*mundus*) over which he ruled (although in reality it was now confined to the lands east of the Dardanelles) was seen as constituting a *universitas* which required one lord to provide it with the ratio "of protection and jurisdiction".[27] It was, as the great nineteenth-century German classicist, jurist, and historian Theodore Mommsen in his massive history of Roman public law put it, "a familiar concept to the Romans that they were not only the first power on earth, they were also in a sense, the only one".[28]

The ideology of universalism and the powerful political *imaginaire* which sustained the Roman conception of the civitas relied not only on a system of civil law governing all the citizens of the empire. It also gave rise to a transnational system of laws – the *ius gentium*, the law of nations – which would prove to be the context in which all subsequent debates over the nature, the legitimacy, and the possible future of empire in Europe would evolve until the nineteenth century. The law of nations had originally been only a law governing the relationship between Roman citizens and non-Roman citizens. It was, in effect, a body of international *private* law. In the sixth century, however, the Roman jurists had made it a secondary natural law – that is, a law which, or so it was supposed, all rational peoples could be brought to accept, had they been in a position to be consulted as to its content; and in this form it became the basis for a law *between* peoples. It was this which allowed Hugo Grotius to argue that for the Roman jurists, "the *ius gentium* and *naturalis ratio* [natural reason] are the same thing".[29] In the account provided by Henry Sumner Maine, jurist, historian, early anthropologist, and Law Member of the Viceroy of India's Council, in his immensely influential study, *Ancient Law* of 1861, it had in fact been Grotius and his successors, from Samuel Pufendorf in the mid-seventeenth century to Emer de Vattel in the late eighteenth, who had misconceived the true, and far more limited, meaning of the "the ancient Jus gentium" so as to provide "them [with] a system of laws for the adjustment of international transactions."[30] And it was this move – although Grotius was not, in fact, the first to make it – which was to provide the theoretical foundations on the which nineteenth-century, and all subsequent, conceptions of "international law" was to be based.

II

Grotius, his successors, and a number of his significant predecessors (who formed no part of Maine's history) were living in a world which had been dramatically transformed in 1492 by the discovery of a hitherto unknown content. The discovery of America – and for Europe it really *was* a discovery – had the effect of unsettling many of the hitherto unquestioned European assumptions about not only geography but also, as we shall see in Chapter 3, human history and anthropology. It also opened up the possibility for the acquisition of new territories overseas – what the twentieth-century German jurist Carl Schmitt described as a "land-appropriation" (*Landnahme*) – which, with the dubious exception of the Crusader States, had effectively ceased to exist more than a millennium earlier.[31] In 1494, the pope Alexander VI "donated" to the Spanish monarchs Ferdinand and Isabel a form of sovereignty over all those lands "as you have discovered or are about to discover", which were not already occupied by another Christian prince. When in 1519, Charles V, who was not only King of Spain and much of central Europe and Italy but also now, in name at least, the sovereign of the entire western hemisphere, was elected Holy Roman Emperor, the claim that the emperor of Rome was "Lord of the World" would seem at last to have been fulfilled. Charles himself, wary of the impression such assertions might make on other European rulers, in particular the French, and on the Papacy, protested to Pope Paul III in 1536 that "some say that I wish to be Monarch of the world, but my thoughts and deeds prove that the contrary is true". His councilors, however, were not so reticent, and Charles V became, in the political imagination of his subjects, if nowhere else, the "last world emperor" supposedly foretold in the Book of Daniel who would bring peace stability and, in various Christian commentaries, Christian unity, to the entire world. (One contemporary image shows Daniel explaining all this in person to the seated figure of Emperor.)[32] As the Neapolitan magus Tommaso Campanella informed the princes of Europe in 1600 in a messianic proposal for a Christian World Empire ruled from Spain: "The monarchy of Spain, which embraces all nations and encircles the world is that of the Messiah, and thus shows itself to be the heir of the universe." (When, however he fled Naples for France, in 1635 Campanella changed his mind and named France as the future world empire.)[33]

It was in this context, and the context of the horror stories of the enslavement and butchery which followed the Spanish occupation of the Antilles, and the brutal conquests of Mexico between 1519 and 1521 and that of Peru between 1532 and 1572, that a group of Spanish theologians at the University of Salamanca – now widely referred to as the "School of Salamanca" – began to question, in the words of the earliest of them, Francisco de Vitoria, "by what right (*ius*) were the barbarians subjected to Spanish rule?" It is with what Vitoria himself called the "Affair of the Indies" and the subsequent attempts to re-work the ancient understanding of the law of nations that Chapter 1 is concerned.

The existence, and subsequent attempt, to occupy America presented Europeans with a wholly new legal challenge. The "donation" by which the entire western hemisphere had been ceded to the Spanish monarchs in perpetuity implied that the papacy exercised jurisdiction not merely over the whole of mankind but also in both the spiritual and the temporal spheres. And this, none but the canon lawyers in the service of the Curia were prepared to accept. With the exception of the early Portuguese incursions into West Africa, which had been similarly justified in terms of a papal donation, the title to all previous "land-appropriation" beyond the frontiers of Christendom had relied on the claim that the territories being occupied had once formed part of the "Christian republic". Catholic natural law maintained that as the power to command derived from nature not grace, the ruler's religious beliefs could have no bearing on his territorial rights. (This understanding of the grounds for sovereignty was one of the main theoretical differences between the Spanish and the English, as we shall see in Chapter 4.) The Sultan was, therefore, as legitimate a sovereign over his own lands as the Holy Roman Emperor. What he, or any other ruler, could not lay claim to, however, was any part of the lands of the former Roman Empire, which was deemed to constitute an inalienable part of Christendom. "We do not", wrote Vitoria, "deny right of ownership (*dominium rerum*) [to "Jews and Saracens"] unless it be the case of Christian lands which they had conquered".[34] In law, then, neither the Crusades, nor the "Reconquista" of Spain were wars of religion: they were – as the word "Reconquest" made explicit – attempts to recover what had been seized illegally. The only way that any of this could be made to apply to the Americas, however, would be to take literally the claim of the Roman emperors to universal sovereignty, which none of the Spanish theologians or the jurists were prepared to do. As the jurist Fernando Vázquez de Menchaca argued, the sheer size of America and its distance from Europe had, between them, proved that "that the sovereignty (*dominium*) over so many regions, peoples and provinces separated from one another by such enormous distances, could not reside with one man".[35] Furthermore in a world which was not only far larger than the ancients had imagined but also seemingly in state of continuous expansion – for who could know what still-to-be discovered territories lay in the vastness of the Pacific – the idea that one ruler, no matter how mighty the source of his authority might be "superior in dignity to all others", was, Menchaca remarked archly, "to be compared to the tales of children, to the advice of the aged and to the shadows of an unquiet sleep".[36] It is an irony that it was precisely the "discoveries" in Africa, America, and Asia and the recognition following Magellan's circumnavigation of the globe in 1519–22 that the "Antipodes" were also probably inhabited, which finally shattered the stable notion of universal rule and with it the possible existence of a single universal culture on which the Roman, and subsequently much of the mediaeval Christian world, had founded its conception of itself.

Vitoria and his successors were often portrayed, particularly in the nineteenth century, as radicals, combatants in a struggle against the settlers and the agents of the Crown, if not the Crown itself, for justice in the Americas.

The fact that the Spanish authorities had listened to the Salamancan theologians rather than "their Christian friends and relations", claimed John Stuart Mill, had led them to "side" with "the Pagans" and to do their best to "protect the natives".[37] Without the moral interference of the "divines of Salamanca", the consequences of the Spanish conquest would have been far more deadly than it was. More recently, however, they, and Vitoria in particular, have been cast less as courageous moralists, than as the earliest in a long line of apologists for a blatant form of Christian imperialism.[38] Neither image is entirely correct. Vitoria himself, as we know from his correspondence, was sincerely outraged by the bahavior of those to whom he referred as the "Peruleros", which, he said, "freezes the blood in my veins".[39] However, his discussion of the legitimacy of the conquest, a subject which he had begun, as Schmitt had seen, in "an astonishingly objective manner", nevertheless ends, in Schmitt's words, "with the claim that the Spanish are waging a just war, and therefore may annex Indian lands if the Indians resist free *commercium* (not only 'trade') and the free mission of Christianity".[40] As we shall see, the first of these claims is not quite right, and the second is simply false. But it is true that for all his objectivity and indignation, Vitoria's concern was not with the morality or the legitimacy of the Spanish settlers' behavior in the Indies. Nor was he much concerned with the ultimate fate of the Indians. His purpose was rather to establish a legal basis for a situation which already existed and which he believed (or at least claimed to believe) had to be morally acceptable because the Catholic Monarchs were clearly beyond reproach in this, as were their successors.

In Vitoria's opinion Charles V could make no claim to sovereignty in the Americas unless these had been acquired by means of a just war, which meant, in effect, in terms of the law of nations, and it was with this that Victoria and his successors were overwhelmingly concerned. Although it had been the Roman jurists in the sixth and Bartolus in the fourteenth century who had initially made what in antiquity had been a purely private body of law into a "secondary" natural law, it was Vitoria – not as Maine had supposed Grotius – who was initially responsible for making the first step toward transforming the law of nations into a law governing what he called "all the world that is a commonwealth"; and it was this move which ensured that all subsequent discussions about the nature of empire would ultimately be cast as discussions over the law of nations.

Vitoria had set an agenda which was to determine the direction that the extended and acrimonious debates over the legitimacy of imperial expansion, and more broadly the laws of war, was to take well into the late eighteenth century. However, he had left the precise nature of his new law of nations troublingly vague. Vitoria had insisted that it was a species of positive law, "found out by reason", and thus binding on all peoples everywhere, which meant that it had to take precedence over the laws of individual states. Yet it was also, like the law of nature of which it was a "secondary" version, deprived of any specific legislative content. In part the problem was, as Thomas Hobbes later pointed out with disdain, that the "Schoolmen" and even "the most learned Authors" had failed to make a clear distinction between a law (*lex*) and a right (*ius*). In Hobbes' view the so-called *law* of nations could, in effect, only constitute a *right* – that is, a "Precept or general Rule found out by Reason" (and, furthermore, one which was identical with the "Right of Nature").[41] And if it was that, then it was hard to see how it could also claim to be a true positive *law*. For Hobbes, and later for Kant (as we shall see in Chapter 7) – although for very different reasons – it did not need to be, if only because there could be no recognized law between states, so long, at least, as all states remained in relationship to one another, as Hobbes vividly put it, "in continual jealousies and in the state and posture of Gladiators."[42] For Vitoria and his followers, however, the *ius gentium* had to be capable of providing some kind of international legislative order, and to do that it had be a body of both rights *and* laws.

The person who offered one answer to this question, and who is the subject of Chapter 2, was the Italian jurist and Professor of Civil Law at Oxford Alberico Gentili. Gentili also conceived the law of nations as universally binding. However, to make it a body of true law, to detach it from the moral and theological precepts which underpinned the law of nature of which it was still a "secondary" version, he set out to demonstrate that it was, in effect, identical with the Roman civil law. This – however historically implausible – might have solved one problem, and had, in fact, been suggested many times before by the Roman jurists themselves who, as Maine phrased it, had looked on the natural law as "a type of perfect law" which "ought gradually to absorb civil laws".[43] It was Gentili's contention that this process of absorption had, in fact, already taken place.[44] The equation of the law of nations with the Roman civil law also had the effect, however, of reducing what was originally believed to be a law derived from reason and, thus, acceptable to all peoples everywhere, to the specific legal practices of one group of peoples – even though that group was said by Gentili to encompass, in some imprecise geographical sense, the peoples of all the world. In arguing, in this way, and by adding the qualification that it was "not necessary to understand the word 'all' ... to mean absolutely every nation", Gentili had taken a step down a road which would lead from Grotius, to the Italians Giovanni Vincenzo Gravina and Giambattista Vico, and the German Christian Wolff in the eighteenth century, to a fully evolved positivist law of nations in the nineteenth century, whereby the law of nations would become, in effect, not the law to which "all the world that is a commonwealth" might be assumed to have given its consent but only, to quote Wolff, "what has been approved by the more civilized nations".[45] It had been this law, Gentili claimed, which Rome's conquered peoples had craved, and even though the empire itself had now vanished, the world still "thirstily gulps down" its laws. It might be argued that that was what it had always been. (*Imperium* is, after all, a legal term). However, on Gentile's reading, and that of nearly all subsequent theorists of empire, whether they had read Gentili or not, "empire" became simply coterminous with "civilization".

## III

The "Barbarians" were by definition those whom, as John Stuart Mill said of them in 1859, "cannot be depended on for observing any rules", and because this deprived them of any place within the law of nation, it clearly meant that they did not, or did not yet, constitute true nations (a point to which I shall return).[46] They stood, on Mill's account, at the beginning of the road which led "the best characteristics of Man and Society" toward the "perfection, happier, nobler, wiser" which had been acquired, more by good luck than innate ability, by the "civilized" people of the globe.[47]

The American Indians evidently belonged to this category. They also, however, had another troubling peculiarity which became a subject of particular anxiety in the sixteenth and seventeenth centuries. Because they inhabited a continent whose very existence had been unimaginable before 1492 – and remained unimaginable to many for multiple years to come – they existed beyond the limits of the traditional Biblical narratives of human history. One of the earliest attempts to account for their very existence in ways which would also justify their subjection was by resurrecting Aristotle's theory of natural slavery. This, which I discuss in Chapter 3, was often interpreted – although Aristotle himself does not seem to have understood it in this way – as constituting a division of the species into two distinct races: the natural masters who were, in Aristotle's terms, fully capable of deliberative action (*prohairesis*) and were thus able to fulfil their ends qua human beings, and "the natural slaves", who although they had some "share" in reason and were obviously human, were not. The fact that Aristotle suggests that those to whom he refers to as the "barbarians" – an uncertain category at best – might be natural slaves seemed to some to offer clear evidence that what he was describing was a category of being which included all non-Europeans and thus, by implication, the American Indians. This, if nothing else, would have placed the Indians irrevocably outside the boundaries of the law of nations. It would indeed have made them a category of being to which no human law could reasonably be said to apply. Vitoria and his colleagues all rejected the idea. They did so, in the first instance, on the purely empirical grounds that nothing that was known about the Indians suggested that they were lacking in a deliberative faculty. Their most telling objection, however, was that the existence of creature which possessed some of the attributes of humanity, but was deficient in the essential, constituted a serious threat to the integrity of the human race and thus a denial of the perfection of the Creation.

The existence of an inhabited landmass so far removed from the geographical spaces in which the narratives of the Creation and the Redemption had supposedly unfolded, however, raised the possibility that, in fact, the human genus might not, as the Church had always insisted, be one and that the Indians might, in fact, not have formed a part of the Creation at all, or at least not a part of Creation recorded in the Book of Genesis which had resulted in the peopling of the earth by the sons of Noah. Might they not, some dared to ask, instead be the consequence of spontaneous generation, like certain kind of insects and other "lower" animals, or, more charitably, might they be the children of another creation, historically distinct from the one that had generated the peoples of Europe, Africa, and Asia? Needless to say that as these suggestions ran contrary to the Biblical account of the Creation and of the peopling of the world after the Flood was only ever considered by the Catholic Church to be heretical. They were also pervasive, however, and they raised serious and prolonged debates over the supposed unity of the human race. In the nineteenth century as the claims of the biblical narrative became increasingly hard to sustain in the face of the evidence, and with the advent of modern biology, the argument that mankind was in fact divided into distinct races all with innate and inheritable properties becomes far more insistent. Even then, however, although race clearly played a significant role in forming a public opinion of non-European (and some European) peoples, it remained at best an ultimately reductionist and empirically weak justification for any kind of imperial rule.[48] As with the Roman Empire before it, the Spanish, and indeed all subsequent European empires at least before the end of the eighteenth century, were committed to the idea that theirs was a society which sought to incorporate all its peoples under one body of law as, if not actually, then at least potentially, equal. For this to be possible, it was a necessary condition that, for all the variety of human cultures and beliefs, there could be only one human *nature*, rational and perfectible.

## IV

The Spanish were not alone, of course, in having to face the intellectual, legal, and moral challenges which the existence and the attempts to occupy the New World presented. By the late sixteenth century, the British, French, and Dutch had also begun to make substantial incursions into the Atlantic Ocean. Like the Spanish, they, too, were driven to provide some account of the legitimacy of their actions. As relative latecomers, however, they were also confronted with a further problem: how to define and control the frequently contentious relationship between the new settler societies now growing up in the Americas and the metropolis. Of all the new European colonial powers, the English (discussed in Chapter 4) faced this question in perhaps its most acute form. The contest between European powers placed the legitimacy of the "conquests" – and role of the law of nations – in a new light. For what was at stake here had far less to do with the rights of the indigenous peoples themselves – for which the British had relatively little concern – than it did with the rights which the settlers might have acquired, or might claim, vis-à-vis the "mother country", on account of their various acts of appropriation. Unlike the laws governing the Spanish, French, Portuguese, and Dutch relations between colony and metropolis, those between the British colonies and the Crown varied greatly all the way from Puritan New England to Catholic Avalon. In theory, however, all the American colonies were, in the eyes of the English (and later British) Crown, "lands of conquest", although in fact very few indeed had been "conquered" in any meaningful sense. This made them legally part of the royal demesne and thus accountable directly to the king. The colonists, therefore, in an effort to rid themselves of the theoretical burden which this supposition imposed began to look for other ways of pressing their claims to territorial rights.

Unlike the Spanish, but broadly in keeping with both Portuguese and French, the English accounts of the acquisition of territory in America generally maintained that title had been acquired, not through conquest, but either through purchase or, far more contentiously, by means of the occupation and "improvement" of "vacant lands" or *terra nullius*. *Terra nullius* – "the land of no one" – was in origin a Roman law which granted possession to the first person to occupy a previously unoccupied territory. In the English formulation of this, which subsequently came to form an integral part of the law of nations, occupation involved usage or, as the settlers phrased it, "improvement". This in turn drew heavily on a far earlier assumption that all of nature was, in Aristotle's terms, potential and waiting only for human agency – human artifice (*techne*) – to make it actual. For the Greeks this *techne* was a form of *logos*; for the Christians, it became a divine obligation. "God", as John Locke phrased it, "when he gave the World in common to all Mankind, commanded Man also to labour, and the penury of his Condition required it of him. God and his Reason commanded him to subdue the Earth, *i.e.* improve it for the benefit of Life".[49] As the American Indians had (on Locke's understanding at least) singularly failed in this duty, they could make no claim to be in legitimate possession of the lands on which they lived. It could also be argued, and frequently was (although not by Locke), that they had also in some degree failed to be fully human. It was certainly the case that without agriculture, and property rights in land, they could form no part of "political or civil society" and thus had no standing under the law of nations.[50] Highly contentious though this argument was – not least, because as many pointed out, it would render the Royal Parks in England liable to appropriation by needy peasants – it was widely accepted as a legitimate grounds for occupation, although only under very circumscribed conditions, and it continued to be used by various European powers and in various parts of the world until well into the early twentieth century.[51]

By claiming to have dispossessed the Indians in this way, the British colonists in America had not only, in their view, carried out what had clearly been God's initial purpose in sending them to the New World; they had also distanced themselves from the hated and supposedly rapacious, boastfully conquering Spanish. More to the point, they had considerably diminished their dependence on the Crown. In retrospect the argument from terra nullius, together with the claim that the settlers had purchased their lands from the Indians, became the principal grounds on which, after the Revolution, the new United States, as the successor state to the Thirteen Colonies, made its arguments for the legitimate appropriation of indigenous lands.

The terra nullius argument was also inescapably linked to an analogous claim which was to have a similarly long history: the right of possession by so-called first discovery. Vitoria had rejected this as any kind of "just title" for seizure precisely because it applied only to unoccupied lands, and in the case of the American Indians "the goods in question already had an owner".[52] For the Portuguese, however, it was crucial. In part because it was a key feature of the bulls granted by Pope Nicholas V to Afonso V in 1454 which had conceded to them sovereignty over the whole of Africa, in part because what mattered most for the Portuguese, in particular in their conflicts first with Spain and then with the Netherlands, was their claim to exercise sovereignty not over the land, but over the sea.[53] For it was not only the newness of the "new" world which created for the Europeans unprecedented legal problems but also its distance from Europe. All legal discourse concerning the relationship between peoples was, as we have seen, in origin Roman. But the Roman Empire had been a land-based empire, and the Roman jurists had thought only in terms of terrestrial space. The empires of early modern Europe, however, were inescapably maritime. This brought them into incessant conflict, real and symbolic, with one another over the degree to which any power could exercise control over the ocean.

In the seventeenth century, the debate crystallized around a short text by Hugo Grotius, *Free Sea* (*Mare liberum*), published in 1609, and intended to be part of the Dutch armoury in the negotiations over the Treaty of Amsterdam of April 9, 1609, by which the Spanish hoped to secure a Dutch agreement to abandon what the Spanish considered to be their piratical activities in the East and West Indies. This, and the subsequent attempt by the Portuguese canonist Serafim de Freitas to refute Grotius' argument, is the subject of Chapter 5. The crucial argument in the debate over the "freedom of the seas" was not merely whether the Portuguese could limit the access of other European powers to the Indian Ocean on the highly dubious grounds that they had been the first to "discover" India, it was the far more significant issue as to whether it was theoretically possible to establish jurisdiction over areas of the world – of which the world's oceans were clearly one – where no jurisdiction could in effect be exercised. It was also the case, which as Grotius pointed out had a long classical pedigree (and had also been raised by Vitoria), that free access to the world's goods was widely deemed necessary for human survival. They could, that is, only be held in common. The law of nations, it was argued, had been established among peoples not merely to regulate the relationships between them but to legislate for those areas over which no one group could make any claim to *dominium*.

V

All of the European overseas empires of the initial period of expansion – from 1492 until the collapse of the British and then Spanish colonies in Americas – were settler societies. To justify their existence they had both to incorporate sometimes very large indigenous populations and to negotiate their relationship with the mother country. By the late eighteenth century, the perception of both of these had begun to change, often in quite radical ways. As the settler populations created increasingly stable, coherent societies, they became less dependent culturally, if not politically or legally, on the metropolis. As the "Physiocrat" Victor de Riquetti, marquis de Mirabeau had already seen as early as 1758, sooner rather than later "the new world would throw off the yolk of the old" unless by some miracle those to whom he referred contemptuously as the "little brains" who held power in London and Madrid should consent to transforming "frequently burdensome subjects" into "powerful brothers always ready to assist".[54] The mounting unease in the relations between the creole populations of both North and South America and their respective metropolizes became even more acute after the end of the Seven Years' War in 1763. To Adam Smith, writing in 1767 on the eve of the Revolutionary War, it seemed that the British Empire in America had "existed in imagination only". It was now time, he added caustically, that "our rulers should either realize their golden dream", or because that was hardly likely ever to be practicable, to "awake from it, themselves and endeavour to awaken the people. If the project cannot be completed, it should be given up."[55] In the end of course, it was the colonists themselves who finally "completed" the project, but not in ways which Smith had fully anticipated.

As we shall see in Chapter 6, what applied in the North applied with equal force in the South. The Spanish monarchy, however, unlike the British, was by the early eighteenth century facing a serious economic and political crisis. The painful transition from the archaic Habsburg monarchy to a more enlightened administration under its new Bourbon rulers had had a devastating impact on the ways in which the Spanish settlements in the Americas were conceived. What began as an attempt to reform the system of government in both the metropolis itself and the "Kingdoms of the Indies" developed rapidly into a bid – in the words of Pedro Rodríguez Campomanes, minister of finance from 1762 until 1783 and governor of the Council of Castile from 1783 until 1792 – to "transform the being" of the monarchy itself. This meant a complete reformulation of the status of the overseas settlements and their relationship with the mother country. It meant, in effect, redescribing what were still looked on as kingdoms within a "composite monarchy" (as it has been called) into fully integrated and dependent colonies.[56] It meant, also, rewriting the history of the conquest from a narrative of Spanish exceptionalism and national glory into a far more complex story of heroic, but unstable, origins and subsequent devastation. Above all it meant modernizing, and for the enlightened reformers of the courts of Charles III and Charles VI, modernizing Spain and its American dependencies meant, in effect, making them more like France and Britain, and that could only be achieved by abandoning the older military virtues of which the sixteenth- and seventeenth-century *conquistadores* had been the model for those of what, in the eighteenth century, came to be called the "commercial society". In practice this involved the implementation of sweeping reforms in the structure of government in both metropolitan Spain itself and its overseas dependencies

The right to extensive self-government which the Spanish Creoles (*criollos*) had previously enjoyed (although not, as they themselves frequently complained, to anything like the same degree as their fellow colonists in the North) were slowly, but extensively, erased, and a new system of colonial government, modelled along French lines, was brought in to replace the sclerotic Habsburg administration. All of this, inevitably, bred a feeling of disaffection from the mother country, among the creole elite, a group for whom the virtues of commerce had no particular appeal and who still looked on the conquest as a glorious moment of foundation. Gradually these dissatisfactions coalesced into a bid for full cultural and political independence. "The New World", wrote the exiled Jesuit Juan Pablo Viscardo from London in 1801, "is our patria; its history is our history".[57]

The revolt against Spain, when it came, therefore rapidly rejected all previous ideological association with the mother country. Spain, said the "Liberator" Simón Bolívar, was an "old serpent", an "unnatural stepmother".[58] Whereas Jefferson's "British Americans" could appeal to the terms of the Glorious Revolution of 1688, and more airily to Magna Carta, to fashion their Revolution as the overthrow of a monarchy which had reneged on the rights which it had itself conferred on them, the Spanish Americans, "strangers to the world of politics", as Simón Bolívar said of them, were driven to create what he called "the liberal state" out of pure theory, which in his case took the form of an uneasy blend of ancient, and modern republicanism.[59] The final outcome, despite Bolívar's fleeting and ultimately doomed attempt to hold the south together as the republic of "Gran Colombia", was the disintegration of the entire southern continent into a number of small, mutually hostile, and unstable states. The legacy of what Bolívar, at the end of his life, called despairingly "half a world gone" mad, survives to this day. There are many Spanish-American reformers and would-be reformers since his death in 1830 who have had cause to repeat his most famous utterance that all those "who serve a revolution plough the ocean".[60]

VI

The collapse of the British Empire in North America strengthened an already growing dissatisfaction with the whole conception of empire – those "Enormous monarchies" which, as David Hume said of them, "are, probably, destructive to human nature; in their progress, in their continuance, and even in their downfall, which never can be very distant from their establishment".[61] In one way or another almost all of the major figures of the Enlightenment agreed with him.[62] One of the most trenchant and influential, and also in many ways perhaps among the most improbable, of these was Immanuel Kant.

The main concern of Kant's extensive, if scattered, thinking on "universal monarchy" was, as I argue in Chapter 7, a bid to replace the law – or *right* – of nations (*Völkerrecht*) with a new transnational system of rights – the *ius cosmopoliticum*. This "cosmopolitan right", which was to be the "womb in which all original predispositions of the human species will be developed", was inescapably a condition of future time, but for it to become an eventual reality, all the peoples of the world would ultimately have to enter into a species of world federation, what he called, "an (always growing) nation of peoples (*civitas gentium*) that would finally encompass all the nations of the earth".[63]

For Kant, as for all of his predecessors since Hobbes, states were believed to exist in relationship with one another as individuals had once existed in the state of nature. And just as individuals had, by means of some kind of political process based on the idea of an "original contract", exited into civil society, so ultimately must states find their way out of their present condition of perpetual war, in which even when they are not actually fighting one another, they "wrong one another by being near one another", into a condition of interstate legality.[64] Hitherto, however, the only attempts that had been made to regulate the relationship between states had been confined to the law of nations which Kant identified as primarily the work of three men, dubbed the "sorry comforters of mankind": Hugo Grotius, the Prussian philosopher Samuel Pufendorf, and the Swiss diplomat Emer de Vattel. The code which these men had devised, he declared, although "couched philosophically or diplomatically [had] not the slightest lawful force and cannot have such force". Worse it was only ever "cited in justification of an offensive war".[65] Because, furthermore, there clearly could exist no law in the lawless condition which is the state of nature, the very concept of a law (*Gesetz*) – or right – of war would seem to be so inherently meaningless that "it is difficult even to form a concept of this or to think of law in this lawless state without contradicting oneself".[66] If the idea of anything resembling the law of nations could be said to have any value at all it was merely as evidence that mankind possessed the "moral disposition" required to overcome the "evil principle within", even if, at present, most individual humans seemed to be incapable of acting on it.

The fundamental flaw in the entire conception of the law of nations was that it supposed "the separation of many neighboring states independent of one another". Exiting from this condition could mean only one thing – namely, the "fusion of them by one power overgrowing the rest and passing into a universal monarchy". For Kant this was worse than the natural condition of war. This was so, however, not so much because universal monarchy inevitably violates the public rights of individual states but because empires are necessarily overextend polities, and the inescapable consequence of overextension is that, "as the range of government expands, laws progressively lose their vigor, and a soulless despotism, after it has destroyed the seeds of good, finally deteriorates into anarchy". Yet despite the melancholy history of all the would-be global empires – Rome in particular – human beings (or at least their rulers) seem to possess an insatiable craving "to attain a lasting condition of peace in this way, by ruling the whole world". Fortunately for humanity, however, "*nature wills* it otherwise". Cultural conditions, above all language and religion, would, Kant believed, always in the end prevent peoples from fusing their identities into one. However, as with Kant's concept of "unsocial sociability" (the principle whereby human beings are compelled to form societies by the very fact that they cannot bear – yet cannot bear to leave – each other) so this seemingly unquenchable desire to "rule the world" would seem to have a potentially positive outcome. For with "increasing culture" the quest for domination might have the effect of bringing peoples closer together, at least in their agreement over principles. While they will remain in separate and independent states, they will, also out of simple self-interest (if nothing else), be driven "to enter into a civil constitution [with one another] in which each can be assured of ... rights". This, however, would create not a "state of nations" – that is an empire – but instead "a *league of nations*" and would be the final outcome of the operation of *ius cosmopoliticum*.[67]

The "cosmopolitan right", however, is limited to what Kant calls, the "right to hospitality", which is defined as "the right to visit", which all human beings enjoy by "virtue of the right of possession in common of the earth's surface on which, as a sphere, they cannot disperse indefinitely but must put up with being near one another".[68] This has some affinity with Vitoria's "right of natural partnership and communication", which we will encounter in Chapter 1, and Grotius' allusion to the right of free passage, discussed in Chapter 5, both of which drew on an ancient pre-social right of all peoples to enjoy free access to all others, and to the world's resources, although Kant makes no mention of either and had almost certainly never heard of Vitoria. But Kant's conception is very much more limited than either Vitoria's or Grotius'. On Kant's account, although the would-be "visitor" must be treated without hostility and all states ought to provide sanctuary for refuges, they only *ought* to, for no individual has a right to enter a foreign territory at will unless invited to do so, let alone to settle.[69] Furthermore the right of hospitality could only apply universally in a world free from the predatory behavior of the European empires. So long as the European powers continued in their course; so long as the "inhospitable behavior of the civilized, especially commercial, states in our part of the world" for whom "visiting" others was "tantamount to *conquering* them" persisted; so long do those others – having "given such guests a try" and found them wanting – have a perfect right to deny them access to their territories. Although the right of every nation to enter into some kind of political association with every other was, indeed, a *right* – no one nation was thereby entitled to force it on any other.

Kant (or at any rate the later Kant) was also fiercely dismissive of any claim that more civilized peoples might have the right to seize the territories of the less civilized, even if he recognizes that this would be a means "to establish civil union with them and bring these men (savages) into a rightful condition (as with the American Indians and the Hottentots and the inhabitants of New Holland)".[70] The only possible ground on which people are able to establish settlements overseas is either by legitimate purchase or on lands that are genuinely vacant. Although Kant allows for the existence of two different kinds of settlement "from home", both can only ever be wholly dependent on the metropolis. And because for Kant what he called "legal continuity" was an essential property of all states, no colony could ever subsequently achieve legitimate independence as a state, unless the metropolis itself decides to make it so. For just as no outsider is entitled to intervene in the affairs of another state even in what Vitoria had called the "defense of the innocent", against the tyrannical action of their own rulers, so no people, however sorely oppressed, is itself licensed to rise up against its legitimate ruler. For Kant the only "rightful constitution among human beings" is one in which the sovereign is constrained to "give his law as if it could have arisen from the united will of an entire people", and this could only happen under what he calls a "representative republic". Yet no struggle for "self-determination" by any people, even if its purpose were precisely to establish such a republic – the American Revolutions for instance – could ever be a legitimate one.[71] Like many potentially revolutionary thinkers, like Rousseau and Locke before him, Kant could never quite bring himself to sanction a popular uprising as such. Empires – "nations of nations" – might be unbearable tyrannies, but they are also, so long as they are bound by some kind of law, legitimate polities. This, as we shall see, presented him with a seemingly intractable problem; for if the "federative state of states" or "world republic", which alone could lead to the "universal *cosmopolitan condition*", is to come into being, it is hard to see how it can be created in any way except by dissolving all existing legal continuities.[72]

Kant seems to have believed that the only means by which the representative republic of the future could come into being would be through the voluntary action of the reigning sovereigns themselves who, like Frederick the Great of Prussia, would transform themselves from autocrats into "servants" of the state. It was this belief which had led him in 1784 to claim, somewhat disingenuously, that his was "the age of enlightenment or the century of Frederick" in which "hindrances to ... humankind's emergence from its self-incurred minority are growing fewer".[73] The only other legitimate means would be a process similar to that which, in Kant's view, allowed the French Revolution, for which he had an apparently unqualified admiration, to be described not as a *revolution* at all but rather as a voluntary transfer of power by Louis XVI to the Estates General in which "the monarch's sovereignty wholly disappeared (it was not merely suspended) and passed to the people."[74]

One of the mechanisms by which, or so Kant hoped, modern states would acquire the "increasing culture" which would eventually allow them to make the transition from the state of nature into a law-governed federation was commerce. In this he was drawing on a widespread eighteenth-century conviction that commercial exchange not only had the power, in Montesquieu's famous phrase "to make people gentle", by bringing them into constant contact with one another but also would render warfare obsolete, simply because no commercial nation could afford to go to war with its trading partners. Kant, although he often looked on the "spirit of commerce" as generally debasing, was as convinced as most of the political economists of the eighteenth century that it "cannot co-exist with war and sooner or later takes hold of every nation" and that it would thus, despite itself, be responsible for finally bringing the bellicose states of the world closer together.[75] Commerce would certainly not eliminate empire. For even if it were true, as Diderot put it, that "[a] war among commercial nations is a fire that destroys them all", this would obviously only eliminate wars among the most powerful of the worlds' states.[76] It was, after all, as Kant had commented acidly, precisely the "commercial nations" which were most at fault in their behavior toward non-Europeans peoples. As Adam Smith, himself no enemy to commerce, observed, it was by no means obvious what benefit, if any, the indigenous peoples of "both of the East and West Indies" would derive from the creation of the great trading networks which had been launched by the voyages of Christopher Columbus and Vasco da Gama.[77]

But for all the scepticism which accompanied the often unrestrained hymns of praise to commerce, during the latter half of the eighteenth century, an attempt was made, in particular by the French who lost much of their actual empire to the British at the end of the Seven Years' War in 1763, to reimagine empire based not on conquest and exploitation but on exchange and reciprocity. In the end this proved to be an illusion. The new trading empires "of liberty" were destined finally to become yet another theatre for the rivalry between the major European states, and, in the Pacific, Africa and Asia, to dissolve into very much the same kind of colonizing exploits which had taken place centuries before in the Americas.

The Enlightenment vision of the creation of future "empires of liberty" overseas collapsed, less because of the failure of any of the European maritime states to establish anything even remotely resembling Diderot's half-ironical fantasy of a world of free exchange in which young Europeans would be sent off to Polynesia to learn from the simplicity and sincerity of its inhabitants and young Polynesians brought back to Europe to acquire the benefits of the arts and sciences.[78] It finally collapsed before the very brevity and bloodiness of the Napoleonic ambition to transform Europe itself into a very different kind of empire. For anyone who had lived through them, the Napoleonic wars seemed to have rendered all imperial projects, no matter what their initial motives, unrepeatable. One of these was the Swiss political theorist, novelist, politician, gambler, and man of letters Benjamin Constant (whom we shall meet in Chapter 8). Like Kant (with whom in 1797 he had a heated exchange over the social consequences of lying), Constant accepted that all empires were essentially unsustainable and that no matter what claims they might make to legitimacy, they were doomed sooner rather than later to collapse into tyranny. His main opposition, however, was to what he saw as the sheer archaism of all forms of conquest. In this of course, Constant shared much in common with the anti-imperialists of the eighteenth century, in particular Montesquieu, but lacked their faith in the autonomous potential of the commercial spirit. Commerce – that "civilized calculation" as he called it – was for Constant not so much a means of softening the manners of an otherwise unruly warrior horde: it was merely warfare by other means, the "attempt to obtain by mutual agreement what one can no longer hope to obtain through violence".[79] Because, however, its costs were very much less than warfare and because in a modern post-Napoleonic state it was the population which now made up the bulk of the fighting force, there was some hope that in the future it would finally make war obsolete. "The only possible guarantee against useless or unjust war", he wrote in 1815, "is the energy of representative assemblies, they grant the conscription of men, they consent to the taxes".[80] And they, it must be supposed, would always choose peaceful trade over war whenever they could. It was not, however, only the mechanism of modern liberal government which would finally limit wars to those that were, in effect, defensive and, in so doing, eliminate imperial expansion altogether. It was also the very private nature of the modern citizen. Empires thrived on heroism and the inflated language of patriotic self-denial. But the principle aim of modern liberal man was "the enjoyment of security in private pleasure" rather than the pursuit of public good, and it made him a very improbable hero.[81]

Constant had also understood, even as early as 1813, that what would finally undo Napoleon's ambition to make Europe an empire was another form of modernity: nationalism.[82] The empires of antiquity, although they may have, in fact, "destroyed entire nations", had nevertheless left intact "men's strongest attachments: their ways of life their customs, their gods". They may have deprived their subject peoples of political autonomy but they had made no attempt to diminish "the feeling of fatherland" in the countries they occupied. Napoleon by contrast, in his ambition to reunite what he sometimes called "the family of Europe", had hoped precisely to eliminate all those things and to replace them by the "same code of law, the same measures, and the same regulations".[83] The outcome had not been, as Napoleon had hoped, an adherence to the new Revolutionary order embodied by the French nation. Instead it had been the reinforcement of the older ties and consolidation of those feelings for the "fatherland", which Napoleon had tried to eradicate – even when these meant, as they did in Naples and Spain, the institution of monarchy and the Catholic Church. Napoleon, as Giuseppe Mazzini, the architect of Italian unity, claimed in 1849, had been "brought down not so much by the brute force that the kings had marshalled against him, but by the strength of a popular idea; by an outburst of the idea of nationality which he had offended by his arrogance".[84] Out of the rubble of the Napoleonic Empire, a new Europe of nations had arisen and, in Constant's view, this Europe would require a very different set of incentives to persuade it to go to war in pursuit of anything so ultimately elusive as empire.

In this changed political world, directed by "public opinion" and compelled to operate, or be seen to operate, very largely in function of whatever the individual citizen conceived to be his – and increasingly her – personal interests, the new aspiring imperialists would have to resort to an entirely new language commensurate with the rising power of the nation. They would, Constant recognized, have to "talk of national independence, of national honour, of the rounding off of frontiers, of commercial interests, of precautions dictated by foresight".[85] Modern man might have no wish to conquer the world if he were asked to participate directly in the conquest, but he had little objection to the benefits which conquest and imperial expansion could bring.

Far from casting a cold eye over the imperial ambitions of their rulers, the subjects of the monarchical order which came to dominate Europe after the Congress of Vienna of 1815 embraced it with apparently unquestioning enthusiasm. The newly self-conscious European states and subsequently the new nations of Europe – Belgium, founded in 1831, Italy in 1861, and the German Empire in 1876 – all began to compete with one another for the status, and the economic gains, which empire was thought to bestow. It was this which persuaded France in 1852 and Germany in 1871 to declare themselves to be, once again, "empires", and which led the Ottoman Sultans to revive the title of "Kayser" first assumed by Mehmed II the conquer of Constantinople in 1453. It was this, too, which led Meiji Japan between the

1850s and the 1910s to re-invent itself as a European-style empire with a semi-scared emperor (something it had not previously had). Even the United States fitfully toyed with the idea of acquiring an extraterritorial empire in the 1890s. The members of this new Empire Club saw themselves as belonging to a new world "civilization" which would henceforth dictate the direction of all the other lesser states and societies on the planet. Colonization had also apparently brought another unforeseen gift to Europe: relative peace. As Henry Maine observed, in 1888, "war appears to be as old as mankind, but peace is a modern invention."[86] (The last major conflict had been the Franco-Prussian War of 1870–71.) However, the invention of peace had only been made possible, as the highly influential political economist Paul Leroy-Beaulieu observed in 1891, because the scramble for empire had indeed channeled much of the competitive, and potentially destructive, energies of the European states outwards. "For ten years", wrote Leroy-Beaulieu, "colonization has become the condition of peace within Europe. ... It has quenched the desire for conquest and the restlessness of peoples: their eyes fixed on the immense spoils to be had in distant lands, they have forgotten their mean quarrels with their neighbors."[87]

By 1898, imperialism was indeed becoming, in the words of Lord Nathaniel Curzon, Viceroy of India, "more and more the faith of a nation".[88] In the new world of nation states which had grown up in Europe after 1815, to be a "patriot" meant increasingly to be an "imperialist". The new empire became the formal expression of Hegel's mystical vision of the nation as an organic whole as "spirit in its substantial rationality, and immediate actuality, and ... therefore the immediate power on *earth*".[89] The ideal of modern "Imperialism", declared the Scottish historian and novelist J. A. Cramb in 1900, was "patriotism transfigured by a light from the aspirations of universal humanity". For Cramb there could be no doubt about at least the British dedication to the nation's "fate-appointed task", to bring stability, unity, and law to the world beyond Europe. Cramb, it is true was given to wild flights of fantasy, and his rhetoric is heavily tinged with a messianic belief in the destiny of the British Empire as not merely the successor of the Roman but also its apotheosis in which "the spirit of Empire receives a new incarnation".[90] But for all his pseudo-poetical verbiage and reinterred allusions to Kant, Lessing and Schiller, Goethe and Coleridge, Cramb's vision of Britain's imperial destiny reflected a widespread, if far cruder, belief in the patriotically enhancing power of the new imperialism – if only for the new imperialists. Even Beaulieu, a less elegiac, if no less convinced, champion of empire, said of colonization that it was "the expansive force of a people: it is the power of reproduction, it is dilatation through space. The people who colonizes the most is the first among peoples, if they are not today, then they will be tomorrow."[91] Empire, as the historian Eric Hobsbawn once remarked, made "good ideological cement".[92]

## VIII

The new imperial calculus also proved to be immensely effective. It has been estimated that in 1500 the future imperial powers of Europe, Spain, Portugal, France, Britain, and Holland occupied, or controlled in one way or another, about 10 percent of the surface of the planet. Over the following two centuries this had perhaps doubled, and by 1800 the major western powers – Britain, France, Germany, Austria, Russia, and the United States – plus what still remained of Spain and Portugal's overseas dependencies – between them occupied or controlled some 35 percent. By 1878, however, they had taken 67 percent and by 1914 over 84 percent. Even if we allow for the fact that all of these figures can only be approximate and that "controlled" can be made to mean many things, this is a remarkable rate of growth.[93]

The new "second empires" differed, however, markedly from their predecessors in a number of crucial ways. For the one lesson which the fate of the older empires had taught the new European imperial powers was that the creation of large-scale overseas settler populations was not in their long-term interests. Similarly the enlightened, vision of a new world order which cast empire as, in the words of the eighteenth-century Anglo-Irish parliamentarian Edmund Burke, a "sacred trust", whose ultimate benefits would be shared by all its "fellow citizens" in which the peoples of Africa and Asia (alas, it was already too late for the poor American Indians) were waiting, in the marquis de Condorcet encouraging image of the future, only to become the "friends and disciples" of new, enlightened Europeans, dissolved into a far starker conception of what divided the civilized European world from the world beyond, and a far more instrumental view of how the one should govern the other.[94]

The "new" empires did not, in general, conceive of their subject peoples as "fellow citizens", and although they were, ideologically at least, committed to their education and improvement, they did not usually think of them as "friends". Neither did they, as their predecessors had done, encourage settlement among them, except in those areas such as southern Africa and Australia, which were held to be "empty lands" (terra nullius). Even British India, which had a more extensive administration and closer ties with the metropolis than any of the settlements in Africa or Asia remained until the end a place visited rather than settled. "The English", observed the French essayist and art historian Élie Faure in 1931, alluding to the railways, "seem to be camping. One only ever sees them from behind a wall of steel."[95] In South Africa, as late as 1936, after successive interwar migrations, European settlers accounted for only 21 percent of the population. In Southern Rhodesia it accounted for less than 5 percent.[96] Even in such places as Algeria, which was something of an exception, by 1931 the *colons* amounted to less than 13 percent of the population. As Alexis de Tocqueville had warned the government in Paris as early as 1841, "without a European population we will be camping in Algeria".[97]

It had been precisely this which Edmund Burke had denounced as "Indianism", a counterpart to "Jacobinism" – the peculiar brand of imperial pillage practiced by the East India Company, which, in his view, threatened not only the welfare of the indigenous peoples of the overseas territories but also the very existence of what he thought of as "the civilization of Europe".[98] By contrast with the British, the Mughal conquerors of India had "made the conquered country their own", and this had "very soon abated their ferocity. They rose or fell with the rise and fall of the territory they lived in. Fathers there deposited the hopes of their posterity; and children beheld the monuments of their fathers." The British, however, had gone to India like birds of prey who swoop down "wave upon wave. ... [With] nothing before the eyes of the natives but an endless hopeless prospect of new flights ... with appetites continually renewing for a food that is continually wanting".[99]

But if the revolutions which had destroyed the earlier empires were to be avoided, "birds of prey" not stubborn creoles – no matter how abated their ferocity – was precisely what the metropolis now needed. To ensure their effectiveness and their survival, the new possessions would, therefore, have to be controlled as far as possible, with the smallest number of European intermediaries. That this had, in effect, always been the practice, as Burke had seen not only of the British in India but also of the Dutch and Portuguese overseas empires, and the fact that none of these had witnessed any creole uprising only helped re-force the point.

Instead, therefore, of creating large settler bureaucracies supervised by visiting metropolitan officials, the new empires attempted, where possible, to govern through what F. D. Lugard, governor and governor-general of Nigeria between 1912 and 1919, was the first to describe as "indirect Rule" but which had, in fact, been the practice in much of Africa since the mid-nineteenth century.[100] Britain was to act as the "custodian on behalf of civilization", but the daily administration of the colonies, protectorates, mandates, and so forth was to be left in the hands of the colonized.[101] It was a policy which since it appeared, whatever its larger political purpose, to be calculated to interfere as little as possible with indigenous systems of government, met with approval from the new anthropologists, who in the early part of the twentieth century began working closely with the imperial administrations. "Indirect rule" declared the "functionalist" anthropologist Bronislaw Malinowski in 1929 was "a complete surrender to the functional point of view" that African society should be tampered with as little as possible since their present ways of life were "functionally" the best suited to the conditions in which the Africans had evolved.[102] Henry Maine, also, had persuaded himself that the traditional Indian village, self-sufficient and to some degree self- governing, constituted a living instance of what the German or Scandinavian *mark* had once been. If he was right, then the "village community", as he called it, was an example of the kind of society from which the prevailing order of the nations of modern

Europe had developed. For those who read him, this was a good reason for protecting and, to some degree, preserving these villages, particularly if they also turned out to be convenient administrative districts. Their supposed similarity with ancient Anglo-Saxon institutions might also serve as a guide into how they might best be governed.[103]

A similar policy known as "politique des races" was applied by the French in West, and in certain areas of North Africa, and by the Dutch, in South-East Asia. The absence of direct control, not only reduced the presence of colonial settlers and thus the danger of future Americas arising in Africa or Asia. It also – or so it was hoped – lessened the likelihood of indigenous uprisings. For as Christiaan Snouck Hurgronje, advisor to the colonial government of the Netherlands East Indies, in 1908 remarked, the "Orientals" were no different from the Irish, the Finns, or the Poles: they preferred to be ruled by their own people, for all their faults, than by foreigners.[104] And what was true of the "Orientals" was probably true of all peoples under colonial rule everywhere. Only perhaps in Algeria did the earlier image of empire still persist with any force. But like so many exceptions, this one, too, proved the rule. Before the French invasion, Algeria was not perceived to have been, in any sense, self-governing, as had most areas of Sub-Saharan Africa. It had been part of the Ottoman Empire. Its people had for so long been "in a state of tyrannical subjection" that, in Tocqueville's opinion, they had "entirely lost the habit of governing themselves" – not that this had apparently made them any the more inclined to allow the French to replace the Turks.[105] The alternative to the rule of some other imperial power was not liberty, but anarchy. If Algeria were ever to be at peace, some order had to be brought to the enormously varied cultural geography of the place. We should not, Tocqueville warned in 1847, "be proposing for Algeria the creation of a colony properly speaking, but the extension of France itself to the far side of the Mediterranean". But even Tocqueville was prepared to admit that "justice is not constituted in Africa as it is in France".[106] What he, in fact, envisaged was a mixture of the old and the new. The coastal cities and the surrounding countryside, because these were the only areas the French had any interest in, would be governed by French officials, under French law. Here Algeria would indeed be a part of France on "the far side of the Mediterranean". The interior, however, occupied by warring unstable Bedouin tribes, whose religion made European law and institutions hard for them to accept, should be allowed within limits to govern its own affairs. He called it "partial colonization and total domination", a phrase which could be applied, mutatis mutandis to most of the colonial projects of the nineteenth century.[107]

## IX

The indeterminate, often shifting, status of the new areas under European control, brought to the fore a question which had remained unanswered for a long time. What in the modern world was, precisely, the nature of sovereign authority within an empire? Ever since 1648, the modern nation state has been one in which sovereignty has been regarded as indivisible. The monarchs of Europe had spent centuries wresting authority from nobles, bishops, towns, guilds, military orders, and any number of other quasi-independent, quasi-sovereign bodies. Indivisibility had been one of the shibboleths of pre-Revolutionary Europe, and one which, as we shall see in Chapter 9, the French Revolution had gone on to place at the centre of the conception of the modern state. The modern person is a rights-bearing individual, but – as the *Déclaration des droits de l'homme et du citoyen* 1791 had made clear – he or she is so only by virtue of being a citizen of a single indivisible state.

A nation state is a piece of territory occupied by a single ethnic group, probably speaking a single language, professing a single religion, and most certainly being ruled by a single indivisible power. Empires, were, by contrast, not only ethically, religiously, and linguistically diverse but also, by definition, societies in which sovereignty was divided between a large number of political authorities. It had been impossible for any empire to thrive for long without sharing at least some measure of sovereign authority with either local settler elites or with the local inhabitants. As Henry Maine, declared in 1887, "indivisibility of Sovereignty. ... Does not belong in International Law".[108] Failure to cede this point had after all been the prime cause of the American Revolution, and, after 1810, the revolt of the Spanish colonies in South America, and it had almost driven the French settlers of St. Domingue, Guadeloupe, and Martinique into the waiting arms of the British.

In the case of the "second empires" the practice of some kind of "indirect rule" made the necessity of shared sovereignty even more essential to the survival of the entire system. "The powers of sovereigns", argued Maine,

> are a bundle or collection of powers that may be separated from one another. Thus a ruler may administer civil and criminal justice, may make laws for his subjects and for his territory, may exercise power over life and death and may levy taxes and dues, but nevertheless he may be debarred from making war and peace, and from having foreign relations with any authority outside his territory.[109]

Constitutionally there were obvious similarities between Maine's account and a claim made by the Virginian Richard Bland – Thomas Jefferson's "most learned and logical man, profound in constitutional law" – and reiterated by Benjamin Franklin in his famous three-hour testimony before the House of Commons in February 1776 that the American colonies constituted, in Bland's words, "a distinct state, independent as to their internal government of the original kingdom, but united with her as to their external policy in the closest and most intimate LEAGUE AND AMITY".[110]

The crucial difference between Maine's use of this argument and Bland's is that whereas Bland is talking about "British -Americans", creoles who are claiming to enjoy the same rights and privileges as native-born Englishmen, Maine is talking about the sovereignty of non-European rulers in territories occupied in one way or another by Europeans. The example he had in mind was

> the native princes of India; and states of this kind are at the present moment rising in all the more barbarous portions of the world. In the protectorates which Germany, France, Italy and Spain have established in the Australasian seas and on the coast of Africa, there is no attempt made to annex the land to found a colony in the old sense of the word, but the local tribes are forbidden all foreign relations except those permitted by the protecting state.[111]

The policy of conceding to indigenous rulers a large, yet vaguely defined, control over their own affairs, so long as they did not conflict with the interests of the metropolis, also explains the variety and imprecision of the names given to the new overseas possessions: colonies protectorates, mandates – not to mention the anomalous systems of de facto European rule in which no direct authority of any kind was recognized, such as the "veiled protectorate" by which the British effectively governed Egypt, although it was formally under the sovereignty of the Ottoman sultan, from 1822 to 1922.[112] Whatever else all these places might be, they could not be described (with exception of Bombay) as allodial lands of the Manor of East Greenwich, as some of the Thirteen Colonies had been or, like the Spanish "Kingdoms of the Indies", as integral parts of a "composite monarchy". "I know of no example of it either in ancient or modern history", wrote an exasperated Benjamin Disraeli in 1878 of the British Empire, "No Caesar or Charlemagne ever presided over a dominion so peculiar". The only thing which united all the parts of the British Empire was their recognition of what he called "the commanding spirit of these islands".[113] And it was not only the British who were peculiar in this way; so, too, were the French, German, Belgians, Spanish and Portuguese.

Behind all these claims there lurked another distinction between the first and second empires, which would ultimately prove to be their undoing. The empires of the pre-Revolutionary world had never envisaged a time in which either the natives, when they were believed to exist at all as separate nations, or the settlers would be self-governing or find themselves enjoying the same international status as the nations of Europe. When, by the Royal Proclamation of 1763, the British Crown classified the peoples living in the lands west of the Appalachians as "the several Nations or Tribes of Indians ... under our Sovereign Protection and Dominion", it was not, as some later commentators have suggested, setting those "nations" on the road to eventual independence. It was merely trying to limit the power of the settlers.[114] At the very most the Spanish had conceded that with time, and sufficient education, the American Indians might come to take their place as the equals of the inhabitants of Castile. All the earlier empires had, broadly speaking, shared the Roman view that while a man might still be ethnically, culturally, and religiously a Jew or a Gaul, politically he would be a Roman. Sovereignty, although it might be exercised by any number of different peoples, remained bound, and defined, by an overarching body of law that, although it might accept many local legal codes, derived ultimately from the metropolis.

Because the new empires, by contrast, were ones in which the conquerors were prepared to share at least some part of Maine's "bundle or collection of powers" which constituted their sovereignty with the "native", they were also supposedly intended to prepare him to take his place among what Maine called the "family of civilized nations".[115] For most of the positivist international lawyers of the second half of the nineteenth century, the new imperialism provided a working definition of what the "civilized nations" of the world might be: they were, tautologically, those who agreed to observe international law, because international law itself had always been determined, in Grotius' terms "by the continual experience and testimony of the Sages of the Law".[116] The new international law, therefore, bound together all those under its aegis into what the great German jurist Friedrich Karl von Savigny described as an "international legal community" (*Völkerrechtliche Gemeinschaft*).[117] To join this community, however, one had first to embrace its values which, for Maine at least, if not quite for Savigny, were identical with "the old order of the Aryan world, dissolved but perpetually re-constituting itself under a vast variety of solvent influences".[118]

The "civilizing" objectives of the later empires, combined with the policies of indirect rule – although this had clearly never been their intention – had made the ultimate self-determination of their subject peoples an inevitable goal. Already by 1861 John Stuart Mill had given an admittedly rather lukewarm endorsement to the idea. Although he believed that "the present slight bond of connection" which existed between Britain and its colonies was "a step, as far as it goes, towards universal peace and general friendly co-operation among nations" and would prevent any independent former colony from falling prey to some less benign imperial power, it could not override the fact that "on every principle of morality and justice, [Britain] ought to consent to their separation, should the time come when, after full trial of the best form of union, they deliberately desire to be dissevered".[119]

"The British Empire is a galaxy of states", declared another liberal and first francophone prime minister of Canada, Sir Wilfrid Laurier, in 1902, within which "only one fixed rule of action seems to exist: it is to promote the interests of the colony to the utmost, to develop its scheme of government as rapidly as possible, and eventually to elevate it from the position of inferiority to that of association". As John Atkinson Hobson, the English economist and one of the fiercest and the most influential of the early critics of empire, acidly commented, in reality this was "quite the largest misstatement of the facts of our colonial and imperial policy that is possible. Upon the vast majority of the populations throughout our Empire we have bestowed no real powers of self-government, nor have any serious belief that it is possible for us to do so."[120]

Hobson was doubtless broadly right in his claim that, for all the protestation that European rule was only ever conducted in the interest of leading the peoples under its tutelage to acquire an ability to govern themselves in an identifiably "civilized" manner, very little effort was actually made by colonial administrators on the ground to achieve this goal even in the long run. Although Thomas Babbington Macaulay could claim in 1833 that the mission of the British East India Company had always been that "by good government we may educate our subjects into a capacity for better government; that having become instructed in European knowledge they may, in some future age, demand European institutions", he relegated this to some comfortingly distant moment which would be "the proudest day in English history".[121] Even as late as 1923, Lugard was prepared to state that, as the Africans did not yet constitute states, "the era of complete independence is not as yet visible on the horizon of time".[122]

But for all the imprecision, or sheer pessimism about the time it would take to raise, in Macaulay's words, "a people sunk in the lowest depths of slavery and superstition" and render them "desirous and capable of the privileges of citizens",[123] the very logic of the language of "civilization" made it effectively impossible to postpone indefinitely the moment when, what Rudyard Kipling had infamously called, those "lesser breeds without the law" would take their place among the civilized ones as nations.[124] One of the inescapable consequences of the imperial view that civilization could never be fully achieved except through nationhood was the assumption that what came to be called "national self-determination" could only be achieved with full state independence. Woodrow Wilson, who is generally credited with having placed the idea inescapably before the imperial nations of the world at the Paris Peace Conference of 1919, stopped off on his way to Paris at Genoa, and in front of the monument to Mazzini, the father of liberal nationalism – if ever there was one – declared that his ambitions at the conference would be to realize the ideals of this lonely thinker who "by some gift of God had been lifted above the common level".[125] If the nation state is today looked on not, in Ernest Gellner's terms, as merely a "contingency" but as a "universal necessity" and something approaching a natural type, then it is the imperial practices of the nineteenth-century states that made it so.[126]

The Paris Peace Conference of 1919 had set the ideological agenda for the eventual dissolution of the great empires of the nineteenth centuries. However, it would take another Europeans "civil war" to so weaken the capabilities of the imperial powers that their colonial subjects, no longer content merely to share sovereignty with their conquerors and usurpers, came to increasingly demand undivided sovereignty for themselves. After 1945, however, the end came swiftly, if uncertainly. The British struggled on ineffectively for a brief while in India and Africa, and even in the eastern Mediterranean. The Spanish were driven out of Morocco in 1956, and the French, after what was perhaps the most brutal war of colonial independence of the century, from Algeria in 1962. The Portuguese held tenaciously to Mozambique until 1974; the British clung to Hong Kong until 1997, and Portuguese to Macao, the last factory in Asia, until 1999. But empire, in any of the senses in which it had been previously understood, was over by the mid-1960s. Today, the British still govern a few isolated outposts (and more contentiously the Falkland-Malvinas Islands and Gibraltar), Spain has military bases on the Moroccan coast, and France preserves several overseas "dominions" (*départements et territoires d'outre-mer*), but all of their inhabitants now have French citizenship and are represented separately in the French National Assembly.

x

With the collapse of Hitler's "Thousand Year Reich" and the Soviet Union, the sole surviving contender for imperial status would seem to be the United States. In this context, as in the case of the Soviet Union, the word "empire" is more often used as a term of abuse than as a descriptive, let alone analytical, category. It is, the French liberal philosopher Raymond Aron observed in 1959, merely a "name given by rivals, or spectators, to the diplomacy of a great power".[127] And most of the now diminishing debates over whether the United States is, or is not, an empire or not, as Eric Hobsbawn has pointed out, "really concerned with the actual histories of empires. They are trying to fit old names to historical developments that don't necessarily fit old realties."[128]

There is, in fact, very little about the objectives, policies, or even ideologies of the modern United States which resembles, except superficially, those of past empires. It is true that the early American Republic shared, if only fitfully, some of the enlightened ambitions to create what Jefferson called an "empire of liberty" in the Americas. Like Alexander Hamilton, Jefferson firmly believed that the new Republic should one day be able to "concur in erecting one great American system superior to the control of all transatlantic force or influence and able to dictate the terms of the connections between the old world and the new".[129] This involved casting a sometimes anxious eye over the events unfolding among "our southern brethren". But the conception of empire invoked by Jefferson's talk of "sister republics" was far closer to Kant's "league of peoples" with the United States acting as what Jefferson called the "nest" for all the others than it was to anything envisaged by the European imperial powers.[130]

It is also true that today the United States, like the "liberal" empires of the nineteenth century, Britain and France, is broadly committed to view that there is only one possible form of government for humankind, one mode of "civilization" – in this case liberal democracy – and that it is its duty to export it. It, too, has a mission, and a burden. As with the earlier British (and French) views on the subject, this mission is also linked to the realization that a civilized world of liberal states will be a safer and more profitable place for those places which are already liberal states. What, with few exceptions, it is not committed to is the view that empire – the exercise of *imperium* – is the best, or even a possible, way to achieve this.

In a number of crucial respects the United States is, indeed, very un-imperial. With very few exceptions, it has no overseas possession and no obvious desire to acquire any. It does not conceive its hegemony beyond its borders as constituting a form of citizenship. It exercises no direct rule anywhere outside these areas; and it has always attempted to extricate itself as swiftly as possible from anything which looks as if it were about to develop into even indirect rule (as the recent occupation of Iraq has demonstrated). As Viscount James Bryce, one of the most astute observers of the Americas both North and South, said of the (North) Americans in 1888, "they have none of the earth-hunger which burns in the great nations of Europe".[131] However, it was not merely a lack of "earth hunger", already amply satisfied in Bryce's view within the American mainland, which made the United States a reluctant empire. It was its refusal to engage in the kind of divided sovereignty which Maine had identified as the determining feature of the new empires of the nineteenth century. True, the federal government shares sovereignty with the individual states of which the Union is composed. But it could not contemplate, as former empires have all had to do, sharing sovereignty with the members of other *nations*.

The internal colonization of the United States had followed a precise pattern of incorporation, unlike any empire in (European) history. By the terms of the Northwest Ordinance in 1787, as each new territory was settled or conquered and its settler population had reached 60,000, it became a new state within the Union – rather than an extension of an existing state. The Ordinance did not, of course, apply to overseas territories. However, it did imply that any settlements that might be acquired overseas, like Hawaii, had to be incorporated fully into the nation or returned to their native rulers.[132] What no American administration has been willing to tolerate for long is any kind of colonialism. Even so resolute an imperialist as Teddy Roosevelt could not imagine turning Cuba or the Philippines into true colonies.[133] Such de facto colonies (the overseas territories) that do exist – Guam, the Virgin Islands, Samoa – are also too small to cause much offence. The major exception to this rule is Puerto Rico. However, the continuing debate over the status of Puerto Rico, the fact that it strikes everyone, even those (the majority of the population) who support a continuation of the present status quo, as an anomaly, largely proves the rule.[134]

Like so many of the enlightened and liberal critics of empire from Montesquieu, through Burke to Tocqueville, many Americans have been, and continue to be, conscious of the fact that what is done in the name of the nation overseas may all too easily creep back to threaten the metropolis. As William Jennings Bryan, Democratic candidate for the presidency in 1900, declared: "We hold that the Constitution follows the flag, and denounce the doctrine that an Executive or Congress deriving their existence and their powers from the Constitution can exercise lawful authority beyond it or in violation of it. ... Imperialism abroad will lead quickly and inevitably to despotism at home."[135]

As Bryan was fully aware, to become a true empire the United States would have had to change radically the nature of its political culture. For, in the end, liberal democracy (as most of the western world now conceives it) and liberal empire (as Alexis de Tocqueville and John Stuart Mill conceived it) – or even a "benevolent" empire – are incompatible. Burke and Smith had understood this, as had Mill and Tocqueville. "Empires of liberty" were empires which existed to enforce the virtues and advantages that accompanied free or liberal government in places which otherwise would only ever be, in Mill's language, "barbarous". Such places would, if they were lucky, eventually become fit for "home rule" through a prolonged process of, often forced, education. The United States, by contrast, believes that its adventures overseas are to enable sundry unfortunate "others" to fulfil – usually through the ballot box – what is seen as their natural human right to self-determination. And although this inevitably requires a great deal of coercion, and certainly involves a measure of what might be called informal hegemony, it is clearly not imperial. For whatever else an empire might be, it is constituted by the exercise of sovereignty, direct or indirect, whole or shared, over a people and its territory. Talk of "indirect" or "informal" or "cultural" empire may be illuminating, and it may be helpful, but it is also, and only, metaphorical. Hegemony, the ability of a state to exercise often unrestrained influence over its politically independent and sovereign allies, is one thing. Imperial rule is quite another.

But if empire is at an end, many of the legacies of the political and legal thinking for which it was responsible during its very long history are still very much alive. International law, as we have seen, evolved out of the need to account for, legitimate, and administer far-flung colonial empires. What we today call globalization is the creation of the modern commercial system, and that began, as did the modern European overseas empires, with what were, in Adam Smith's description, the "greatest and most important" events in the history of mankind: the voyages of Columbus and Vasco da Gama.[136]

Paradoxically, one of the most influential of the contemporary legacies of empire which involves questions of both law and sovereign political authority has been the seemingly anti-imperial conception of "human rights". The idea of a "human" right, a right that a person possesses not because he or she occupies a position within a particular political order but merely because he or she is a person, is, I argue in Chapter 9, the successor to the concept of the "natural" or "subjective" right of the late middle ages. And this, I argue in Chapter 1, first acquired real significance beyond the frontiers of Europe in the context of the highly contested claim that there existed a universal law which was binding on all the peoples of the world no matter what their religious beliefs or local forms of government and which, as far as rights were concerned, took precedence over all local positive law. Today there exists, even if it is only of very recent creation, an unmistakable and universal "human rights' culture". This is, as those from the Ayatollah Khomeini to Singapore's Lee Kuan Yew, who have opposed it in the name of theocracy or of some variant of communitarian "Asian" values, have repeatedly insisted, the intellectual progeny of European universalism, and European universalism is the handmaiden of European imperialism. This does not mean, however, as Khomeini Lee Kuan Yew and many Western communitarians have supposed, that this necessarily renders the entire category an empty one, a mere subterfuge for the interference by more powerful military or economic bodies in the affairs of lesser, weaker, powers.

What it does mean is that if we are prepared to argue that all the peoples of the world can make certain claims, however limited, against their governments, as individuals, and that they can – in theory at least – press those claims before a supranational court, then we have also to recognize that this depends on the assumption that there must indeed exist a universal law, however minimal, for all mankind, and that there must also exist an "international community" charged with interpreting and upholding that law. That this is inescapably the creation of a Western conception of law, and of specifically Western belief in the existence of a single human nature, and that those, in turn, are the enduring legacies of the European empires cannot easily be denied. Neither, however, should their genealogy be counted as grounds for dismissing them altogether. For if the form which international law and most international organizations currently take are undeniably "Western", the idea, and the ideal, of universalism is itself clearly universal.

### Endnotes

1 Jan Zielonka, *Europe as Empire: The Nature of the Enlarged European Union* (Oxford: Oxford University Press, 2006), 1–20. Also see the comments by Harold James, *The Roman Predicament: How the Rules of International Order Create the Politics of Empire* (Princeton: Princeton University Press, 2008) 119–40.
2 Cf., Charles Maier, *Among Empires: American Ascendancy and Its Predecessors* (Cambridge: Harvard University Press, 2006), 33. Empires are "a particular form of state organization in which elites of differing ethnic or national units defer to and acquiesce in the political leadership of the dominant power."
3 *Islands of History* (Chicago: Chicago University Press, 1985), 75–6.

4 Jane Burbank and Fredrick Cooper, *Empires in World History: Power and the Politics of Difference* (Princeton: Princeton University Press, 2010), 2–3, and see David Armitage, *Foundations of Modern Political Thought* (Cambridge: Cambridge University Press, 2013), 191–214.

5 Herfried Münkler makes a somewhat opaque distinction between "world" empires and "great" ones, but although he accepts that "a power that does not dominate a significant area cannot be seriously considered as an empire", this depends less on actual size as on duration. The important feature of a "world" empire would seem to be its capacity to outlive the "charismatic qualities of its founder". *Empires*, Patrick Camiller trans. (Cambridge: Polity Press, 2007), 9–17.

6 *The Expansion of England: Two Courses of Lectures* (Macmillan: London, 1883), 239.

7 Quoted in Bernard Cohn, "The Command of Language and the Language of Command" in Ranajit Guha ed., *Subaltern Studies* (Delhi, 1985), IV, 295. Jones, however, died in April 1794 before he could complete the task.

8 This has been described by Clifford Ando, *Imperial Ideology and Provincial Loyalty in the Roman Empire* (Berkeley, Los Angeles, London: University of California Press, 2000).

9 *Ab urbe condita* 8.13.16.

10 Quoted in Peter Brown, *The World of Late Antiquity* (New York and London: W.W. Norton and Company, 1989), 123.

11 "A Few Words on Non-Intervention", in *Essays on Equality Law and Education*, in J. M. Robson ed., *Collected Works of John Stuart Mill* (Toronto: University of Toronto Press, 1984), XXI, 119.

12 *Discorsi sopra la prima decada di Tito Livio*, II. 2.

13 *The Rights of War and Peace [De Jure Belli ac Pacis]* Richard Tuck ed. from the edition by Jean Barbeyrac (Indianapolis: Liberty Fund, 2005), III, XV, 1500–1.

14 *Decline and Fall of the Roman Empire*, David Womersley ed. (London: Penguin, 1994), I, vi.

15 Quoted in A. N. Sherwin-White, *The Roman Citizenship* (Oxford: Oxford University Press, 1973), 435.

16 Claude Nicolet, *The World of the Citizen in Republican Rome*, P. S. Falla trans. (Berkeley and Los Angeles: California University Press,1980), 22.

17 *Aeneid* VIII, 319–23.

18 "The Roman Oration", in James H. Oliver, *The Ruling Power A Study of the Roman Empire in the Second Century after Christ through the Roman Oration of Aelius Aristides* (Transactions of the American Philosophical Society New Series, 23) (Philadelphia: American Philosophical Society, 1953), 59–60.

19 Tacitus *Annals* II, 23–4.

20 See my *Lords of All the World: Ideologies of Empire in Spain, Britain and France c.1500-c.1899* (New Haven and London: Yale University Press, 1995), 149–51.

21 *On the Fortune of Alexander*, 329.

22 *De Finibus* II, 24.

23 *Decline and Fall of the Roman Empire*, 103, chap. III.

24 Quoted in Ando, *Imperial Ideology and Provincial Loyalty in the Roman Empire*, 63.

25 *De Republica* 3.15.24.

26 *Aeneid* I, 277–9, "His ego nec metas rerum nec tempora pono; imperium sine fine dedi."

27 *Digest*, 6.1.1.2.

28 *Le Droit publique romain [Romisches Staatsrecht]*, P. F. Girard trans. (Paris, 1896) VI, 478–9.

29 *The Rights of War and Peace*, II VIII, 636n. See Peter Stein, "The Development of the Notion of *naturalis ratio*", in A. Watson ed., *Daube Noster: Essays in Legal History for David Daube* (Edinburgh: Edinburgh University Press, 1974), 305–16, and Max Kaser, *Ius gentium* (Cologne, Weimar, Vienna: Böhlau Verlag, 1993), 59–70.

30 *Ancient Law* (London, 1861), 58.

31 Defined as "a process of order and orientation that is based on firm land and establishes law" as distinct from *Kolonisation*, which involved active settlement. *The Nomos of the Earth in the International Law of the Jus Publicum Europaeum*, G. L. Umen trans and ed. (New York: Telos Press, 2003), 80–3.

32 On Charles' place in the legend of the "Last World Emperor", see Marie Tanner, *The Last Descendant of Aeneas: The Habsburgs and the Mythic Image of the Emperor* (New Haven and London: Yale University Press, 1993), 119–30.

33 On Campanella's vision, see Jean-Louis Fournel, *La Cité du soleil et les territoires des hommes: Le savoir du monde chez Campanella* (Paris: Albin Michel, 2012).

34 "On the American Indians", in *Vitoria: Political Writings*, Anthony Pagden and Jeremy Lawrance eds. (Cambridge: Cambridge University Press, 1991), 251.

35 *Controversiarum illustrium aliarumque usu frequentium, libri tres* [1563], Fidel Rodriguez Alcalde ed. (Valladolid, N.P.,1931–5), II, 25.

36 Ibid., I, 17.

37 *Considerations on Representative Government*, [1861] in *Collected Works of John Stuart Mill*, XIX,

38 See, e.g., Antony Anghie, *Imperialism, Sovereignty and the Making of International Law* (Cambridge: Cambridge University Press, 2005).

39 Letter to Miguel de Arcos, 8 November 1534, in *Vitoria: Political Writings*, 331.

40 *The Nomos of the Earth in the International Law of the Jus Publicum Europaeum*, 92.

41 *Leviathan*, I, XIV, and II, xxvi, Richard Tuck ed. (Cambridge: Cambridge University Press, 1991), 91–2 and 200. See Noel Malcolm, "Hobbes's Theory of International Relations", in *Aspects of Hobbes* (Oxford: Oxford University Press, 2002), 432–56.

42 *Leviathan*, I, XIII, 90.

43 *Ancient Law*, 45.

44 See Benjamin Straumann, "The *Corpus iuris* as a Source of Law between Sovereigns in Alberico Gentili's Thought" in Benedict Kingsbury and Benjamin Straumann eds., *The Roman Foundations of the Law of Nations* (Oxford: Oxford University Press, 2010), 101–23.

45 *Jus gentium methodo scientifica pertractatu*, (Oxford: Clarendon Press, 1934). II, 17. And cf., Grotius' contention that "The Law of Nations is a more extensive right, deriving its authority from the consent of all, or at least of many nations.... Now the Law of Nations is proved by the same manner as the unwritten civil law,

and that is by the continual experience and testimony of the Sages of the Law."
*The Rights of War and Peace*, I, I, xiv, 162–3. Such "sages" clearly were only to
be found among the "civilized" peoples of the world.

46 "A Few Words on Non-Intervention", in *Essays on Equality Law and Education*,
in *Collected Works of John Stuart Mill*, XXI, 118.

47 "Civilization", in *Essays on Politics and Society*, in *Collected Works of John
Stuart Mill*, XVIII, 119.

48 See Thomas McCarthy, *Race, Empire and the Idea of Human Development*
(Cambridge: Cambridge University Press, 2009), 171–7, discussing John Stuart
Mill's view on race.

49 *Second Treatise on Government*, V, 26, in *Locke's Two Treatises of Government*, Peter Laslett ed. (Cambridge: Cambridge University Press, 1960), 304.

50 The chief end of what he called "civil Society" was as he said, "the preservation of
Property", *Second Treatise on Government*, VII, 85, p. 341. Also see James Tully,
"Aboriginal Property and Western Theory: Recovering a Middle Ground", *Social
Philosophy and Policy* 11 (1994), 153–80, and *An Approach to Political Phil-
osophy: Locke in Contexts* (Cambridge: Cambridge University Press, 1993).

51 See R. Y. Jennings, *The Acquisition of Territory in International Law* (Manches-
ter: Manchester University Press, 1963), 16–20, and Gregory Claeys, *Imperial
Sceptics: British Critics of Empire 1850–1920* (Cambridge: Cambridge University
Press, 2010), 15–19.

52 "On the American Indians", *Vitoria: Political Writings*, 264.

53 See pp. 136–7.

54 *L'Ami des hommes, ou traité de la population* (The Hague, 1758), III, 241–2.

55 *An Inquiry into the Nature and Causes of the Wealth of Nations*, W. B. Todd ed.
(Oxford: Clarendon Press, 1976), II, 946–7 (V. iii).

56 For the use of this term, see H. G. Koenigsberger, "*Dominium regale* or *Dominium politicum et regale*" in *Politicians and Virtuosi: Essays in Early-Modern
History* (London: Hambledon Press, 1986), 12.

57 *Carta derijida [sic] a los Españoles Americanos por uno de sus compatriotas*
(London, 1801), 2.

58 "Carta de Jamaica", September, 1815, in *Obras completas*, Vicente Lecuna and
Esther Barret de Nazaris eds. (Havana: Editorial Lex, 1950), I, 160.

59 Letter to the *Royal Gazette* of Kingston, Jamaica, 1815, in *Obras completas*,
I, 176.

60 See my *Spanish Imperialism and the Political Imagination. Studies in European
and Spanish-American Social and Political Theory 1513–1830* (New Haven and
London: Yale University Press, 1990), 152–3.

61 "Of the Balance of Power", in *Essays, Moral, Political, and Literary* [1777],
Eugene F. Miller ed. (Indianapolis: Liberty Fund, 1985), 340–1.

62 See, in general, Sankar Muthu, *Enlightenment against Empire* (Princeton and
Oxford: Princeton University Press, 2003).

63 See pp. 176–7.
"Toward Perpetual Peace. A Philosophical Project", in *Practical Philosophy*,
Mary Gregor trans. and ed., *The Cambridge Edition of the Works of Immanuel
Kant* (Cambridge: Cambridge University Press, 1999), 328 (AK 8:357).

64 Ibid., 325–6 (AK 8:354).

65 Ibid., 326 (AKA 8:355).
66 "The Metaphysics of Morals", *Practical Philosophy*, 485 (AK 6:347).
67 "Towards Perpetual Peace: A Philosophical Project", *Practical Philosophy*, 336 (AK 8:367).
68 On this see p. 178.
69 See Pauline Kleingeld, "Kant's Second Thoughts on Colonialism", in Katrin Flikschuh and Lea Ypi eds., *Kant and Colonialism: Historical and Critical Perspectives* (Oxford: Oxford University Press, 2014), 43–67.
70 See p. 181, and Muthu, *Enlightenment against Empire*, 88–9. On Kant's change of mind from his earlier, and overtly racist, position, see Pauline Kleingeld, *Kant and Cosmopolitanism: The Philosophical Ideal of World Citizenship* (Cambridge: Cambridge University Press, 2012), 111–117.
71 "On the Common Saying: That May Be Correct in Theory, But It Is of No Use in Practice", *Practical Philosophy*, 296 (AK 8:297). For Kant "republicanism" was to be understood as "the political principle of the separation of the executive power (the government) from the legislative power" and was not to be confused with "a democratic constitution (as usually happens)". "Towards Perpetual Peace: A Philosophical Project", *Practical Philosophy*, 324 (AK 8:352).
72 "Idea for a Universal History with a Cosmopolitan Aim", in *Anthropology. History, and Education*, Günter Zöller and Robert B. Louden, eds., *The Cambridge Edition of the Works of Immanuel Kant* (Cambridge: Cambridge University Press, 2007), 118 (AK 8:28).
73 "An Answer to the Question: What Is Enlightenment?", *Practical Philosophy*, 21 (AK 8:40).
74 See my *The Enlightenment – and Why It Still Matters* (New York: Random House, 2013), 309–13.
75 On the complexities and ambiguities in Kant's views on commerce, see Lea Ypi "Commerce and Colonialism in Kant's Philosophy of Nature and History", in Flikschuh and Ypi, *Kant and Colonialism*, 99–129.
76 "Histoire des Deux Indes," in *Œuvres*, Laurent Versini ed. (Paris: Robert Laffont, 1994), III, 689.
77 See p. 194.
78 See my *European Encounters with the New World from Renaissance to Romanticism* (New Haven and London: Yale University Press, 1993).
79 See p. 199.
80 "Principles of Politics applicable to all Representative Governments," in *Constant: Political Writings*, Biancamaria Fontana ed. and trans. (Cambridge: Cambridge University Press, 1988), 256.
81 "The Liberty of the Ancients Compared with that of the Moderns", *Constant: Political Writings*, 317.
82 See pp. 201–2.
83 "The Spirit of Conquest and Usurpation and their Relation to European Civilization", *Constant: Political Writings*, 72–3.
84 "Towards a Holy Alliance of the Peoples", in Stefano Recchia and Nadia Urbinati eds., *A Cosmopolitanism of Nations. Giuseppe Mazzini's Writings on Democracy, Nation Building and International Relations* (Princeton: Princeton University Press, 2009), 118.

85 "The Spirit of Conquest and Usurpation and their Relation to European Civilization", *Constant: Political Writings*, 64.
86 *International Law: A Series of Lectures Delivered before the University of Cambridge 1887* (London: John Murray, 1888), 8.
87 *De la colonization chez les peuples modernes* (Paris: Guillaumin, 1902, 5th edition), I, viii. Preface to the 4th edition of 1891.
88 *Speeches by Lord Curzon of Kedleston, Viceroy and Governor General of India* (Calcutta, 1900), I, ii.
89 *Elements of the Philosophy of Right*, H. B. Nisbet trans. (Cambridge: Cambridge University Press, 1991), 367, 368 (331, 335).
90 *Reflections on the Origins and Destiny of Imperial Britain* (London: Macmillan, 1900), 16, 262, and see the essays in Mark Bradley ed., *Classics and Imperialism in the British Empire* (Oxford: Oxford University Press, 2010), and Richard Hingley, *Roman Officers and English Gentlemen: The Imperial Origins of Roman Archaeology* (London and New York: Routledge: 2007), 87–95.
91 *De la colonization chez les peuples modernes* (Paris, 1874), 605–6.
92 *The Age of Empire, 1875–1914* (London: Abacus, 1987), 70.
93 Paul Kennedy, *The Rise and Fall of the Great Powers* (New York: Random House 1987), 148–9.
94 "Speech on Nabob of Arcot's Debts, 28 February 1785", in *The Writings and Speeches of Edmund Burke*, P. J. Marshall ed. (Oxford: Clarendon Press, 1981), V, 519. He also refers to the "the sufferings of our fellow creatures and fellow subjects in that oppressed part of the world" (549). On Condorcet, see my *The Enlightenment – and Why it Still Matters*.
95 *Mon périple* (Paris: Seghers, 1987), 142.
96 For these figures, see Jacques Frémeaux, *Les empires coloniaux dans le processus de mondialisation* (Paris: Maisonneuve & Larose, 2002), 168–76.
97 "Travail sur l'Algérie", in *Tocqueville sur l'Algérie*, Seloua Luste Boulbina ed. (Paris: Flamarion, 2003), 126.
98 Quoted in David Bromwich ed., *On Empire, Liberty and Reform. Speeches and Letters of Edmund Burke* (New Haven and London: Yale University Press, 2000), 15–16.
99 Quoted in Uday Singh Mehta, *Liberalism and Empire: A Study in Nineteenth-Century British Liberal Thought* (Chicago: University of Chicago Press, 1999), 139–40.
100 On the ideological origin of "indirect rule", see Karuna Mantena, *Alibis of Empire: Henry Maine and the Ends of Liberal Imperialism* (Princeton: Princeton University Press, 2010), who argues very powerfully that the new policies, and the claims – Maine's in particular – which sustained them, represented a move away from "liberal imperialism".
101 Frederick John Lugard, *The Dual Mandate in British Tropical Africa* (London: Blackwood, 1923), 61.
102 T. S. Smiley, "Social Advance in Non-Autonomous Territories", in *Principles and Methods of Colonial Administration, Colson Papers* (London: Butterworth Scientific Publications, 1950), 212.
103 On Maine's invention of "traditional society", see Mantena, *Alibis of Empire*, 56–88, and Clive Dewey, "The Influence of Sir Henry Maine on Agrarian Policy

in India", in Alan Diamond ed., *The Victorian Achievement of Sir Henry Maine* (Cambridge: Cambridge University Press, 1991), 353–75.

104 J. S. Furnivall, *Netherlands India: A Study of Plural Economy* (Cambridge: Cambridge University Press, 1939), 291.

105 "Second lettre sur l'Algérie", *Tocqueville sur l'Algérie*, 57.

106 "Rapport fait par M. Tocqueville sur le projet de la loi relative aux crédits extraordinaires demandés pour l'Algérie", *Tocqueville sur l'Algérie*, 228.

107 "Travail sur l'Algérie", *Tocqueville sur l'Algérie*, 106.

108 *International Law*, 58. And, in general, on the issue of divided sovereignty, see Edward Keene, *Beyond the Anarchical Society: Grotius, Colonialism and Order in World Politics* (Cambridge: Cambridge University Press, 2002).

109 *International Law*, 57-8

110 *An Enquiry into the Rights of the British Colonies* (London, 1766), 16, and on Franklin, see Bernard Bailyn, *The Ideological Origins of the American Revolution*, (Cambridge, MA: Harvard University Press, 1967), 213.

111 *International Law*, 58–9.

112 The phrase "veiled protectorate" was coined by Lord Alfred Milner, who occupied the ambiguously named position of "under-secretary of finance".

113 Quoted in R. Koebner and H. Schmidt eds., *Imperialism: The Story and Significance of a Political Word, 1840–1960* (Cambridge: Cambridge University Press, 1964), 136–7.

114 In W. P. M. Kennedy ed., *Documents of the Canadian Constitution* (Toronto, New York: Oxford University Press, 1918), 20.

115 *International Law*, 37–8. He is commenting on the view put forward in Francis Wharton's *A Digest of the International Law of the United States*, but it is obvious that he also endorses it.

116 See pp. 56–7.

117 Maine, *International Law*, 38. On Savigny, see Jean-Louis Halperín, *Entre nationalisme juridique et communauté du droit* (Paris: Presses Universitaires de France, 1999), 46–66, and Martti Koskenniemi, "Ruling the World by Law (s): The View from around 1850", in Martti Koskenniemi and Bo Strath eds., *Europe 1815–1914: Creating Community and Ordering the World* (Helsinki: University of Helsinki, 2014), 16–32.

118 *The Effects of Observation of India in Modern European Thought* (London: John Murray, 1875), 30.

119 *Considerations on Representative Government* Cap, XVII. See Duncan Bell, "John Stuart Mill on Colonies", *Political Theory*, 38 (2010), 34–68, and R. N. Ghosh, "John Stuart Mill on Colonies and Colonization", in *John Stuart Mill*, John Cunningham Wood ed. (London: Croom Helm, 1987), IV, 354–67.

120 *Imperialism: A Study* (London: James Nisbet, 1902), 120.

121 Quoted in Ronald Hyam, *Britain's Imperial Century 1815–1914: A Study of Empire and Expansion* (London: B. T. Batsford, 1976), 220.

122 *The Dual Mandate in British Tropical Africa*, 197–8. Although Lugard did not look on African rulers as sovereign in the same way that the Indian princes were, but rather as collaborators, the relationships both involved what Maine thought of as divided sovereignty.

123 Quoted in Ronald Hyam, *Britain's Imperial Century 1815–1914*, 220.

124 *The Recessional*, line 22.
125 Quoted in Denis Mack Smith, *Mazzini* (New Haven and London: Yale University Press, 1994), 221.
126 *Nations and Nationalism* (Oxford: Blackwell, 2006), 6–7.
127 Quoted in Tzvetan Todorov, *Le Nouveau désordre mondial: Réflexions d'un Européen* (Paris: Robert Laffont, 2003), 38.
128 *On Empire: America, War and Global Supremacy* (New York, London: New Press, 2008), 61.
129 "Federalist 11", in Alexander Hamilton, James Madison, and John Jay, *The Federalist Papers*, Isaac Kramnick ed. (Harmondsworth: Penguin Books, 1987), 133–4.
130 Letter to Lafayette May 14, 1817, in *Writings* (New York: Library of America, 1984), 1408, and see Robert W. Tucker and David C. Hendrickson, *Empire of Liberty: The Statecraft of Thomas Jefferson* (Oxford: Oxford University Press, 1990), 159–61 and 312–3.
131 *The American Commonwealth* [1888] (New York: Cosmo Classics, 2007), II, 530.
132 There are exceptions. Alaska, for instance, which had been purchased from Russia in 1867, was administered first as a federal district and then, in 1912, as a territory, and only became a state, after a prolonged struggle, in 1959.
133 Frank Ninkovich, *The United States and Imperialism* (Malden: Blackwell Publishers, 2001), 75.
134 See Christina Duffy Burnett and Burke Marshall eds., *Foreign in a Domestic Sense: American Expansion and the Constitution* (Durham: Duke University Press, 2001).
135 Quoted in Kal Raustiala, *Does the Constitution Follow the Flag? The Evolution of Territoriality in American Law* (Oxford: Oxford University Press, 2009), 4.
136 *An Inquiry into the Nature and Causes of the Wealth of Nations*, 626 (IV. vii).

# Defending Empire

## *The School of Salamanca and the "Affair of the Indies"*

The conquest, occupation, and settlement of the Americas were the first large-scale European colonizing ventures since the fall of the Roman Empire. From Columbus' first landfall on a still unidentified island in the Caribbean, which its inhabitants called Guarahani, on October 12, 1492, the Spanish – followed by the Portuguese, the French, the British, the Dutch, the Germans, and even briefly the Russians, the Swedes, and the Danes – established settlements in territories where they had no clear and obvious authority. Before long, and in varying degrees of intensity depending on the circumstances of the initial settlement, this gave rise to considerable anxiety as to what kind of rights, if any, these states might have in the lands they had occupied. In some cases the overseas territories had been acquired by treaty or purchase. In the case of the most significant in terms of sheer size and wealth, however – the Spanish, French and British in the the Americas – they had been acquired by forceful occupation. Their acquisition had, that is, involved warfare, and within the European legal tradition, violence by one group of people against another could only be legitimate when it was defensive. "The best state", as Cicero had observed in a much-quoted phrase, "never undertakes war except to keep faith or in defense of its safety".[1] Of course, as Cicero well knew, the Roman state had frequently acquired clients, "allies" (*socii*), the need to "keep faith" with whom could be employed as a justification for what was in effect a war of conquest. But what the arguments from defence clearly could not easily do was legitimate attacks on remote populations whose very existence, in the most contentious case, had previously been entirely unknown. The debates over the legitimacy of the much publicized European "conquests" in the Americas therefore turned, inevitably, on the question of how what seemed uncontestably to be wars of occupation and dispossession could be presented as wars of defence.[2] This involved an extensive reexamination, and sometimes reworking, of whole areas of the legal systems of early-modern Europe, just as it threw into question earlier assumptions about the nature of sovereignty, utterly transformed international relations, and was ultimately responsible for the evolution of what would eventually come to be called international law.

The earliest, and most influential, contributors to this enterprise were a group of theologians who have become known as the School of Salamanca, or since some of them had only a slight connection to the University of Salamanca itself, the "Second Scholastic". Theologians from Domingo de Soto (1494–1560) and Melchor Cano (1509–60) to the great Jesuit metaphysicians, Luís de Molina (1535–1600) and Francisco Suárez (1548–1600) – whom Leibniz claimed (improbably) to be able to be read with as much pleasure as most people read novels – were, for the most part, the pupils, and the pupils of the pupils, of Francisco de Vitoria who held the Prime Chair of Theology at Salamanca between 1526 and his death in 1546.[3] "Insofar as we are learned, prudent and elegant", wrote Cano, "we are so because we follow this outstanding man, whose work is an admirable model for every one of those things, and emulate his precepts and his example."[4] Although they are sometimes described vaguely as "theologians and jurists", they were all, in fact, theologians.[5] The discussion of the Roman law played a large role in their work, and their influence can be seen in particular in canon lawyers such as Diego Covarrubias y Leyva (1512–67) and in the civil lawyer Fernando Vázquez de Menchaca (1512–69), whom Hugo Grotius called the "pride of Spain".[6] But jurists were members of a distinct and, in the opinion of most theologians, inferior faculty. In the early-modern world, theology, the "mother of sciences" because it dealt directly with first causes, was considered to be above all other modes of inquiry and superior to everything that belonged to what today is called jurisprudence, as well as to most moral and political philosophy.[7]

Many of the more prominent members of the School of Salamanca acted not only as university professors but also as advisors primarily, but not exclusively, on matters of conscience to a wide range of public and private bodies. Vitoria was asked about the justice of the Portuguese slave trade, the validity of clandestine marriages, and the legitimacy of increasing the price of corn during a poor harvest. Cano advised Philip II in his struggle with Pope Paul IV and was even consulted on how best to defend the Canary Islands against attacks by French pirates. Suárez was questioned innumerable times on the Immaculate Conception, the election of the Pope, benefices, marriage contracts, and the preaching rights of the Dominicans.[8] Vitoria once told a correspondent that his views were rarely heeded, for kings were necessarily pragmatic beings driven to think "from hand to foot and their counselors even more so".[9] Theology and philosophy, he claimed, should ideally be confined to professional deliberations. "I sometimes think", he wrote, "how very foolish it is for one of my kind to think, let alone to speak, about government and public affairs. It seems to me even more absurd than a grandee pronouncing on our philosophies."[10] There was, however, something disingenuous in these claims. Most of the topics on which the Salamanca theologians and jurists were asked their opinion had clear policy implications, and many of the major figures of the "School" – Vitoria himself, Cano, and Domingo de Soto – were taken away from their lecture halls for long periods to become diplomats (Soto was a member of the Spanish delegation at the Council of Trent) and councillors or members of that select body of spiritual-cum-political advisors, the royal confessors.

It was, however, their views on the legitimacy of their sovereign's conquest of the Americas, and more broadly on the nature of the polity that has come to be called the Spanish Empire, for which they were best known by later generations. The involvement of the School of Salamanca in the "Affair of the Indies" had a wide and long-lasting resonance, sufficient even for that staunch anti-imperialist Samuel Johnson to remark as late as 1763: "I love the university of Salamanca, for when the Spaniards were in doubt as to the lawfulness of their conquering America, the University of Salamanca gave it as their opinion that it was not lawful."[11] Johnson was being overenthusiastic. The University of Salamanca never went that far. On occasions, however, some of its members came perilously close. And their reputation as upholders of the rule of law against an otherwise unprincipled monarch, and an overambitious Pope, endured. "It is difficult for us in the present age", wrote Sir Travers Twiss, former British Advocate General and salaried champion of Leopold II's occupation of the Congo in 1856,

> to measure the degree of courage and noble principle which impelled these excellent monks [Francisco de Vitoria and Domingo de Soto] to vindicate the right of the oppressed against the authority of the Church, the ambitions of the Crown, the avarice and pride of their countrymen, and the prejudices of their own Order. These were the early streaks of dawn, the earnest of the coming day.[12]

Twiss was referring initially to a now celebrated public lecture, *relectio* "On the Indies" (*De Indis*) or "On the American Indians", delivered by Vitoria in January 1539.[13] It is a text that has, ever since, been held to be the earliest attempt to transform the Roman law of nations into something that later generations would recognize as an international law.

Vitoria's objective, he claimed, had been merely to find an answer to the question: "By what right (*ius*) were the barbarians subjected to Spanish rule?" He began, however, with a caution. "It may first of all be objected", he admitted,

> that *this whole dispute is unprofitable and fatuous* not only for those like us who have no warrant to question or censure the conduct of government in the Indies irrespective of whether or not it is rightly administered, but even for those whose business it is to frame and administer their government.

Could it be possible that Ferdinand and Isabella, "most Catholic Monarchs", and Charles V, officially entitled "most righteous and Christian prince", might have failed "to make the most careful and meticulous inquiries" into a matter of such concern to both their security and their conscience? "Of course not", Vitoria retorted, "further cavils are unnecessary, and even insolent."[14]

However, he went on, in cases where some reasonable doubt might exist as to the lawfulness of a particular case, "it is pertinent to question and deliberate" the issue. No one, that is, was casting doubt on the righteousness of Ferdinand and Isabel's or Charles V's acts. For if the "verdict of the wise" is that an act is lawful, "anyone who accepts their opinion may be secure in his conscience *even if the action is in fact unlawful*" (emphasis added). This, in Vitoria's cautious assessment, was the position in which Ferdinand and Isabel and Charles V had all found themselves. What was at issue, then, was not the conscience of a king, but the legal facts of the case. And although the previous "wise men" who had decided in favour of the legality of the issue might have been in good faith, it is nevertheless the case that any decision will be binding only "until such time as an equally competent authority pronounces a conflicting opinion which reopens the case or leads to a contrary verdict". As facts change over time, so, too, will the laws and the kind of government they sustain. "For the law in such things", wrote Vázquez de Menchaca, "is for one day only, and on another day it dies."[15] This was precisely what had occurred in the case of "this business of the barbarians". For now, it would seem, in the light of all the evidence which currently existed, that "the matter is neither so evidently unjust of itself that one may not question where it is just, nor so evidently just that one may not wonder whether it might be unjust". Under these circumstances, it was perfectly legitimate to reopen the case, for although

> we may readily suppose that, since the affair is in the hands of men both learned and good, everything had been conducted with rectitude and justice. ... When we hear subsequently of bloody massacres and innocent individuals pillaged of their possession and dominions, there are grounds for doubting the justice of what has been done.[16]

Most of the previous cavils had been proposed by the jurists. The Indians, however, were not, as Vitoria put it, "subjects [of the Spanish crown] by human – [i.e., positive] law", and the jurists – he went on, pulling academic rank – were, therefore, "not sufficiently versed" in the matter to "form an opinion on their own". This was clearly "a case of conscience", and as such it was a question for the theologians (although in fact, the substance of Vitoria's arguments are legal rather than theological). It was also the case that "theo-logical disputations", as distinct from legal ones, "are of the deliberative kind – undertaken that is not to argue about the truth, but to explain it".[17]

By posing his question in terms of a *right*, however, Vitoria was clearly aware – as his overextended piece of self-justification makes plain – that he was raising a far wider, and for his royal master potentially far more damaging, doubt about the nature and the possible legitimacy not only of the Spanish monarchy in the Americas but also of all empires everywhere. He was also raising questions about what right, if any, a state had to a make war against another which had not caused it any direct harm. More generally he pointed to issues, which have still not been resolved, about the right of any people to impose on others what it believes to be the natural rights of all humankind or to intervene in affairs of another state in the defence of those whom it believes to be oppressed.

It was this which led the German jurist Carl Schmitt to declare in 1951 that "for four hundred years from the sixteenth to the twentieth centuries the structure of European international law (*Völkerrecht*)" had been "determined by a fundamental course of events; conquest of a new world". It was this "legendary and unforeseen ... and unrepeatable historical event", he claimed, that had given rise to what he called "the traditional Eurocentric order of international law". For the discovery of America by presenting the jurists and theologians of Christian Europe with a truly novel problem had dramatically altered the nature of the legal and moral arguments concerning what Schmitt described as the "justification of European land-appropriation as a whole".[18] And it was this which, in 1780, Jeremy Bentham had christened "international law".

For America, and its inhabitants – despite ingenious attempts to prove that it had once been occupied by stranded Carthaginian sailors – was indisputably, in Vitoria's words, "previously unknown to our world".[19] Whatever else the Amerindians might be, they, therefore, could clearly not be "subjects by human law".[20] This meant that the only categories of law under which they might be subject were the divine, the natural, and the law of nations, all of which were believed to be binding, in different ways on all humankind. Any argument that might grant the Spanish any kind of *rights* in the Americas would, *therefore*, have to be expressed in terms of some kind of universal claim.

The earliest, and politically most contentious, of these had been papal donation. Ever since the ninth century, the canon lawyers in the service of the Curia had held that the pope as "Vicar of Christ" enjoyed both spiritual and secular authority over all the peoples of the world whatever their religious beliefs. If this were the case then the pope was in a position to grant sovereignty over a non-Christian people to a Christian prince. Acting on this belief, in 1454, Pope Nicholas V had granted to Afonso V of Portugal rights of settlement over all "provinces, islands, ports, places and seas, already acquired and which you might acquire in the future, no matter what their number size or quality" in Africa from Cape Bojador and Cape Nun, "and thence all southern coasts until their end".[21] After Columbus returned from his second voyage in 1493 and it became clear to all – except Columbus himself – that what he had discovered was not the outer fringes of "Cathay" but some new world whose size and potential wealth was as yet unknown, the Castilian crown hastily secured from Alexander VI five bulls which granted it territorial rights over all those lands "as you have discovered or are about to discover" and which were not already occupied by another Christian prince.[22]

One year later Spain and Portugal signed a treaty at the Spanish border town of Tordesillas, which divided the entire globe into two discrete spheres of jurisdiction, along a line set at 370 leagues west of the Cape Verde Islands. This corresponded approximately to 46°30′W, although at the time, before the invention of the marine chronometer, this could not be established with any accuracy. By means of what William Paterson, first governor of the Bank of England, contemptuously dismissed in 1701 as "certain imaginary mathematical lines between heaven and earth", the western half of the globe went to Castile, which believed that it now controlled an unhindered route to Asia.[23] The eastern half went to Portugal, intent mainly on keeping its Castilian rivals out of the South Atlantic, which thereby came into possession of Brazil.

The treaty, however, as the English astronomer John Dee gleefully pointed out, said nothing about what happened to the line once it emerged on the far – eastern – side of the globe. Furthermore, by continuing around the globe it had, in effect, violated the terms of the bulls, which had spoken only of lands to the west.[24] Because both the bulls and the treaty were cast in the future tense, they also assumed that the actual inhabitants of all those territories had no legitimate claim to them. These had now become merely caretakers biding their time until the arrival of their true owners. Any attempt to resist could, therefore, be met with legitimate force.

Needless to say, most of the other rulers of Europe were generally dismissive of any such claims. The Treaty of Tordesillas was recognized to be binding between its two signatories but worthless elsewhere. As for the bulls, they, as Dee colorfully put it, "importeth not a Portingale fig". Queen Elizabeth, said William Camden, "could not perswade her selfe the Spaniard had any rightfull title to the Bishops of *Romes* donation, in whom she acknowledged no prerogative, much less authority in such causes".[25] In the bulls the English also believed that they could see clear evidence of a characteristically papist collusion between church and state. Alexander VI was, as the English geographer Richard Hakluyt pointed out, himself a Spaniard and "therefore no marvell thoughe he were ledd by parcialitie to favour the spanish nation though yt were to the prejudice and dommage of all others".[26]

Despite the absurdities and duplicities involved, on which the Spanish scholastics themselves dwelt at length, the Bulls of Donation remained for the Spanish monarchy itself the principle and, in its mind, only undisputable claim to sovereignty in the Americas until the final demise of the Kingdoms of the Indies in the nineteenth century. The *Recopilación de leyes de los reynos de Indias* of 1680, which constituted a distinct law code for the Americas, states, "By donation of the Holy Apostolic See and other just and legitimate titles We [the King of Spain] are Lord of the Western Indies and the Mainland of the Ocean Sea, which has been discovered or is still to be discovered, and has been are incorporated into our Royal Crown of Castile."[27]

The Salamanca theologians, however, had no doubt that whatever other status the Americas might have, they were certainly not a gift from the pope as God's legate on earth. Twiss was overdramatizing the case when he claimed that it had been the "scandal given by [the] extreme reach of the authority on the part of the See of Rome coupled with the cruel and rapacious abuse of the Donation made by the Spaniards" that had "provoked" a "champion from amongst the ranks of the theological casuists to step forth in [sic] behalf of the native inhabitants of the newly discovered countries".[28] He was right, however, in seeing the need to deprive the papacy of its plenitude of power in secular matters, as among the first of their concerns. For whereas it might be acceptable to grant the Church some measure of precedence over the secular authority on spiritual and even moral grounds, the idea that the papacy could make grants of sovereignty ran directly counter to the hallowed, if often abused, injunction of Jesus himself to "Render ... unto Caesar the things which are Caesar's; and unto God the things that are God's" (Mathew 22:21), and it raised questions about the spheres of jurisdiction shared by pope and emperor, both of whom, at one time or another, made mutually incompatible claims to universal sovereignty.

The canon lawyers, for their part, rested their claims on an argument which had been made most forcefully by the decretalist Hostiensis in the thirteenth century. If, as they assumed, the Roman Emperors had, by the terms of Justinian's decree *Bene a Zenon*, been granted exclusive rights of property in "the world", then the popes, as their sole true heirs, could likewise lay claim not only to sovereignty over the entire world, Christian and non-Christian, but also the right of ownership (*dominium ac proprietatem bonorum omnium*) to everything in it.[29] This, in turn, allowed the papacy the right to distribute that property among its subjects as it so wished. It was on this presumption that the Holy See had given jurisdiction and property rights over one half of the world to Afonso V and to Ferdinand and Isabella over the other half. Clearly, however, only the most committed champion of papal supremacy could find any unassailable reason for endorsing such a claim. It was, said Soto bluntly, nothing other than a prescription for tyranny. In practice, only the Turks had ever exercised such rights. A Christian prince, by contrast, whose rule was absolute but not arbitrary, could not make use of the goods (*bona*) of his subjects "except where it is necessary for the defence and government of the community".[30]

To exercise universal *dominium* the pope would, as Vitoria pointed out, have had to have acquired it through one of the three forms of law: divine, natural, or civil. Clearly, on the canon lawyers' own evidence, papal *dominium* could not derive from either civil or natural law. And, "as for divine law, no authority is forthcoming", wrote Soto, hence, "it is vain and willful to assert it".[31] All the references to secular authority in the Bible would indeed seem to suggest a clear distinction between the domain of Christ and that of Caesar. The pope's authority, as Innocent III had decreed, was confined to spiritual rather than secular matters, except where strictly moral issues were involved.[32] "It is clear from all that I have said", concluded Vitoria bluntly and categorically, "that the Spaniards when they first sailed to the lands of the barbarians carried with them no right at all to occupy their territories."[33]

Papal claims to plenitude of power over the whole world, furthermore, like all universalist claims supposed the existence of a stable and recognizable cosmos. If, as Soto argued, the Latin term *terra* (or *orbis terrarum*) was taken to describe nothing more than the territorial limits of the jurisdiction of the Roman people, and if "Christendom" was deemed to be coextensive with the Empire, there were grounds for supposing that the pope might be in a position to act as an adjudicator between Christian rulers, and such rulers "are bound to accept his judgment to avoid causing all the manifold spiritual evils which must necessarily arise from any war between Christian princes".[34] (It was precisely this claim, widely accepted by all Christians before the Reformation, which was effectively abandoned by the Treaty of Westphalia in 1648.[35])

The analogous claim of the rulers of the oxymoronic "Holy Roman Empire", of which Charles V was of course one, to exercise *dominium* over all the world as the heirs of Augustus suffered from similar defects.[36] It was Soto who first addressed this question in a *relectio* entitled *De dominio* of 1534.[37] On the first argument he pointed out that the Romans had certainly never, in fact, exercised jurisdiction over the entire world, for "many nations were not then subjugated as is attested by Roman historical writing itself; and this point is most obvious with regard to the other hemisphere and the lands across the sea recently discovered by our countrymen". And if that were so, then clearly they could have no a priori jurisdiction over places which were previously unknown to them, nor could they claim to have exercised sovereignty over the entire world.[38] And even if it had been the case that the Romans had had an exact geographical knowledge of what they freely called the *orbis terrarum*, they could not, even then, claim to exercise sovereignty over any part of it, other than that which they actually administered.

The frequently cited (Christian) supposition that "God handed the world over to the Romans on account of their virtues" necessarily implied, Soto argued, that all the nations of the world had "willingly handed themselves over to the Romans on account of their zeal for justice". In historical fact, however, "[f]rom their own historians we learn that their right was in force of arms (*ius erat in armis*) and they subjugated many unwilling nations through no other title than that they were more powerful, and one cannot find where God gave them such a right".[39] Furthermore, the collective *virtus* of the Romans (assuming it to have existed at all) had been constituted by purely secular and civil qualities, such as justice and fortitude, which retain their intrinsic merit, even when they are pursued for the wrong reasons. The Romans might have had the capacity for instructing the less able in the path of secular virtue, but that did not make their empire a divinely sanctified state. The supposition which had underpinned so much Christian thinking about the pagan empire was clearly false. It had been a purely human creation limited, like all such creations, in both time and space. As such, of course, its historical existence offered no possible legitimization for future imperial projects, especially those supposedly pursued in the interest of evangelization.[40]

For Soto, however, there was a further, and in the long run far more compelling, reason why there could exist in the world no ruler of any kind with universal sovereignty. All the neo-Thomists were insistent that civil power could only be transferred by society acting as a single body. What was known as the "efficient power" of the commonwealth because it is "founded upon natural law" ultimately derived from God. But the "material cause" of civil power – that is, the actual task of administration and of the choice of who is to rule – must rest with the commonwealth, for, in Vitoria's words, "in the absence of any divine law, or human elective franchise (*suffragium*) there is no convincing reason why one man should have power more than another".[41] To create a truly *universal* empire, therefore, it would be necessary, said Soto, for "a general assembly to be called on which at least the major part consented to such an election". No one, however, could possibly imagine a general assembly of literally all the world. Even if, as the prehistory of civil society seemed to require, some such meeting had once been called, the new discoveries would have subsequently nullified its decisions, if only because, as Soto reiterated, "neither the name nor the fame of the Roman Caesars reached the Antipodes and the islands discovered by us".[42] The whole idea of any kind of universal rule was, as Hugo Grotius said later, nothing more than a "silly notion".[43]

The Roman Empire itself, however exceptional it might have been, was merely, in fact, a very large state – although this is not, of course, how any of the neo-Thomists phrased it. Soto was prepared to accept that "the imperial authority ... surpasses all others, [and] it is the most excellent of all", but only because it involved the rule of more than one people (*natio*). It did not, however, he continued, "follow from this that it is the only one to dominate the world".[44]

II

Vitoria and his successors had established beyond any doubt that, in Vitoria's words, "it is clear ... that the Spaniards when they first sailed to the land of the barbarians, carried with them no right at all to occupy their countries".[45] The question now then was, did there exist any other claim that the Spanish might have which could be said to have been acquired after their arrival in the Americas? Any such "titles" could only be valid under one of the four kinds of law: divine, civil, natural, and the law of nations. As we have seen, no European ruler was in a position to claim rights in America under civil law because no civil, or positive law, could apply beyond the territorial limits of the state in which it had been promulgated. Divine – that is, revealed – law made no mention of the Americas.[46] This left the natural law and the law of nations, the *ius gentium*, and it is because of their rewriting of the latter that the School of Salamanca is most often accredited with having laid the basis for a law which would be something more far-reaching than a simple domestic law applied to the wider world.

Initially the *ius gentium* had been the law used by the Romans in their dealing with the *gentes* – that is, non-Roman citizens. It was based on the *mos maiorum* or the customs of the majority, for, as Cicero had observed, "there is a fellowship that is extremely widespread shared by all with all".[47] By the second-century CE, however, its reach had been considerably expanded and it had become enmeshed in the natural law. The jurist Gaius is widely accredited with having made it into a general law which "natural reason establishes among all men and is observed by all peoples alike [this] is called the *ius gentium*, as being the *ius* which all nations employ".[48] In the fourteenth century, Bartolus of Sassoferato and the commentators then divided the *ius gentium* into two: a "primary law of nations" (*ius gentium primaevum*) and a secondary one (*ius gentium secundarium*). The first of these would seem to be indistinguishable from the natural law. The second, however, since it was clearly arrived at by human agency and was generally deemed to be made up of the assembled customs of all the peoples of the world, was a species of positive, or human, law.[49]

The distinction between Bartolus' two kinds of *ius gentium* is primarily an historical one. The *ius gentium primaevum* belongs to the natural law in that it corresponds to untutored human reason and, thus, could be known to all human beings – all *homines* – everywhere, even to those living in some hypothetical pre-social condition, and is, consequently, in Vitoria's terms, "equitable of itself". The *ius gentium secundarium*, however, is a species of positive law which, as Vitoria said of it, "is not equitable of itself but has been established by human statute grounded in reason".[50] Parts of the law of nations clearly derive unproblematically from the natural law, and these are "manifestly sufficient to enable it [the law of nations] to enforce binding rights". However, he went on, "even on the occasions when it is not derived from natural law, the consent of the greater part of the world, is enough to make it binding, especially when it is for the common good of all men".[51]

We might say, then, that the law of nations was that law which *could* have been agreed on by all the peoples of the world had anyone been in a position to discover what the collective reasoning of its members might be. "Reason", as Domingo de Soto put it, "dictates what are its particularities."[52] This distinguishes it from the purely civil law of individual states which requires either "a council of the commonwealth or the will of the prince" for it to be binding.[53] Or, in Francisco Suárez's words, it "had been introduced not by evidence [as was the case with the civil law] but by the probable and common estimation of men", and then enacted, if only *ex hypothesi*, by what Vitoria famously called "the whole world which is in a sense a commonwealth [*respublica*]", a version of Cicero's "human society" and "common human law".[54] In the slightly different formulation offered by Soto, whereas a civil law had to be supported, as Soto put it, by "the council of the state or the authority of the prince", acting on behalf of the collective will of the peoples of that state, the law of nations clearly did not: "To constitute the law of nations", he concluded, "no assembly of men in one place is required." In Martti Koskenniemi's words: "The pre-lapsarian *ius naturae* . . . was adjusted in the world of real human beings by a consensual and historical *ius gentium*."[55] This allowed the *ius gentium* the universality of the natural law, but not its immutability. "That which may be inferred from the absolute necessity of things, belongs to the natural law", wrote Soto, "but those matters which do so not through absolute consideration of things but because they are determined by a particular end, belong the law of nations."[56] This meant that "although some things which pertain to the law of nations, contribute to human relations, so that there can be no dispensation from them, and indeed any such dispensation would be considered null", others clearly do not. A positive *ius gentium*, however, grounded in reason, was still subject to change and abrogation. It was – provisionally at least – subject to the *dominium* of individual princes, and it had to respond to circumstances. What the "whole world which is in a sense a commonwealth" might decide to do at one moment in time might not be the same as what it would decide to do, even in like circumstances, at another. As Jeremy Waldron has phrased it, "like the *ius civile*, the *ius gentium* is a matter of history and contingency—what happens to have been established among men." In much the same way, Aquinas had accepted that even the natural law might be changed if only by addition or "in its secondary principles".[57]

Vitoria's world *respublica* takes the form of a single legal person, with *de iure* at least, full powers of enactment – the *vis legis* – so that, in Vitoria's words, "the law of nations does not have the force merely of pacts or agreements between men, but has the force of a positive enactment (*lex*)".[58] This, of course, makes of the "whole world which is in a sense a commonwealth" a quasi-legal body at least *de iure* even if the right of actual enactment belongs to the sovereign princes of the world. For "if the commonwealth has these powers [of punishment] against its own members, there can be no doubt that the whole world has the same powers against any harmful and evil men. And these powers can only exist if exercised though the princes of the commonwealth."[59]

Despite this insistence that the *ius gentium* belongs with the positive law, the fact that it was still ultimately grounded on an expression of human reason rather than consent or enactment meant that there was a good deal of slippage between it and the natural law in the ways in which this was understood. As a consequence in the manner it is handled by the School of Salamanca – and later by Grotius – the *ius gentium* often comes out looking less like an inter-*national* law than and inter-*personal* law applied on a universal scale.[60]

It is this which allows Vitoria, for all that he was insistent that the prince enjoyed unfettered authority within his own territory, to claim that the community of all humanity took precedence over the nation. This then conferred on the *ius gentium* precedence over the local legislative practices of individual states so that no "kingdom may chose to ignore this law of nations".[61] Furthermore, because one of the eight reasons Vitoria offers for the legitimacy of warfare itself is "the good of the whole world", it followed that any "war which is useful to one commonwealth or kingdom, but of proven harm to the world or to Christendom [is] by that very token unjust".[62] And since any state which wages an unjust war may legitimately be resisted, this would seem to confer, if only by implication, a clear right on any state under threat from what today would be called a "rogue state" to intervene in the affairs of another to prevent "further harm".[63] In all cases where there arose a conflict between the law of nations and the civil law, the former would appear to trump the latter.

It might be argued, however, that if the law of nations really was a positive one, it could only ever have been arrived at by peoples who were already in some kind of juridical condition. Vitoria's *respublica* – if only by virtue of being a *respublica* – clearly cannot be the state of nature. And any people living in a *respublica* would have to be bound by some kind of civil law, however primitive. Such peoples were also unlikely to come up with laws which were simultaneously licit as civil law and illicit (although they might be inapplicable) as part of the *ius gentium*. And if they did, it did not necessarily follow that the *ius gentium* took precedence.

III

It was in the terms of this rather shaky and unstable understanding of the law of nations that Vitoria, and his successors, set out to try to explain how it was that the Spanish Crown had come to exercise "private and public *dominium*" in the Americas. As Schmitt (and Hegel before him) had seen, the Spanish occupation of what was before 1492 a wholly unknown landmass had been the outcome of what, in particularly after Hernán Cortés' seizure of the "empire" of Montezuma in 1519–21, had been a highly publicized conquest. The word "conquest" caused the Spanish Crown, as it was later to cause the English, considerable legal anxiety, and in 1680 the *Recopilación de leyes de los reynos de las Indias* required that "this word conquest be omitted, so that it should not be the case of, or provide an excuse for, force or harm being given to the Indians".[64] For all the triumphalism involved in the studious comparison with ancient Rome, a "conquest" could only be justified if it could be shown to be the outcome of a just war. Such a war conferred on the aggressor a right to wage war – the *ius ad bellum* – and was governed by a set of agreements about how the war should be conducted and the benefits which the victor was entitled to derive from it – the *ius in bello*.[65] As the Roman jurists had maintained that war could only be just if it was waged defensively, it could only be conceived as a means of punishing an aggressor and seizing compensation for damages suffered by the victor who was, by definition, the injured party. Wars, said St. Augustine, in one of the most frequently cited passages on the subject, "are just which revenge the injuries caused when the nation or *civitas* with which war is envisaged has either neglected to make recompense for illegitimate acts committed by its members, or to return what has been injuriously taken".[66]

Clearly no war could be just if it were pursued for personal gain or for the sake of glory. "When we are fighting for empire and seeking glory through warfare", Cicero had insisted, war may be "waged less bitterly" than with a true enemy, but that did not alter the fact that, in these cases also, the condition of a just war "should be wholly present".[67] For a war to be just, it had therefore to begin as an act of self-defence. "Reason has taught to the wise," wrote Cicero, "necessity to the barbarians, custom to the *gentes* and nature to brute beasts that they should repulse on every occasion by every means all violence to their bodies their heads and their lives."[68] War, Cicero had also said, might similarly be waged on behalf of allies or clients, which is what he meant by "fighting for empire"; it could also – a point to which I shall return – be waged against those who are believed to have offended not merely an individual or a state but also humanity itself by violating the law of nature.

The question for Vitoria was, how could such conditions possibly apply to wars against a distant people who had manifestly caused no harm to any European prior to their arrival and then had only apparently acted in self-defence? One possible answer was that, for some reason, the Indians had not been in legitimate "public and private *dominium*" – that is, property rights and sovereignty – over the territories they occupied before the Europeans arrived, in which case their lands might be considered "empty". The Indians' refusal to make way for the Spanish would then constitute grounds for a just war under the law of nature.

If this argument were to apply, it would have to be shown that *either* the Indians were in some sense less than fully human (or fully adult), in which case they could not be said to be true masters either of themselves or of their goods, or that, although both fully human and fully adult, they had somehow failed to fulfill the necessary conditions by which human beings were believed to acquire ownership over land.[69] In the first case, they would have to be either mad, or in some other way irrational. It is under this heading that perhaps the most contentious attempt to deny the Indians their natural rights, Aristotle's theory of natural slavery, was introduced – a point to which I shall return in

Chapter 3. But, although it clearly was, in Vitoria's estimation, the case that if such a thing as a natural slave were to exist, no single group fitted Aristotle's definition better than the Indians; it was also "self-evident" from the "order in their affairs" that they "have judgment just like other men".[70] Vitoria was prepared to adduce from the related argument that *if* the Indians were all truly mad, they could make no more claim to be able to govern their own affairs than a group of children, in which case the Spanish king would possess a highly constrained right to take "them into his control". Since, however, this would be due under the terms of the obligation we all have to our neighbors, it could only be done "for the benefit and the good of the barbarians and not merely for the profit of the Spanish".[71]

This suggestion was to have a long afterlife. Despite its tentative and imprecise formulation, despite the fact that Vitoria himself introduces it "merely for the sake of argument", it was translated by later jurists into an embryonic theory of "trusteeship". After the creation of the Mandate System by the League of Nations in 1919, international lawyers struggling to find some historical pedigree for what in the twentieth century came to be called a "suspension of sovereignty" turned to Vitoria's argument as a way of challenging the arguments of nineteenth-century positivists that "uncivilized" peoples might legitimately be appropriated by "civilized" ones, because only the latter could claim to constitute states and thus to exercise sovereignty.[72]

In the specific case of the Spanish occupation of America, however, where "care" had, in fact, taken the form of colonization and settlement, it could not provide any grounds for the suspension, much less the acquisition, of sovereignty. As the theologian Melchor Cano argued in 1546, even if were true that the Indians were some kind of children in need of civic education, the Christians would not be entitled to "take them into their care" if they had to conquer them first to do so. For any act whose purpose is to secure the good of another is a precept of charity, and no act of charity can ever involve coercion. The position of the Castilian Crown, Cano concluded, somewhat unflatteringly for his monarch, was like that of a beggar to whom alms may be due, but who is not empowered to extract them.[73] Vitoria's argument would also seem to imply that the gold and silver which the Spaniards had extracted in massive quantities from the mines in Mexico and Peru could not legitimately be shipped back to Europe to pay for costly wars fought against other Christian princes.

If, as Vitoria concluded briskly at the beginning of "On the American Indians", "it is clear that from all that I have said that the Spaniards when they first sailed to the land of the barbarians, carried with them no right at all to occupy their countries", then the only legitimate grounds would have to derive from the claim that the wars waged against them constituted just ones.[74] In Question 3 of the *relectio* he, therefore, considers on what grounds such an argument might be made. He offers eight possibilities. The only ones to which he seems to have been prepared to give any credence, however, are

Articles 1 and 5. Both were to have a long afterlife, and it is on them that Vitoria's somewhat airy claim to have been the "father of international law" largely rests. I shall begin with Article 5. This is a version of what today comes under the general heading of the "Responsibility to Protect", or what Vitoria calls "the defence of the innocent". The Spanish might, he wrote – and only might – have a right to intervene in the Americas "either on account of the personal tyranny of the barbarians' masters towards their subjects or because of their tyrannical and oppressive laws against the innocent". As in Vitoria's words, "the Spaniards are the barbarians' neighbors, as is shown by the parable of the Samaritan (Luke 10: 29–37); ... the barbarians are obliged to love their neighbors as themselves" and vice versa. Under the terms of what Edmund Burke in the eighteenth century – in the hope of persuading his listeners that the French Revolution constituted a European civil war – called the "law of civil vicinity", neighbors have an obligation to assist each other in times of crisis.[75] Now the rulers of an individual state have, for Vitoria at least, an unassailable right to "punish those of its own members who are intent on harming it with execution or other penalties". From this it followed that, as the law of nations always overruled mere civil law: "If the common-wealth has these powers against its own members, there can be no doubt that the whole world has the same powers against any harmful and evil men." But although, as we have seen, the world *respublica* does possess *de iure* the "power to enact laws" (*potestas ferendi leges*), there clearly exists no insti-tutions that could transform this into a de facto authority.[76] The question then arises: who, in the absence of some analogue of the United Nations, has the right to do the job for "the whole world"? Vitoria's answer is "the prince", by which he apparently means any legally established ruler capable of assuming the legislative authority of the entire world for "these powers can only exist if exercised though the princes of the commonwealth".[77]

"It should be noted", he wrote,

> that the prince has the authority not only over his own people, but also over foreigners to force them to abstain from harming others; this is his right by the law of nations and the authority of the whole world. Indeed, *it seems he has this right by natural law*: the world could not exist unless some men had the power and authority to deter the wicked by force from doing harm to the good and the innocent. (Emphasis added.)

Under the appropriate conditions then, it would appear that any sovereign was in a position to draw on the authority of both the law of nations *and* the natural law in defence of the world *respublica*.[78] In the case of the Americas the Spanish are merely acting on behalf, and by the authority, of a supposed international community. They are in America by historical contingency, and the task of defending the innocent has thus fallen to them. But this responsibility could just as easily have been assumed by any other ruler, Christian or – since unbelievers have just as much right to exercise *dominium* as unbelievers – non-Christian.[79] (The argument is, however, decidedly odd, since it implies that the authority to act on behalf of one legal entity – the international community – can only derive from another which historically is a subsequent creation.)

The principal evidence to support Vitoria's claim that the American Indians were being forced to live under "tyrannical and oppressive laws" were the much-discussed practices of human sacrifice and cannibalism. Vitoria accepts that there is no prohibition against cannibalism "in divine or civil law". It is not, therefore, a mortal sin "provided that it is not against charity to God, or ones' neighbour" (although it is not clear who one is going to eat if not one's "neighbour"). Because, however, it "is held in abomination by all nations who have a civil and humane life", it is clearly contrary to the *ius gentium* since.[80] Human sacrifice was more tricky if only because the biblical stories of Abraham and Jephthah seemed to suggest that under certain circumstances human sacrifice might not only be natural but even pleasing to God. Vitoria's response was that it was contrary to natural law and, of course, *eo ipso* against the law of nations on the grounds that no man may "deliver himself up to execution" (unless justly convicted of a crime), for the same reason that he may not commit suicide, because possession in his own body (*dominium corporis suuis*) belongs not to him, but to God.[81]

It is important, however, that although human sacrifice, at least, constitutes a violation of the law of nature, it is not that which, in Vitoria's view, might justify intervention, any more than a Christian prince might legitimately make war on another Christian prince because his subjects are "adulterers or fornicators, perjurers or thieves because these things are against natural law".[82] As Suárez observed, it was not man's task to vindicate the Almighty. If God wishes to take revenge on the pagans for their sins, he remarked acidly, "he is capable of doing so for himself".[83]

The truly significant difference between "unnatural" activities practiced among individuals in Christian states and the cannibalism and human sacrifice practiced in the Americas is that whereas the former are forbidden by law, the latter were sanctioned by the state. They are, that is, a part of law, and it is this which makes them tyrannical. The *harm* which the rulers of the barbarian are prepared to inflict on their own subjects in this way clearly constitutes a breach not of the natural law but of the *ius gentium*. And it is because of this, not because of the gruesome nature of the practices themselves, that the human community may intervene to prevent them.

It is also the case, Vitoria insisted, that: "It makes no difference that all the barbarians consent to these kinds of laws and sacrifices, or that they refuse to accept the Spaniards as their liberators in this matter". For as Soto phrased it, "that which nature teaches is not within the reach of everyone, but only those who have serene reason and are free from all obscurity (*nebula*)".[84] Prolonged habit is capable of distorting every human being's understanding of the natural law and, by implication, the law of nations. "For sometimes, due to bad customs, and in those who have fallen profoundly into evil, the knowledge of the natural law may be changed."[85] Clearly, then, if the rulers of the "barbarians" refuse to abandon their crimes against their own peoples, "their masters may be changed and new princes set up".[86]

Vitoria's "defence of the innocent" suffered from some very obvious defects. In common with all attempts to justify armed intervention in the interests of others, it fails, of course, to specify very clearly what would count as "tyranny" and "oppressive laws" outside the two specific – and extreme – cases he cites. It was, too, an innovative move because, in general, theories of the "just war" avoided claims made on behalf of third parties, unless these were specifically involved as "allies". The Indians might, for instance, quite reasonably have sought the assistance of the Europeans in their (legitimate) struggles against other Indians. This had indeed, as Vitoria points out, happened in the case of the Tlaxcalans who had – at least in Hernán Cortés' account of events – sought Spanish aid in their struggle against the Aztecs.[87] But no subsequent writer on the law of war from Grotius to Kant accepted that one ruler had the authority to decide what constitutes an "offence against the innocent" in another state, nor to intervene on their behalf, and even against their will. Intervention was only licit if the actions of that state also in some way constituted a clear and direct threat to the belligerent, and even here there was much disagreement over what might count in such instances as what was called "just fear".

What the international community – however defined – clearly could not do, therefore, was precisely what Vitoria was arguing that the Spaniards could – that is, to make war on a foreign power to set up new princes more to their liking, and what they believed the liking of their subjects to be. Intervention "in defence of the innocent" required, much as the claim to trusteeship did, a suspension of sovereignty, and very few were prepared to sanction that as a prior condition of war – as part, that is, of the *ius ad bellum* – rather than a legitimate (but not inevitable) *outcome* of a just war, and thus a part of the *ius post bellum*. Vitoria himself in an earlier *relectio*, *On Civil Power*, delivered in 1528, had asserted vehemently that even if an entire commonwealth collectively decided to rid itself of an established power "their agreement would be null and void as contrary to natural law which the commonwealth cannot abolish".[88] And this of course is precisely what any hypothetical delegation of the "innocent" seeking assistance against their legitimate if tyrannical rulers would in fact be doing. In other words, no individual or group of individuals can decide to break what Kant later called "legal continuity" without violating the law of nature.[89]

There was a further problem with this line of argument as a justification for *conquest*. For although it might provide grounds for initial intervention, it offered no charter for effective colonization. Since anything resembling "humanitarian" intervention could only be for the good of those supposedly afflicted, once the "integrity of the state" had been established, the invading power should logically withdraw. The victor was only entitled to seize such moveable goods as he deemed necessary to compensate for the loses he had incurred. He might also seize goods, and even persons, as punishment for wrongdoing. However, what were termed "immovable goods" – that is, territory, cities, and, crucially in the Spanish case, what lay beneath the land – were another matter. Vitoria accepted that

> it is sometimes lawful to occupy a fort or town, but the governing factor in this case must be moderation, not armed might. If necessity and the requirements of war demand that the greater part of enemy territory or a large number of cities be occupied in this way, they ought to be returned once the war is over and peace has been made, only keeping so much as may be considered fair in equity and humanity for the reparation of losses and expenses and the punishment of injustice.[90]

All of which was ultimately to present all those who hoped to use some version of the "defence of the innocent" to justify intervention in the affairs of sovereign states with considerable difficulties. But the inter-personal rather than international aspect of Vitoria's understanding of the law of nations, its vacillating proximity to the law of nature, and the power which this conferred on the world republic and its self-appointed agents allowed his successors to extend substantially the possible applications of the same argument. It allowed Suárez, for instance, to argue that the law of nations might sanction war against Henry VIII of England. For although by breaking with Rome, Henry had harmed no state other than his own, the offences he had caused his own people were already, or so Suárez claimed, so severe that he might legitimately be attacked to prevent further collapse.[91] "War", as Suárez phrased it, "is permitted so that the state may preserve the integrity of its rights", even if that war had been initiated by a foreign power, against its own sovereign.[92] Furthermore, St. Augustine had endorsed wars that were fought to "acquire peace" – peace in this context being defined as a "work of justice" (*opus justitiae*) for the restoration of the "tranquility of the order of all things".[93] In such circumstances, argued Suárez, "the natural power and jurisdiction of the human republic" could be mobilized as a "reason for universal conquest".[94] Under these circumstances, the scope of the jurisdiction exercised by the "human republic" had thus, potentially at least, become very wide indeed.[95]

IV

The second – although in fact it is the first – of Vitoria's "just titles" is similarly grounded on the assumption that the law of nations is a form of interpersonal law and that it trumps the civil law. It is based on the claim that the "division of things" (*divisio rerum*) – that is, the carving up of the world into autonomous (and sovereignty-bearing) nations which had taken place after mankind's departure from the state of nature – had not obscured certain natural rights, which remain the common property of all human beings.[96] On Vitoria's account these rights, precisely because they survived from man's primitive condition, cannot be abrogated by merely human legislation, since they pre-date state sovereignty.[97] Among these were what he called "the right of natural partnership and communication" (*ius naturalis societas et communicatio-nis*).[98] This describes a complex set of claims divided into five propositions. At the core, however, lies an allusion to the ancient obligation to offer hospitality to strangers. For "Nature" claimed Vitoria, quoting the *Digest*, "has decreed a certain kinship between men (*Digest* I.i. 3). . . . Man is not a 'wolf to his fellow men' – *homo homini lupus* – as the comedian [Plautus] says, but a fellow."[99] All of this brings with it an obligation to friendship, for "amity between men is part of the natural law". "In the beginning of the world", he continued, "when all things were held in common, everyone was allowed to visit and travel through any land he wished. This right was clearly not taken away by the division of property; it was never the intention of nations to prevent men's free mutual intercourse with one another by its division." This allowed Vitoria to transform the ancient concept of hospitality – the authority he cites is Virgil – into a right under the law of nations and the natural law.[100] "Amongst all nations", he wrote, "it is considered inhuman to treat travellers badly without some special cause, humane and dutiful to behave hospitably to strangers." This, of course, meant that the Indians could not "lawfully bar them [the Spaniards] from their homeland without due cause".[101] If they attempted to do so, then a just war might be waged against them.

Expressed as a right under the terms both of the natural law and of the *ius gentium*, this was an original – if also highly debatable – claim. In making it, Vitoria was drawing on a long ancient and humanist tradition, which is, like the natural law itself, Stoic in origin. Clearly individuals, no matter how rude and barbarous they might be, had an inalienable right to communicate with their fellow beings. This is the historical underpinning for the modern concern with freedom of speech. The fact that such communication was also perceived as a means of civilizing the barbarian in no way altered its standing as a right.

Vitoria, however, extended the same argument to commerce. The natural right of communication delivers a right under the law of nations for all travelers (*peregrini*) to engage in trade with whoever they please "so long as they do not harm the citizens" of the lands through which they are traveling. Therefore, he added, "they [the Spaniards] may import the commodities which they [the Indians] lack and export the gold and silver and other things which they have in abundance". And at the very end of his lecture Vitoria pointed out that the Portuguese had done just as well out of a licit trade "with similar sorts of people", without conquering them, as the Spaniards had done by possibly illicit occupation. Something which, he tentatively suggested, the Spanish Crown might think of emulating.[102]

The transition from passage to trade was, however, at best, a shaky one because the right of passage, as a natural right, could only be understood as both a "prefect" (one that is binding in all possible circumstances) and negative one, in that every individual has a natural right not to be hindered. On Vitoria's account, the right to free trade, by contrast, comes out looking very much like an "imperfect" obligation. As the eighteenth-century Swiss diplomat Emer de Vattel said of it later: "The obligation of trading with other nations is in itself an imperfect obligation, and gives them only an imperfect right. ... When the Spaniards attacked the Americans under a presence that those people refused to traffic with them, they only endeavored to throw a colourable veil over their own insatiable avarice."[103]

Furthermore, Vitoria's last inference, as Soto, generally more radical on most such issues than his predecessor, pointed out, confused a mere right of passage – or even of settlement – with rights of property. The Spanish Crown, even if it could make an unassailable claim to sovereignty in the Americas, could still not take possession of the gold and silver or any other goods which they might find there, for

> the law of nations established a division between the regions [of the earth], and therefore, even if the inhabitants of those regions held such things to be common [property], foreigners cannot take possession of them without the consent of those who live there. For neither can the French enter for this reason into Spain, nor we into France, without the consent of the French.[104]

The Spaniards, in other words, had, in effect, been mining illegally, and logically they should now restore what they had taken to their rightful owners.

In Vitoria's account, however, merchants were not the only class of person to possess a right to travel, so too, and far more problematically, were missionaries. They, like all humans, enjoyed a natural right to "teach the truth if they [in this case the Indians] are willing to listen". By implication, however, while the Indians are under an obligation to allow the Christians to be heard, they are themselves under no obligation to listen, much less, of course, to believe what they hear. For "whether or not they accept the faith it will not be lawful to attempt to impose anything on them by war or otherwise conquer their lands".[105] And despite Vitoria's evocation of Mark, "Go ye into the world and preach the gospel to every creature" (which would seem to make the "right to preach" one in divine law), it is still the case that the only right, in fact, invoked here is a further appeal to both the "law of civil vicinity" and the "defence of the innocent". For "brotherly correction is as much a part of natural law as brotherly love" and the non-Christian is always, by definition, in need of correction. Furthermore, if the Indian princes were actively to oppose the conversion of their subjects "by deterring them with threats or any other means", they may be resisted by force because this would constitute a harm inflicted by the rulers on the ruled so that "the Spaniards could wage war on behalf of other subjects for the oppression and wrong which they were suffering, especially in such important matters".[106] In other words, Indian converts, or would-be converts, could be considered as a class of "innocents" requiring protection. Furthermore it would seem that were there a sufficient number of converts, then "it would be neither expedient nor lawful for our prince to abandon altogether the administration of those territories".[107]

As with all claims made under the law of nations, it was crucial for their coherence that they should be applicable to the entire world. This would mean that Indian missionaries – should such persons have existed – or far more contentiously Muslim ones, should have been allowed a similar access to Spain. In reality, however, as the jurist and historian Arthur Nussbaum has claimed: "Admission of non-Christian missionaries to Spain would of course have been unthinkable." He is, of course, quite right. It would. But Vitoria does not, and in the logic of his argument could not, say so.[108]

There are, it need hardly be said, a great many problems with this argument. Samuel Pufendorf pointed out in 1672, as Soto had done, that both Vitoria's and Grotius' understanding (which I discuss in Chapter 5) of the right of hospitality confused transit with property.[109] This "natural communication", he wrote scathingly, "cannot prevent a property holder from having the final decision on the question, whether he wishes to share with others the use of his property." It was also, in Pufendorf's view, "crude indeed" to claim that everyone, irrespective of "the numbers in which they had come" or "their purpose in coming", possessed such a right. In 1546, Melchor Cano had made a similar point. The Spaniards might have natural rights as travelers, or even as ambassadors. But they had gone to America as neither. They had gone as conquerors. "We would not", he concluded dryly, "be prepared to describe Alexander the Great as a *peregrinus*."[110]

For Pufendorf, however, the key issue was precisely the degree to which the law of nations, if it was a positive law with an international reach, could really override the civil laws of individual states. If it had been created by a consensus among nations, and not among single individuals in the state of nature relying solely upon their natural reason – that is, if it was indeed a "secondary" natural law and not a primary one – then it was clear to Pufendorf that it could not, as Vitoria insisted it should, take precedence over other forms of positive law. It would, as Cano had argued, clearly be absurd to suggest that there might exist a law which would forbid a prince from controlling the passage of foreigners over his own territories. Vitoria himself, after all, had recognized that if the "barbarians" could not interfere with the right of the Europeans to travel among and trade with them, then it must follow that no European state could prevent another from doing the same thing. The French, he admitted, could not lawfully "prevent the Spaniards from traveling to or even living in France and vice versa".[111] This would, of course, have given the French as perfect a right to wage war against Charles V as he had to make war on the Indians.

Any such right would in fact, however, be contrary to actual practice and a violation of the civil laws of Castile. Did it mean, then, that the civil laws of Castile were in some sense in violation of the common wisdom of the commonwealth of the world? Clearly the answer could only be no. In Vitoria's account it would appear that rights that derived from the *ius gentium* must trump any laws derived from a purely civil code, because, as we have seen for Vitoria, the "whole world which is in a sense a commonwealth" is prior to, and must take precedent over, any individual state. For Pufendorf, however, it was clear that there simply could be no right which had somehow survived the *divisio rerum*, since this had been precisely the moment in history in which the *ius gentium* had come into being. And this meant that the *ius gentium* was what its name claimed it to be: a law which governed the relationships between states (and peoples), not a universal law governing the behaviour of individuals in a hypothetical stateless condition. As Pufendorf understood it, Vitoria's claim that any prince might possess the right to force the rulers of states "to abstain from harming others" came down to the claim that what were, in fact, private rights – such as the *ius peregrinandi* –could be used not merely to trump the rights of states but also to legitimate wars in their defence which could, of necessity and by right, only be waged by states. "Most writers", concluded Pufendorf, "feel that the safest reply to make is this: Every state may reach a decision, according to its own usage, on the admission of foreigners who come to it for other reasons than are necessary and deserving of sympathy." Refugees clearly possessed some kind of claim to permanent settlement, if only on the grounds of charity. But refugees had no right to behave as conquerors, and they certainly did not have any prior claim over any portion of their land of adoption. "Such persons", he concluded, "must recognize the established government of that country, and so adapt themselves to it so that they may be the source of no conspiracies and revolts."[112] The Spanish could make no claim to be "refugees" and certainly had not recognized the established government of the Indians. Therefore, they clearly had no right to be in the Americas at all.

All of this seemed to dictate the need for some distinction between those who were, so to speak, fully covered by the law of nations and those who were not. None from the School of Salamanca make any such distinction explicit. Some recent historians, however, have tried to locate the distinction between "civilized" and "barbarian" peoples, which became the staple of the new international law in nineteenth century to a supposed distinction by Vitoria and others between Christian and pagan peoples. But had Vitoria held any such position, he would, on his own account, have fallen prey to the heresy of deriving *dominium* from grace not law.[113] As the French jurist Gaston Jèze had rightly seen in 1896, all of the Salamanca theologians had, in fact, consistently maintained that "civilized powers have no more right to seize the territories of savages than savages have to occupy the European continent. The law of nations does not admit any distinction between the barbarians and the so-called civilized."[114]

Jèze was clearly right as far as Vitoria and his successors were concerned; nevertheless it was not at all clear that it had not been they who had at least prepared the way for the notorious barbarian and civilized distinction he was arguing against. As Vázquez de Menchaca pointed out, Bartolus' *ius gentium secundarium* must originally have been the laws adopted by the different *gentes* of the world. And then "with the passage of the ages", these had become "the practice of most of those peoples that are governed by customs and laws". At first then, it was "a purely civil law" but subsequently became "accepted by all or most of the peoples of the world".[115]

It is not a very large step from this to the claim that this aboriginal "civil law" was in fact the law of one particular people, the most obvious candidate being the Romans. As we shall see in Chapter 2, this was an augment deployed slightly later by the Italian jurist Alberico Gentili who makes of the Roman civil law a kind of *summa* of all the laws of all the peoples of the world.[116] But even if we ignore the claim that this aboriginal civil law is identical with Roman law, it was very hard to avoid the supposition that it must, at least, have been the law of a very gifted – or to use another language – civilized people. Both Grotius and Pufendorf had been driven to much the same conclusion, and it was repeated with various nuances until Wolff and Vattel in the eighteenth century.

The division of the *gentes* into civilized and uncivilized posed a further, if rather obvious, problem. As the eclectic German jurist and philosopher Christian Thomasius asked in 1705:

> Who will determine if a nation is civilized or barbarian? For all peoples are equal amongst themselves, and this latter term [civilized] has its origins in the arrogance of the Greeks and the Romans, and among those nations who imitate them and who stupidly despise all other nations. The customs of the so-called civilized nations can be very much crueler than those of the Barbarians, as one can see from the treatment of Protestants by a Catholic prince.[117]

In the end the only possible reply had been to reduce the law of nations still further into a body of purely positive contract or treaty law between consenting states. As Robert Ward, whose *Enquiry into the Foundation and History of the Law of Nations in Europe* was the first systematic attempt to write a history of the subject, warned in 1795:

> We expected too much when we contended for the *universality* of the duties laid down by the Codes of the Laws of Nations. ... However desirable such universality might be ... what is commonly called the Law of Nations ... is not the Law of *all* Nations, but only of particular classes of them; and thus there may be a *different* Law of Nations for *different* parts of the globe.[118]

But that was precisely what Twiss and many of the other members of *Institut de droit international* were seeking to avoid. What they wanted was precisely what the Salamanca theologians had seemed to offer, namely the possibility of a truly universal human consensus, which would be capable of delivering a universal law of nations with a powerful prescriptive component inferred not from any presumptions about the natural law but from the actual civil laws of a large number of diverse peoples "who have a civil and humane life". For many this would have included both the Muslims (or at least the Ottomans) and Chinese. This, in turn, would be capable of providing the basis for a law which could then be applied to all peoples everywhere. It was for this reason that Vitoria was described in 1927, by James Brown Scott, founder of the American Society of International Law and secretary of the Carnegie Endowment for International Peace, as having provided "a summary of the modern law of nations".[119]

## Endnotes

1 *De Republica* 3.34.
2 I have discussed these at length in *Lords of All the World: Ideologies of Empire in Britain, France and Spain, 1400–1800* and "The Struggle for Legitimacy and the Image of Empire in the Atlantic to c. 1700" in Nicholas Canny ed., *The Oxford History of the British Empire*, I, *The Origins of Empire* (Oxford: Oxford University Press, 1998), 34–54. See also Richard Tuck, *The Rights of War and Peace. Political Thought and the International Order from Grotius to Kant* (Oxford: Oxford University Press, 1999), 51–78.
3 Leibniz's remark is in "Vita Leibnitii a seipso" in Foucher de Careil, *Nouvelles lettres et opuscules inédits de Leibniz* (Paris, 1857), 382.
4 *De locis theologicis* (Salamanca, 1536), XII, *Proemium*.
5 Antony Anghie, for instance, mistakenly describes Vitoria as a "theologian and jurist", as did James Brown Scott, the international lawyer who was responsible for the revival of interest in the School of Salamanca in the Anglophone world in the early twentieth century and for the re-edition of many of its works. Anghie, *Imperialism, Sovereignty and the Making of International Law*, 13.
6 "Vázquez decus illud Hispaniae", *The Free Sea* [*De Mare Libero*], Richard Hakluyt trans., David Armitage ed. (Indianapolis: Liberty Fund, 2004), 43. Also see Annabel Brett, *Liberty, Right and Nature* (Cambridge: Cambridge University Press, 1997), 245. "Vázquez should be read neither in isolation from, nor as a continuation of, the School of Salamanca, but rather as a positive response to its achievements, and particularly to that of Soto."
7 See the discussion in Francisco Suárez, *Tractatus de legibus ac Deo Legislatore* [1612], Luciano Pereña ed. (Madrid: CSIC, 1971), I, 2–8.
8 For these, see my "The 'School of Salamanca' and the 'Affair of the Indies'", *History of Universities* 1 (1981), 71–112.
9 "Los reyes piensan a las veces del pie a la mano, y mas los de consejo" in reply to Miguel de Arcos' question as to why political authorities pay so little attention to their advisors. In Vicente Beltrán de Heredia, "Coleción de dictámenes inéditos", *Ciencia tomista* 43 (1931), 1743.
10 Letter to Pedro Fernández de Velasco, *Vitoria: Political Writings*, 337.
11 James Boswell, *Boswell's Life of Johnson*, G. B. Hill ed. (Oxford: Oxford University Press, 1934), I, 45.

12 *Two Introductory Lectures on the Science of International Law* (London: Longmans, 1856), 8, and quoted in Marti Koskenniemi, *The Gentle Civilizer of Nations: The Rise and Fall of International Law 1870–1960* (Cambridge: Cambridge University Press, 2001), 78.

13 A *relectio*, literally a "re-reading", was a lecture given not on a particular text, as were most lectures, but instead on a specific problem.

14 "On the American Indians", I, Introduction, *Vitoria: Political Writings*, 233–4.

15 *Controversiarum illustrium aliarumque usu frequentium, libri tres*, I, 18.

16 Ibid., 234–8.

17 Ibid., 238.

18 *The Nomos of the Earth in the International Law of the Jus Publicum Europaeum*, 39, 69.

19 "On the American Indians", I, Introduction, *Vitoria: Political Writings*, 233.

20 Ibid., 238.

21 "Romanus pontifex" in *Monumenta hericina* (Coimbra: Comissao Executiva das Comemorações do V Centenario da Morte do Infante D. Henrique, 1960–74), XII, 71–9. On the importance of these for the Portuguese claims to sovereignty in Africa, see Giuseppe Marcoci, *L'invenzione di un imperio: Politica e cultura nel mondo portoghese (1450–1600)* (Rome: Caroci editore, 2011), 69–88.

22 There were five bulls in all. They are printed in "Bulas Alejandrinas de 1493 texto y traducción" in Juan Gil and José Maria Maestre eds., *Humanismo latino y descrubrimiento* (Seville: Universidad de Sevilla and Universidad de Cadiz, 1992), 16. Also see Hans-Jürgen Prien, "Las Bulas Alejandrinas de 1493" in Bernd Schröter and Karin Schüller eds., *Tordesillas y sus consecuencias: La política de las grandes potencias europeas respecto a América Latina (1494–1898)* (Frankfurt: Vervuet Iberoamericana, 1995), 12–28.

23 *The Writings of William Paterson, Founder of the Bank of England*, S. Bannister ed., 2 vols. (London, 1858), I, 121.

24 *The Limits of the British Empire*, Ken MacMillan (with Jennifer Abeles) eds. (Westport, CT; London: Praeger, 2004), 92–3.

25 Quoted in Tuck, *The Rights of War and Peace*, 111.

26 "A Discourse on Western Planting" in *The Original Writings and Correspondence of the two Richard Hakluyts*, E. G. R. Taylor ed. (London: Hakluyt Society, 1935), II, 302. For a wider discussion of the English rejection of the bulls, see Ken MacMillan, *Sovereignty and Possession in the English New World: The Legal Foundations of Empire, 1576–1640* (Cambridge: Cambridge University Press, 2006), 67–9.

27 3. I. i. and quoted in Francisco A. Ortega Martínez, «Entre 'constitución' y 'colonia', el estatuto ambiguo de las Indias en la monarquía hispánica» in *Conceptos fundamentales de la cultura política de la Independencia* (Bogotá: Universidad Nacional de Colombia, 2012), 61–91 at 64. The Papal Bulls are also the only justification for the Spanish presence in America offered by the Historiographer Royal, Antonio de Herrera, in his massive official history of the conquest of the Americas, *Historia general de los hechos de los Castellanos en las islas y tierra firme del Mar Océano* of 1601–1615. See David Brading, *The First America: The Spanish Monarchy, Creole Patriots and the Liberal State, 1492–1867* (Cambridge: Cambridge University Press, 1991), 205–10.

28 *Two Introductory Lectures on the Science of International Law*, 9.

29 *Codex*, VII, 37, 3.
30 *De iustitia et iure, libri decem*, IV. IV. i. (Salamanca, 1556), 301.
31 "On the American Indians", 2.2., *Vitoria: Political Writings*, 260. Vitoria uses the same arguments in "On the Power of the Church", I. 5.1., *Vitoria: Political Writings*, 83–4.
32 See Brian Tierney, *The Crisis of Church and State 1050–1300* (Toronto: Toronto University Press, 1988), 127–38.
33 "On the American Indians", 2.2., *Vitoria: Political Writings*, 264.
34 *De iustitia et iure, libri decem*, III. IV. iii. (262).
35 See Anne Orford, *International Authority and the Responsibility to Protect* (Cambridge: Cambridge University Press, 2011), 148–9.
36 Vitoria, who similarly rejected the claim, pointed out that Charles V styled himself "Divine Maximilian or Eternally August Charles Lord of the World (*orbis dominus*), "On the American Indians", 2.1., *Vitoria: Political Writings*, 252. Also see Juan Carlos D'Amico, *Charles Quint maître du monde: entre mythe et réalité* (Caen: Presses universitaires de Caen, 2004).
37 See David A. Lupher, *Romans in a New World: Classical Models in Sixteenth-Century Spanish America* (Ann Arbor: University of Michigan Press, 2003), 344–7, *passim*.
38 Quoted in Lupher, *Romans in a New World*, 63. The argument is made again in Soto, *De Iustitia et iure*, IV. IV. II. (304).
39 Quoted in Lupher, *Romans in a New World*, 65. As Lupher points out, what he calls the "starkly paradoxical phrase" (*ius erat in armis*) could not be read as meaning that the Roman Empire had been based, independently of divine decree, on the pursuit of the *ius belli*. But merely that the Romans owed their success, as did the Spanish, to "brute military superiority".
40 *De Iustitia et iure*, IV. IV. Ii. (305). A more detailed analysis of Soto's argument on this point is in Lupher, *Romans in a New World*, 64–5.
41 This is Vitoria's formulation, but the others of the School of Salamanca were in broad agreement. Indeed it is a conventional Thomist explanation of the sources of political power and the basis of the scholastic distinction between power and authority, which Hobbes ridiculed. "On Civil Power", I. 3, 4, *Vitoria: Political Writings*, 10–12.
42 *De Iustitia et iure*, IV. IV. ii. (304).
43 *The Rights of War and Peace*, II, xii, 13. Also see "'Elephant of India': Universal Sovereignty through Time and across Cultures" in Peter Fibiger Bang and Dariusz Kolodziejczyk eds., *Universal Empire. A Comparative Approach to Imperial Culture and Representation in Eurasian History* (Cambridge: Cambridge University Press, 2012), 7.
44 *De Iustitia et iure*, IV. IV. Ii. (305).
45 "On the American Indians", 2. 2. *Vitoria: Political Writings*, 264.
46 Ibid., I, Introduction, 238.
47 *De Officis*, III, 69.
48 "Quod vero naturalis ratio inter omnes homines constituit, id apud omnes populos peraeque custoditur vocaturque ius gentium, quasi quo iure omnes gentes utuntur." *Institutes* II. I.1. In Justinian's *Institutes* (made up largely of quotes from Gaius), the *ius gentium* is similarly described as "those rules prescribed by natural reason for all men are observed by all peoples alike".

49 See Annabel Brett, *Changes of State. Nature and the Limits of the City in Early-Modern Natural Law* (Princeton: Princeton University Press, 2011), 76.

50 *Comentarios a la Secunda Secundae de Santo Tomás*, Vicente Beltrán de Heredia ed. (Salamanca: Biblioteca de teólogos españoles, 1934), III, 89–90.

51 "On the American Indians", 3.1, *Vitoria: Political Writings*, 281.

52 "On Civil Power" 3.4, *Vitoria: Political Writings*, 40. Soto, *De iustitia et iure* III, II, iii (205)

53 *De iustitia et iure*, III. 1. iii. (197)

54 *De Republica* 2, 26 and *De Finibus* II 24.

55 "International Law and *raison d'état*: Rethinking the Prehistory of International Law", in Benedict Kingsbury and Benjamin Straumann eds., *The Roman Foundations of the Law of Nations*, 303.

56 *De iustitia et iure*, III. 1. iii. (198).

57 "*Ius gentium*: A Defence of Gentili's Equation of the Law of Nations and the Law of Nature", in Benedict Kingsbury and Benjamin Straumann eds., *The Roman Foundations of the Law of Nations*, 283–96, and Aquinas, Ia IIae. q. 94 a. 5.

58 Suárez, *Tractatus de legibus ac Deo Legislatore* II. xix. 4, and "On Civil Power", 3.4, *Vitoria: Political Writings*, 40. See also *Comentarios a la Secunda Secundae de Santo Tomás*, III, 89–90. For a more detailed account, see Daniel Deckers, *Gerechtigkeit und Recht. Eine historisch-kritische Untersuchung der Gerechtigkeitslehre des Francisco de Vitoria (1483–1546)* (Freiburg: Universitätsverlag Freiburg, 1991), 345–94.

59 "On the Law of War", 1.4, *Vitoria: Political Writings*, 305.

60 Martti Koskenniemi, *From Apology to Utopia: The Structure of International Legal Argument* (Cambridge: Cambridge University Press, 2005), 98 n. 95, and the authorities cited therein.

61 "On Civil Power", 3.4, *Vitoria: Political Writings*, 40.

62 Ibid., 1.10, p. 21.

63 "On the Law of War", 1.1, *Vitoria: Political Writings*, 298.

64 *Recopilación de leyes de los reynos de las Indias*, Bk. 4 Tit. I Ley 6 (Madrid, 1791), II, 4. For the English case, see 105–12.

65 See, in general, S. Albert, *Bellum Iustum* (Frankfurter Althistorische Studien 10) (Kallmunz, 1980); Frederick H. Russell, *The Just War in the Middle Ages* (Cambridge: Cambridge University Press, 1975) l and Jonathan Barnes, "The Just War" in *Cambridge History of Later Medieval Philosophy*, Norman Kretzmann, Anthony Kenny, and Jan Pinborg eds. (Cambridge: Cambridge University Press, 1982), 775–8.

66 *Quaestionum in Heptateuchem*, VI. X. and cf. "War should be waged only as a necessity, and waged only that God may by it deliver men from necessity and preserve them in peace. For peace is not sought in order to kindle war, but war is waged in order that peace may be secured. ... So it should be necessity not desire, that destroys the enemy in battle." *Epist.* 189.6 [to Bonifatius], *Patrologia latina*, XXXIII. Col. 856.

67 *De Officis*, 1, 35, 38. See also *De Republica*, III, 34a–b, and Tuck, *The Rights of War and Peace*, 201

68 *Pro Milone*, XI. 30.

69 The term *dominium* employed by all the Spanish scholastics described, in Soto's definition, "a faculty and right [*facultas et ius*] that [a person] has over anything,

to use it for his own benefit by any means that are permitted by law". *De iustitia et iure*, III. II. Ii (280). The term "sovereignty", which I have used here rather loosely and which did not enter the language until later, translates *dominium iurisdictionis*, that is, the "faculty and right" which a sovereign has over jurisdiction or government.

70 "On the American Indians", 1.1 and 1.6, *Vitoria: Political Writings*, 239 and 250.

71 Ibid., 3.8, pp. 290–1.

72 Antony Anghie claims that "virtually every book written on the mandates make some reference to Vitoria's work" but does not offer any examples. *Imperialism, Sovereignty and the Making of International Law*, 144–5.

73 *De Dominio indorum*, printed in Luciano Pereña, *Misión de España en América* (Madrid: Consejo Superior de Investigaciones Scientíficas, 1956), 107. For a more extensive reading of Cano's *relectio*, see Lupher, *Romans in a New World*, 85–93.

74 "On the American Indians", 2. 2, *Vitoria: Political Writings*, 264.

75 "First Letter on a Regicide Peace" in *Selected Works of Edmund Burke*, E. J. Payne ed. (Indianapolis: Liberty Fund, 1990), III, 117.

76 "On Civil Power", 3.4, *Vitoria: Political Writings*, 40, and see Adolfo Miaja de la Muela, "El derecho *totius orbis* en el pensamiento de Francisco de Vitoria", *Revista española de derecho internacional* 18 (1965), 341, 348–52. Vitoria, like most scholastics, accepted the traditional distinction between *potestas* and *auctoritas* (on which Hobbes heaped such scorn). On this issue, see Andreas Wagner, "Francisco de Vitoria and Alberico Gentili on the Legal Character of the Global Commonwealth", *Oxford Journal of Legal Studies* 31:3 (2011), 565–82, who describes *potestas* as a "factual power reflexively embedded in a legal order".

77 "On the Law of War", 1.4.19, *Vitoria: Political Writings*, 305.

78 In doing so, however, he was not exercising the purely private right which Grotius later found most useful – that "any person even a private citizen may declare and wage a defensive war" – since he had not himself been harmed by the behavior of the barbarians. "On the Law of War", 1.2, *Vitoria: Political Writings*, 299. On Grotius' use of this claim, see Tuck, *The Rights of War and Peace*, 81–3

79 D. J. B. Trim's claim that "The Spanish commentators restricted the application of this right [to defend the innocent] to 'barbarians', i.e. the indigenous inhabitants of the New World", although factually accurate, at least in this particular instance since all that Vitoria – and Vitoria is the only source Trim cites – was concerned with were precisely the "barbarians" is nevertheless misleading, as is the subsequent claim that "in the second half of the sixteenth century, however, the right to act against tyranny and oppression was extended to Christian princes, and was chracterised as a duty". For Vitoria and his successors, Christian princes enjoyed the same natural rights and were bound by the same duties as non-Christian ones, and "defending the innocent" had always been as much a right as a duty. "'If a Prince Use Tyrannie Towards His People': Interventions on Behalf of Foreign Populations in Early-Modern Europe" in Brendan Simms and D. J. B. Trim eds., *Humanitarian Intervention: A History* (Cambridge: Cambridge University Press, 2011), 25–66.

80 "On Dietary Laws", 1.3, *Vitoria: Political Writings*, 209.

81 Ibid., 1.4, p. 215.

82 Ibid., 1.5 p. 218.
83 *Disputatio xii. De Bello*, from *Opus de triplice virtute theologica, fide spe et charitate* [Paris, 1621], printed in Luciano Pereña Vicente, *Teoria de la guerra en Francisco Suárez*, II, 149–52.
84 *De iustitia et iure*, III I ii, (195).
85 *De legibus. Comentarios al tratado de la ley*, Francisco Puy and Luís Núñez ed. and trans. (Granada: Universidad de Granada, 1965), 94.
86 "On the American Indians", 3.5.15, *Vitoria: Political Writings*, 287–8. This is the fifth "just title".
87 "On the American Indians", 3.7, *Vitoria: Political Writings*, 289.
88 "On Civil Power", 1–7, *Vitoria: Political Writings*, 19. This, however, contrasts sharply with his argument in "On the American Indians", 3.6, that "true and voluntary election ... might be a legitimate title in natural law". He refrains, however, from saying whether he truly believes that the American Indians had, in fact, "decided to accept the king of Spain as their prince". *Vitoria: Political Writings*, 288–9. On the legitimacy of Cortés' alliance with the Tlaxcalans, see Richard Tuck, "Alliances with Infidels in the European Imperial Expansion" in Sankar Muthu ed., *Empire and Modern Political Thought* (Cambridge: Cambridge University Press, 2012), 61–83.
89 See pp. 171–89, *passim*.
90 "On the Law of War", 3. 7, *Vitoria: Political Writings*, 324.
91 See my *Spanish Imperialism and the Political Imagination*, 31.
92 *Disputatio xii. De Bello*, 126–7.
93 *De Civitate Dei*, XIX. 13.
94 *Disputatio xii. De Bello*, 238.
95 Ibid., 158–61.
96 See my "Stoicism, Cosmopolitanism and the Legacy of European Imperialism", *Constellations* 7 (2000), 3–22.
97 See Brett, *Liberty, Right and Nature*, 205–6. On natural rights of this kind and modern "human rights".
98 "On the American Indians", 3. 1, *Vitoria: Political Writings*, 278. As he defines it, this seems to have been Vitoria's own creation. St. Augustine had suggested that denial of a right of passage might be sufficient *injuria* for a just war. However, this has none of the structure of Vitoria's argument. (*Quaestiones in Heptateuchum*, IV. 44; *Decretum* C.23. 2.3).
99 "On the American Indians", 3. 1, *Vitoria: Political Writings*, 280.
100 Ibid., 278, citing Justinian, *Institutes* I.2.1, "What natural reason has established among all nations is called the law of nations." See note 48.
101 "On the American Indians", 3. 1, *Vitoria: Political Writings*, 279.
102 Ibid., 291–2.
103 *The Law of Nations or, Principles of the Law of Nature* [1797], Béla Kapossy and Richard Whatmore ed. (Indianapolis: Liberty Fund, 2008), 275. The original, *Le droit des gens. Ou principes de la loi naturelle*, was first published in 1758.
104 *De iustitia et iure*, V. III. iii. (423).
105 "On the American Indians", 3.1, *Vitoria: Political Writings*, 285.
106 Ibid., 285.
107 Ibid., 292.

108 *A Concise History of the Law of Nations* (New York: Macmillan, 1954), 81.

109 See p. 135.

110 *De Dominio indorum*, 142, "nisi vocetur Alexander peregrinus".

111 Ibid., 280.

112 *De iure naturae et gentium libri octo*, C. H. Oldfather and W. A. Oldfather trans. (Oxford: Clarendon Press, 1934), II, 364–6. I would like to thank Theodore Christov for drawing my attention to this important passage.

113 Antony Anghie, for instance, claims that "Vitoria bases his conclusion that the Indians are not sovereign on the simple assertion that they are pagan". *Imperialism, Sovereignty and the Making of International Law*, 29. Cf. Sharon Korman who infers from Vitoria's claim that non-Christian rulers were bound to admit Christian missionaries under the *ius peregrinandi* implied that non-Christian states did not possess the same legal standing as Christian ones. *The Right of Conquest: The Acquisition of Territory by Force in International Law and Practice* (Oxford: Clarendon Press, 1996), 53. There is, in fact, nothing in Vitoria's discussion of the *ius perigrinandi* to deny the obvious inference that Christian rulers had a corresponding obligation to admit Muslim missionaries – although clearly he could not say as much. Quincy Wright's claim that "Francis of Vitoria and other writers of the Naturalist School of international law ... held that Montezuma of Mexico and other non-Christian states had equal rights [with Christian states] under natural law", which Korman denies, is, in fact, perfectly correct. "The Goa Incident", *American Journal of International Law* 56 (1962), 629 n. 37.

114 *Étude théorique et pratique sur l'occupation* (Paris, 1896), 103.

115 Quoted in Brett, *Liberty, Right and Nature*, 78.

116 See pp. 70–1.

117 *Fundamenta juris naturae et gentium ex sensu communi deducta* (Halle, 1718), 161 (LXXII).

118 *An Enquiry into the Foundations of the Laws of Nations in Europe from the Time of the Greeks and Romans to the Age of Grotius* (London, 1795), 1 xiii–xiv and 169, and see Jennifer Pitts, "Empire and Legal Universalism in the Eighteenth Century", *American Historical Review* 117 (2012), 92–121.

119 *The Spanish Origin of International Law: Lectures on Francisco de Vitoria (1480–1546) and Francisco Suárez (1548–1617)* (Washington, DC: School of Foreign Service, Georgetown University [1928]), 21.

## 2

# "Making Barbarians into Gentle Peoples"

## *Alberico Gentili on the Legitimacy of Empire*

I

The great debates over the status and nature of what later came to be called international law may be said to have begun, as we have seen, with an attempt by some of the members of the School of Salamanca to reconfigure the law of nations so as to provide a normative justification for the Spanish presence in America. Francisco de Vitoria's arguments had, of course, been intended to be applicable to all nations everywhere. However, the specific conditions with which the School was primarily concerned were narrowly defined by the circumstances of the Spanish "discovery" and the peoples they had discovered. The first writer to bring some of the arguments which Vitoria in particular had identified to bear on the wider issue of the justification for universal empire was the Italian jurist Alberico Gentili.

Gentili was born in the town of San Ginesio in the Marche in central Italy in 1552. In 1580, having converted to Protestantism, he fled first to the relative safety of Ljubljana and then to Germany. He arrived in England in 1580, by which time he had acquired a considerable international reputation and, in 1587, was appointed Regius Professor of Civil Law at Oxford. He joined Gray's Inn in 1600 and in 1605 was appointed advocate for the interests of the Spanish Crown in cases before the Admiralty Court. Gentili wrote widely on a number of related topics, a defence of the traditional method of legal exegesis, the *mos Italicus* against the new humanist *mos Gallicus* (*De iuris interpretibus dialogi sex*), a treatise on embassies (*De legationibus*), a collection of reflections on his experiences as advocate for the Spanish Crown (*Hispanicae advocationis libri duo*), and a dialogue on the justice of Roman imperial expansion, *The Wars of the Romans* (*De armis Romanis*).

The best-known and by far the most influential of his writings, however, was *On the Laws of War* (*De iure belli*), which first appeared in 1598. It is, as its title claims, a study of the laws governing warfare, but since for Gentili, as for Vitoria, the legal and morally most troubling instance of warfare occurred not within but between nations, it was inevitably also a treatise on the law of nations and, thus, inescapably on the legitimacy of empire.

Gentili clearly owes a great deal to his Spanish predecessors, and in particular to Vitoria; but his approach, and the conclusions to which he ultimately comes, are very different, in part at least, as we shall see, by distorting the thrust of Vitoria's central argument. *De iure belli* opens with the characteristically assertive claim that the laws of war are not to be found in the "books of Justinian" (that is in the Roman Law). Neither, however, "does it appear to be the function either of the moral or of the political philosopher to give an account of the laws which we have in common with our enemies and with foreigners". The reason given for this last assertion is that the philosopher or the moralist always "confines himself within the city state, and rather limits himself to the foundations of the virtues than rear lofty structures", whereas in Gentili's view, "this philosophy of war belongs to that great community formed by the entire world and the whole human race".[1] But if the philosopher and the moralist are not competent to judge matters concerning the "whole human race", who is? There would seem to have been only two possible candidates: the theologians and, despite Justinian's apparent silence on the subject, the jurists. The theologians will not do because, Gentili remarks cuttingly, despite their grand claims, they are confined to the "sacred writings" and are bound by "the word of God". Or at least they should be, although as Gentili knew full well, they constantly, as he famously remarked, meddled "in other people's business" – *in munere alieno* – most often in that of the jurists. The jurists, themselves, by contrast, are not confined to the texts of the law "any more than physicians are limited to those of Galen, or philosophers to the writings of Aristotle".[2] From this Gentili concluded that, even if Justinian's famous codes contained no set of laws governing warfare as such, any attempt at understanding the nature of human conflict and all its myriad consequences – and it is, of course, with them rather than the rules of combat that Gentili is concerned – could only be the task of the jurist.

Gentili has repeatedly been described as a "humanist", the assumption being that this made him *eo ipso* the enemy of the theologians. True, he was indebted to (although not uncritical of) both Machiavelli and Jean Bodin, both of whom might be described as "humanists", *sensu lato*. Published in 1599, *The Wars of the Romans*, a sustained panegyric of the Roman Empire, is written as a humanist dialogue – although hardly in humanist Latin – and also makes extensive use not only of the classical poets but also of the moderns.[3] Yet there are also perhaps more significant ways in which Gentili was clearly not a humanist.[4] He was consistently hostile to French legal humanism and to most humanist textual criticism, and he seems to have been unaware of, or most probably simply ignored as the Salamanca theologians themselves had done, Lorenzo Valla's celebrated debunking of the "Donation of Constantine", an eighth-century forgery and a key document in the ideological armory of the papacy, by which the Emperor Constantine the Great is supposed to have bequeathed the *imperium* of the Roman Empire in the West to the Holy See. Then it is also the case that the more one examines the humanist/scholastic or humanist/theologian distinction, the more fuzzy it becomes. The various members of the School of Salamanca were, for instance, by no means consistent in their opposition to humanism. The theologian Melchor Cano used recognizably "humanist" textual methods in his major work *De locis theologicis* (1563), an historical and philological inquiry into all the sources of theology and a project which was, in itself, a recognizably humanist one. Vitoria, although he condemned Erasmus, did so not because he was a humanist but because he was, in Vitoria's view, a jumped-up grammarian – "ex grammatica fecit se theologum", he said of him – who dared to speak on matters of theology about which, Vitoria supposed, he knew nothing.[5] And although a text by any one of the Salamanca theologians certainly looks very different from one by, say, Bruni, Ficino, or Pomponazzi, it does not look so very unlike one by Gentili. Both drew extensively on recognizable humanist sources, on the poets, the Roman moralists, and the historians – in particular Cicero and Livy – and on the Roman orators, when it suited them. (Vitoria even cites the comic playwright Plautus, hardly an orthodox theological *auctoritas*.) And neither, it must be said, paid much heed to the niceties of Ciceronian Latin. As Noel Malcolm has pointed out, many of Gentili's seemingly secular, and thus supposedly humanist, views on religious toleration and the legitimacy of non-Christian regimes, most significantly the Ottomans, "can themselves be found within the theological tradition". It is also clearly true that whereas the scholastic/humanist distinction generally represents the scholastic tradition as if it were a set of unwavering doctrines (as, it must be said, do many of the humanists themselves) in the hands of the Spanish neo-Thomists at least, it was, in Malcolm's words, "a flexible system, in which judgment had to be used to apply principles in different ways to different circumstances".[6]

Gentili's hostility toward both the humanists, or as he calls them, "the philosophers", and the theologians derived not from any really substantive disagreement over method, nor from any dispute over Latin style (Gentili's Latin is, if anything, worse than Vitoria's) nor even consistently over sources. In part, at least, it belongs to an ongoing early modern academic turf war. The theologians, in particular, made repeated claims to omniscience and persisted in denying the jurists any right to an opinion in matters which we would now think of as belonging broadly to moral and political philosophy. The humanist philosophers for their part were generally scathing about all forms of knowledge associated with the schools, whether theological or legal. What was ultimately at stake, however, was far more than the status of an academic discipline. It was Gentili's conviction that, if it was fully and properly interpreted, it was the law, not theology, much less "philosophy," which would provide an understanding of the condition of the "whole human race".

Just as, in an earlier work of 1583, on the problematic passages in Roman law, he claimed to have demonstrated, to his own satisfaction, that a proper reading of the Roman law would yield a far better definition of the idea of liberty than any provided by "a thousand philosophers", so in *De iure belli* he insists that a full account of the laws of war could be arrived at without appeal to the theologians.[7] In this respect Gentili, together with Vitoria and Hugo Grotius, is not only, as he has so often been described, one of the founders of modern international law; he also belongs in a genealogy which runs through Montesquieu and Giambattista Vico and Gravina and down to Friedrich Carl von Savigny and Henry Sumner Maine in the nineteenth century of jurists who sought to make the study of the law into a recognizable human science.

II

Gentili's immediate concern was precisely to find a satisfactory account "of the laws which we have in common with our enemies and with foreigners", those laws, that is, which could be said to transcend purely domestic law because they did not make "any distinction between nations"; and what this meant was a re-working of the current understanding of the law of nature and its always troubling – and troubled – relationship with the law of nations.[8] The problem for the jurist (although not for the theologian or the philosopher) was how to come up with a conception of the law of nations which would possess both a clearly established, and seemingly indisputable, body of first principles, but which would, at the same time, have some real legal content. Vitoria and his successors had, as we have seen, offered a compelling account of the nexus between the natural law and the law of nations, which made of the latter a hypothetically positive version of the former. If the human community is governed by a law to which all its members have access, then the law which applies between nations, however remote they might be from one another, must be that to which they all would have agreed on had they been consulted about it beforehand. What the Salamanca theologians had created was, in effect, a heavily ontologized moral argument based on a counterfactual claim which could plausibly allow any people from Finns to Fuegians to recognize a properly binding law when they saw one. What it singularly failed to do was to provide the law of nations with any legal content – with, that is, a body of *leges* – or to see where any such content might come from. And only a thorough under-standing of the sources of the law could provide this.

The problem with every attempt to formulate an international law which would be something more compelling than a simple set of treaty agreements between states was to establish what Immanuel Kant later called "a common external constraint".[9] Without some such restraint, any law of nations is inevitably reduced to what Clausewitz referred to dismissively as those "imperceptible limitations, hardly worth mentioning known as international law and custom".[10] External constraints demanded the presence of a sovereign, and sovereigns, however defined, were only to be found within individual states. The only species of law which could be made binding was, therefore, in the first instance, always private or domestic, and nearly all forms of the law of nations have, in effect, been conceived initially as a transfer of one of another kind of domestic law to the international sphere. The real problem with this, of course, was how to make a body of laws initially devised by, and for the use of, one group of people, valid for all peoples.

This problem confronts all those who have any kind of significant and extended dealings with groups outside their own communities. But, when these relationships are, at best, limited, mutual agreements can be reached in much the same way in which domestic laws are established. The emphasis given in the ancient world on the obligations of hospitality, and the rights of passage, together with the immunity granted to ambassadors – all subjects on which Gentili has much to say – assured an, albeit limited, degree of common accord between otherwise highly bellicose communities. It is no accident that the Trojan War – the first great war in (Western) history – began precisely because of a violation of the code of hospitality.

The problem evidently becomes far more acute when the relationship is one between large numbers of different peoples and crucially when that relationship involves not only trade and reciprocity but also active political control by one group over another: in other words, when the relationship involves "empire". It becomes most acute of all when, as in the Roman case, that empire is held to be, potentially at least, identical with the human community itself. The Romans, who had frequent contacts, albeit often indirect ones, with peoples as far afield as China knew full well that "the world" was far more extensive than the Roman Empire. Furthermore, it was obviously the case that, with very few exceptions, whatever definition one gives to "empire", most empires, and the Roman in particular, had been acquired through warfare. A law, therefore, which applied to an empire of supposedly universal extent – as the Roman law was intended to be – must be at once linked to the laws of war and coextensive with what Gentili, echoing Vitoria, calls the "law of human society" (*ius societatis humanae*).[11]

The need to establish a supranational legal agreement of this kind was the theoretical problem of empire. It inevitably involved not only the creation of a universal law, which could be applied to all peoples (even to those who, as yet, lay outside the empire) but also the extinction of the sovereignty of others. In its simplest form the question was, in the formulation Vitoria had employed vis-à-vis the American Indians: How could a sovereign people be deprived of "true dominion public and private" by another?[12] The initial answer was either through voluntary surrender, which rarely if ever occurred in practice, or more usually by means of what the victors at least held to be a "just war".[13]

Although Gentili makes a passing allusion to the condemnation by Augustine of the "lust for dominion", he is, by and large, a robust champion of (legitimate) imperial expansion. "Those Spaniards," he said, referring to Seneca and Lucan, who had denounced Alexander the Great as a brigand and "who condemned the empires not only of Alexander alone, but of all nations and all times which sprung from humble beginnings and are increased by the art of war ... were inept and lacked the stomach of the modern Spaniards".[14] The moderns (by whom he appears to have understood principally Vitoria and his fellow theologian Diego de Covarrubias), in Gentili's understanding of them at least, strongly endorsed the claim that empire could legitimately be acquired through the pursuit of a just war and that victory in such a war granted to the victor not only rights over the movable property of the vanquished but also over their territory, and thus sovereignty over their persons. (As we have seen, Vitoria, in fact, makes no such claim, but Gentili's reading of him is highly tendentious.)[15]

For the empire to be a legitimate one, however, it had, of course, to have been acquired in accordance with the laws of war. For Gentili, what he called that "branch of the law which is buried in obscurity" constituted a distinct domain of jurisprudence; but it was one which belonged firmly with the *ius gentium*, so that "we hold the firm belief that that question of war ought to be settled in accordance with the law of nations".[16] Famously, however, Gentili, who has little time for the metaphysical niceties of the theologians, makes no distinction between this and the natural law:

> Abundant light is afforded us by the definitions which the authors and founders of our laws are unanimous in giving to this law of nations which we are investigating. For they say that that the law of nations is that which is in use among all the nations of men, which native reason has established among all human beings, and which is equally observed by all mankind. This law is the natural law. The agreement of all nations about a matter must be regarded as a law of nature.[17]

As we have already seen, Gentili was not, of course, the first to make this move. As he himself observes, both the *Institutes* and the *Digest* speak of the law of nations as one, as had Bartolus. Gentili, however, goes far beyond the claims of the jurists, for whom the law of nations had been in origin customary by making his *ius gentium/ius naturae* into a body of innate ideas, a fully developed *innata lex*. "The civil law", he wrote,

> is an agreement and bond of union among citizens, but the same is true of the law of nations as regards nations, and the law of nature as regards mankind. The founders of our laws are not to be censured for defining natural law as that which nature teaches to all animals, even though there is no law, that is, no interaction (*communio*) between man and the lower animals. For to say nothing of the law which is common to us with the brutes, of our dominion over them, we surely cannot deny that what is natural to men is common to all men.[18]

Like the theologians, Gentili takes the broadly Stoic view that the world is a single "commonwealth". This held all men together in bonds of mutual obligation.

> All this universe which you see, in which things divine and human are included, is one, and we are members of a great body. And in truth the world is one body. Moreover nature has made us all kindred, since we have the same origin and the same abode. She has implanted in us love for one another and made us inclined to union.[19]

Or, as the principal speaker, and in most respects Gentili's mouthpiece, in *The Wars of the Romans*, identified simply as the "Apologist", puts it, "the original source of the law of nations, ... is that of human fellowship".[20]

Initially, Gentili would also seem to have been broadly in agreement with Vitoria's and Cicero's claim that the law of nature – and thus also of nations – is constituted by "the agreement of all nations about a matter". This should not, however, be taken to mean that

> all nations actually came together at a given time, and thus that the law of nations was established. The writers to whom I refer [that is, the authors of the *Digest*, the *Institutes*, and Cicero] do not make any such statement and it is not necessary to understand the word "omnes" in such a way that when one speaks of the usage of all nations it should be considered to mean absolutely every nation; since countless numbers of these, in regions widely separated from us and utterly different in their customs, and of different tongues, remain unknown.[21]

From this it would seem that, like the Salamanca theologians, Gentili would be prepared to accept the practices of the majority of the nations of the world, or at least of a representative part of them, as evidence of what his "great body" could reasonably be supposed to have chosen in any given instance, had they, in fact, been able to have "come together at a given time".

Gentili's objective, however, was to establish "a system of law ... which is regarded as natural and definite".[22] To do this, and to ensure that this system is indeed a system of *law* and not merely a moral or epistemological device, he had to identify the *consensus gentium* as it manifested itself in the customs of the majority, in an immutable and irrefutable law of nature. Grotius and others would make a not dissimilar argument by employing the Glossators' and post-Glossators' distinction between a primary and second-ary natural law—the *ius naturale prius* and the *ius naturale posterius*.[23] On this account the *ius gentium*, although not natural "in a primary sense", could be considered so "in a secondary sense". Gentili, however, makes no use of this slippery distinction. For him the *ius gentium* becomes not merely a part of the law of nature. It becomes, in effect, the definition of the law of nature itself. This is what he means by saying that the *ius gentium* "is a part of the divine law which God left with us after our sin".[24]

Two centuries later Giambattista Vico (with no allusion to Gentili) was to make much the same move to create what he called simply "the natural law of nations".[25] Like Gentili, although with far more elaborate self-justification, Vico was trying to create a new kind of science on the basis of a study of the law and similarly applicable to all human beings. Like Gentili, Vico also turns the law of nations into something like the actual content of the natural law, which he described as "the record of divine [or natural] and human things".[26] On this account, most of the positive laws of individual nations can be thought of as purely domestic arrangements, in keeping with reason, but essentially contingent and, thus, changeable. But those domestic laws which turn out on examination to be common to a large number of peoples must have their origins in some kind of innate disposition, and in consequence, be immutable. It was what Henry Maine, in 1887, called "the creation of a real and determinable Law of Nature". (Surprisingly, however, Maine ignored Gentili altogether and ascribed the attempt to use this configuration of the "the Law of Nature Law of Nations, Jus Naturae, Jus Gentium, as the most admirable, the most dignified portion of Roman Law" to create "the system which lies at the basis of the rules now regulating the concerns of states *inter se*", to "Grotius and his successors".)[27]

Although the sources of this natural law/*ius gentium* are, for Gentili, "hidden in a well", the law (*lex*) itself can still be known, and the method of knowing consists of an inquiry into what "the authors and founders of our laws" claimed it to be.[28] To substantiate this claim, Gentili embarks on a rambling historical illustration of his assumption that, although the peoples of the world are myriad, "our jurists (*nostri iurisconsulti*) could properly speak of all the nations, since the empires of the Romans, Alexander, and of the Parthians could bring these to light, and did in fact reveal them". In Gentili's historical vision of the origin of law, conquest and trade had, in effect, opened up the entire world to the Romans, so that "knowledge could be gained of all peoples, thus the law of nations could be defined, thus many other matters could be settled". All of which led him to the conclusion that "our jurists, then, have been able to compile this law [of nations] from absolutely all nations; for if the Romans, Greek, Jews and barbarians, in short, all known peoples, have made use of a certain code of laws, it must be assumed that all men have made use of that same code".[29] Who, however, are our jurists, and why was the Roman law as codified under Justinian silent on such an important issue as the laws of war? The only possible answer to both questions – since Gentili nowhere returns to the supposed absence of the laws of war in "the books of Justinian" – is that the body of law devised by "our jurists" includes not only the Roman law codes themselves but also all of the work of later commentators together with a good deal of Cicero. On this account the Roman civil law becomes not merely the reflection of the law of the Romans themselves but instead a kind of summa of all the laws of all the peoples of the world.

There would, however, appear to be one important exception to Gentili's argument that "our jurists" could "properly speak of all peoples", namely, America. If America had been truly "unknown" before the fifteenth century, and, if, as seemed to be the case, its peoples lived by "codes" which, in certain crucial respects, lay well outside the hypothetical universal human law, then its very existence posed a threat to any supposition that the natural law, and thus the law of nations, could be inferred from the laws compiled by our jurists. This, as Gentili must have known, was in part the argument used by both Domingo de Soto and Vázquez de Menchaca against the Roman Emperor's claim to be "lord of all the world".[30] For Soto and Vázquez as for Gentili, the law – positive or natural – could only be existential. It made no sense to speak of peoples being subjects of the emperor, by *law* but not so in *fact*. The presence, therefore, of an entire continent which was by law subject to the law of nations, but in fact was not, would have constituted a serious objection to the claim that "our jurists could properly speak of all nations".

This might explain Gentili's otherwise unintelligible claim that: "No-one doubts to-day that what we call the New World is joined to our own and has always been known to remote India."[31] Gentili's assertion appears to be based on a 1590 commentary on Hippocrates' *Airs, Waters and Places* by the Milanese doctor Lodovico Settala which identifies Peru as both Plato's "Atlantis" and the Biblical "Ophir" – the mythical location of King Solomon's mines.[32] By the 1590s, however, notwithstanding such claims as these, and the only marginally less fantastical supposition that the Americas had been settled by shipwrecked Carthaginian sailors, it was abundantly clear to all informed persons that the New World had, in fact, been unknown to the ancients and that at no point was it "joined to our own". Indeed, all the initial premises of Vitoria's "On the American Indians" had been based on the assumption that the argument which had regularly been used to justify incursions into territories occupied by the Ottoman Turks, that these were lands which had once formed part of the Roman empire and of the *Respublica Christianorum* and thus fell under the jurisdiction of the Pope and Emperor, could not apply to the Americas precisely because they were, in Vitoria's words, "previously unknown to our world".[33] If, however, as Gentili claims to believe, the Americas had indeed been known to the ancients, then it would be reasonable to suppose that they, too, could be said to have fallen under the same "code of laws" as those studied by our jurists. (The Chinese – unless they are also included in "remote India" – he seems simply to have ignored.)

Gentili had thus made the laws devised by our jurists on the basis of their survey of all human laws into something like the codified content of the natural law. This unsurprisingly comes out, as it would for Vico, as identical with the Roman law, hence, Gentili's description of the Roman law as "the most excellent kind among human laws" and the allusion to "Justinian's law" as containing "much that is drawn from the natural law and the law of nations".[34] For Vico, however, this was not because the Roman law some-how embodied the customary laws of all the peoples of the world but because the history of the Roman empire constituted an "ideal eternal history", "traversed in time by the histories of all nations", (except that of the Jews whose history, as that of the chosen people, is governed by divine law), a measure which could therefore be employed to adjudicate all other forms of human behaviour.

Gentili has, of course, no recourse to ideal types. For him the history of the Romans, and above all the history of the Roman law, constituted what was in effect the civil expression of the law of nature.[35] And this was because the labour of our jurists, patiently collating all the civil codes from all corners of the known world, had come up with a code which corresponded to what nature had inscribed in the minds of men. The truth of this could be demonstrated from the study of the history of the expansion of the Roman Empire and of its laws.

The "natural law of nations" is not, however, simply the accumulated customs of all the peoples of the entire world; it is by implication limited to those which also conform to "natural reason", and it is the Romans – our jurists – who determine what is and what is not in conformity with natural reason. Gentili is stating what, if it was not already so by his day, would certainly soon become commonplace: that the Romans had invented law as surely as the Greeks had invented philosophy and the natural sciences. As Aldo Schiavone has put it, it is only because Rome had succeeded in creating a category, and a conception to go with it, of "the law" that we are able to describe the prescriptions derived from "theological apparatuses more or less connected to kingship, kinship-relations and political institutions", observed by ancient Greeks, Persians, Egyptians, Hawaiians, Aztecs, and so on, as "juridical" at all.[36] Gentili's contribution is to claim that the Romans were fully conscious of this fact. By inventing *ius* the Romans had, in effect, codified the natural law.

Furthermore having created a law which was commensurate with what was supposedly in accord with the wishes of the "human community", they had set out to export it – as we might say – to all those places where it was not properly observed. The Apologist, in *The Wars of the Romans*, makes the point over and over again that it was the capacity of Roman arms to make the law applicable to all which made the empire not only legitimate but also a blessing for all, most especially, of course, to those whom they had conquered. Over and over again we are told that this or that people were "brought over by our laws to a more cultivated way of life". As he reminds Picenus – his interlocutor in the dialogue, – it was a Goth who "said of our empire, it was sought out by just arms and preserved by just laws".[37]

And even when the Empire itself had vanished, the law remained. The world which, though deprived of that blessed good luck of our empire, nevertheless tenaciously hangs onto and thirstily gulps down Roman laws, with which it renews for itself the sweet memory of its ancient happiness under Roman rule and alleviates the sadness of these times by this little bit of pleasure that has been mixed in. By those arts did Rome grow; by those arts did Rome stand firm.[38]

What this meant, of course, was more than simply the imposition of a rule of law; it meant incorporation into a political society, into the *libertas publica*. It meant, in short, becoming a Roman citizen. "The Roman people", enthuses the Apologist,

have bestowed citizenship upon other defeated peoples as well, who acknow-ledged our own manifest kindness but did not ascribe anything to their own excellence, and therefore always remained more easily in obedience to our state. This was the true secret of that empire, and it was indeed a just one, in that it was owing to exceptional Roman excellence.

The Roman Empire was not merely a conquering state as were, for instance, the Spanish and the Ottoman Empires – in Gentili's view the two great tyrannies of his day. It was, instead, a body of citizens, for instead of subjugating the peoples it had conquered, it transformed them.

"How fortunate", enthuses the Apologist,

were all our subject peoples, who in our empire did not only accept, but also gave us emperors—even the very Africans themselves, and the Syrians, and the Thracians, and the remotest Britons. ... The whole world lay open, allowing passage to Roman courage, and humbly yielded in defeat. But the world was defeated by us in such a manner that it was to its advantage to have been defeated, so that it could be ruled by this scepter of ours.[39]

All of this had been made possible because the Romans possessed excel-lence – virtue, in other words – by reason not so much of their superior arms but because of their superior understanding of the law. Nothing, as Plutarch would say, had come to them initially from Fortune. The Apologist is prepared to admit that "after celebrating its virtue, we are not ashamed to admit the good fortune of our state, a good fortune that has at one and the same time made the empire lucky and the ages of the world most blessed".[40] But it was Roman virtue "that produced universal dominion", and Roman virtue thus became "the good luck of all the world".[41]

The Roman Empire was an open society: multinational (we might say), multilingual, multicultural, and multi-religious. Even its Emperors, as the Apologist points out, had not always been Romans. Thus, the Apologist, taking a swipe at the loathed Spaniards, observes that

Rome wanted all to be citizens; it has wanted barbarians to turn into gentle peoples. I shall make note only of Spain. Barbaric and wild was that people, whose minds are said to be closer to those of animals than men; for whom in such a long series of ages there is said to have been no great leader, apart from that one of a robber band (this was the Spanish specialty), Viriathus. That people was brought over by our laws to a more cultivated way of life and, trained by service in our army, produced triumphators over the nations and rulers of the world: men like Balbus, Trajan, Theodosius.[42]

To this Picenus replies that one of the major injustices of the Romans had been precisely their willingness to grant refuge to every kind of criminal and barbarian. Their state had no shape or form, he complains. It was merely the archetypical cosmopolitan society, a robber band, made up in this case of

> the sole base dregs of base barbarians, if Plato was right when he observed that barbarians are those who are united by no commonality of customs and language. Romulus used to receive everyone in sanctuary. He wouldn't give a slave back to a master, a debtor [*nexus*] to a creditor, a guilty man to magistrates. "Romulus filled the walls with the disreputable grove" as Lucan, a truer historian than a poet, wrote. And a poet—if Juvenal, who doesn't know how to lie, is really a poet—wrote: "Yet, for all that, if you trace and unscroll your name way back, you derive your race from a base asylum. The first of your ancestors, whoever he was, was either a shepherd or something I'd rather not name." He didn't want to say "robber" or some other criminal and wicked type.[43]

Picenus is here being made to echo those members of the Roman Senate who, when in 40 CE the Emperor Claudius proposed that a number of transalpine Gauls be granted citizenship, objected that this would be to have "a nation of foreigners, a troop of captives ... so to say ... forced upon us". To this Claudius had replied: "What else proved fatal to Sparta and Athens, in spite of their power in arms, but their policy of holding the conquered aloof as alien-born? But the sagacity of our own founder Romulus was such that several times he fought and naturalized a people in the course of a single day."[44] Romulus, as the Apologist puts it, had invited "the whole world into his state". Picenus' objections are not merely groundless and promoted to no small degree by his resentment at the exclusion of his own people. They reveal a profound misunderstanding of the purpose for which the empire was created. Roman inclusiveness became the basis, at least in the political imagination of the Roman historians and jurists, for the success and duration of the empire. As opposed to the Athenians and Spartans who had closed their societies against all those who were not native-born, the Romans had not only tamed the barbarians by exporting their way of life – what the first-second-century theologian, Tertullian, called their *Romanitas*, their "Romaness"; to them, they had drawn strength from them. As Immanuel Kant was later to remark, as a warning to the newly emergent nation states of Europe, it had been precisely the tendency of the Greeks – as opposed to the Romans – to isolate themselves from the rest of humanity, which had been the "perfect source that contributed to the decline of their states".[45]

The openness of the Roman world had made it a truly universal society, and it is this which has bestowed on the world the blessings of peace and prosperity. This, it must be said, was a common theme in the literature on which Gentili draws most heavily: Plutarch, Polybius, and above all Claudian and Prudentius. It was what the Greek rhetorician, Aelius Aristides (who made use of some of the same sources), in his famous eulogy to the "grandeur and magnificence" of Rome delivered 143 or 144 CE, called "your wonderful citizenship" to which "[n]either sea nor intervening continent" was a bar. "No one", he went on, "worthy of rule or trust remains an alien, but a civil community of the World has been established as a Free Republic under one, the best, ruler and teacher of order; and all come together as into a common civic centre; in order to receive each man his due."[46] You have, he concluded, "caused the word 'Roman' to be the label, not of membership in a city, but some common nationality".[47] As the Apologist, in very much the same vein, and quoting both Claudian and Prudentius, tells Picenus:

> We have wished our enemies to be friends, allies, citizens. Behold, gradually the citizenship was given to all who lived in the Roman world Behold: Rome, the common fatherland. O the immeasurable glory of Roman citizenship! … These are testimonies that agree with the actual results of historical fact. These are testimonies of the blessed Roman Empire and of Roman virtue.

If these were the criteria which made an empire just, then the Spanish empire (or even the Ottoman) might be as laudable as the Roman. True the Spanish had no analogous concept of citizenship, but they did have a common system of imperial law which applied throughout all of their territories. (Not that Gentili makes any reference to this.) They had also, it could be argued, made war on the American Indians to civilize, or Christianize, them. What, for Gentili, renders the Spanish Empire a tyranny is the fact that the perfectly laudable end of taming the barbarians had, in brute fact, been pursued for illicit reasons. And here Gentili applies the same basic criteria which Picenus had applied to the Romans. Had the Romans indeed fought wars to spread the rule of law and to free the barbarian from their barbarism, had they in fact incorporated all foreigners into their "wonderful citizenship", then their empire would indeed have been a just one. But they had not. They had fought wars for their own personal gain and, far from incorporating everyone, they had even excluded from citizenship men, such as Picenus himself, who had fought for the Romans to acquire it. "It is contrary to nature and contrary to the laws of peoples", he protests, "for one to increase his own advantage to the disadvantage of another man. Even if one had to undergo all sorts of disadvantages that did not involve one in wrongdoing—disadvantages for one's possessions, for one's body, even for one's own life—even then one is not allowed to detract from the advantages of others."[48]

The Spanish too, in Gentili's view, had gone to America merely to enrich themselves rather than for the good of their conquered peoples. For both they and the Turks are "planning and plotting universal dominion". True the American Indians, because of their crimes against nature, fully deserved their fate. However, because the empire which the Spanish had built in America had been constructed on nothing other than naked greed, it could never be made legitimate in the same way that the Roman had, since, the Apologist assures Picenus, that had been founded on "this excellence of ours [which] was not inhumane, not proud, not the sort which would be unwilling to spread most liberally every sort of goodwill and benevolence".

That the benefits of Roman rule rested predominantly on the concept of citizenship which in turn rested on its laws was hardly a novel claim. But what, for Aristides and Claudian, had been merely the imposition of an indisputably superior mode of justice – one which had brought peace and prosperity to the entire inhabited world – became for Gentili the expression of "the original source of the law of nations" which in turn derived from the consensus of the "human fellowship" of the entire world.[49]

## IV

Gentili's bid to create a legitimate basis for imperial expansion in the law of nations becomes clearer from an examination of his seemingly contradictory treatment of Vitoria's arguments for the legitimation of the Spanish conquest and occupation of the Americas. This is a mixture of judicious distortion, willful misreading, and outright misrepresentation. Assuming, however, that Gentili had actually read "On the American Indians" – the only work of Vitoria's he cites – we must also assume that the uses to which he puts it are not purely casual. They take the form of two distinct but related claims. The first concerns the Indians' supposed "crimes against nature".

Gentili would, initially at least, seem to have been in broad general agreement with the Salamanca theologians that

> the cause of the Spaniards is just when they make war upon the Indians, who practised abominable lewdness even with beasts, and who ate human flesh slaying men for that purpose. For such sins are contrary to human nature, and the same is true of other sins recognized as such by all unless perhaps by brutes and brutish men.[50]

However, as we have seen, Vitoria's argument does not, in fact, justify war on grounds of crimes against nature in themselves, because these are widely practiced even within Christian states, which would give just as much right to, say, the king of France to invade Spain because of his subjects' persistent violations of the natural law, as it would the Spanish to invade the Americas. Vitoria's claim is that, in sanctioning such things as human sacrifice and cannibalism (Vitoria makes no mention of "abominable lewdness"), the Amerindian rulers were endorsing "tyrannical and oppressive laws against the innocent".[51]

Gentili's misreading of Vitoria is initially puzzling because elsewhere, and with no allusion to "On the American Indians", he himself makes much the same point. "It is the duty of man to protect men's interests and safety," he wrote. "This is due to any man from any other, for the very reason that they are all alike men; and because human nature, the common mother of the all, commends one to the other." And, like Vitoria, he also accepts that the "innocent" may legitimately be protected even from themselves. "Even the defense of one who neglects to protect himself is approved; nay even one who refuses to be protected by another, whether a kinsmen defend him or an alien, or even an enemy."[52]

For Gentili, the problem with Vitoria's formulation of this claim would seem to be that whereas the "Responsibility to Protect" was clearly part of the law of nations, it was also clearly a positive law. What was at stake in America for both Vitoria and Suárez was what the latter called the "order of the world", and it fell to the "commonwealth of all the world" to ensure its continuity. Vitoria's argument, as we have seen, lays great stress on the legitimacy of the sovereign authority. He is clear that even if the sovereign's power comes from the somewhat nebulous "whole world that is a commonwealth", only a sovereign can exercise it. By contrast, Gentili, in claiming that the Spanish conquest was a legitimate attempt to punish crimes against the natural law, is in effect pressing the private law case that any person, sovereign or not, possessed an inherent right of intervention since crimes against nature, as crimes against humanity, are a threat to all mankind, and thus, by implication to the individual.[53]

To underscore the point, Gentili links the American case to another much discussed example of what in the sixteenth century was held to be a supreme manifestation of inhumanity and one with which Gentili was himself closely involved, namely, piracy. Piracy, Gentili says, is "contrary to the law of nations and the league of human society". Because this also makes it a violation of the natural law, the destruction of pirates becomes a duty which falls on "all men, because in the violation of that law we are all injured and individuals in turn can find their personal rights violated is this not so?"

Piracy then clearly belongs to the same category of violation of the natural law as those crimes supposedly perpetrated by the Indians: "And if a war against pirates justly calls all men to arms because of a love for our neighbour and the desire to live in peace, so also do the general violation of the common law of humanity and wrong done to mankind."[54] For this reason the duty to punish – and since a violation of natural law posed a threat to the natural right of all mankind, the *right* to punish – now fell as much on the individual as on the state: "Therefore since we may also be injured as individuals by those violators of nature, war will be made against them by individuals. And no rights will be due to these men who have broken all human and divine laws and who, though joined with us by a similarity of nature, have disgraced this union with abominable stains."[55] From this it would seem to follow that a violation of the law of nature would thus make it legitimate for any person to judge as to the rightness or wrongness of the supposed offence and to take up arms in defence of his own natural rights.

Gentili, therefore, comes very close to the conclusion arrived at later by Grotius, and then again by Locke, and described by the latter as a "very strange doctrine" that, in Grotius' formulation, "the right of chastisement was held by private person, before it was held by the state".[56] (The same might be said of Vitoria's claim – which Grotius had found most useful – that "any person even a private citizen may declare and wage a defensive war".)[57]

It is even stranger in Gentili's case since it would seem to contradict his definition of war as a "public contest" and his insistence that "war on both sides must be public and official, and there must be sovereigns on both sides to direct the war".[58] The structure of Gentili's argument is, however, quite unlike that of either Grotius or Locke. He also clearly does not, as they do, allow to every person in the state of nature the right to punish. For Gentili, a violation of the law of nature (and thus the law of nations) would seem to transform warfare, which between civil beings would have been a resolution of differences following an initial attempt at a solution through dialogue, into a struggle for survival.[59] If that is indeed what Gentili had in mind then, although he nowhere makes the claim, this would have granted the English, indeed any English subject, as much right to wage war against, and claim sovereignty over, the American Indians as any Spaniard.

Whereas the positive law is made by sovereigns and applies to persons as members of particular states, the natural law applies to individuals, as human beings. We might say that whereas Vitoria's *ius gentium* was, in effect, something close to what we today might call an international law, in that it was a law between, and binding on, states, Gentili had transformed this into something much closer to what some might call a cosmopolitan law – that is, one which was universally binding upon individuals.[60]

Gentili's second engagement with Vitoria's account of the natural law concerns the discussion of what Vitoria termed "the right of natural partnership and communication" (*ius naturalis societatis et communicationis*). This, as we saw in the previous chapter, granted to all human beings a natural right of access to all parts of the globe so as to enable all peoples to "communicate" with one another. Travelers who wish to visit, or even to settle in a territory other than their own, had, therefore, a natural right to do so. This right – the *ius peregrinandi* – applied, however, only "so long as they do not harm the citizens" of the lands through which they are travelling.

Gentili's response to this depends, once again, on the question of motive. He is prepared to allow that Vitoria's argument would be an adequate defence of the conquest of America, if his account of the Spaniards' intention had been true. It was not, however, because "the Spaniards were aiming not at commerce but at dominion. And they regarded it as beyond dispute that it was lawful to take possession of those lands which are not previously known to us; just as if to be known to none of us were the same thing as to be possessed by no one."[61]

As Benjamin Straumann has pointed out, this is in fact a conflation of two quite distinct arguments. The first concerns the right of free passage. And although Vitoria's argument is vastly more complex than he suggests, Gentili is, in effect, pointing to the same flaw which a number of Vitoria's colleagues and pupils had already seen for themselves.[62] The second, however, is an allusion to a quite separate claim: the much debated principle of *res* or *terra nullius*, the argument that unoccupied territory (and moveable goods) became the property of the first person to take possession of them, although in the case of territory, just what that might involve was highly contentious (to which I shall return in Chapter 5).[63]

Gentili seems to have been prepared elsewhere to accept that, as "the law of nature abhors a vacuum", such land might legally be occupied by the first person to take up residence there. His conclusion, however, was that whereas this might create legal condition of ownership, it could not involve a transfer of sovereignty to the settlers. "Things which are common to all so far as their use is concerned are the property of no one; their jurisdiction and protection [however] belong to the sovereign."[64] (Similar objections were made to the claim of the English settlers in America that, because they had supposedly acquired their lands through legitimate purchase or treaty with the Indians, they were no longer subjects of the English Crown.)

The same, of course, would have to have applied to the Spaniards in America, if they had ever made such claims. However, all of Vitoria's arguments in defence of a war against the Indians are, in fact, based precisely on the supposition that their territories were, in every possible sense, occupied and that, as he set out in great detail in the first part of "On the American Indians", before the arrival of the Spanish "the barbarians undoubtedly possesses as true dominion both public and private, as any Christians".[65] For Vitoria, the right to *terra nullius* formed part of the "the right of discovery" (*de iure inventionis*) which he gives as one (the third) of his "unjust titles", and although it was "with this pretext alone Columbus of Genoa first set sail", he dismissed it with the contemptuous observation that "it provides no support for possession of these lands, any more than it would if they had discovered us".[66]

The point of conflating these two distinct issues, as with the earlier distortion of Vitoria's argument over the right to punish crimes against nature, seems to have been a wish to deny the Spaniards any claim to sovereignty in the Americas, not because their arguments for dominion are in themselves false, but because they, like the Turks, "are planning and plotting universal dominion". They do not constitute a threat to the Native

Americans, who as violators of the law of nature, deserve to lose their liberty and their *dominia*, but to the rest of Europe which does not. Against such people preemptive strike is not merely justified; it is imperative.[67] At the same time, however, Gentili wished to uphold what he – correctly in the case of the *ius naturalis societatis et communicationis* – takes to be Vitoria's insistence that the Spanish conquest of America had been conducted, throughout, as a form of punishment for violations of the natural law.

The conquest of America, together with the legitimacy of the war against Islam, was the most hotly disputed moral and legal issues of Gentili's day. True, Gentili was employed in the service of a crown whose own acts of conquest on the same continent were based, as we shall see in Chapter 3, on quite distinct premises to those employed by the Spanish.[68] But at least in *De iure belli*, his ambition was to establish a quasi-moral legal domain which would contain both a body of legal principles and, at the same time, be free of what he saw as the theologians' concern with abstractions derived from Holy Scripture. To achieve this, he chose to represent Vitoria as an advocate of the idea that the Spanish conquest had been grounded on a universal law of nature which was also identical with the law of nations, while at the same time denying the legitimacy of the arguments which the Salamanca theologians might have drawn from this claim, had they in fact ever made it.

Gentili's elevation of the *ius gentium* to the status of a natural law provided what amounts to a quasi-theological, quasi-moral underpinning for the positive legislation of the Roman world. In this he is, as he himself understood it, very close to the classical sources he cites approvingly: Cicero, the *Institutes* and the *Digest*, the Glossators and post-Glossators, and in particular Baldus. The difference is that his conception of the natural law was in essence that of the theologians. By insisting that violations of this law granted the right to any state, or individual, to exact punishment and thus wage a just war against the violators and by insisting that *dominium* over both persons and moveable goods could be acquired in such wars, he was handing the European powers a licence to conquer virtually any peoples whose behaviour did not conform to the codes established by our jurists.

The theologians' conception of the law of nations, and Vitoria's in particular, because they held it to be a species of positive law, was consensual and thus changeable. Gentili's understanding of the *ius gentium/ius naturale* is, in effect, the precise opposite. By making the law of nations into the content of the natural law, he had dispensed with any need for "moral discernment". By making that content in all significant respects identical with the Roman law, he had also eliminated any need for further development. As far as its basic principles were concerned, it could only remain where our jurists had left it: unchanged and unchanging for all time. It is thus a law which could hardly be further removed from any modern conception of a consensual positive law between nations. Although Gentili was rudely dismissive of what he took to be the Greek idea that humanity is divided, by nature, into two mutually hostile groups – the Greeks ("designating reason and not a nation") and the "barbarians" – and that the conflict between them is perennial and immutable, it is hard to resist the conclusion that, in this respect at least, he belongs, as does Vitoria (very much *malgré lui*) to a tradition which will culminate in the nineteenth century with the conception of a world composed of "civilized nations" who are governed by international law, and all the rest – the "barbarians" – who, by definition, are not.[69]

## Endnotes

1 *De iure belli*, John Rolfe trans. (Oxford: Clarendon Press, 1933), 1.1, 1. In general, I have followed the translation by John Rolfe, (printed with an introduction by Coleman Phillipson), although I have made some adjustments against the text edited by Thomas Erskine Holland, *Alberici Gentilis, De Iure Belli* (Oxford: Clarendon Press, 1877).

2 *De iure belli*, 1.3, 26.

3 See Diego Panizza, "Political Theory and Jurisprudence in Gentili's *De Iure Belli*: The Great Debate between 'Theological' and 'Humanist' Perspectives from Vitoria to Grotius", *International Law and Justice Working Papers*, 15:5 (2005), at http://www.iilj.org/publications/2005-15. Richard Tuck claims that the now conventional distinction between "humanist" and "scholastic" traditions would best be described as one between "oratorical" and "theological" traditions. *The Rights of War and Peace*, 17.

4 See Benjamin Straumann "The *Corpus iuris* as a Source of Law between Sovereigns in Alberico Gentili's Thought", in Benedict Kingsbury and Benjamin Straumann eds., *The Roman Foundations of the Law of Nations*, 101–23, and Noel Malcolm "Alberico Gentili and the Ottomans", ibid., 127–45.

5 *De Justitia* [part of the lecture course for the years 1534–7, covering *quaestiones* 57–88 of the *Secunda secundae*], Vincente Beltrán de Heredia ed. (Salamanca, 1932), I, xxxi.

6 "Alberico Gentili and the Ottomans", in Benedict Kingsbury and Benjamin Straumann eds., *The Roman Foundations of the Law of Nations*, 127–45 at 136.

7 Annabel Brett, *Changes of State. Nature and the Limits of the City in Early-Modern Natural Law* (Princeton: Princeton University Press, 2011), 153–4, and see Diego Panizza, *Alberico Gentili, giurista ideologico nell' Inghilterra elisabettiana* (Padua: la Garangola, 1981), 43.

8 "Of Commerce with the Turks", in *Hispanicae advocationis libri duo*, Frank Frost Abbott trans. (New York: Oceana Publications, 1964), 117.

9 "Toward Perpetual Peace: A Philosophical Project", *Practical Philosophy*, 326 (AK 8:355).

10 Quoted in Michael Howard, "Temperamenta belli: Can War be Controlled?", in *Restraints on War* (Oxford: Oxford University Press, 1979), 1.

11 Diego Panizza, "Alberico Gentili's *De armis Romanis*: The Roman Model of the Just Empire", in Benedict Kingsbury and Benjamin Straumann eds., *The Roman Foundations of the Law of Nations*, 85–100.

12 "On the American Indians", 1.1, *Vitoria: Political Writings*, 239.

13 Vitoria allows that "true and voluntary election" might be a legitimate title in natural law. He refrains, however, from saying whether he truly believes that the American Indians had, in fact, "decided to accept the king of Spain as their prince". "On the American Indians", 3.6, *Vitoria: Political Writings*, 288–9.

14 *De iure belli*, 3.4, 496.

15 Cf. "On the Law of War", 3.7, *Vitoria: Political Writings*, 324.

16 *De iure belli*, 1.1.5.

17 *De iure belli*, 1.1.10. The quotation is from Cicero, *Tusculan Disputations*, 1.13.30.

18 *De iure belli*, 1.25.202.

19 *De iure belli*, 1.15, 107f., citing, *inter alios*, Lactantius and Augustine.

20 *The Wars of the* Romans, A Critical Edition and Translation of *De armis Romanis*, Benedict Kingsbury and Benjamin Straumann, eds. David Lupher trans. (Oxford: Oxford University Press, 2011), 147. The relationship between the Apologist, his interlocutor Picenus, and Gentili himself is, however, complicated. See David Lupher, "The *De Armis Romanis* and the Exemplum of Roman Imperialism", Benedict Kingsbury and Benjamin Straumann eds., *The Roman Foundations of the Law of Nations*, 85–100.

21 *De iure belli*, 1.1.10f.

22 *De iure belli*, 1.1.4.

23 "There exists a species of mixed law, compounded of the [primary] law of nations and the civil law, and designated in correct and precise terminology as 'the secondary law of nature'." *De iure praedae commentarius (Commentary on the Law of Prize and Booty)*, G. L. Williams trans. (Oxford: Oxford University Press, 1950), I, 10–11. On the distinction between a *ius gentium primaevum* and a *ius gentium secundarium*, see pp. 45–7.

24 *De iure belli*, 1.1, 10.

25 Vico claims a Roman precedent for this by arguing that Justinian's *Institutes* had originally been called not, *De iure naturali, gentium et civili* but *De iure naturali gentium, et civili* – the removal of the comma making "On the natural law, the law of nations and the civil law" into "On the natural law of nations and the civil law". Vico's argument, however, is vastly more complicated than Gentili's and crucially supposes that, while the rational principle in mankind is unchanging, the "natural law of nations" is not. See my "Ley y sociabilidad en Giambattista Vico: hacia una historia crítica de las ciencias humanas", *Agora Papeles de Filosofía* 16:2 (1997), 59–80.

26 "De nostri temporis studiorum ratione", in G. B. Vico, *Opere*, F. Nicolini ed. (Bari: Laterza, 1911–41), I, 101.

27 *International Law*, 20–2.

28 *De iure belli*, 1.1, 10; see Jeremy Waldron, "*Ius gentium*: A Defence of Gentili's Equation of the Law of Nations and the Natural Law", in Benedict Kingsbury and Benjamin Straumann eds., *The Roman Foundations of the Law of Nations*, 283–96.

29 *De iure belli*, 1.1, 11–13.

30 See pp. 9–10.

31 *De iure belli*, I.19.144.

32 I would like to thank David Lupher for pointing this out to me.

33 "On the American Indians", 1, Introduction, *Vitoria: Political Writings*, 233. There are other instances of very late claims that America was in fact a part of Asia, but in every one the author clearly had some ulterior motive in making it.

34 *De iure belli*, 1.3. 26f. and 1.19, 147f.

35 See Benjamin Straumann, "for Gentili the *ius gentium* is not simply shorthand for custom, but rather shorthand for those norms and rules contained in the *Corpus iuris civilis*". "The *Corpus iuris civilis* as a Source of Law between Sovereigns in Alberico Gentili's Thought", Benedict Kingsbury and Benjamin Straumann eds., *The Roman Foundations of the Law of Nations*, 101–26.

36 Aldo Schiavone, *Ius: L'invenzione del diritto in Occidente* (Turin: Einaudi, 2005), 5.

37 *The Wars of the Romans*, 355.

38 Ibid., 351.

39 Ibid., 349.

40 Ibid., 335.

41 Ibid., 349.

42 Ibid., 349.

43 Ibid., 19.

44 Tacitus *Annals* II, 23–4. For a detailed account of these events, see Sherwin-White, *The Roman Citizenship*, 237–50.

45 "Kant on the Metaphysics of Morals: Vigilantius' Lecture Notes", in *Lectures on Ethics*, Peter Heath trans. and ed. (Cambridge: Cambridge University Press, 1997), 406 (AK 27:674).

46 "The Roman Oration", *The Ruling Power*, 59–60.

47 "The Roman Oration", *The Ruling Power*, 63.

48 See, in general, Kaius Tuori, "Alberico Gentili and the Criticism of Expansion in the Roman Empire: The Invader's Remorse", *Journal of the History of International Law* 11 (2009), 205–19.

49 "The *Corpus iuris* as a Source of Law between Sovereigns in Alberico Gentili's Thought", in Benedict Kingsbury and Benjamin Straumann eds., *The Roman Foundations of the Law of Nations*, 101–123

50 *De iure belli*, 1.25, 198–9.

51 See pp. 50–1.

52 *De iure belli*, 1.15, 111–12.

53 See Andreas Wagner, "Francisco de Vitoria and Alberico Gentili on the Legal Character of the Global Commonwealth", *Oxford Journal of Legal Studies* 31:3 (2011), 565–82.

54 *De iure belli*, 1.25, 202.

55 Ibid.

56 *De iure praedae commentarius*, I, 91–2, and Locke, *Second Treatise on Government*, II, 9, 272. On this, see Richard Tuck, who describes the similarity between Grotius' and Locke's argument as "the most striking example of intellectual convergence". *The Rights of War and Peace*, 82. But as Benjamin Straumann has pointed out, while Locke could not have read *De iure praedae*, Grotius uses a similar argument in *De iure belli ac pacis* which Locke could, and probably did, know. If he did, this "convergence" would seem to be a simple case of plagiarism. Benjamin Straumann, "The Right to Punish as a Just Use of War in Hugo Grotius' Natural Law", *Studies in the History of Ethics* 2 (2006), 1–20.

57 "On the Law of War", 1.2, *Vitoria: Political Writings*, 299.

58 *De iure belli*, 1.3, 22.

59 Ibid. "For whereas there are two modes of contention, one by argument and the other by force, one should not resort to the latter if it is possible to use the former."

60 See Seyla Benhabib et al., *Another Cosmopolitanism* (Oxford: Oxford University Press, 2004), 15–16: "Cosmopolitan norms of justice, whatever the conditions of their legal origination, accrue to individuals as moral and legal persons in a worldwide civil society. . . . Their peculiarity is that they endow individuals rather than states and their agents with certain rights and claims."

61 *De iure belli*, 1.19, 144f.

62 "The *Corpus iuris* as a Source of Law between Sovereigns in Alberico Gentili's Thought", in Benedict Kingsbury and Benjamin Straumann eds., *The Roman Foundations of the Law of Nations*, 114.

63 For a critique of many of the positions taken in the debate, see Lauren Benton and Benjamin Straumann, "Acquiring Empire by Law: From Roman Doctrine to Early-Modern European Practice", *Law and History Review* 28:1 (2010), 1–38.

64 *De iure belli*, 1.19, 148. See Benedict Kingsbury, "Confronting difference: the puzzling durability of Gentili's combination of pragmatic realism and normative judgment", *American Journal of International Law* 92:4 (1998), 713–23.

65 "On the American Indians", 1. Conclusion, *Vitoria: Political Writings*, 250.

66 Ibid., 2.3, 264–5.

67 *De iure belli*, 1.14, 103.

68 For these, see pp. 105–12.

69 *De iure belli*, 1.12, 87f. On the nineteenth-century international lawyers, see Koskenniemi, *The Gentle Civilizer of Nations*, 98–166. Gentili's dismissal of the Greek/barbarian distinction does not, however, alter the view that although "barbarians" may have had binding laws, those were, when in accordance with natural law, included in the Roman law.

# 3

## The Peopling of the New World

## *Ethnos, Race, and Empire in the Early-Modern World*

In discussing the status of the American Indians, the School of Salamanca and their successors habitually referred to them as "barbarians" (*barbari*). The word derives from the Greek *barbaros*, an onomatopoeia which described all those who could not speak Greek and whose languages sounded, to Greek ears, merely like people stuttering *bar bar*. It thus, by implication, meant an outsider, a foreigner, and since on the most extreme interpretation, only the Greeks had articulate speech, it implied both social and political inferiority. What, however, it did not imply, at least for the Europeans of the sixteenth century, was a racial distinction. The American Indians, as we have seen, may have been barbarians; they may even have been, as Vitoria said of them, "unsuited to governing even their own households; hence their lack of letters, of arts and crafts ... and in many other things useful, or rather indispensable, for human use". But they still belonged biologically and psychologically to the same category of person as all the other peoples of the world.[1] They did not, that is, despite the reiterated claim that all modern early-modern empires were organized along broadly racial lines, belong, nor were they generally thought to belong, to district races.

In part, this is because neither Vitoria, nor any of his contemporaries, possessed anything like a fully developed conception of race. This is not to deny that an awareness of something amounting to racial or ethnic differentiation is to be found in all cultures and at all times. In the form the word is most often employed today, however, a race is taken to be a genetically specific group of people – a biological, or rather pseudo-biological – not a cultural entity.[2] Because of this, and the properties which each supposedly possesses, races cannot vary too much over time or space. Racism, thus understood, is clearly the product of nineteenth-century positivism, and any attempt to apply the term to an earlier period would, therefore, seem to be simply anachronistic. The development of race as a category has also persuasively, if not uncontentiously, been linked to the rise of the concept of the "nation" in the nineteenth century, the assertion of whose unique identity, the concept of distinct races, was intended to ensure.[3]

It is certainly the case that without any reference to some degree of physiological, biological, or even psychological determinism, the very notion of race in the ancient or early-modern world becomes highly problematical. With a few obvious exceptions – most obviously those applied to Sub-Saharan Africans – most of the classificatory schemes dreamt up before 1700 were not in any obvious modern sense "racial". True, the peoples of the globe were organized into large groups, nations, tribes, and so forth, and each one ascribed a number of defining features. But all of the characteristics which these groups were supposed to possess were essentially what we today would call "cultural". The word "race" – *race*, (French) *razza*, (Italian) *raza* (Spanish), and so forth – and their equivalents are also of relatively recent coinage. Race has some affinities with the term *ratio* in the sense of "the order of things"; in its modern sense, however, it derives from the Arabic *ras* – whose root meaning is "head" or "origin" – and, not insignificantly, it probably reached Europe via Spain. It is also significant that it first achieves widespread recognition during the sixteenth century at the time, of course, when the cultures of southern Europe, Spain, Portugal, and Italy were coming increasingly into contact with a large number of "new" – or at least unfamiliar – "races".

Its earliest uses are zoological, having first been applied to falcons and horses. The transference from animals to humans was, at least initially, seemingly both unproblematic and non-prejudicial. It was used, for instance, by Edmund Spenser in the *Faerie Queene* in 1589:

And thou, fair, imp, spring out from English race
How ever now accompanied Elfin's son
Well worthy doest they service for her grace
To aid a virgin desolate foredone
(X.6)[4]

It seems clear that Spenser attached no particular importance to the word and that a number of other terms would have done just as well – in particular "nation" – had the rime scheme, and the meter, called for it. And race continued to be used in this way as a synonym for "people", "nation", "breed", or even "kind", until at least the early nineteenth century. Lord Byron, in 1823, could even speak of stone statues as "a race of mere impostors".[5]

It was probably the French doctor, Bernier François, who, in 1648, first used the term in something like its modern meaning by equating the word "race" with the unambiguously biological "species" in a brief essay entitled, "A New Division of the Earth by the Different Species or Races of which Inhabit It". Bernier was a disciple of the French empiricist philosopher Pierre Gassendi and an intermediary between Gassendi and Locke. He was tireless traveler (he spent twelve years as physician to the Mughal emperor Aurang-zeb), and one of those rare creatures, in the opinion of Diderot, who generally looked on travelers with suspicion, who was also at the same time a *philosophe*.[6] Geographers, said Bernier, have hitherto divided the world into countries or regions, but his "long and frequent travels" had suggested to him another way of classifying humankind. Men, he noticed, as far as their appearance is concerned, might vary greatly from one to another, even within the same nation. "I have nevertheless observed that there are four or five Species or Races of men, the difference between whom is so marked, that it may serve as the basis for a new division of the Earth". The first of these groups include the Europeans, most of the peoples of North Africa, India, and much of the Far East: the second, all the Africans, except the coastal peoples; the third those living in areas of the Far East, central Russia, and Mongolia; and in the fourth – by themselves – the Laps. (No fifth group is mentioned.) The Amerindians, although they are olive skinned and "have faces which are cast differently from ours", are said to be "not sufficiently unlike us to constitute a separate species". In fact, however, Bernier, nowhere suggests that his division could be employed to impute different mental characteristics to his four races. Much of the essay is taken up with a discussion of female beauty, and although it is obvious that his aesthetics are wholly European, such beauty, he says, can be found in every race, "even among the blacks of Africa".[7] There is nothing here, except the word itself, which clearly distinguishes "race" from "species" or "variety". There is nothing which approaches Immanuel Kant's famous (or infamous) essays from the 1770s and 1780s – "Of the Different Races of Human Beings" (1775, 1777), "Determinations of the Concept of Human Race" (1785), and "On the Uses of Teleological Principles in Philosophy" (1788) – all of which employed a concept of race as a part of what Pauline Kleingeld has described as an attempt to solve "pre-Mendelian biological questions regarding the heritability of bodily features". They also ascribed a hierarchy of different intellectual and physiological capacities to the different races of the world, which was, of course, to become a salient feature of all later attempts at a biological racial classification.[8]

The closest approximation to anything like modern racial classifications in the early-modern, pre-Enlightenment world are, perhaps, to be found in the "national characters" supposedly possessed, largely if not consistently, by the various peoples of Europe. The English were perfidious, the Germans brutal, but courageous, the Italians cunning, and so on. The multinational mercenary armies of early-modern Europe were often organized along these line, although non-racial qualities were frequently muddled in with the apparently racial ones. The Germans were put out in front not only because they were ferocious but also because they were good pikemen; the English were placed a little way behind to prevent them from sneaking off in the heat of battle as well as because they were skilled archers, and so on.

But supposed natural attributes could, in this way, easily became confused with acquired skills. Were the Germans, for instance, good pikemen because they were ferocious and the English good archers because they were cowardly and unsuited for hand-to-hand combat? Whatever the answer, the source of "national character" was not anything which could plausibly be derived from race but rather from custom and education – from culture, that is, not nature. "As to *physical* causes", wrote David Hume, "I am inclined to doubt altogether of their operation in this particular; nor do I think that men owe anything of their temper or genius to the air, food or climate."[9]

There was also the question of the bloodline. Although the transference of identity via blood has no place in ancient medicine, by the late middle ages, if not earlier, the idea that certain features of a person's identity could be passed down in this way appears to have become a commonplace. However, this was less a means of distinguishing between peoples from different races than it was a way of marking distinctions within the same race. *Holinshed's Chronicles* of 1577 defined gentlemen as "those whom their race and blood, are at least their virtue doo make noble and knowne", which suggests that the qualities a person exhibits might make him a member (albeit, if we are to take that "at least" seriously, a slightly inferior one) of the same group as those who belong to it by lineage.[10] As the European aristocracy lost its traditional military role in the late Middle Ages, so it increasingly came to defend itself against the newer aristocracies of commerce and service by appealing to origins: *ex nobili genre ex nobili prosapia*. Even the notorious *limpieza de sangre* statues in Spain aimed at preventing *conversos*, Christians of Jewish ancestry, from acquiring positions in the Church or the administration – although it would be absurd to deny that they were in some sense racist – belong to this category.[11] They were, in effect, the extension to a particular people of what was in origin an essentially social differentiation.

Take – only because it is usefully conventional – the classification provided by the canon lawyer Regino of Prüm, writing about 900. He offers four ways of classifying what he calls the "various Nations" of the world: they are "descent, custom, language and law".[12] If we add to this list religion, with relatively few modifications these criteria will remain largely unchanged until the eighteenth century.[13] Of these only the first, descent, really qualifies as a true racial category. Ever since Hesiod – perhaps ever since mankind has been organized into societies – descent, lineage, genealogy, mostly spurious and contrived, have been employed to establish differences, generally of course differences of status.[14] Yet, even here the usage is problematical. Certainly to be, say, German "by descent" distinguished one from those who were Norman "by descent". Yet, precisely because there was no theoretical argument underpinning the notion of descent, the only way to differentiate one descent group from another was by reference to the other categories in Regino's list. If, that is, we were to ask what made the lineage of Germans distinct from the Normans all we could reply would be: "custom language and law".

The whole thing becomes, in the end, inescapably circular. In 1539, the Portuguese chronicler Joâo de Barros – who evidently had not given much thought to these matters – describes, or makes Vasco da Gama describe, the Hindus as being "all from one race (geração)" precisely because they were "very alike in their customs", and, he added, because they shared a belief in the Trinity, they were also "friends of the Christians *by nature*". This was enough for Barros to lump together all the peoples of southern India as belonging to a single descent group.[15] What obviously did *not* matter was any supposed biological difference between Europeans and Indians whether carried by blood or some other means.

If race is ultimately a matter of languages, customs, laws – and even religions – it is evidently highly unstable. Customs can be acquired; laws can be accepted and observed. Languages may also, of course, be learned. However, language-acquisition presented a rather more complex problem since for most language theorists, from Aristotle in the fifth century BCE to Étienne Bonnot de Condillac in the eighteenth CE, speech was believed to provide something akin to a cognitive map of the mind of the speaker. Initially, as we have seen, "barbarian" (*barbaros*) had been a linguistic category, and the widely held assumption was that if you lacked a word for something, then you probably also lacked the understanding of that thing. Similarly, if the Inuit famously have dozens of words for "snow" (they, in fact do not), this is not because they are highly imaginative but because they cannot formulate general categories.

This supposed deficiency may, perhaps, broadly be understood as a racial characteristic. It may, on the other hand, be merely a consequence of history. Although some supposedly primitive peoples, such as the Tahitian "Aotourou" whom the French navigator Antoine de Bougainville took with him to France in 1769, might have found it impossible to master a more "advanced" language (in this case French), this was never attributed to anything resembling race. In Aotourou's case it was ascribed by Bougainville to the simplicity and transparency of the world in which he lived. He would, he said of his Tahitian guest, have had to "create, so to speak, in a mind as indolent as his body, first a world of ideas, before being able to adapt them to the words in our language which corresponded to them".[16] And it was not certainly his race or his descent which prevented him from doing this, but rather the incommensurability of his culture with the French, and the brevity of his exposure to European mores.

The most extreme expression of cultural transformation, which was clearly and crucially open to all, was religious conversion. Conversion, to Christianity, after all – if St. Paul was to be believed – guaranteed admission to a community in which the distinctions between "Greek or Jew, circumcision and uncircumcision, barbarian, Scythian, bondman, freeman" would all be dissolved.[17] Lineage may not change. The Christian Scythian remains a Scythian, but his character, his *ethos*, has become something else. As the Jesuit historian José de Acosta, one of the first to attempt a systematic analytical history of the peoples of the Americas, said in 1590, what he called the "Ethiopians" – that is, black Africans – brought up "in a palace" would be in all respects, save the colour of their skin, "just like other men".[18] If this were the case, what significance could race possibly have?

The answer would seem to be none. But what is it then that leads certain peoples to adopt certain kinds of customs, laws, languages, even religions and not others? If (in Greek eyes) the laws and customs of the Persians inclined them to slavishness and those of the Greeks to liberty, is this something inherently Persian and Greek or, if given other circumstances, could Greeks become slavish – as it was later believed that they had done under Turkish rule – and the Persians freedom loving? One obvious answer, offered by Aristotle, embellished by Polybius, picked up by Aquinas and his Spanish commentators, by Jean Bodin in sixteenth century, and elaborated into full-scale theory of cultural – not racial – differentiation by Montesquieu in the eighteenth century, was, of course, climate, or to be rather more precise since a significant number of factors other then simply climate were involved, "environment".

Crudely stated this argued that those, the Asians who lived in hot climes, reacted to this by becoming lethargic and indolent. Those who lived in the cold northern climes became hyperactive aggressive and uncouth. Only the Greek and, in later versions, Europeans generally, because they were poised midway between these two extremes, could achieve the necessary balance to remain free, in control of their passion, reflective, and morally active.

But even climate could determine only disposition. Aristotle's lethargic Asians, and uncivil northerners, might well become perfectly balanced Greeks were they to take up residence in the Mediterranean – not perhaps within a single generation, but certainly within two. Similarly, those Europeans born in places remote from Europe might, it was feared, lose something of their identity under unfamiliar skies and in extreme climates. The debilitating force of the environment, so obvious in the lethargic and indolent lives of the Native Americans, was clearly visible to the (Spanish-born) Franciscan Bernardino de Sahagún, the first European to attempt a systematic description of a Mesoamerican people. Those Europeans born in the Americas, he wrote, "are born very much like the Indians, for in appearance they are Spaniards, but in disposition they are not ... and I believe that this is due to the climate and constellations of this land".[19] For this same reason, the provincial council of the Jesuits in Lima ruled in 1582 that Creole neophytes should not be admitted to the order until they were twenty years old – the age for those born in Europe was eighteen – and they should be subjected to a more rigorous training.[20]

One more deterministic and, I think genuinely racist – or as it has been characterized, "proto-racist" – theory to come out of antiquity was to have a longer afterlife even than the theory of climates: Aristotle's account of natural slavery in the *Politics*.[21] This has been much discussed, and given the fragmentary nature of Aristotle's argument, it is unlikely that any consensus will ever be reached as to just what he intended by the category.[22] On the most minimal account it assumed that natural slaves were, not by chance and circumstance but by their very nature, inferior beings to their masters. Aristotle makes a distinction between a "natural" slave and what he calls a slave "by convention" – that is, one who, by "the convention by which whatever is taken in war is supposed to belong to the victors", finds himself in a legal condition of servitude. The "natural" slave, by contrast, because he is one who, contrary to the norm, possesses no independent autonomous self, is a being whose status is defined not by his legal standing but by his psychological identity.[23] And no matter how nuanced Aristotle's own arguments, in particularly in the context of his ethical works, it seems clear that his Roman and Christian readers, from Cicero to Aquinas, believed that what he had identified was a species of being who, while not mentally defective, was nevertheless severely limited in both his powers of reasoning and even his technical capacities.[24]

The definition of this anomalous creature was grounded in a distinction between what, in Greek psychology, was called the "rational" and the "irrational" souls. For "all things rule and are ruled according to their nature". Since "such duality exists in living creatures, but not in them alone; it originates in the constitution of the universe".[25] In fully developed human males (although not in either children or women), the rational will invariably triumph over the irrational, unless it is diseased. This is what it means to possess the capacity for deliberation or moral choice. The natural slave, however, lacks this capacity. In this respect he is akin – but also inferior to – women and children, "for the slave has no deliberative faculty at all; the woman has but it is without authority and the child has but it is immature".[26] While he is clearly a fully developed adult male, he nonetheless has, as Aristotle characterizes it, only a share in the faculty of reason, without being in full possession of it. He is said to be incapable of *prohairesis* – deliberative action – and consequently of *eudaimonia*, often misleadingly rendered as "happiness", or what Aristotle's Christian commentators called "blessedness" and some modern philosophers "human flourishing".[27] A natural slave is therefore unable, by his very nature, to attain the ends for which (true) human beings are intended. Furthermore, because he lacks that part of what it is to be human, so long as he remains free, he is violating what nature has intended him to be, for his master is supposed to do his thinking for him; and he is himself almost literally a "living but separate part of his master's frame".[28]

Slaves are a feature of the natural world, and a necessary requirement for the proper functioning of the only true political form, the *polis*. There could never exist a *polis* composed only of slaves – just as there could not be one made up solely of women and children.[29] On the other hand "a *polis* cannot be administered without them".[30] The slave also benefits by being enslaved, although he may not immediately be aware of it, since this is the proper fulfillment of his nature. Thus he is said to "share his master's life" to such a degree that he "only attains excellence in proportion as he becomes a slave".[31]

What this could be taken to mean is that the slave is a kind of useful automaton, a creature who is said to be capable of carrying out commands, but not of initiating them. He is, as Aquinas said later, "almost an animated instrument of service".[32] (Aquinas, however, was by no means committed to the actual existence of such beings.) As such there is nothing inherently racist about such a claim, since individual "natural slaves" just might crop up in any ethic group or nation. It is merely condescending. Most European aristocrats until recently would have said something similar about their servants. What makes it racist – or "proto-racist" – is Aristotle's identification of the slave with a particular group of people: namely, what he calls "the barbarians". "Among barbarians", he said, "no distinction is made between women and slaves, because there is no natural ruler among them: they are a community of slaves male and female. That is why the poets say 'it is meet that the Hellenes should rule over the barbarians.'"[33]

The barbarians, then, could be taken to be merely communities of unmastered slaves. And war on them is not only justified. It may be likened to hunting.[34] They might plausibly be described as a race of slaves, and that is certainly how some of Aristotle's later commentators came to see them. But one crucial element of race is missing from Aristotle's description: heredity. Nature may have indeed wished that natural slaves should always give birth to natural slaves. But nature for Aristotle is not always able to achieve her objectives, and consequently like does not always beget like.

Then there was the further difficulty of the precise identity of barbarians. Aristotle leaves this problem unresolved, but given the general use of the term to mark a clear distinction between Greeks and non-Greeks, it would seem to include the peoples of Asia described conventionally as "more servile than those in Europe". Although being more servile would not necessarily make them natural slaves, only beings more suitable to tyrannical rule, and thus unsuitable to self-government. However, on Aristotle's account, the further away from Greece one goes, the more likely one will be to encounter peoples who lack rationality and live by perception alone, like nonhuman animals.[35] The entire argument is highly allusive, but the explicit association between natural slaves and barbarians made it an extremely serviceable category for future generations. The best-known case in antiquity is Cicero's discussion of justice in the state in *De Republica* in which he argues that "the provincials" – that is, all those peoples who have been incorporated into the Roman empire as allies or clients – although they may not be formerly chattels, are nevertheless rightly subject to Rome, as they are servile by nature.[36] Again both parties benefit from the relationship which is why Cicero elsewhere insists, in a passage that was eagerly adopted by the British after the mid-seventeenth century, that the Roman Republic exercised over its provinces not *imperium* but *patrocinium* (protectorate) – although for Cicero, it was very much *patrocinium* by the more able over the less.[37]

Aristotle's account of slavery occurs in a discussion of the household. Aristotle, however, as we all know, was Alexander's tutor, and Plutarch – an unreliable source to be sure, but not entirely implausible in this instance – tells us that Aristotle advised his tutee before leaving on the Persian campaigns to treat only the Greeks as humans and all other peoples he might encounter as animals or plants. As later commentators pointed out – something which became one of the arguments used to discredit it – in the theory of natural slavery, Aristotle had, in effect, handed his pupil a reason for subjugating the vast Achaemenid Empire, more serviceable than a desire to avenge Xerxes' burning of the Acropolis. (Alexander, however, had other ambitions than to rule over animals and plants and ignored his tutor's advice – wisely, as Plutarch remarked, because otherwise he would have "filled his kingdoms with exiles and clandestine rebellions".[38]) Cicero, for his part, was of course, explaining the right of Rome to constitute the *orbis terrarum* in its own image. Both Aristotle and Cicero, that is, bring us to the place where a conception of a world divided into different, and differently endowed, races will have its most lasting purchase will be, so to speak, most urgently needed, but where also, I want to argue, it will encounter what will in the end prove to be insurmountable difficulties: namely, the creation of empires.

## II

In 1519, a Scottish theologian at the Collège de Montaigu in Paris, John Major, or Mair, published what was to become an immensely influential commentary on Peter Lombard's *Sentences*. In discussing the justice of Christian rule over pagans, he made a passing comment on the newly discovered American Indians:

"These peoples", he said,

> live like beasts on either side of the equator. ... And this has now been demonstrated by experience that the first person to conquer them, justly rules over them because they are by nature slaves. As the Philosopher [Aristotle] says in the third and fourth chapters of the first book of the *Politics*, it is clear that some are by nature slaves and some are by nature free. On this account the Philosopher says ... that this is the reason why the Greeks should rule over the barbarians, because the barbarians and slaves are the same.[39]

By this argument the inhabitants of the Antilles are barbarians, ergo they are slaves, ergo it is just that the first people to conquer them – in this case the

Spanish – have a right, which might also amount to a duty, to rule over them. This brief comment set in motion an attempt to classify the peoples of the New World as belonging to a quasi-distinct species of man – a race if you will – set down by God to perform at least some of the tasks without which, as Aristotle had duly observed, the true *polis* could not function adequately.

Here, it seemed, was a category which had been empty since the Greeks – neither Major nor any of those who took up his suggestion mention Cicero – which could conveniently be used to classify a people who had been unknown to Antiquity.

Natural slavery appeared at first to provide a neat argument from an authoritative – indeed *the* authoritative – source to justify the Spanish presence in a part of the world over which, as we have seen, neither the Spanish Crown nor any other European people could claim to exercise any clear or uncontestable a priori right to sovereignty, much less property rights of the kind which their exploitation of the resources of the Americas would necessarily entail. If the Indians were natural slaves, they could they could be said to possess neither sovereign authority over themselves nor rights over the lands on which they happened to reside. The Spanish might, therefore, legitimately conquer and subdue them, deprive them of their goods and lands, and exploit their labour to introduce them, so to speak, to their proper place in the natural world.

Identifying the Indians as natural slaves, however, posed certain difficulties which Major passed over in silence. Aristotle had argued that external appearances should have been sufficient to distinguish the natural slave from the natural master. "Nature would like", he said, "to distinguish between the bodies of free men and slaves, making the one strong for servile labour, the other upright and although useless for service, useful for the political life and the arts of both peace and war." But as we have seen, nature, in Aristotle's world, is often unable to fulfill her purposes, and as he admitted, "the opposite frequently happens".[40] Despite this note of caution, at least one Spanish "expert" on Indian affairs was gauche enough to inform Philip III that

> [t]he Indians can be said to be slaves of the Spaniards ... in accordance with the doctrine in Aristotle's *Politics*, that those who need to be ruled and governed by others may be called their slaves. ... And for this reason Nature proportioned their [the Indians'] bodies so that they should have strength for personal service. The Spanish, on the other hand, are delicately proportioned, and were made prudent and clever, so that they should be able to lead a political and civil life.[41]

The Indians, declared the chronicler Gonzalo Fernández de Oviedo, had heads three times thicker than Europeans, "and as they have thick skulls so their understanding is that of the beasts" – although he failed to draw any very precise conclusions from this.[42] Few, however, were prepared to take such arguments seriously. As many Spanish observers pointed out, the Indians could be just as "delicately proportioned" as the Spanish and sometimes a great deal more so. It was also the case that, although the canonist Diego de Covarrubias was prepared to argue that "the slaves who are born of slave women are natural slaves", few, in the face of Aristotle's own denial that this was always the case, seem to have been prepared to accept anything resembling the genetic transmission of conditions fitting to servitude.[43] The absence, furthermore, of any secure exterior markers – the colour, size, and physiognomy of the Indians only becomes of any real concern in the eighteenth century – tended ultimately to throw all those who hoped to identify the Indians as "natural slaves" back on some version of the items on Regino's list: "custom language and law".

One of the earliest commentators on the condition of the Indians, and the earliest to recognize the full implications of Major's suggestion, was the jurist Juan López de Palacios Rubios. In 1512, at the request of King Ferdinand, he wrote an opinion on the legal status of the Spanish Crown in America. The Indians, he said, on the evidence which he had read appeared to be "rational, gentle and peaceful men capable of understanding our faith". They owned no property and apparently dwelt in peace with nature. "They loved the birds and the animals, as if they were children, and they would not eat them, for that would have been as if they devoured their own offspring". An ideal world it would seem – all peace and light and harmony, not too far removed from the image which some have tried to paint of modern Amerindian tribes.

But Palacios Rubios was no sentimentalist, and America was no Eden. In the real world after the Fall, such behaviour indicated not an admirable oneness with nature, but only ineptitude. In the real order of things, ownership was a mark of humanity, and animals were for eating not for play. If the Indians did not understand that, it was hardly surprising that they also did not understand the vastly more complex laws and customs which governed human societies. Look again, said Palacios Rubios, and you will see behind this apparently Edenic exterior, a world in which everyone went naked and the men took several wives, in which the women "gave themselves readily considering it shameful to deny themselves". It was hardly surprising, therefore, that they also failed to observe the limits of consanguinity – sisters mating with brothers, daughters with fathers – had no religion worth the name, and in their daily lives were simple hedonists. Thus, he concluded, they "are so inept and foolish that they do not know how to rule themselves". History, furthermore, had contrived to pass them by. Had they been a more worthwhile people would not God have sent them news of the arrival of Christ before now, as he had sent St. Paul to the Corinthians and St. Augustine to the English?[44] Such a people, he concluded, were therefore, "broadly-speaking called slaves as those who are almost born to serve and not to rule".[45]

Despite its obvious deficiencies, the theory of natural slavery was widely used to bolster Spanish claims to the Indies, most famously, by the humanist Juan Ginés de Sepúlveda. It was certainly important enough for Francisco de

Vitoria, Domingo de Soto, and Melchor Cano, among others, to spend a good deal of time publicly refuting it.[46] The implication, made explicit by some, that if these Indians were such a race of men, they must also lack immortal souls, or at least the ability to understand the teachings of the Gospels, so alarmed the Papacy that in May 1537 Paul III issued a bull, *Sublimis Deus*, denouncing the idea that "the Indians of the West and South, and other people of whom We have recent knowledge should be treated as dumb brutes created for our service" as the invention of the Devil and confirming their rationality and humanity and, thus, "that they may and should, freely and legitimately, enjoy their liberty and possession of their property".[47]

The only jurist who seems to have been prepared to support some form of natural slave argument in this context was Alberico Gentili (whom we met in Chapter 2). In a brisk endorsement of what he saw as Vitoria's defence of the Spanish conquest, Gentili was apparently prepared to endorse the idea that certain groups of people who have "violated the common law of nations" – something which, although the group he is discussing are pirates, would certainly apply to the American Indians – might be so far outside the "league of human society" as to justify enslavement on those grounds alone and with which he claimed to believe "a disquisition of Aristotle on the natural origin of slavery is in harmony". But Gentili undermines his own case by going on to say that "although the philosopher is speaking of those who have servile dispositions, yet his arguments apply to those who become natural slaves because of their wickedness and sins".[48] It is certainly true that Aristotle accepts that persons can be made brutish through habituation (*ethismos*) – that is, through custom rather than instruction – and although this may indeed, in time, become a "second nature", no amount of exposure to "wickedness and sins" could make of a natural master a *natural* slave.

No version of Aristotle's theory was ever, in fact, adopted as a justification for conquest, without considerable qualification, and it never once appears in any official description of the Indians. Even those who were most convinced of the Indian's natural deficiencies, even Sepúlveda, – who described them as *homunculi* and compared them to pigs and monkeys – in the end backed away from claiming that these slavish beings constituted a wholly different subspecies of humanity.[49]

There were two immediate and obvious reasons for this reluctance. The first was simply the evidence. The Tainos and the Arawak of the Antilles, of whom Major and Palacios Rubios had some, albeit fragmentary and frequently fantastical knowledge, might conceivably, when measured against contemporary European expectations, seem to conform to some notion of creatures without deliberative capacities. But this could hardly be said for all their barbarism of the Aztecs and the Incas. The ethnography disproved the case. From this some, such as Juan de la Peña, Vesper Professor of Theology at Salamanca, concluded in 1561 that the natural slave was a purely hypothetical category. There might still exist such creatures in the world, and if they did, they would be justly enslaved. "But no such people (*natio*) has even been discovered." (He went on to remark that "some say that with these words Aristotle was adulating Alexander the Great" in which case they "were not worthy of interpretation".)[50]

Ethnography, however, could be, and frequently was, merely ignored. A far more serious objection lay in the fact that for the Christian – who believed in the existence of a single, and remote creator – the very existence of inferior races also posed an insuperable problem. Another expert to give his opinion to Ferdinand in 1512 was Bernardo de Mesa, later bishop of Cuba. He shared Palacios Rubios' generally dismal view of the behaviour of the Indians but drew a very different conclusion from it. "The incapacity we attribute to the Indians", he wrote, "contradicts the bounty of the creator, for it is certain that when a cause produces its effects so that it is unable to achieve its end, then there is some fault in the cause; and thus there must be some fault with God."[51] How could a being with no deliberative faculty, and on Aquinas' version of Aristotle, no share in "blessedness", possibly be described as having been made in the image of his creator, if that creator was the Christian God? The existence of races, of separate and distinct groups of peoples, who stand in an evaluative relationship to one another, is, obviously, an inescapable threat to the existence of a single human species. True, the harmonious and perfect natural world this God had created was capable of throwing up the odd anomaly – madmen, dwarves, and so on. But an entire continent – or possibly because there was still a lot of the world still to be discovered, *continents* – filled with people who had no moral agency, who merely shared in reason but did not possess it, who were only "a living but separate parts of their masters body" would be to imagine an imperfect creation. It would also have made the work of Christ – who had been sent to save *all* mankind and not just a favoured part of it – similarly incomplete. And both were, of course, unthinkable. As Francisco Suárez, put it, the existence of such beings would constitute a threat to human nature itself.[52]

III

However problematical Aristotle's theory of natural slavery might be, it seemed to provide, for those who were prepared to overlook its daunting inconsistencies, an explanation not only as to why it was just for the Europeans to deprive the Amerindians of what would otherwise be considered to be their natural rights: it also appeared to explain the very startling differences between their behaviour and all that was held to be in accordance with natural law in Europe. There was, however, another dimension to this story. The American Indians were not only socially anomalous beings, supposedly capable of unthinkable crimes – human sacrifice, cannibalisms, incest, bestiality, and so on – but also had no obvious place in any known historical account of the origins of humanity. The diversity which existed between the various "nations" of the world had hitherto been explicable in terms of two Biblical myths: the Tower of Babel and the separation of the sons of Noah – Shem, Japhet, and Ham – after the Flood. Shem had repopulated Asia; Japhet, Europe; and Ham, Africa. The story of Noah's curse on Ham, that his son, Canaan, and all his descendants, should be "a servant of servants unto his brethren" had been used to account for the blackness of the Africans, their alleged inferiority to the peoples of Asia and Europe, and their God-allotted role as slaves.

None of this, however, could be made to apply, obviously at least, to the American Indians, nor later to the peoples of the South Pacific. Neither, clearly, were the descendants of Ham; yet, it was also by no means obvious whose descendants they were. Surely, said Jacques Cartier in 1534, when he reached the inhospitable coast of Labrador, as his ships stuck fast in the ice, their flimsy wooden hulls cracking like nuts, this must be the land to which God had banished Cain, a land of perpetual wandering in whose soil nothing would grow. But no one took him up on the idea if only because the "land of Nod" lay to the east – not the west – of Eden.

If the integrity of the Biblical account of the peopling of the world were to be maintained, the Indians had to have come from some region of the old world. Could they possibly be the descendants of shipwrecked Carthaginians, alluded to in a popular pseudo-Aristotelian text, *De mirabilibus auscultationibus*, or of the Vikings? Might they perhaps be the last survivors of Atlantis or, as Hugo Grotius supposed, a band of migrant Tartars, or – one of the most enduring suppositions – the descendants of the Ten Lost Tribes of Israel?[53] (This last idea, quite apart from the geographical and chronological difficulties it presented, finally faltered on the fact that, as the Jesuit comparativist Joseph François Lafitau noted in 1724, it was inconceivable that two of the tribes of Israel had lost nothing of their Judaism despite centuries of dispersion and persecution, whereas the other ten, on reaching America, had shed all trace and all memory of their ancestry.)[54]

The uncertainty over the origins of the Indians could perhaps only be resolved by answering another question: How had they come to America? Had they, as some suggested, drifted there on rafts or perhaps even been carried across by angels? And if that were the case, how then could one explain all that proliferation of nonhuman life, the anacondas and the pumas, not to mention the tarantulas, and a thousand different kinds of venomous snakes? Surely no man, nor angel, in his right mind would have taken the trouble to transfer such creatures from the old to the new world?

The problem had, in fact, been solved in the late sixteenth century by a number of writers, the most influential being José de Acosta, who had come to the conclusion that the presence in the American continent of any life form which could not be accounted for by spontaneous generation could only be explained by the existence of a northern-land bridge – whose precise location was yet to be discovered – which joined, or at least had once joined, America to Asia.[55] Today we know, from the fossil record, that this is, broadly speaking, true. The peoples of the Americas, in fact, migrated across what is now called the Bering Strait in successive waves beginning sometime, probably, although this is hotly contested, between 12,000 to 13,000 years ago. (It is a striking case of a true conclusion being arrived at from an entirely false premise. It is also significant that it was only in the late eighteenth century, with the arrival of a true physiological racism, that the physical similarities between the peoples of eastern Mongolia and the American Indians became a factor in the debate.)

But although Acosta's solution gradually gained acceptance and became, indeed, the basis for a substantial diffusionist literature throughout the eighteenth century, it did not entirely dispel the suspicion that the peoples of America might be some quite different species of human being. What if the Biblical account were simply wrong or perhaps incomplete? Few if any Spaniards dared contemplate such a move. In the ecclesiastically more relaxed circles of Italy and northern Europe, however, this possibility increasingly seemed to become the only likely answer. In 1537–8, in two works on astronomy, the German doctor-magus Theophrastus Bombast, best-known as Paracelsus, considered the question. "We are all", he wrote, "descended from Adam, and are those creatures called men, whose ancestor was generated directed by God, without the intervention of the stars." But he went on,

> We must not forget those who have been discovered on remote islands, many of which are still hidden, and are still to be discovered. ... It cannot be demonstrated that the men that occupy these unknown lands derive from Adam [for] no one can easily believe that they are the line of Adam, since the sons of Adam could not have reached such remote places.[56]

Therefore, he concluded, it must be accepted that "the sons of Adam do not occupy all the earth". This, he explained elsewhere, did not deny them a soul, only a common ancestor with the rest of the species.

So, if they were not the descendants of Adam, who were they?

Two alternative versions presented themselves. Aristotle had argued that certain lower creatures, insects, reptiles, and fish might be generated either from the soil or from putrid matter. The orthodox view was that this excluded all higher animals and in particular humankind – a point on which Aquinas had insisted – since man was the only creature, of course, to be endowed with an immortal soul. But there were those who thought otherwise. One was the Bolognese Aristotelian Pietro Pomponazzi. Had not God himself made Adam out of "the dust of the ground?" he asked. And if that were the case why should not humanity also have been created, as Plato had claimed, *ex putri materia* – from rotting matter? Plato, knowing nothing of the Bible, had assumed that it had been the stars which had been responsible for the final act of generation. We, said Pomponazzi, now know better. But the fact that Adam and his descendants had been created by the hand of God did not necessarily exclude the possibility of later non-divine acts of creation. "That man is perfect and thus cannot be generated out of rotting matter", he told his students, "is a probable argument, but it does not exclude the possibility that it might occur."[57]

The theory of spontaneous generation was taken up by the doctors who found in it a satisfyingly economical solution to the problem of polygenesis, by Paracelsus himself, by Girolamo Cardano, by Andrea Cesalpino, who believed that the climate had something to do with it – "in the torrid zone", he claimed, "perfect animals are constantly generated spontaneously" – and by the arch magus Giordano Bruno, who was burned at the stake, in part for harboring similar beliefs. Had the Americans, and who knows who else besides, been the product of spontaneous generation, this might explain their servility, because it was hard for any of these authors to escape the conclusion that even if the higher animals could be generated from putrefaction, they were not, for that very reason, of an inferior kind to those which had stepped out of the Ark. The Americans on this calculation became not merely a race but, in effect, an entire species apart.

There was, however, another more benign explanation for their origins and incidentally of the origins of other remote peoples such as the Chinese.

In 1655, a treatise entitled *Prae-Adamitae* by Isaac Le Peyrère, a nominally French Huguenot of Jewish descent, was published in Holland (having been refused a licence by Richelieu ten years earlier).[58] Based on a detailed analysis of the account of the creation in Genesis – and a stray comment from St. Paul's Epistle to the Romans (V. 13) – Le Peyrère pointed out that the Book of Genesis contained not one, but two accounts of the creation: the first, 1. 27, speaks of the simultaneous creation of Adam and Eve, "male and female created he them"; the second 2–7: 21–2 describes the creation of Adam and *then* of Eve from Adam's rib. (Le Peyrère was not the first, nor the only, exegete to notice this. Furthermore, the existence of two similar but often contradictory stories is not unusual in creation myths. The *Timaeus*, for instance, also offers two contrasting versions.)[59] The claim that Adam was "the first man" should be understood, he argued, in the same sense as the claim that Christ was "the second man" (or the second Adam) was understood: not literally, but figuratively. Adam and Christ are archetypes each of which contains within himself the whole of humankind.[60] God had also charged Adam with naming everything on the earth. But that, reasoned Le Peyrère, in a moment of uncharacteristic literal-mindedness, would have been impossible given the variety of the species and the huge distances which separated them. Therefore there must have been two creations divided by a vast amount of time.

The races of Europe and Asia were the obvious descendants of the better documented of the two Adams, and all the other peoples of the earth, of the other, earlier, Adam. This theory proved instantly controversial and also immensely popular. Within a year of its publication *Prae-Adamitae* had been translated into English, elicited at least a dozen refutations, been condemned by the Parliament of Paris, and been burnt by the public executioner. Le Peyrère himself went on to become perhaps the most celebrated heretic of his day, and although his work has now been largely forgotten, the controversy it aroused rumbled on well into the eighteenth century.[61] For those who were prepared to ignore its obvious heterodoxy, however, it had a lot to recommend it. It provided an answer to all those who were already beginning to recognize that no species could have been created from a single pair, and it solved not only the American question but also the increasingly troubling Chinese question. The traditional Biblical chronology had set the date of the creation at 5199 BCE, which does not allow much time in which to compress the whole of human prehistory. In the sixteenth century, furthermore, the Jesuits had discovered that the Chinese had sacred books which recorded far longer periods of time. (Le Peyrère seems to have believed that the American Indians also had similar records.) This, as Voltaire over-optimistically thought, would put an end to the presumption of the Church once and for all. (It did not. However, it did seriously upset the Church's sense of its hold over human history and, via Leibniz and others, launched the Sinophilia of the eighteenth century, which argued that Confucius was the witness to a theological tradition which pre-dated Moses.)

By positing the existence of two creations, separated by perhaps thousands of years, Le Peyrère had effectively resolved this difficulty. It was not something which any traditional Christian theologian could make use of. But it was to have a marked influence on a slightly later generation of English deists, William Petty and Thomas Burnet in particular, who in 1681, for the first time, linked what might be described as a theory of race with an attempt to reevaluate the geological history of the earth.[62]

By establishing two distinct descent groups for all humankind, Le Peyrère had, in effect, divided the species into two separate races. In itself, however, Le Peyrère's thesis was not, in any obvious modern sense, racist. It was strictly non-evaluative – since the progeny of both Adams were treated as exactly equal, insofar as their mental and moral capacities were concerned. If anything, at a time when antiquity could be used to establish authority, the peoples of America and China might be thought to be superior to those of Europe and Asia, west of the Himalayas, by virtue of their greater age.

The separation of what would come to be called the "white" races into one descent group, and of all the others into another, had obvious racial implications nevertheless. There was a further point. If there were two Adams, it was clear that only the second had fallen into original sin – or at least in the way it is described in Genesis. This implied not that the progeny of the second was without sin (for if they were, they could only be angelic beings, something which no one was prepared to sustain) but rather that they could not have benefited from Christ's sacrifice. To get round this problem, Le Peyrère had insisted that God's grace had been extended "mystically" to the descendants of both Adams and that the Chinese, and the American Indians, although denied immediate access to the Gospel because of the unfortunate geographical distance between them and Palestine, could be counted as beings in the same condition of those – the "virtuous pagans" – who had led blameless lives before the birth of Christ. Not much attention, however, was paid to this part of Le Peyrère's argument, and the idea that all those people who had not originated somewhere west of the Euphrates were not merely descended from a separate progenitor to all the others but had also been excluded by God from grace appealed strongly to later racial theorists who were lumbered with being both Christian fundamentalists and anti-Darwinians.

All three of these claims – that the Indians were natural slaves, that they had been generated spontaneously, or that they were the descendants of another Adam – led, however, inexorably to a conclusion that even the most virulent of their detractors could not quite bring themselves to accept.

For not only did all three propositions threaten the idea of a single human kind; they also had the effect of placing those races outside the course of human history – the *operatio Dei* – in Augustine's words, which ran from a single act of creation until the end of human time. And although this might serve the purpose of later exclusionists – true racists, that is – it was deeply inimical to the early European ideologues of empire, since the only ethical and theological justification for the European oversees expansion had been precisely incorporation. This had been made clear in Columbus' charters. It had been made clear in the Bulls of Donation of 1493. It was set out in the Laws of Burgos of 1513, which states:

> Whereas it may so happen that in the course of time . . . the Indians will become so apt and ready to become Christians, and so civilized and educated, that they will be capable of governing themselves and leading the kind of life that the said Christians lead . . . [they] shall be allowed to live by themselves and shall be obliged to serve in those things in which our vassals in Spain are accustomed to serve.[63]

This could only mean that the Indians would one day come to enjoy the same legal status as the inhabitants of Castile. Even slavery was conceived as means to make the enslaved more like their masters, not as Aristotle had conceived it, as a way of rectifying a discrepancy in the natural order. As the Nertherlandish, Spanish humanist Sebastian Fox Morcillo pointed out in 1536, the Spanish had conquered America not to exploit or denigrate its inhabitants but so that they "should be civilized by good customs and education and led to a more human way of life".[64] And by making them more civilized, they would also be made fit to take their place in the course of human (and divine) history. Even so firm a champion of the political rights of the American Indians as Bartolomé de las Casas had insisted that the entire course of the Spanish overseas empire could only be justified on the grounds that it had brought these "countless peoples" into history, that Columbus' voyages had "broken the locks that had held the Ocean Sea fast ever since the Flood".

This is why, in the end, even Sepúlveda was prepared to concede that, "now that they have received our law, our rule our customs and have been imbued by the Christian religion", they are as unlike their former selves as "as human men are to barbarians, as those with sight to the blind, as savages are to the gentle as the pious are to the impious and, I say again, almost as men are to beasts".[65]

Broadly speaking, this remained the case until the collapse of the European empires in the twentieth century. Even when some notion of a civilizing process came to replace the Christian mission, any theory which implied that the conquered peoples of Europe's overseas empires belonged to a distinct race – defined in term of psychology, descent, or origin – ran directly counter to the declared ideological objective of the colonizing power. So long as they were committed either to evangelizing or to preparing the non-Christian, non-European subject for life in a "civilized" polity as a civilized being, apologists for empire were inescapably committed to a single indivisible human nature. Any claim that the colonized peoples might belong to separate, and inferior, races necessarily excluded them from history whether it was conceived as divine or – in terms of the history of "civilization" – secular. Had the American Indians been a race apart, natural slaves or the sons of another Adam, their history would have been very different, and there could have been no justification whatsoever for the European attempt either to Christianize or to civilize them. For this reason, paradoxical though it may seem, race plays no ultimately determining role part in the early modern ideologies of empire. That is not, of course, to deny that there were many who served the interests of the European overseas empires who were, on any understanding of the term, the most virulent racists. Nor is it to deny that there were many who sought to justify the European exploitation of non-Europeans on grounds which were, under any heading, clearly racial. But none of these voices, loud though they were, ever received any official recognition. The imperial ideologies of Spain, Britain, France, and Portugal were grounded on the assumption of a single human nature; and while such a nature can be divided – to return one last time to Regino of Prüm's list, by "custom, language and law" – it cannot be divided by "descent", that is, in the modern sense of the term, by race.

## Endnotes

1 "On the American Indians", 3. 8, Introduction, *Vitoria: Political Writings*, 290.
2 The general consensus among modern biologists, however, is that no such thing as race actually exists. An excellent account of the current scientific debate is to be

found in Colin Kidd: *The Forging of Races: Race and Scripture in the Protestant Atlantic World, 1600–2000* (Cambridge: Cambridge University Press 2006), 1–18.

3  The now classic statement of this claim is Ruth Benedict, *Race and Racism* (London: G. Routledge, 1942), and see Etienne Balibar "Racism and Nationalism" in Etienne Balibar and Immanuel Wallerstein, *Race, Nation, Class: Ambiguous Identities* (London: Verso, 1991), 37–67.

4  The earliest recorded use of the word in English is in a poem of 1508 by the Scot, William Dunbar who, like Spenser, used it to refer to a descent group. See Michael Banton, *Racial Theories* (Cambridge: Cambridge University Press, 1987), 17.

5  A race of mere impostors, when all's done –
I've seen much finer women, ripe and real
Than all the nonsense of their stone ideal
*Don Juan*, II, 942–4

6  See, in general, Siep Stuurman,"François Bernier and the Invention of Racial Classification" *History Workshop Journal* 50 (2000), 1–21.

7  « Nouvelle division de la Terre, par les différentes Espèces ou Races d'hommes qui l'habitent » *Journal des Scavans* 12 (April 1684), 148–55.

8  "Kant's Second Thoughts on Colonialism", *Kant and Colonialism: Historical and Critical*, 43–67 at p. 63, and see Robert Bernasconi, "Who Invented the Concept of Race? Kant's Role in the Enlightenment Construction of Race", in *Race* (Oxford: Blackwell, 2001), 11–36.

9  "Of national characters", *Essays, Moral, Political, and Literary*, 200. This, however, is the essay that contains the infamous footnote which begins, "I am apt to suspect that Negroes, and in general all other species of men ... to be naturally inferior to the whites", which has earned Hume a reputation as a racist. But the note, inserted in the essay in the edition of 1753 – five years after it was written – is a denial of the basic premise of all of Hume's anthropology, which assumed a universal and unchanging human nature. For a balanced analysis – despite the title – see Andrew Valls, "A Lousy Empirical Scientist": Reconsidering Hume's Racism", in *Race and Racism in Modern Philosophy*, Andrew Valls ed. (Cornell: Cornell University Press, 2005), 127–49 and cf. Kidd, *The Forging of Races*: 93–4.

10  Quoted in Ivan Hannaford, *Race: The History of an Idea in the West* (Baltimore: Johns Hopkins University Press, 1996), 173 and, in general on race as lineage, see 168–82.

11  See Albert A. Sicroff, *Les Controverses des status de "pureté de sang" en Espagne du XIVe au XVIIe siècles* (Paris: Didier, 1960), 290–7, and Gil Anidjar, "Lines of Blood: Limpieza de Sangre as Political Theology", in Mariacarla Gedebusch Bondia ed., *Blood in History and Blood Histories* (Florence: Edizioni del Galluzzo, 2005), 119–136, and María Elena Martínez, *Genealogical Fictions: Limpieza de Sangre, Religion, and Gender in Colonial Mexico* (Stanford: Stanford University Press, 2008) on the influence of the concept on the creation of the *casta* system in Spanish Mexico.

12  Quoted in Robert Bartlett, *The Making of Europe* (Harmondsworth: Penguin Books, 1994), 197.

13  Colin Kidd is surely right, however, in saying that the "absence of racialist doctrine did not mean that racist prejudice was similarly invisible. Racist attitudes

existed, but, significantly, did not rest upon clearly articulated theories of racial difference. Race – like ethnicity and even national consciousness (as distinct, say, from allegiance to one's monarch) – was a matter of second order importance behind primary commitments to church and state." *The Forging of Races*, 54.

14 See the comments by Judith Shklar in "Subversive Genealogies", in *Political Thought and Political Thinkers*, Stanley Hoffman ed. (Chicago: Chicago University Press, 1998), 132–60.

15 *Asia de Joam de Barros dos feitos que os Portugueses fizeram no descobrimento e conquista dos mares et terras do Oriente* (Lisbon, 1781), I, 154–5 (I.iv.9).

16 Louis-Antoine de Bougainville, *Voyage autour du monde par la frégate la Boudeuse et la flûte l'Étoile; en 1766, 1767, 1768 et 1769* [1771], Michel Bideaux and Sonia Faessel eds. (Paris: Presses de l'Université de Paris-Sorbonne, 2001), 161–2, and see my *The Enlightenment – and Why It Still Matters*, 223–26.

17 *Colossians* 3:11.

18 José de Acosta, *De promulgatione evangelii apud indos, sive De procuranda indorum salute libri sex* (Cologne, 1596), 150–1. Also see Marcel Bataillon, "L'Unité du genre humain de P. Acosta à P.Clavigero", in *Mélanges à la mémoire de Jean Sarrailh* (Paris: Institut d'Études Hispaniques, 1966), 1, 175–86.

19 *Historia de las cosas de la Nueva España* (Mexico City: Fondo de Cultura Económica, 1938), III, 82.

20 *Monumenta historica societatis Iesu* (Rome, 1954), III, 687. For more details see my "Identity Formation in Spanish America", in Nicholas Canny and Anthony Pagden eds., *Colonial Identity in the Atlantic World, 1500–1800* (Princeton: Princeton University Press, 1987), 81–3.

21 On proto-racism, see Benjamin Isaac, *The Invention of Racism in Classical Antiquity* (Princeton: Princeton University Press, 2004), 15–23.

22 See Malcolm Schofield, "Ideology and Philosophy in Aristotle's Theory of Slavery", in *Saving the City: Philosopher Kings and Other Classical Paradigms* (London: Routledge, 1999), 115–40, and Malcolm Heath, "Aristotle on Natural Slavery" *Phronesis* 53 (2008), 243–70.

23 *Politics*, 1255a 5–6. For the most compelling modern discussion of the implications of Aristotle's views, see Bernard Williams, *Shame and Necessity* (Berkeley, Los Angeles, Oxford: California University Press, 1993), 110–16.

24 Aristotle himself, however, makes it clear that natural slaves can be a perfectly skilled craftsmen. On this last point, see Eugene Garver, "Aristotle's Natural Slaves: Incomplete *praxeis* and Incomplete Human Beings", *Journal of the History of Philosophy* 32 (1994), 175–96.

25 *Politics*, 1254a 28 f.

26 *Politics*, 1324b 21–2.

27 *Politics*, 1280a 31–4. See Heath, "Aristotle on Natural Slavery".

28 *Politics*, 1254a 8.

29 In *Politics* 1252b 5, however, the *barbaroi* are said to be made up entirely of slaves. This, however, cannot possibly be meant to apply to all non-Greeks. Aristotle recognized that the Egyptians had invented mathematics, and the Babylonians astronomy. He was also well aware that the Persians had very nearly overrun Athens. On this point, see Heath, "Aristotle on Natural Slavery".

30 *Politics*, 1283a 14–23.

31 *Politics*, 1260b 1, and see Giulia Sissa, "La Génération automatique", in Barbara Cassin and Jean-Louis Labarrière eds., *L'Animal dans l'antiquité* (Paris: Vrin, 1997), 95–111.
32 *In decem libros ad Nicomachum expositio*, R. M. Spiazzi ed. (Rome-Turin, 1964), 1447 (*lectio*, 7.I.9).
33 *Politics*, 1252b 5.
34 *Politics*, 1255b 34; cf. 1333b 38.
35 *Nichomachean Ethics*, 1149a 9–11, and Heath, "Aristotle on Natural Slavery".
36 In Augustine, *De Civitate Dei*, XIX 21. In *De provinciis consularibus*, Cicero alludes to the Jews and Syrians as "peoples born to be slaves", which, as Benjamin Isaac says, would hardly have been intelligible to his audience if "a popular version of Aristotle's doctrine of natural slavery had not been common ground for at least a large number of people in antiquity". *The Invention of Racism in Classical Antiquity*, 225
37 *De Officis*, II. 27. Also see Richard Koebner, *Empire* (Cambridge: Cambridge University Press, 1961), 4–11.
38 *On the Fortunes of Alexander*, 329b.
39 *In secundum librum Sententiarum* (Paris, 1519), f.clxxxvijr.
40 *Politics*, 1254b 27f.
41 Quoted in J. H. Elliott, *The Old Word and the New, 1492–1650* (Cambridge: Cambridge University Press, 1970), 44.
42 *La Historia general de las Indias, primera parte* (Seville, 1535), f.xliiiiv.
43 *Opera omnia* (Geneva, 1697), I, f.39v. This might also be nothing more than confusion with the Roman law that the offspring of slave women are the property of that woman's owners. On this, see my *The Fall of Natural Man: The American Indian and the Origins of Comparative Ethnology* (Cambridge: Cambridge University Press, 1986, 2nd revised and enlarged edition), 46.
44 *Insularum mari Oceani tractatus*, in *De las islas del mar Océano por Juan López de Palacios Rubios*, Augustín Millares Carlo ed. (Mexico City: Fondo de Cultura Económica, 1954), 24.
45 Ibid., 127. "quapropter largo modo possunt dici servi, quasi nati ad serviendum, non autem ad imperandum." The highly qualified phrasing is significant. Few, even at this early stage before the discovery of Mexico and Peru had revealed the existence of highly complex Amerindian cultures, were prepared to accept the full force of Aristotle's claims.
46 See pp. p.49.
47 The full text is available on www.papalencyclicals.net/Paulo3/p3subli.htm.
48 *De iure belli*, 35. As usual, however, Gentili is making fast and loose with his sources. In fact, Aristotle makes a very clear distinction between the two kinds of slave; neither, of course, was slavery held by any ancient author to be a just punishment for "wickedness" or "sin".
49 See my *The Fall of Natural Man*.
50 "An sit iustum bellum adversus insulanos", in Luciano Pereña ed., *Misíon de España en América* (Madrid: Consejo Superior de Investigaciones Scientíficas, 1956), 301.
51 Quoted by Bartolomé de las Casas in *Historia de las Indias*, Augustín Millares Carlo ed. (Mexico: Fondo de Cultura Económica, 1951), II, 461–2. Compare the

declaration made by the World Council of Churches in 1968: "Racism is a blatant denial of the Christian faith. (1) It denies the effectiveness of the reconciling work of Jesus Christ …(2) it denies our common humanity in creation and our belief that all men are made in God's image." Quoted in Kidd, *The Forging of Races*, 274.

52 *Opus de triplici virtute theologica. Fide spe et charitate* (Paris, 1611), 630.

53 For Grotius' suggestions that the various Indian groups came from different parts of the Old World, see Joan-Pau Rubies, "Hugo Grotius' Dissertation on the Origins of the American Peoples, and the Use of Comparative Method", *Journal of the History of Ideas* 52 (1991), 221–44.

54 On this see my *The Fall of Natural Man*, 198–209.

55 *Historia natural y moral de las Indias* [1590], Edmundo O'Gorman ed. (Mexico: Fondo de Cultura Económica, 1962), 324–30. See Saul Jarcho, "Origin of the American Indian as Suggested by Fray Joseph de Acosta", *Isis* 59 (1959), 430–8. As Joan-Rubies has pointed out, Acosta's account, despite his claim to originality, in fact follows that of the chronicler-royal Juan López de Velasco's *Geografía y descripción universal de las Indias* of 1574. A northern land bridge also appears on maps from 1550 by the Venetian cosmographer Giacomo Gastaldi. ("Hugo Grotius' Dissertation on the Origins of the American Peoples, and the Use of Comparative Method", 224–5.) But almost every learned man in Europe had read Acosta, whereas very few had read Velasco, and fewer still had seen Gastaldi's maps.

56 Quoted in Giuliano Gliozzi, *Adamo e il nuovo mondo* (Florence: La Nuova Italia, 1977), 309–10.

57 In Bruno Nardi, "Pietro Pompnazzi e la teoria di Avicenna intorno alla generazione spontanea del uomo", in *Studi su Pietro Pompanazzi* (Florence: F. Le Monnier, 1965), 319.

58 The volume was made up of two works: the *Preadamitae, sive Exercitatio super Versibus duodecimo, decimotertio, et decimoquarto, capitis quinti, Epistolae D. Pauli ad Romanos, quibus inducuntur Primi Homines ante Adamum conditi* and the longer *Systema theologicum ex Praeadamitarum hypothesi*.

59 See the comments on this and its implications for our conceptions of time in Aldo Schiavone, *Storia e destino* (Turin: Einaudi, 2007), 14–19.

60 *Preadamitae*, cap. xxiii. For a more detailed discussion of the text, see Giuliano Gliozzi, *Adamo e il nuovo mondo*, 535–66, and "Poligenismo e razzismo agli albori del secolo dei lumi", in *Differenze e uguaglianza nella cutura europea moderna* (Naples: Vivarium, 1993), 255–87.

61 For his life and work, see Richard Popkin, *Isaac La Peyrère (1596–1676): His Life, Work and Influence* (Leiden, New York: Brill, 1987).

62 On this, see Kidd, *The Forging of Races*.

63 Article 4 of an appendix of July 28, 1513. Text in Charles Gibson, *The Spanish Tradition in America* (New York: Norton, 1968), 81.

64 *Brevis et perspicua totius ethicae, seu de moribus philosophiae descriptio* (Basle, 1566), 252.

65 *Democratus secundus, sive de justis causis belli apud Indos*, in *Democrates Segundo, o justas causas de la guerra contra los indios*, Angel Losada trans. and ed. (Madrid: Consejo Superior de Investigaciones Científicas, 1951), 33, 120.

# 4

## Conquest, Settlement, Purchase, and Concession

### *Justifying the English Occupation of the Americas*

I

Of the five major European powers to establish large-scale and enduring settlements on the American mainland – Spain, Portugal, Holland, France, and England – the English were relative latecomers. Although there are more similarities between them and the other European colonial powers than has sometimes been supposed, in many respects both the legal character and the administration of their colonies were unusual. The overseas possessions of the Spanish, despite early incorporation into the Crown of Castile, were legally identified as separate kingdoms – the *reinos de Indias* – governed by a separate body of legislation (codified in 1680) and administered by a royal council whose functions were similar to those of the councils that administered the European regions of the Monarchy: Italy, Flanders, and Castile itself. As the Milanese jurist Camillo Borello, looking at the Monarchy from the view of one of its most autonomous dependencies, remarked, "the kingdoms have to be ruled and governed as if the king who holds them all were only the king of each one of them".[1] The Spanish possessions were thus a separate but legally incorporated part of a single imperium, embodied in the person of the monarch – what has often been referred to as a "composite monarchy".[2] The Portuguese overseas dependencies were, with the exception of Brazil, trading stations (*feitorias*) not dissimilar to the factories the English later established in Asia and were under the direct control of the Crown. The French kings looked on New France – what would later become Canada – as part of the royal demesne, but, unlike their English neighbors, the French settlers were governed according to the body of local administrative law, the *Coutume de Paris*, which prevailed in most of northern France, a situation that would determine the ideological shape of the empire until the collapse of the monarchy itself. The Dutch Republic's possessions in America, both in the New Netherlands and, while it lasted, New Holland (a part of Portuguese Brazil that the Dutch occupied between

1630 and 1654) were held by the Dutch West Indian Company, which had a monopoly on all land and trading concessions. The governors appointed to the regions by the Republic were officers in the company's employ. The laws they administered were those of the Republic, and Dutch settlers in the Americas never thought of themselves as anything other than Dutchmen overseas.

By contrast, each of the thirteen colonies that were eventually to make up the United States, from Puritan New England to Catholic Avalon, had a different foundation and a different form of administration and represented different demographic and cultural aspects of the British Isles. The legal status of the English colonies was also both more varied and much less precisely defined than that of their Spanish, Portuguese, French, or Dutch (or even later their Swedish, Russian, and German) counterparts. Some colonies were proprietary, like Maryland; some were corporate in which the king had granted powers of self-government to a company or to a body of settlers, like Massachusetts. Virginia and New York (after 1648) were administered directly by the Crown (as was Maryland between 1689 and 1715). As Edmund and William Burke noted in 1757, "there is scarce any form of government known, that does not prevail in some of our plantations."[3] The same applied to the various legal systems employed throughout the colonies. "No one can tell", complained one anonymous settler in Virginia in the early eighteenth century, "what is law and what is not in the Plantations."[4] The English common law, unlike the law in Spain and France during the sixteenth century, was uncodified. The absence of any accepted body of legislation made the resulting conflict between the Parliament, the Crown, and the various colonies and overseas dependencies hard to resolve. It was this lack of any single constitutional definition of empire which led J. R. Seeley in 1883 to make his famous remark that it seemed as if England had, "conquered and peopled half the world in a fit of absence of mind".[5] And it would remain a defining feature of the British Empire until its final demise in the twentieth century.

There was a further difference between the English and their European rivals. From the beginning of their colonizing ventures, the English seem to have taken a far more detached view of the possible relations between the "mother country" and its colonies than their continental neighbors. Spain, quite obviously, and France less certainly, represented themselves as the true heirs to Rome. Britain, which at least until the eighteenth century had a very weak sense of itself as an "empire" – a word, which as John Adams said later, belonged "not to the language of the common law, but the language of newspapers and political pamphlets" – held to a far stricter distinction between a "colony," on the one hand, and a separate, if distinct kingdom, within a "composite monarchy" on the other.[6] But if there was, in effect, no true "British Empire" before Disraeli created one for Queen Victoria in 1878, if the American colonies were not, as were those of both Spain and

France, united to the mother country by a shared *ius publicum* embodied in the legal person of the king, what was their relationship to the metropolis? On the answer to this question hinged the entire nature of their legal identity.

To understand just how the English colonies in America acquired their distinctive legal character, we have to begin where the colonists themselves had *a fortiori* to begin: with the question of legitimacy. From the early sixteenth century until well into the eighteenth, in Spain, France, and Britain, a moral, theological, and legal struggle was waged over the legitimacy of the conquest and settlement of the Americas. At one level – as we have seen – this was concerned with the justice of the treatment of the indigenous peoples. But that was only one aspect of the question and, arguably for the British, the least pressing. Although the Puritan divine John Eliot has been compared to Bartolomé de las Casas, and even shared with him the title of "Apostle to the Indians", he was in John Elliott's words, "a Las Casas in a minor key". And none of his interventions on behalf of the Native Americans had any of the intellectual implications of Las Casas' for the possible future of the Spanish presence in the Americas, nor for the moral conscience (such as it was) of the Crown.[7] Far more troubling (and fare more enduring) for the British, because it had an immediate and direct impact on the political conduct of the metropolitan power, was the question of the juridical status of the colonial settlements, with regard to both the metropolis itself and other rival European powers.

Like their European rivals the English could make no a priori claims to rights of any kind in the Americas. "[We] shall be put to defend our title," the Virginia Company early recognized, "not yet publicly quarreled, not only comparatively to be as good as the Spaniards, but absolutely to be good against the Natural people."[8] Claims to both sovereignty and property in the Americas had, that is, to be sustained on two fronts: first against prior claims by another European power – in this case Spain – and then against all those others, the "Natural people," whose rights would seem to be antecedent to those of any European. Because no argument from English civil law could be applied anywhere outside the jurisdiction of the English courts, the English had to find some argument that would be considered valid in either natural law or the law of nations, laws that were believed to be binding on all humankind no matter what their civil constitution might be. The complex and extended attempts to do this rumbled on well into the nineteenth century and are still being discussed in Canada and Australia to this day.

Both the Spanish and the French, in their different ways, had attempted to establish not colonies but overseas dependencies and had tried to incorporate the indigenous peoples into new multiethnic societies. The Spanish policy had been based on the phrase in Luke 14: 23: "Go out into the highways and hedges, and compel [them] to come in, that my house may be filled." The Indians were to be driven "in" not only as Christians but also as civilized, that is, Europeanized, beings. They were to be peasants, serfs, sometimes allies.

A few could even be landowners with European servants, and at least in the early years in Spanish America, they could occupy semi-bureaucratic positions in the new overseas dependencies. Something similar also applied in French America. Under a law of 1664, all native inhabitants of New France who had converted to Christianity were held to be "denizens and French natives, and as such entitled for all rights of succession, goods laws and other dispositions, without being obliged to obtain any letter of naturalization".[9] For the English, by contrast, the indigenes were always only of secondary importance – persons who were to be displaced, not incorporated. Few sustained attempts were made to convert them. It was up to them, as John Cotton wrote in the 1630, "to believe willingly or not to believe at all".[10] For the most part they were classified as "savages," in the terms of Charles II's charter to settle Carolina, who belonged in the same general category with "other enemies pirates and robbers".[11] It was the manner of their displacement which was crucial because that raised substantial legal questions about the status of those who were engaged in – and benefiting from – the displacing.

Unlike the Spanish, furthermore, and to some degree the French, the English also lacked any initial founding charter issued by an international authority. Henry VII's letters patent to John Cabot of 1496 were to some degree an attempt to replicate the language of Papal legislation, as were the grants made by Elizabeth I to Sir Walter Raleigh in March 1584. But for all their assumed authority neither Henry nor Elizabeth were pontiffs; neither could make the least claim to excise any degree of jurisdiction beyond their realms. In the end, possession or sovereignty in the Americas could only be made legitimate on three distinct grounds: by right of conquest; by "discovery", which crucially, as we shall see, implied that the territory being "discovered" was also unoccupied; or by purchase from, or voluntary concession by, the native and legitimate owners or rulers.

II

Of these, the most contentious was indisputably conquest, since for the English no less than for the Spanish, no conquest could be legitimate unless it were the consequence of a just war, and there were no immediate or obvious reasons for considering the European invasions of America as in any sense just. In general, conquest as prior grounds for claims of property rights or sovereignty was looked on with mistrust throughout the entire history of the European overseas empires.[12] "The Sea", as the Scottish political theorist and soldier of fortune Andrew Fletcher declared in 1698, "is the only Empire which can naturally belong to us. Conquest is not our Interest".[13] The Portuguese spoke of "conquering" the seas, but rarely of the land, and even the Spanish, whose American empire was so obviously, and in the early years so proudly, based on conquest, banned all official use of the term in 1680.[14] In England, furthermore, there existed a long-standing distrust of conquest – to which I shall return – that originated in the Norman occupation after 1066 and resulted in the "continuity theory" of constitutional law in which the legal and political institutions of the conquered are deemed to survive a conquest.

Although very few of the English settlements in America were in fact "conquered" in any meaningful sense, conquest nevertheless remained the basis of the English Crown's claim to its American colonies until independence. In many instances the terms "occupy" and "conquer" were taken to be synonymous. "Occupation", as the great seventeenth-century jurist Sir Edward Coke explained, "signifieth a putting out of a man's freehold in time of warre ... *occupare* is sometimes taken to conqueror."[15] It could also be taken to legitimate grounds for *de iure* occupation even if, de facto, none had taken place (something which, as we have seen, the Spanish jurists firmly denied). As late as 1744, in the negotiations which led to the treaty of Lancaster with the Iroquois, the Virginia delegation declared that "the King holds Virginia by right of conquest, and the bounds of that conquest to the westward is the great sea". "Virginia", that is, reached all the way to the Pacific, much of which was at the time neither occupied, in any formal sense, nor even charted.[16] This repeated insistence that America was a land of conquest was but one stage, of which the annexation of India by the British Crown in 1858 was to be perhaps the last, of a long series of "conquests" – that of Wales, completed in 1536; the conquest, or at least the seizure, of the Channel Islands (although this was not completed until 1953); the conquest of the Isle of Man in 1406; the prolonged conquests of Ireland between 1175 and 1603; and the initial attempt at union with Scotland which was to become one of the issues at stake in the Civil War in 1603. For more than two centuries before the first colonies were established on the eastern seaboard of North America, England had been in a state of constant and determined expansion. It was to remain more or less uninterruptedly in this state until the First World War.

There were good political reasons for this. Land acquired by conquest passed under the jurisdiction of the Crown. Lands acquired either through terra nullius or purchase could, and frequently were, said to have been acquired by private agreements which conferred property rights on the discovery or the purchaser and, therefore – or so it could be argued – made them subject to Parliament and not directly to the Crown. Conquest was also, of course, the means which the Spanish had employed to great rhetorical effect in their occupation of Americas. Conquest conferred political status. As the polymathic English astronomer John Dee had told Elizabeth in 1578, if she was going "to recover the premises" seized from her by the Spanish, she had to be prepared to "make entrances and conquestes vpon the heathen people".[17] As this phrase implied, if the still imaginary "British Empire" were to be a match for the Spanish, it, too, had to be founded on conquest.

It had also, as had the initial Spanish settlements in the New World, to be tied to evangelization. As the English were fully aware the Papal Bulls of Donation had granted sovereignty over territory in exchange for sovereignty over souls and had charged the Catholic Monarchs "to subjugate (*subdicere*) with the aid of divine clemency the aforesaid mainlands and islands and their dwellers and inhabitants, and to reduce (*reducere*) them to the Catholic Faith".[18] If the English conquests were to be legitimate, they, too, had to follow – or at least claim to follow – a similar path. In 1606 First Charter of the Virginia Company proclaimed in 1606 that its purpose was to serve in "propagating of Christian religion to such people, [who] as yet live in darkness and miserable ignorance of the true knowledge and worship of God, and may in time bring the infidels and salvages living in these parts to humane civility and to a settled and quiet government".[19] In a similarly self-congratulatory vein, Hakluyt told Sir Walter Ralegh that "no greater glory can be handed down than to conquer the barbarian, to recall the savage and the pagan to civility, to draw the ignorant within the orbit of reason, and to fill with reverence for divinity the godless and the ungodly".[20] Both the Virginia Company and Ralegh, however, carried an additional burden that the Spanish did not. For whereas the Spaniards were "papists", the English were, of course, Protestants. Their monarch's "Christian duty" thus became a double one; not merely to Christianise, but to seize for the reformed religion the initiative lost to its Catholic rival. The "Kinges and Queenes of England", in Hakluyt's strained analogy, as they "Nowe … have the name of Defenders of the Faithe; By which title I thinke they are not onely charged to mayneteyne and patronize the faithe of Christe, but also to inlarge and advaunce the same".[21] As the title *fidei defensor* – bestowed first on Henry VIII by Pope Leo X in 1521, then revoked by Paul III, and subsequently re-bestowed on Edward VI and his successors by Parliament in 1544 – had been transformed from a papal benediction into a patent to defend Protestantism against Catholicism both in the Old World and the New it became a further incentive for the English to overtake the Spanish. "Now yf they in their superstition and by meanes of their plantinge in those parts", asked Hakluyt, "have don so greate thinges in so shorte space, what may wee hope for in our true and sincere Relligion?", particularly because, or so he claimed to believe, the English, unlike the Spanish, were concerned with neither "filthie lucre nor vain ostentation", but instead with "the gayninge of the soules of millions of those wretched people and reducing them from darknese to lighte, from falsehoodde to truthe, from dombe Idolls to the lyvinge god, from the depe pitt of hell to the highest heavens".[22] This, then, was to be, at least as far as the indigenous populations were concerned, an entirely peaceful "conquest". Between them, Ralegh and Hakluyt set in motion an idea to which the English would revert over and over again: once they had understood their true intentions the Indians would look on these new European interlopers not as invaders, but as saviours from the Spanish, and then from their own barbarous ignorance.

"Riches and Conquest, and renown I sing", wrote Robert Chapman, in his best Virgilian manner, in the ode *De Guiana carmen epicum*, which was prefixed to Laurence Keymis' narrative of his voyage to the Orinoco, but added, "Riches with honour, Conquest without bloud".[23]

In Hakluyt's imagination, trade, precious metals, the foundation of permanent settlements, and conversion were all but parts of a single enterprise: those who sought to plead the Gospel in the newfound lands would be rewarded materially for their pains.[24] That was the only reason why God had filled the Indies with such wealth. A "group of barbarous nations", the biblical scholar Joseph Mede told the Calvinist theologian William Twisse in 1635, had wandered across the Bering Strait and down into the New World, where they now awaited the coming of the English, drawn by the promise of infinite riches, to reveal to them the truth of their particular brand of Christianity.[25] Or as Edward Winslow, the governor of Plymouth, wryly commented in 1624, America was a place where "religion and profit jump together".[26] In performing this valuable and godly service, the English colonists were replicating what their Roman ancestors had once done for the ancient Britons. The American settlers, argued in 1612, were like Roman generals in that they, too, had "reduced the conquered parts of our barbarous Island into provinces and established in them colonies of old soldiers, building castles and towns in every corner, teaching us even to know the powerful discourse of divine reason".[27] Except that whereas the Roman had brought only civilization, the English were bringing both civilization and Christianity.

For the more extreme Calvinists, however, all infidels, together presumably with all Catholics, lay so far from God's grace that no amount of civilizing would be sufficient to save them. Such "barbarous" peoples might, therefore, legitimately be conquered, because in Edward Coke's dramatic phrasing:

> A perpetual enemy (though there be no wars by fire and sword between them) cannot maintain any action or get any thing within this Realm. All infidels are in law *perpetui inimici*, perpetual enemies, (for the law presumes not that they will be converted, that being *remota potentia*, a remote possibility) for between them, as with devils, whose subjects they be, and the Christians, there is perpetual hostility and can be no peace.

Like all Calvinists, Coke adhered to the view that as "infidels" the Native Americans could have no share in God's grace, and because authority and rights derived from grace, not nature, they could have no standing under the law. Their properties, and even their persons, were therefore forfeit to the first "godly" person with the capacity to subdue them. "If a Christian King," he wrote, "should conquer a kingdom of an infidel, and bring them [sic] under his subjection, there *ipso facto* the laws of the infidel are abrogated, for that they be not only against Christianity, but against the law of God and nature contained in the Decalogue."[28] Grounded as this idea was, not only in the writings of Calvin himself but also in those of the fourteenth-century

English theologian John Wycliffe, it enjoyed considerable support among the early colonists. As the dissenting dean of Gloucester Josiah Tucker wrote indignantly to Edmund Burke in 1775:

> Our Emigrants to *North-America*, were mostly Enthusiasts of a particular Stamp. They were that set of Republicans, who believed, or pretended to believe, that *Dominion was founded in Grace*. Hence they conceived, that they had the best Right in the World, both to *tax* and to *persecute* the *Ungodly*. And they did both, as soon as they got power into their Hands, in the most open and atrocious Manner.[29]

Despite Tucker's belief that it was this which was steadily pushing the colonists toward outright rebellion against the Crown, by the end of the seventeenth century, much of the essentially eschatological aspect of the argument had generally been dropped. If anything, it was now the "papists" (because the canon lawyers shared much the same views as the Calvinists on the binding nature of divine grace) who were thought to derive rights of conquest from the supposed ungodliness of non-Christians. The colonists themselves, in particular when they came in the second half of the eighteenth century to raid the older discussions over the legitimacy of the colonies in search of arguments for cessation, had no wish to be associated with any argument which depended uniquely on their standing before God. For this reason, if for no other, the idea that right derived from grace, was, as James Otis noted in 1764, a "madness" which, at least by his day, had been "pretty generally exploded and hissed off the stage".[30]

Otis, however, had another more immediate reason for dismissing this account of the sources of sovereign authority. For if America had been "conquered", it followed that the colonies, like all other lands of conquest, were a part not of the king's realm but of the royal demesne. This would have made them the personal territory of the monarch, to be governed at the king's "pleasure," instead of being subject to English law and to the English Parliament. It was this claim that sustained the fiction that, in the words of the rebuke of one "Vindex Patriae" to Benjamin Franklin in January 1766, "New England lies within England", which would govern the crown's legal association with all its colonies until the very end of the empire itself. As late as 1913, for instance, Justice Isaac Isaacs of the Australian High Court could be found declaring that at the time Governor Arthur Phillip received his commission in 1786, Australia had, rightly or wrongly, been conquered and that "the whole of the lands of Australia were already in law the *property* of the King of England," a fact which made any dispute over its legality a matter of civil, rather than international, law.[31]

It was precisely because all conquered territories were a part of the royal demesne that the monarch was able to grant charters to the colonies in the first place. For however empty those charters might have been considered by some, they were indisputably concessions made by the Crown. Charters, wrote Thomas Hobbes, "are Donations of the Soveraign; and not Lawes but exemptions from Law. The phrase of a Law is *Jubeo, Injugo, I Command* and *Enjoyn*; the phrase of a Charter is *Dedi, Concessi, I have Given I have Granted*".[32] If this were so, and Hobbes is here stating a legal commonplace, then in one quite specific sense the English colonies had feudal foundations. Most of the lands in America had originally been granted in "free and common socage" as of the manor of East Greenwich in Kent. This formula allowed for what were, in effect, allodial grants – grants which while they derived from a contract between the Crown and the landowner, at the same time avoided the duties of feudal tenure, such as the need to provide military assistance to the sovereign. In this way the colonies were both free and unencumbered while at the same time remaining legally part of the royal demesne, and every part of the *terra regis* had to form a constitutive part of a royal manor in England. Land in Ireland, for instance, was held as of Carregrotian, or Trim or Limerick or the Castle of Dublin, and when Charles II made over Bombay to the East India Company, this, too, was granted in "free and common socage" of the manor of East Greenwich. In the proprietorial colonies, by contrast, a large area of land was granted to single individuals who then allocated lands more or less as they pleased. Even here, however, the Crown still maintained that it possessed the ultimate rights of ownership and that it could, therefore, dispose of the territory in question as it wished.

The English king's persistent belief that the overseas dependencies remained his personal property, despite the charters which the monarchy itself had granted to each of its parts, led to some strain in the relationship between king and Parliament. When, in 1660, Charles II acquired Jamaica, together with Dunkirk and Tangier, he immediately moved that these were also part of the royal demesne and thus his to dispose of as he willed. As a preemptive move, on September 11, 1660, the House of Commons passed a bill "for annexing Dunkirke ... and the Island of Jamaica in America to the Crown of England". Charles rejected this, and on October 17, 1662, sold Dunkirk to Louis XIV for five million pounds. Selling off what Parliament held to be parts of the realm was an extreme measure, but there was little Parliament could do about it at the time. What was at stake here was the status of private rights of the monarch, as against the sovereign rights of the monarchy. The royal claim created obvious difficulties when, after the end of the Seven Year's War, Parliament attempted to tighten its hold over the fiscal and commercial activities of the colonies.

The exceptions to the rule were those areas, Maryland and the Carolinas, which had been created as palatinates, "as of any Bishop of Durham, within the Bishopric, or County Palatine of Durham".[33] Although much reduced in power since 1535, Durham itself remained a palatinate until 1836. The bishop had, in effect, powers very similar to those of the Spanish viceroys.

The charter of Maryland also offered its proprietor, Lord Calvert, "free and common socage." In exchange for a nominal rent of two Indian arrows and one-fifth of all gold and silver ore payable annually to the Crown, the proprietor was given the right to grant or lease any portion of the territory in fee simple or fee tail. Among other privileges he could also erect manors with courts baron and courts leet.

Both approaches, however, still preserved lands as part of the royal patrimony, albeit at one remove; consequently, both denied inhabitants any right of appeal against their immediate proprietor. For as both the bishop and the proprietor were, in effect, delegates of the Crown, the colonists could make no claim to constituting an independent sovereign body. This resulted in some very strained interpretations of the historical facts of conquest. In 1694, the inhabitants of Barbados argued before the House of Lords that they were entitled to rights under English law as "their birthright" because Barbados had been, quite literally, uninhabited when they arrived. They were told that, notwithstanding the facts of the matter, Barbados was nevertheless held to be a "conquered territory". Any protection the settlers might have under English law was therefore at the discretion of the monarch. As Coke put it, "if a king come to a Christian kingdom by conquest, seeing that he hath *vitae et necis potestatem*, he may at his pleasure alter and change the laws of that kingdom" – a statement which, of course, was a direct contradiction of the "continuity theory" of conquest.[34] If Coke were right, then the same would apply to the Americas, even if there was, in effect, no prior recognizable system of legislation. Indeed, in Coke's view it would apply with even greater force in a country of "Infidels" such as America, since the laws of such peoples had no basis in right at all.

Here the long-standing suspicion of conquest, which originated in the Norman Conquest of Britain, could be turned to the Crown's advantage. If America had been conquered, its laws could only be made by royal decree, and its inhabitants would be bound by those laws. Furthermore, since those laws were royal decrees, they would not be subject to the provisions of Magna Carta or any of the subsequent constraints which parliament had succeeded in imposing on the monarchy. This did not much appeal either to the settlers or to Parliament, which took the view that, although such laws might have been made by the monarch acting very much as, to use the Roman term, "unfettered by law" (*legibus solutus*), once they had been enacted they became, in effect, laws passed by Parliament. In Coke's view, for instance, although King John had introduced the laws of England into Ireland without parliamentary consent, "no succeeding king could alter the same without Parliament." It was for this reason that Sir William Blackstone, in what has become perhaps the most celebrated statement on the subject, declared: "Our American plantations" had been

obtained in the last century either by right of conquest and driving out the
natives (with what natural justice I shall not at present inquire) or by treaties.
And therefore the common law of England, as such, has no allowance or
authority there, they being no part of the mother country, but distinct though
dependent dominions. They are subject, however, to the control of
Parliament.[35]

On occasion the same was also said of Ireland, which although indisputably
a land of conquest was nevertheless frequently described as a "dominion
separate and divided from England". "Of all the objections raised against
us," complained William Molyneux in 1698 of the various attempts to
classify Ireland as a colony and thereby to remove it from the legal jurisdiction of Parliament,

> I take this to be the most extravagant: it seems not to have the least foundation
> or colour from reason or record. ... Do not the Kings of England bear the Stile
> of Ireland amongst the rest of their Kingdoms? Is this Agreeable to the nature
> of a Colony? Do they use the title of Kings of Virginia, New England or
> Maryland?[36]

The same was true of the Isle of Man, which, although governed by its own
laws, could be bound to Westminster any time Parliament chose because it
had originally been acquired under Henry IV "by conquest".

What Blackstone's claim implied, of course, was that in the case of both
conquest and treaty (for a treaty could only be entered into by a sovereign
state) New England was not "within England." Nor was it the case that
English law – English common law at least – followed Englishmen wherever
they went, as was so often stated. Paradoxically, the consequence of such a
view was that whereas the colonies were themselves nothing other than
extensions of the royal demesne, the laws by which they were ruled were,
in the terms of the various charters by which they had been established, the
creation of the colonists themselves. It was this situation which led Andrew
Fletcher in 1704 to compare the British *overseas* empire to the leagues of the
Greek city-states, a semi-federal structure in which each community was
responsible for its own internal affairs, and consequently its own legislative
order, while being dependent, or semi-dependent, on a central power for its
external regulation. It was a model which offered Antoine Barnave, the most
forceful of the spokesmen for the interests of the French *colons* of the
Caribbean, an argument with which to compel the Revolutionary government to mitigate, if not entirely abolish, the restrictive trade laws by which
the colonies were bound and, crucially, to ward off any attempt to emanci-
pate the slaves. The British, he told the French National Assembly in 1791,
had always treated their colonies as "co-states as far as their internal laws
were concerned", whereas they were "purely subject" with regard to their
"exterior regime". Had they continued to honor this distinction, he added

darkly, they would have had their colonies still. The error of the *ancien regime* in France had been to allow for no distinction between "these two classes of laws which should never be confused".[37] If the new government in Paris wished to retain control of its Caribbean possessions, however, it would now have to recognize the legitimacy of the colonists' claims to full representation on the newly established *Corps lesgislatif national*. For Barnave himself, it was to be the beginning of the road to the guillotine.

The external/internal division would also be invoked by James Madison and James Wilson in their proposals for a federal structure for the United States. This quasi-independent status, both political and legal, with respect to the metropolis did not make the American colonies distinct from other colonial settlements within the British Empire, despite repeated attempts by American historians in pursuit of the origins of American exceptionalism to demonstrate that it did. Similar patterns would later be repeated in India, Africa, and Australia. But, it did distinguish them from the colonial settlements of other European powers in the Americas. Their freedom had, however, been conceded to the settlers either directly by the crown or by those to whom the crown had made grants or charters. And because they were not a part of what Francis Bacon had called "one imperial crown", they could not enjoy the benefits of the English common law.[38]

This position involved, of course, a great deal of incoherence, which was captured nicely by Benjamin Franklin when he demanded of the House of Commons in February 1776 to know, "What have these inhabitants of East Greenwich in Kent done, that they, more than any other inhabitants of Kent, should be curbed in their manufactures and commerce?"[39] For if the colonists were virtual residents of East Greenwich, then they should have enjoyed *all* the rights enjoyed by the English, just as any labourer on the East Greenwich estate would necessarily have done. The argument that because the colonies were the personal property of the monarch, their inhabitants could be denied the rights and freedoms enjoyed by those of other places within the British monarchy was also perceived by many to be a short road to the establishment of the kind of unfettered legislative powers which the British constitution had struggled so hard for so long to prevent. It was one of the reasons why Edmund Burke upheld the rights of self-determination claimed by the American revolutionaries. "In order to prove that the Americans have no right to their liberties," he wrote in 1776, "we are every day endeavoring to subvert the maxims which preserve the whole Spirit of our own."[40]

No matter what the legal status of the colonies was thought to be in England, in America de facto self-government in most of the settlements meant that the colonies enjoyed a great deal of autonomous legislation. This led, inexorably, to a political climate in which, in Burke's words, the colonists tended to "augur misgovernment at a distance and sniff the approach of tyranny in every tainted breeze".[41] The conflict over the status of the relationship between the crown and its overseas subjects first came to a head in the years after the Restoration in 1660 when an attempt was made to transform the scattered American colonies into something resembling the Spanish empire, with a centralized structure. Between 1651 and 1696, a series of Navigation Acts were passed whose purpose was to restrict trade between the colonies and the mother country and to exclude the Scots from what was, in effect, an English mercantile system. A new authority of the Privy Council, called the "Lords of Trade and Plantations", was also established to administer the colonies, which was far closer to the Spanish Council of the Indies than anything which had previously existed. More significantly, the royal charters of the corporate colonies were revoked by royal decree. The crown had already resumed the charter of the Virginia Company in 1624, and between then and the 1680s, various, although frequently inconsistent, attempts were made to establish crown sovereignty over all the remaining settlements.

From the late seventeenth century until the eve of the Revolution, the crown or its more legally minded officials had looked with envy at the degree of administrative and judicial authority the Spanish excised in their colonies. In the opening years of the eighteenth century, the English political and economic theorist Charles Davenant, although one of the fiercest critics of what he saw as Spanish cruelty and Spanish popery, nevertheless recommended that "a constitution something like what we call the Council of the Indies in Spain" should be established in Britain. "Whoever considers the laws and political institutions of *Spain*," he went on, "will find them as well formed, and contrived with as much skill and wisdom, as in any country perhaps in the world."[42] In accordance with this sentiment, by the 1670s the Crown had begun to put into operation a plan to divide the thirteen colonies into four separate viceroyalties.

As it turned out, only one was ever established. In 1686, the former colonies of New England, Massachusetts, Plymouth, Maine, New Hampshire, Rhode Island, and Connecticut were combined with New Jersey and New York to form the Dominion of New England. Like the Spanish viceroyalties, the Dominion was ruled by a single individual appointed by the Crown, who governed with a council but without a locally elected assembly and who exercised certain legislative as well as executive powers. After the Glorious Revolution of 1688 and the demise of the Stuart monarchy, the colonists threw the governor, Sir Edmund Andros, and the members of his advisory council into jail, and the Dominion ceased to be. Nevertheless, by 1776, only three of the thirteen mainland colonies – Massachusetts, Rhode Island, and Connecticut – still had charters. Two others, Maryland and Pennsylvania, had proprietors. All the rest, mainland and Caribbean, had become royal territories.

In the eyes of the Crown, then, the American colonies were in all legal respects lands of conquest. They were so not because any actual conquests had occurred but because the definition enabled the Crown to assert unlimited rights to grant concessions or, if it so wished, repeal them without consultation, just as, when the time came, it would assert an unlimited right to raise exceptional taxes without consent. The claim of the American revolutionaries that taxation without representation in Westminster was illegal amounted to a denial of the status which the Crown had conferred on them since the beginning. Their denial was predicated on an alternative narrative of the legal foundations of the settlements that had begun to emerge during the eighteenth century, one which would have a powerful and enduring hold on the legal history of the revolution and indeed of the fledgling United States.

III

In 1804, in the first volume of his misleadingly entitled *Life of Washington*, Chief Justice John Marshall stated categorically: "There is not a single grant from the British Crown from the earliest of Elizabeth down to the latest of George III that affects to look at any title except that founded on discovery, Conquest or cession is not once alluded to."[43] Conquest, in Marshall's view, only became grounds for possession in the eighteenth century when the thirteen colonies which would make up the new United States had already been securely established and most of their remaining indigenous populations effectively dispossessed. This claim seems to have been based very largely on Marshall's reading of Henry VII's letters patent to John Cabot of 1496, which had echoed exactly the terms of the bulls by which Pope Alexander VI had granted to the Catholic Monarchs of Spain, Ferdinand and Isabella, dominion over all territories in the western hemisphere not already occupied by another Christian prince. In Marshall's understanding, the right to occupation derived not from the conquest of such territories (although Cabot is explicitly charged with conquest) but from the absence of occupation by any power that the English were prepared to recognize as sovereign.

Even if such an interpretation of Henry VII's letters were warranted, it is difficult to see how a man of Marshall's learning could have insisted that "discovery" had continued to be the *sole* justification employed by the English Crown in view of all the subsequent evidence. Marshall, however, was not the first to make this claim. In 1754, faced with the prospect of a French invasion, the delegates to the Albany Congress agreed: "That his Majesty's title to the northern continent of America appears founded on the discovery thereof first made, and the possession thereof first taken, in 1497 under a commission from Henry 7th. of England to Sebastian Cabot."[44] In 1774, James Abercromby, as influential a jurist as Marshall in his own day, stated: "The point of Territorial Right in America at first turned totally, on the priority of Discovery."[45] These statements would seem to suggest that from the moment the colonists began to distance themselves from the Crown, until well after independence, there existed a movement to redefine the question of legitimacy in such a way as to remove the notion that America had ever been, de facto or *de iure*, a land of conquest. Marshall's argument from prior discovery provided the historical basis for his celebrated ruling in *Johnson v. M'Intosh* (1823) that private citizens could not purchase lands from Native Americans.[46] Thereafter it became a commonplace. Two decades later, in 1844, the former governor of Tennessee, Aaron V. Brown, in his report to Congress concerning the Oregon territory, confidently declared of the Indian tribes in the region that they enjoyed "no higher title to the soil than that founded by simple occupancy" and to be therefore "incapable to transfer their title to any other power than the Government which claims the jurisdiction of their territory by right of discovery".[47]

The colonists, and the citizens of the still nascent United States, had good reason for wishing to distance themselves for any territorial claim based on conquest. Marshall clearly shared with his near contemporary Joseph Story and with John Adams the widespread unease that the United States might have been created on lands which had been seized illicitly from their original occupants, who might, therefore, at any time attempt to claim them back again.[48] In view of recent developments in Canada, and the ruling of the Australian High Court in *Mabo v. The State of Queensland* in 1992, conceding that the land of the Meriam peoples of the Murray Islands in the Torres Straits had been unjustly taken from them, he had some grounds for anxiety.[49] For all that he is represented as one of the earliest defenders of aboriginal rights, Marshall, like most of his contemporaries, looked on Indians as what he called "domestic dependent nations",[50] who might possess the "right to retain possession of it [the land] and to use it according to their own discretion" but nevertheless enjoyed greatly diminished "rights to complete sovereignty, as independent nations."[51] If then the English settlers – and by implication the United States as the successor state to the Thirteen Colonies – were to make any claims to have acquired their rights to Indian lands legitimately, they had to have acquired them by any means other than force.

Abercromby, Story, Adams, and Marshall all knew that of all the claims to sovereignty made by the European powers in America, "discovery" had, in what by Marshall's day had become known as "international law", been the most easily discredited. As the English jurists of the seventeenth century were quick to point out, even the Spanish had been reluctant to base assertions of either sovereignty or possession on anything so flimsy. But flimsy or no, discovery had the advantage not only of securing rights of occupation "in nature" but also of distancing the history of the English settlements in America from those of the Spanish, which successive generations of English jurists had maintained were, in fact, little more than usurpations. It was for precisely these reasons that the settlers in Barbados had argued that their lands, genuinely unoccupied, could not possibly be counted as conquests.

Both Marshall and, more immediately, Abercromby were also the beneficiaries of an Enlightenment attempt to detach the legacy of the crumbling
Spanish Empire from that of the more robust and prosperous British and
French settlements. As we shall see in Chapter 6, by the middle of the
eighteenth century it was widely assumed across Europe – even by the
Spanish themselves – that it had been precisely the Spanish obsession with
conquest that by the 1740s had reduced Spain, in Montesquieu's terms, to
little more than a dependency on its own colonies.[52] In his condemnation of
what he took to be the Spanish conception of empire, Montesquieu was
himself picking up on the seventeenth-century English republican James
Harrington's definition of Britain as a state which exercised not *imperium*
over its various dependencies but *patrocinium* (protectorate). This, too, was
how Marshall and Abercromby wished to see it. But if the British Empire –
as it was coming to be named – was now what Edmund Burke called "an
empire of liberty," it could hardly continue to insist that it had been founded
on the same legal grounds as the Spanish. Discovery thus had two distinct
advantages. It distanced the English settlers from their Spanish, Catholic,
and consequently despotic neighbors. And it was one of two grounds –
contract or purchase being the other – that settlers could plausibly cite to
deny usurpation in either natural law or the law of nations.

The trouble with discovery as a title to possession, however, lay not only in
its lack of credibility. Even if it were accepted as a legitimate claim in the way
Marshall insisted it had been, it could never amount to more than something
like a right to first refusal. For behind Marshall's attempts to resuscitate the
argument from discovery lay another legal debate, one which would prove the
most contentious and most widely discussed of all European assertions to
rights in overseas colonies, from Africa to Australia: the debate over terra
nullius, "land of no-one" – the argument that whoever first came on or
discovered unoccupied land could claim rights or property over it.

Although it was never formally adopted by the Crown, some version of
this claim was widely alluded to by the English during the sixteenth and
seventeenth centuries and was still sufficiently compelling as late as 1754 to
prompt the delegates to the Albany Congress, when faced with the prospect
of a French invasion, to argue: "That his Majesty's title to the northern
continent of America appears founded on the discovery thereof first made,
and the possession thereof first taken, in 1497 under a commission from
Henry 7th. of England to Sebastian Cabot."[53] Like the Spanish, and the
French, the English also made use of far-fetched arguments for sovereignty in
the New World on the basis of a supposed dynastic succession from some
earlier, and generally mythical, act of discovery. In 1578, John Dee presented
Queen Elizabeth with a brief treatise entitled the *Limits of the British
Empire*. It is one of the earliest attempts to demarcate the frontiers between
the Spanish and British spheres in the Atlantic and to sketch out a role for the
still largely hypothetical "British Empire" (as well as being the first text to

use the phrase).[54] Elizabeth, Dee argued, had a right to occupy America not only because of the Cabots' "prior discovery" but also because the first European to land in America had not, in fact, been Columbus, but a Welsh Prince named Lord Madoc. In about 1170, Madoc, "sonne of *Owen Gwynedd*", had sailed to America in a coracle and founded a colony "in the province then named *Iaquaza* (but of late Florida) or into some provinces and territories neere ther aboutes".[55] With the accession of the Tudors and the Acts of Union between England and Wales in 1536 and 1543, Madoc had become a direct ancestor of Elizabeth. The use of this myth has an analogy, although Dee makes no reference to it, in the Spanish claim that America had first been colonized by shipwrecked Carthaginians, had thus been absorbed into the Roman Empire, and subsequently by translation, had become a part of the domains of Charles V as Holy Roman Emperor.[56]

The Madoc story became ever more picturesque with every retelling. In his *True Report of the New Found Land* of 1583, George Peckham went so far as to argue that when in 1520, according to the story provided by Hernán Cortés in his *Second Letter of Relation* describing his conquest of Mexico, the "Aztec Emperor" Moctezuma surrendered his lands to Cortés on the grounds that (in Peckham's rendering) "we are not the naturally of this Countrey ... our forefathers came from a farre Countrey, and their King ... returned again to his natural Countrey saying, he would send such as should rule and governe us", he could only have been referring to Madoc – not, as Cortés had claimed, to Charles V, who had never set foot in America.[57] This hypothesis was then backed up by some bogus etymology to the effect that the word "penguin" had the same meaning in both Welsh and Nahuatl, implying that the latter language was a derivation of the former. The Madoc story, of course, also implied that, in terms of the *translatio imperii*, the English might lay claim not only to all the lands north of Florida but also to the entire American continent.[58] Despite its vagueness, the thinness of the evidence, and the fact that no serious claim to regions which the English Crown always officially accepted as sovereign Spanish territory was ever made on the basis of the story, it was repeated by Richard Hakluyt in the opening chapters of the American volume of his *Principal Navigations* with the claim that it showed that "the West Indies were discovered and inhabited 322 yeares before Columbus made his first voyage", and it was still being deployed as late as the 1730s as, if nothing else, in David Armitage's words, a "stick with which to beat the Spanish".[59] The Spanish for their part, however, appear to have ignored it entirely.

Both the claims on behalf of the Cabots and the Madoc myth shared another inconvenience besides their inherent implausibility. For even if the Cabots could possibly be said to have discovered the whole of North America, even if anyone so unlikely as Prince Madoc had in fact sailed there and claimed it for the Tudor dynasty, it would still be the case that, on general agreement, such an act would have had no legal force without some measure of actual occupation. As Hugo Grotius argued in 1608 against, in this case, the Portuguese claim to sovereignty in the Indian Ocean, "discovery" (*invenio*) implied not merely seeing for the first time but also possession. Discovery, he claimed, "be not sufficient for dominion, because possession is also required, seeing it is one thing to have a thing, another to have a right to obtain it".[60] On the whole both the Spanish and the British agreed with him. As Francisco de Vitoria had concluded of his own sovereign's claims on these grounds: "Discovery of itself provides no support for possession of these lands, any more than it would if they had discovered us."[61] In both cases the premises were as evidently absurd as the conclusion.

Over a century later, Richard Price would make the same point in exactly the same language. "If sailing along a coast can give a right to a country", he wrote in 1776, "then might the people of Japan become, as soon as they please, the proprietors of Britain."[62] This, as Price also pointed out, was the real theoretical weakness of the arguments set out in the Spanish Bulls of Donation. For "it is not a donation that grants *dominium* but consequent delivery of that thing and the subsequent possession thereof". "Nothing but possession by a colony, a settlement or a fortress," Arthur Young had written a few years earlier, "is now allowed to give a right from discovery."[63] Clearly the setting up of stone crosses, planting flags, burying bottles and other such devices to which generations of Europeans had resorted were quaint and wholly insubstantial as legally recognizable claims to possession. "To pass by and eye", as the French king François I once icily informed the Spanish ambassador, "is no title of possession."[64]

Before the English could claim that discovery had made them legitimate masters of America, therefore, they had not only to have been there first but also to have exercised some kind of actual sovereignty. It was in implicit recognition of this that when Richard Hakluyt (who as the translator of *The Free Sea* was fully aware of the force of Grotius' arguments) drew up a document, laying out "the true limits" of the Spanish and Portuguese domains, he went to some length to stress that the English were in North America not only "by right of first discovery performed by Sebastian Cabot at y$^e$ cost of King Henry ye 7$^{th}$" but also on grounds of "actual possession taken on y$^e$ behalf and under ye sovereign authoritie of hir Mat$^{ie}$ by y$^e$ severall deputies of Sir Walter Ralegh. ... As likewise of Sir Humphrey Gilbert, Sir Martin Frobisher and Mr. John Davies and others."[65]

In fact, however, in a great many of the areas to which the English laid claim, their presence was merely proclamatory or cartographic. In 1609, at a time when the only English presence consisted of a handful of settlers in the malarial swamps along the banks of the St. James River, the first Royal Charter for the Virginia Company declared it exercised jurisdiction over all

territories in America either appertaining unto us, or which are not now
actually possessed by any Christian prince or people, situate, lying and being
all along the sea coasts between four and thirty degrees of northerly latitude
from the equinoctial line and five and forty degrees of the same latitude, and in
the main land between the same four and thirty and five and forty degrees, and
the islands thereunto adjacent or within one hundred miles of the coast
thereof.[66]

In fact, the English knew little either of the real extent of these territories or
of the nature of their inhabitants. The charter's outlandish territorial claims
belonged to the language of international diplomacy and were intended to
establish primacy over any other European power in the region, in particular
the French. As the drafters of the charter would have known, no right of
discovery could ever be made undisputedly against any prior occupant.
Sovereignty, that is, required not only discovery and a real presence. It also
required that the territories being occupied should be truly vacant, or terra
nullius. "I like a plantation in a pure soil," Francis Bacon had written in
1625, "that is, where people are not displaced to the end to plant in others.
For else it is rather an extirpation than a plantation."[67]

*Terra nullius* is a principle which has been much discussed, and it remains
a key issue at stake in contemporary Australian and Canadian disputes over
the rights of indigenous peoples.[68] It therefore requires some clarification.
The term itself, although widely used by historians in reference to claims
made in the early modern period, does not, in fact, appear in legal documents linked to the settlement of the Americas before the nineteenth century.[69] It originates in Justinian's *Digest XLI.* 1 and the – more often cited –
law *Ferae bestiae*, of the *Institutes* (II. 1. 2), which simply states: "Natural
reason admits the title of the first occupant to that which previously had no
owner." It is also significant that the idea of vacancy, of being "of no-one",
is one in natural law that, in common with many such general claims,
Justinian's lawyers had absorbed into the Roman civil law. No such process
was available, however, in English law, and precisely because it was in origin
a *natural* right, whose only codification is Justinian's brief entries, the
principle of terra or res nullius is expressed in a number of different and
sometimes frankly contradictory ways. This has led some modern historians
to argue that, as a legal claim to possession in America, terra nullius was
devised ex post facto – as indeed it seems to have been done by Marshall. But
although Marshall was clearly, for good political reasons, overstating the
case, some version of the terra nullius argument, if not the term itself, had
been in use since at least the early seventeenth century.

What constituted a terra nullius posed considerable legal difficulties and
had far-reaching political and ethical implications. What did it mean for a
land to belong to "no-one?" In Roman law any territory which had not been
formally enclosed in some manner and could not be defended, or had once

been occupied but was now abandoned, was held to be vacant. "In the Law of Nature and of Nations," John Donne told the members of the Virginia Company in 1622, "a land never inhabited by any, or utterly derelicted and immemorially abandoned by the former inhabitants, becomes theirs that will possess it."[70] In the American context, however, such an account would have left very little space for European occupation. Most, if not quite all, of the eastern seaboard of North America was clearly neither uninhabited nor "utterly derelicted" nor "immemorially abandoned," no matter what the Virginia Company might think.[71]

This argument raised other difficulties. As its opponents frequently pointed out, even in Europe there existed large tracts of land – the most contentious being the royal forests – which were essentially "vacant," yet they did not therefore become the property of anyone who chose to settle on them. The same general argument was also applied to the territories within the Ottoman Empire, which were widely believed to be effectively "unused" and thus might similarly be claimed as terrae nullius by Europeans. But even Alberico Gentili, although a firm proponent of the claim that "God did not create the world to be empty" and generally prepared to concede extensive rights to Europeans over non-Europeans on the grounds of their greater technical capacities, was certain that, although the occupation of lands formally under the jurisdiction of the Ottoman State would be licit, the settlers would, nevertheless, be bound to accept the sovereignty of the Sultan.[72]

A more demanding criterion had, therefore, to be found. This was based upon what came to be called "improvement". The obligation on any holder of land deemed to be terra nullius to "improve" it was applied literally, by both the English and the French. In 1648 the General Court of Massachusetts decreed that anyone who received a grant of land by what the court termed *vacuum domicilium* but did not build on or "improve" it within a space of three years would lose it.[73] The concept of improvement also had its origins in natural law. Since antiquity, it had been assumed that one of the features of mankind was the uniquely human ability to transform nature, or, in conventional Aristotelian terms, to make actual what was otherwise only potential. This was the root meaning of "technology." Possession and sovereignty were consequently acts which established relationships between persons and their external and social worlds. Because those who failed to develop nature's potentiality could not be counted as true persons, they could not possibly establish such relationships. "God and his Reason," wrote John Locke in what was to become in English the most influential formulation of this supposition,

commanded him to subdue the Earth, *i.e.* improve it for the benefit of Life, and therein lay something upon it that was his own, his labour. He that in his Obedience to this Command of God, subdued, tilled and sowed any part of it, thereby annexed to it something that was his *Property*, which another had no Title to, nor could without injury take from him.[74]

Locke's celebrated theory of property is, in effect, a development of *Ferae bestiae*, and it clearly evolved in the context of the debates over the rights of the American Indians in the years preceding the Glorious Revolution. What Locke had done, however, and which no previous writer on the topic had attempted, was to associate the claims to possession with those of sovereignty, because now what was being argued was that only persons who lived in civil society could possibly exercise property rights. What this implied in the American context was far-reaching. Nothing short of agricultural exploitation and a recognizable civil society could provide grounds for legitimate political control. The Native Americans, by general consent, lacked the capacity to employ culture in this manner. They might live on the land. But since, in Robert Cushman's words, "they run over the grass as do also the foxes and wild beasts," they could not be said to possess it.[75] And because they did not possess it, any attempt on their part to prevent the Europeans from putting it to its proper, natural, and in the terms employed by Locke, also God-ordained use, constituted a violation of the natural law. As such they could, in Locke's celebrated denunciation, "be destroyed as a *Lion or a Tiger*, one of those wild Savage beasts, with whom Men can have no Society nor Security". Furthermore, under the terms of the *ius ad bellum* (the law, that is, which governs the condition under which a war may be waged), the would-be settlers might make war on such peoples "to seek reparation upon any injury received from them".[76] In other words, the seizure of the lands from "those wild Savage beasts" might indeed involve conquest. But now it would be wholly legitimate under natural law, rather than a status established under English civil law.

Despite the considerable difficulties it presented, and for all that it involved a necessarily slippery distinction between possession and sovereignty, some version of the argument from improvement became perhaps the most enduring of the natural rights claims to overseas occupation. The colonists who throughout the seventeenth, and well into the eighteenth, century had maintained that their rights depended on purchase from legitimate indigenous land owners gradually began to turn to one or another version of the "agriculturalist" argument – as it has come to be called – to support what were, in effect, claims to both legal and political independence from the Crown. As the New Jersey jurist, Robert Hunter Morris, put it in the mid-eighteenth century: "If the people settling ... the British Dominions in America can derive property in soil or powers of government from any source other than the Crown which by the laws of England is the fountain of powers and property then they are as much independent of the Crown & Nation of Britain as any people whatever."[77]

There was a further feature of terra nullius: it belonged to the same essentially existential juridical argument as an equally enduring Roman conception, namely, prescription. This allowed for long-term de facto occupation *(praescriptio longi temporis)* to be recognized *de iure* as conferring retrospective rights of property and of jurisdiction. In other words, it came as close as was humanly possible in historical fact to the condition of auto-chthony. Despite its Roman origins, it was entirely in keeping with most English constitutional thinking and with the process of the English common law. "Our Constitution is a prescriptive Constitution" declared Edmund Burke:

> It is a Constitution, whose sole authority is that it has existed time out of mind. ... Prescription is the most solid of all titles, *not only to property, but, which is more to secure that property to Government.* ... It is a better presumption even of the choice of a nation, far better than any sudden or temporary arrangement by actual election. Because a nation is not an idea only of local extent and individual momentary aggregation, but it is an idea of continuity, which extends in time as well as in numbers, and in space.[78] [Emphasis added.]

The legitimacy of a state or condition, that is, depended on its continual and successful existence. Crucially, because prescription relied on objective conditions, it was able to transform natural into legal rights; and in the end, in America, it was always legal rights which were under discussion. Prescription, however, also presented considerable difficulties of interpretation, particularly in the American context. One of the most obvious was the length of time required to establish title. The English, claimed Robert Johnson in 1609, had been in Virginia "long since without any interruption or invasion either of the Savages (the natives of the country) or any other Prince or people," which conferred on James I the right to grant "rule or Dominion" over all "those English and Indian people."[79] In fact, "long since" amounted to little more than two years' continuous presence, and it is unlikely that any jurist, however zealous, would have accepted that as sufficient. Furthermore, as Grotius was to claim against the Portuguese, prescription, like discovery required some act of settlement to be binding. In 1580 an anonymous agent acting for the Crown replied to the Spanish demand that the English should stay out of America and that the existence of a few settlements and the naming "of rivers and capes" in the Americas did not constitute possession because "prescription without possession is not valid".[80]

Despite all its obvious legal flaws, however, prescription, like terra nullius, was generally accepted by a large number of English jurists. Like terra nullius, it has had a long life in the subsequent history of international law. And because it was also widely held to be a part of the law of nations, it could be said to apply to all peoples everywhere. Robert Ferguson, one of the champions of the abortive scheme to create a settlement of Scotsmen in the Isthmus of Darien in 1699, acknowledged that the only rights which the Spaniards might have in America derived exclusively from their "claim and upon the foot of prescription thro' their having inhabited, occupied and inherited them for 200 years without interruption, disseizure or dispossession".[81] This implied that Ferguson's own attempts to supplant them would be invalid in law, unless, as he hoped would happen, the indigenous people turned out to welcome the Scots as saviors from Spanish tyranny – which, unsurprisingly perhaps, they failed to do.


IV

The other argument, which John Marshall claimed was "not once alluded to" in any "single grant from the British Crown" until the eighteenth century, is cessation. In fact, however, British colonists, like their French and Dutch, and later Swedish and other European counterparts, made wide and varied use of land purchases and of several kinds of land grants arrived at through treaty. Indeed, for most colonists, purchase, gift, or treaty was the most usual way in which individual colonists had acquired their land, and had been so from the beginning.[82] Whether in the Chesapeake or in Massachusetts, the earliest settlers purchased land whenever controversies over occupancy threatened. As with all such claims, the Crown's right to grant a patent in the first place was not in question. Sovereignty, however, did not provide rights to property. Even after independence when much of the semi-independent status granted to the Indians by the Crown had been swept away, the new United States claimed only the right to preempt attempts by other nations to take possession. In their recognition of aboriginal title, as in so much else, the British were following French and most immediately Dutch examples, in particular after the Anglo-Dutch conflicts in the Connecticut valley in the 1630s. The Dutch West India Company, eager as always to distance itself from the behaviour of the Spanish "less we call down the wrath of God upon our unrighteousness beginning," insisted that all land had to be "righteously" acquired without "craft or fraud," so that, in the words of the colony's governor, Willem Verhulst, in 1625, none of the Algonquin inhabitants of the Delaware and Hudson rivers should be "driven away by force or threats, but by good words be persuaded to leave, or be given something therefore for their satisfaction". In accordance with this general principle, the following year Vrehulst's successor, Pieter Minuit, famously purchased Manhattan Island for sixty guilders.[83]

The Dutch may have preferred the idea of cessation because of religious scruples and because their presence in America was always overstretched. The British had similar motives for denying their own official status as conquerors. They were also aware, however, that a conqueror in the service of a monarch could only ever be a subject, and, at least by feudal contract, a vassal. If, in contrast, the settlers had purchased their lands, they might claim some measure of independence from the Crown or, where this applied, from the proprietary holder of the colony. It was for this reason that in 1639, the proprietor of Maryland declared all lands purchased from the Indians subject to forfeiture.

Furthermore, if the colonists had purchased their lands, or acquired them through treaty, it followed that the indigenous peoples must have been in legitimate possession of them, otherwise the lands would not have been theirs to sell. The English, insisted Edward Rawson in *The Revolution in New England Justified* (1689), had "purchased from the Natives their right to the soil in that part of the world, not withstanding what right they had by virtue of their charter from the kings of England." Rawson was a supporter of the revolt against the Dominion of New England – to which the title of his pamphlet refers, and in his eyes, one of the more heinous crimes of the late governor Sir Edmund Andros had been precisely to dissolve all land claims on the basis of what Andros had dismissed as "pretended purchases from the Indians" on the grounds that "from the Indians no title can be Derived". If that were allowed to stand, a group of prominent Bostonians protested, "no Man was owner of a Foot of Land in all the Colony".[84] As Rawson stressed elsewhere, any attempt by the Crown to limit the rights to self-determination which the English had acquired by "venturing their lives overseas to enlarge the King's Dominions" made them a conquered people "deprived of their English liberties and in the same condition with the slaves in France or Turkey". In 1721, Jeremiah Dummer, the agent for the New England colonies, reiterated the same point. There could exist "no other right than that in which the honest New-England planters rely on having purchased it with their money. The Indian title, therefore, as much as it is decry'd and undervalued here, seems the only fair and just one."[85]

If, however, America were a land of conquest, and thus a part of the royal demesne, any contract to dispose of any part of it between parties who were both subjects of the Crown was necessarily invalid. In addition, even if such purchases were considered to be merely private agreements, they were, as many subsequent historians have pointed out, generally fraudulent. At least by implication, this was the point made by the Royal Proclamation of 1763, which set out the principles of government for the lands acquired by the British by the Treaty of Paris at the end of the Seven Years' War and which would become one of the principal grievances leveled against the crown by the colonists.

The purpose of the Proclamation was to bind the former New France much more tightly to the Crown than the original English settlements in North America. It had been established, declared the Board of Trade in 1772, for "the preservation of the colonies in due subordination to, and dependence upon, the mother country". To achieve this objective the Crown was compelled to limit the damage that might be inflicted on Native American interests by colonists' intrusions on their lands. Hence, the Proclamation conferred on what came to be called the "Aboriginal Peoples of America", a form of ill-defined *de iure* nationhood that ceded a large measure of autonomy to "the several Nations or Tribes of Indians." The Proclamation accepted that the Indians had use – but not true possession – of "such Parts of our Dominions and Territories as, not having been ceded to or purchased by Us, are reserved to them, or any of them, as their Hunting Grounds". The Proclamation also defined all the lands west of the Appalachians as "under our Sovereign Protection and Dominion for the use of the said Indians", and it forbade any future settlement there.[86] This last injunction reinforced the Treaty of Easton of 1758, which had prohibited any settlement west of the Alleghenies. The bans were unworkable in practice, not least because the Iroquois, the Cherokee, and the Creek all had ancestral lands to the east of the line, while by 1763 there were already settlements from Virginia to the west.

The Proclamation was not, however, merely an attempt to limit the colonists' powers of acquisition. Nor was it an isolated case. In many ways it can be seen as the final resolution to a legal dispute dating from the 1690s between the Mohegan nation and the government of Connecticut, to which John Bulkley's *An Inquiry into the Right of the Aboriginal Natives to Land in America* had been a contribution. The Mohegans had argued that they were a sovereign nation and, as such, could not be deprived of their lands by the claim that they "lack such thing as a civil Polity, nor [do they possess] hardly any one of the circumstances essential to the existence of a state".[87] On August 24, 1705, the Privy Council had decided in favor of the Mohegans. Despite fierce lobbying from the colonists, it reaffirmed the decision the following year. Not until 1763, however, was the matter decided by a formal royal decree intended to be irrevocable. It also had a long subsequent history. It was incorporated into the British North America Act of 1867 (now renamed the Constitution Act, 1867) and still forms the basis for much of the dealing between the Canadian federal government and Canada's Aboriginal Peoples. As recently as 1982, Lord Denning declared that the Proclamation was as binding today "as if there had been included in the statute a sentence: "'The aboriginal peoples of Canada shall continue to have all their rights and freedoms as recognized by the Royal Proclamation of 1763'."[88]

The Proclamation was clearly intended to grant a measure of legal autonomy to the Native Americans, as successive interpreters have supposed. However, the repeated reference in the document to the "sovereignty", "protection", and "dominion" that the British Crown exercised across the whole of America, north of New Spain, Florida, and California makes it clear that this autonomy was also intended to be severely limited. The Indian "nations" may have been self-governing communities with rights over their own ancestral lands. But they certainly could make no claims to independence from His Majesty, and because their rights did comprise the king's seisin fee, they were, in effect, perpetual tenants. They exercised, in effect, only what Marshall later deemed, in *Johnson v. M'Intosh*, a "right of occupancy" – use, rather than full property rights – because they lacked, in Marshall's words, the "ultimate dominion" which had been granted to the "nations of Europe ... a power to convey the soil, while yet in possession of the natives".[89] Similarly, their political status was severely restricted by the presence of an "ultimate" form of jurisdiction that, in the Romanized formulation in which these distinctions were made, was also conceived as a form of property – *dominium jurisdictionis*. They were, in Bruce Clark's words, "sovereign in the same way that the colonial government was sovereign – that is vested with a delimited jurisdiction independent of all other governments except as against the imperial government".[90] As John Pocock has pointed out, it was only by assuming that the United States had acquired the imperial authority formerly exercised by the Crown that Marshall was able to make his famous and still authoritative ruling that the Native American peoples constituted nations.[91]

Although the Proclamation does not explicitly restate the rights of the Crown through conquest, it does insist that, because "great frauds and abuses have been committed in purchasing lands of the Indians, to the great prejudice of our interest, and to the great dissatisfaction of the said Indians", all further purchases had to be made "for Us in our name at some public meeting or assembly of the said Indians". They had, that is, to be a matter of public law, rather than private contract.

But the argument from purchase was too powerful to be disposed of so easily. As Richard Price argued in 1776, if the lands of the settlers had indeed been purchased and developed – and he was in no doubt that they had – "It is, therefore now on a double account their property, and no power on earth can have any right to disturb them in the possession of it, or to take from them, without their consent, any part of its produce."[92] Price was a staunch defender of the cause of the American colonists and his arguments, like Dummer's before him, were intended not only to clear the original settlers of the charge, which so many English writers leveled against the Spanish, of illicit occupation on the basis of conquest; they were also meant to give greater weight to the supposition that the colonies had been original and thus effectively independent foundations, over which, in Dummer's words, "the English king could give ... nothing more than a bare *right of preemption*".[93] For the argument from purchase or concession, backed by the claim to have improved the land, also gave added force to the colonists' resistance to a government that had denied them the right of representation in Parliament.

There was further advantage for the colonists to any claim based on free sale or concession. For if they had acquired their lands in this manner, they might also, thereby, evade the monarch's right to limit the movement of his subjects – the right of *ne exeat regno* – which the monarch held under common (and, many would argue, under natural) law. Later opponents of colonial rule, such as Richard Bland, whom Jefferson described as a "most learned and logical man, profound in constitutional law", would argue that in fact the colonies had been Lockean foundations created like the first human societies, quite literally out of the state of nature. "When subjects are deprived of their civil rights, or are dissatisfied with the place they hold in the community", he wrote in 1766, they have a natural right to quit the society of which they are members, and to retire into another country. Now when men exercise this right of withdrawing themselves from their country, they recover their natural freedom and independence; the jurisdiction and sovereignty of the states they have quitted ceases; and if they unite, and by common consent take possession of a new country and form themselves into a political society, they become a sovereign state, independent of the state from which they separated.[94]

Once established in their new country, their rights, which could only of course be natural rights, could be based only on terra nullius or purchase or a combination of both. Only then would the settler population be in a position to demand for themselves the same kind of sovereign rights that the Crown was claiming to exercise on their behalf.

V

In the end, the prolonged dispute over the legality of the occupation of America resolved itself into a dispute over the sources of sovereign authority. Who, in other words, had the right to make the law, and on behalf of whom? In 1776, Adam Smith complained that the rulers of Great Britain

have for more than a century past, amused the people with the imagination that they possessed a great empire on the west side of the Atlantic. This empire, however, has hitherto existed in imagination only. It has hitherto been not an empire but the project of an empire; not a gold mine, but the project of a gold mine; a project which has cost, which continues to cost, and which, if pursued in the same way as it has been hitherto, is likely to cost, immense expence, without being likely to bringing any profit.[95]

In Smith's view, the de facto situation in the colonies, where every individual settlement enjoyed its own peculiar rights, where laws were made at a local level, and where separate constitutions and even separate semi-feudal hierarchies (think of the Carolinas with its Caribbean Caciques, and Hanoverian Landgraves) might be established, could hardly be an "empire" as the term was currently employed. All that Britain had acquired in the pursuit of this doomed project was a substantial public debt and the burden of having to fight evermore costly colonial wars against its European rivals. This imaginary British Empire had been brought into being largely because, unlike the French or the Spanish, the English Crown had never had any clear conception of what the grounds for the occupation of the Americas were. As we have seen, the Crown had generally insisted that its colonies overseas were lands of conquest, even though very few acts of conquest had actually taken place. Under English common law, conquest made them integral parts of the royal demesne and subject directly to royal command, not Parliament. Logically the colonists were not, as was later claimed, represented "virtually" in Parliament; they were represented literally, just not in person but by the "King in Parliament". Yet the Crown regularly set its own jurisdictional claims aside and not only made grants of lands to its subjects, but also permitted those subjects to make their own laws – something which none of the other European monarchies, all of whose colonies were governed by codes issued in the metropolis, ever did. What this meant was that in practice, if never in law, the Crown shared sovereignty with its settler populations. As an anonymous contributor to the *Pennsylvania Journal and Weekly Advertiser* in March 1766 expressed it: "In a confederacy of States independent of each other yet united under one head, such as I conceive the British empire at present to be, all the power of legislation may subsist full and complete in each part, and the respective legislatures be absolutely independent of each other."

After 1763, when they found themselves faced with a government determined to regain full sovereignty over all its domains, both within the British Isles and overseas, the American colonists turned to those arguments that, in natural rather than civil law, could help them to secure the survival of their de facto rights. This demanded that they reexamine, and very substantially rewrite, the legal history of the original settlements. For questions as to how and by what authority indigenous peoples had been deprived of what in natural law was usually conceded to be their *dominium* would in the end determine not so much the status of whatever remained of *those* peoples as the future legal status of the English colonies and their inhabitants and, more importantly, the status of what the successors to those colonies might be. The "British-Americans" – as Thomas Jefferson called them – waited until the early eighteenth century before they began to contemplate the awful possibility of separation from the "mother country". But as many of those from the Count to Aranda in the 1770s to Simón Bolívar in the 1820s – both whom we shall meet again – who watched to see what the consequences of independence would ultimately be for the Spanish settlements to the south had seen very clearly, the forms of government and the legal system in effect in the British colonies had from the beginning established a de facto independence that no other European monarchy had permitted its settler populations.

### Endnotes

1 *De regis catholici praestantia, eius regalibus, iuribus et praerogatiuis commentari* (Milan, 1611), 332.
2 See p. 16.
3 Edmund and William Burke, *An Account of the European Settlements in America* (London, 1757), II, 288–9.
4 Quoted in Craig Yirush, *Settlers, Liberty and Empire: The Roots of Early American Political Theory 1675–1775* (Cambridge: Cambridge University Press, 2011), 79.
5 *The Expansion of England*, 12.
6 *Works*, Charles Francis Adams, ed. (Boston, 1850–6), IV, 37.

7 John Elliott, *Empires of the Atlantic World: Britain and Spain in America 1492–1830* (Yale: Yale University Press, 2006), 76.

8 Quoted in Stuart Banner, *How the Indians Lost Their Land: Law and Power on the Frontier* (Cambridge, MA: Belknap Press, 2005), 13.

9 "Etablissement de la Compagnie des Indes Occidentales", in *Edits, ordonnances royaux, déclarations et arrêts du conseil d'état du Roi concernant le Canada* (Quebec, 1854–6), I, 46.

10 Quoted in John Elliott, *Empires of the Atlantic World*, 75, and on the difference between Spanish and English attitudes to conversion, see pp. 74–8.

11 "The Second Charter Granted by Charles II to the Proprietors of Carolina", in *Historical Collection of South Carolina; Embracing Many Rare and Valuable Pamphlets and Other Documents Relating to the State from Its First Discovery until Its Independence in the Year 1776* (New York, 1836), II, 44.

12 Locke, *Second Treatise on Government*, 2.175, 403.

13 "A Discourse on Government with Relation to Militias", in *The Political Works of Andrew Fletcher* (London, 1737), 66.

14 On the Portuguese, see pp. 136–7.

15 *First Institute of the Laws of England* (Philadelphia, 1826–7), 249b.

16 Quoted in John Thomas Juricek, "English Claims in North America to 1660: A Study in Legal and Constitutional History", unpublished Ph.D. thesis, University of Chicago, 1970, 512, 669–71.

17 "Unto your Majesties Tytle Royall to these Forene Regions and Ilandes do appertayne 4 poyntes", in *The Limits of the British Empire*, Ken MacMillan (with Jennifer Abeles) eds. (Westport, CT; London: Praeger 2004), 48.

18 The wording is from *Inter caetera*, printed in *Bulas Alejandrinas de 1493 texto y traducción*, 19.

19 "The First Charter of Virginia; April 10, 1606", The Avalon Project http:// avalon.law.yale.edu/17th_century/va01.asp

20 "Epistle Dedicatory to Sir Walter Ralegh", in *The Original Writings and Correspondence of the Two Richard Hakluyts*, E. G. R. Taylor ed. (London: Hakluyt Society, 1935), II, 368.

21 "A Discourse on Western Planting", *The Original Writings and Correspondence of the two Richard Hakluyts*, II, 215.

22 Ibid., 216.

23 *A Relation of the Second Voyage to Guiana* (London, 1596), A1b.

24 On this, see David Armitage, *The Ideological Origins of the British Empire*, (Cambridge: Cambridge University Press, 2000), 73–5. Richard Tuck is clearly right, however, in saying that religion generally played a far lesser role in English motives for colonization than it did in the Spanish. *The Rights of War and Peace*, 110.

25 *The Works of the Pious and Profoundly-Learned Joseph Mede* (corrected and enlarged according to the author's own manuscripts) (London, 1672), 980–1.

26 Quoted in Karen Ordahl Kupperman, *Settling with the Indians: The Meeting of English and Indian Cultures in America, 1580–1640* (Totowa, NJ: Rowman and Littlefield, 1980), 166.

27 William Strachey, *The Historie of Travell into Virginia Britania*, Louis B. Wright and Virginia Freund eds. (London, 1953), 24. I am grateful to David Armitage for drawing my attention to this text.

28 *The Reports of Sir Edward Coke*, Book VII (London, 1658), 601–2.

29 *A Letter to Edmund Burke, Esq., A Member of Parliament for the City of Bristol . . . in Answer to his Printed Speech* (Gloucester, 1775), 18–20.

30 "The Rights of the British Colonies Asserted and Proved" [Boston, 1764], in Bernard Bailyn ed., *Pamphlets of the American Revolution*. I: 1750–1765 (Cambridge, MA: Harvard University Press, 1965), 422.

31 Quoted in Kent Mcneil, "A Question of Title: Has the Common Law Been Misapplied to Dispossess the Aboriginals?", *Monash University Law Review* 16 (1990), 91–110 at 100.

32 *Leviathan*, I, XXVI, 200.

33 "Fundamental Constitutions of Carolina", in *John Locke: Political Essays*, Mark Goldie ed. (Cambridge: Cambridge University Press, 1997), 161–2.

34 *The Reports of Sir Edward Coke*, Book VII, 601–2.

35 Sir William Blackstone, *Commentaries on the Laws of England*, Stanley Katz ed. (Chicago: University of Chicago Press, 1979), I, 105.

36 Howell, *State Trials*, II, 648; *The Case of Ireland's Being Bound by Acts of Parliament* (London, 1698), 148.

37 "Rapport fait à l'Assemblée Nationale, sur les colonies, au nom des Comitées de Constitution, de Marine, d'Agriculture, de Commerce et des Colonies, le 23 Septembre, 1791" [Paris], 6–7.

38 "The parliament doth recognize that these two realms of England and Scotland are under one imperial crown. The parliament doth not say under one monarchy or one king, which might refer to the person, but under one imperial crown, which cannot but be applied to the sovereign power of regiment comprehending both kingdoms." "The Case of the Post-Nati of Scotland", in *The Works of Francis Bacon*, James Spedding ed. (London, 1857–74), VII, 670–1.

39 "On the Tenure of the Manor of East Greenwich" [January 11, 1766], in Benjamin Franklin, *The Papers of Benjamin Franklin*, William B. Wilcox ed. (New Haven and London: Yale University Press, 1959–1993), XIII, 21.

40 Quoted in P. J. Marshall, *The Impeachment of Warren Hastings* (Oxford: Oxford University Press, 1965), 74.

41 Quoted in Gordon Wood, *The Creation of the American Republic 1776–1787* (New York and London: W.W. Norton, 1972), 5.

42 "On the Plantation Trade", in *The Political and Commercial Works of that Celebrated Writer, Charles D'Avenant LL.D.* (London, 1771), II, 30–1.

43 *The Life of George Washington: Commander in Chief of the American Forces during the War Which Established the Independence of His Country, and First President of the United States* (to which is prefixed, an introduction containing a compendious view of the colonies planted by the English on the continent of North America) (London, 1804–7), I, 106–7. (The second part was later re-issued as *A History of the Colonies Planted by the English on the Continent of North America*.)

44 "Representation of the Present State of the Colonies", *The Papers of Benjamin Franklin*, V, 368.

45 "An Examination of the Acts of Parliament Relative to the Trade and the Government of Our American Colonies" (1752) and "*De Jure et Gubernatione Coloniarum*, or An Inquiry in the Nature, and the Rights of Colonies, Ancient,

and Modern" (1774), Jack P.Greene, Charles F. Mullett, and Edward C. Papenfuse, Jr., eds. (Philadelphia: American Philosophical Society, 1986), 200.
46  U.S. (8 Wheaton) 543.
47  Quoted in Steven T. Newcomb, "The Evidence of Christian Nationalism in Federal Indian Law: The Doctrine of Discovery, *Johnson v. McIntosh* and Plenary Power", *New York Review of Law and Social Change* 20 (1993), 303–41 at 319.
48  "The European power which had first discovered the country and set up marks of possession was deemed to have gained the right, though it had not yet formed a regular colony there." *Commentaries on the Constitution of the United States* (Boston, 1891), vol. 1 [first published 1833], 106.
49  This is the celebrated Mabo case. *Commonwealth Law Reports* (Australia) 175 (1991–2). In this case, however, the High Court was disputing the British government's original claim to land rigths in Australia under *terra nullius*, which for Marshall was an entirely legitimate means of acquiring territory.
50  *Cherokee Nation v. Georgia*, U.S. (5 Peters) 1 (1831).
51  *Johnson v. M'Intosh*, U.S. (8 Wheaton) 591–2.
52  See p. 153.
53  "Representation of the Present State of the Colonies", V, 368.
54  What he meant by this, however, was the ancient empire of the British kingdoms supposedly founded by the Trojan soldier Brutus – an Anglo-Saxon counterpart to Aeneas – and the mythical ancestor of King Arthur. Arthur was believed to have conquered thirty kingdoms of the North Atlantic and Scandinavia to form the "British Empire". Ken MacMillan, *Sovereignty and Possession in the English New World, Sovereignty and Possession in the English New World: The Legal Foundations of Empire, 1576–1640* (Cambridge: Cambridge University Press, 2006), 59–60.
55  *The Limits of the British Empire*, 43–4.
56  David Lupher, *Romans in a New World*, 175–7.
57  For the original version of this story and a discussion of the controversy which surrounds it, see Hernán Cortés, *Letters from Mexico*, Anthony Pagden ed. and trans. (London and New Haven: Yale University Press, 1986), 84–7 and 467–9.
58  Quoted in Andrew Fitzmaurice, *Humanism and America: An Intellectual History of English Colonization 1500–1625* (Cambridge: Cambridge University Press, 2003), 151–2. On the history and sources of the myth, see Gwyn A. Williams, *Madoc: The Legend of the Welsh Discovery of America* (London: Methuen, 1979). The Carthaginian origins of America are also mentioned by Hakluyt in the preface to the first part of the *Principal Navigations* (*The Original Writings and Correspondence of the Two Richard Hakluyts*, II, 435). There were other similarly fantastical stories of pre-Columbian "discoveries". The sixteenth-century chronicler Gonzalo Fernández de Oviedo, whom both Dee and Hakluyt had read, claims that the Indies were in fact the mythical Hesperides, supposedly named for the Visigoth King Hespéro. Similarly, the French humanist Guillaume Postel claimed America for France by arguing that America, or "Atlantis" had been colonized by the descendants of Noah's son Japheth who, in Postel's version of the peopling of the world after the Flood, had come from Gaul. See David Armitage, "The New World and British Historical Thought from Richard Hakluyt to William Robertson", in *America in European Consciousness 1493–1750*,

Karen Ordahl Kupperman ed. (Chapel Hill and London: University of North Carolina Press, 1995), 58.

59 "The New World and British Historical Thought from Richard Hakluyt to William Robertson", 58.

60 *The Free Sea*, 13. On the circumstances of Hakluyt's translation, see pp. xxi–xxii.

61 "On the American Indians", 2.3, *Political Writings*, 264–5.

62 "Observations on the Nature of Civil Liberty, the Principles of Government, and the Justice and Policy of the War with America", *Political Writings*, D. O. Thomas ed. (Cambridge University Press: Cambridge, 1991), 40.

63 *Political Essays Concerning the Present State of the British Empire* (London, 1772), 472.

64 Quoted in Marcel Trudel, *The Beginnings of New France, 1524–1663*, Patricia Claxton trans. (Toronto: Toronto University Press, 1973), 38.

65 "The True Limites of All the Countries and Provinces at This Present Actually Possessed by ye Spaniards and Portugales in the West Indies', *The Original Writings and Correspondence of the Two Richard Hakluyts*, II, 423. This was probably intended for use in the peace negotiations with Spain in 1600.

66 *The Three Charters of the Virginia Company of London with Seven Related Documents*, with an introduction by Samuel M. Bemiss (Williamsburg: Jamestown 350th Anniversary Historical Booklets, 1957), 1.

67 "On Plantations", *The Works of Francis Bacon*, VI, 457.

68 See Andrew Fitzmaurice, "The Genealogy of *Terra Nullius*", *Australian Historical Studies* 38 (2007), 1–15 and *Humanism and America*, 140–4, and cf. Michael Connor, *The Invention of Terra Nullius. Historical and Legal Fictions in the Foundation of Australia* (Sydney: Macleay Press, 2005).

69 I would like to thank David Armitage for pointing this out to me.

70 *A Sermon Preached to the Honourable Company of the Virginia Plantation 13 Nov. 1622* (London, 1623), 26.

71 Cf. Jeremiah Dummer's argument that "prior Discovery or Pre-Occupancy as the Civilians speak" was invalid "because that gives a Right only to derelict Lands, which these were not, being full of Inhabitants, who undoubtedly had as good a Title to their own Country, as the Europeans had to theirs". Quoted in Yirush, *Settlers, Liberty and Empire*, 100.

72 *De Iure belli*, 131.

73 *Records of the Governor and Company of the Massachusetts Bay*, Nathaniel Shurtleff ed. (Boston: William White, 1853–4), II, 245.

74 *Second Treatise*, 7, p. 309.

75 *Reasons and Considerations Touching the Lawfullness of Removing out of England into Parts of America* (London, 1622), f.2v.

76 *Second Treatise*, 7, p. 292.

77 Quoted in Brendan McConville, *These Daring Disturbers of the Public Peace: The Struggle for Property and Power in Early New Jersey* (Ithaca: Cornell University Press, 1999), 166.

78 "Speech on the State of Representation of Commons in Parliament", in *Writings and Speeches* (New York: J. F. Taylor, 1901), VII: 94–5.

79 Nova Britannia, Offering Most Excellent Fruites by Planting in Virginia (London, 1609), 47.

80 Quoted (from Camden's *Annales*) by Edward P. Cheyney, "*International Law under Queen Elizabeth*", *English Historical Review* 20 (1905), 659–72, at 660.

81 *A Just and Modest Vindication of the Scots Design, for Having Established a Colony at Darien* (n.p., 1699), 72–5, and for a wider account of the origins of the scheme, see David Armitage, "The Scottish Vision of Empire: Intellectual Origins of the Darien Venture", in *A Union for Empire: Political Thought and the British Union of 1707*, John Robertson ed. (Cambridge: Cambridge University Press, 2006), 45–118.

82 Banner, *How the Indians Lost Their Land*, 10–48.

83 Benjamin Schmidt, *Innocence Abroad: The Dutch Imagination and the New World, 1570–1670* (Cambridge: Cambridge University Press, 2001), 247, 384 n.9.

84 Quoted in Banner, *How the Indians Lost Their Land*, 41–2.

85 Jeremiah Dummer, *A Defence of the New-England Charters* (London, 1721), 14. On Dummer, see Yirush, *Settlers, Liberty and Empire*, 83–112.

86 The text of the Proclamation is printed in Kennedy, *Documents of the Canadian Constitution*, 20–1.

87 Joseph Henry Smith, *Appeals to the Privy Council from the American Plantations* (New York: Columbia University Press, 1950), 434.

88 *R. v. Secretary for Foreign and Commonwealth Affairs* [1982] Law Rep. Q.B. 892, 914.

89 *Johnson v. McIntosh*, U.S. (8 Wheaton) 574. Although the concept of a "right of occupancy" exists in Roman law, Stuart Banner argues that it only came into use in America after Independence and only gained currency with American lawyers in the early nineteenth century. *How the Indians Lost Their Land*, 150–90.

90 *Native Liberty, Crown Sovereignty: The Existing Aboriginal Right of Self-Government in Canada* (Montreal: McGill-Queen's University Press, 1990), 41n.

91 "A Discourse on Sovereignty: Observations on the Work in Progress", in Nicholas Phillipson and Quentin Skinner eds., *Political Discourse in Early-Modern Britain* (Cambridge: Cambridge University Press, 1993), 377–428. It should be noted, however, that the status of "Indian Nations" was subsequently redefined as one which "falls within the description in terms of our Constitution, not of an independent state or sovereign nation, but of an Indian tribe". *Choctaw v. United States*, 119 U.S. 1 (1886) 27.

92 "Observations on the Nature of Civil Liberty, the Principles of Government, and the Justice and Policy of the War with America", *Political Writings*, 40.

93 *A Defence of the New-England Charters*, 13.

94 *An Enquiry into the Rights of the British Colonies*, 12.

95 *An Inquiry into the Nature and Causes of the Wealth of Nations*, II, 946–7 (V. iii). Also see the comments in Harold James, *The Roman Predicament*, 20–1.

# 5

## Occupying the Ocean

### Hugo Grotius and Serafim de Freitas on the Rights of Discovery and Occupation

Adam Smith – echoing the Abbé Guillaume Raynal – famously described the voyages of Columbus and Vasco da Gama as the "greatest and most important" events in the history of mankind.[1] The origin of this conceit, although neither man mentions it, was the Spanish historian Francisco López de Gómara, and some version of it was still being repeated, albeit in a modified form, in the mid-nineteenth century by the Hegelian geographer Ernst Kapp and in the twentieth by Carl Schmitt.[2] But whereas Gómara had seen the discovery of America (he makes no mention of Vasco de Gama) as an event in the history of the spread of Christianity, and Kapp was to see it, together, in his case with the circumnavigation of the globe, as marking the final stage of evolution of human civilization, what both Smith and Raynal understood by their claim was that the discovery of America and of a sea route to India marked the creation of the modern commercial system, of which Raynal's best-selling *Philosophical and Political History of the Two Indies* was both a history and a celebration. Columbus and Gama had, furthermore, not merely transformed geography and hugely increased the amount of transactionable merchandise in the world; they had united mankind, by linking together the four (major) continents of which the world had hitherto been divided.

The story of what the "discovery", and in this context it truly was a discovery not an "encounter", by Europeans of the worlds beyond Europe – first Africa, America, and India, and finally the Pacific – have meant for the European perception of their own environments is a narrative (or rather a series of narratives) whose origins are to be found in the ancient geographical vision of the world.[3] In antiquity this world, the *cosmos* or *mundus* or *orbis terrarum* had traditionally been conceived as an island surrounded by the Ocean – *Okeanos* – an encircling river which constituted the final *periodos* and *peirata*, the boundaries and the limits which enclosed all humanity. This single enclosed landmass was divided into three continents:

Europe, Africa, and Asia. To this hypothetical collectivity the Greek historian Herodotus gave the name *oikoumene*, the "inhabited world". This lent
to what was in fact a vast unknown space some semblance of apparent
cohesion. The *oikoumene* was not merely inhabited but also, in some sense,
unified, which led Herodotus to complain that he could not understand
"why three names, and women's names at that, should have been given to
a tract which is in reality one".[4] What, however, seems most to have
troubled Herodotus, and his Roman heirs as they attempted to exercise
political control over as much of it as they were able, was the isolation in
which most of the denizens of this *oikoumene* actually lived.

   In Cicero's *Somnium Scipionis*, one of the most popular of the Latin texts
which sought to capture some of this anxiety about the limits of human
space, the Roman general Scipio Aemilianus is visited by the shade of his
dead grandfather, the general Scipio Africanus, and granted a vision of a
globe divided into not three, but four inhabited but separate landmasses.
"You see", says, the elder Scipio,

> that the earth is inhabited in only a few portions, and those very small, while
> vast deserts lie between them. ... You see that the inhabitants are so widely
> separated that there can be no communication whatever among the different
> areas; and that some of the inhabitants live in parts of the earth that are
> oblique, transverse and sometimes directly opposite your own, from such
> you can expect nothing surely that is glory.[5]

For Cicero the lesson to be learned from Scipio's dream had been the relative
futility of earthly fame. When, however, Macrobius in the fifth century wrote
his Neoplatonic commentary on Scipio's dream voyage, his concern – and it
was one which would be repeated again and again as the European understanding of the world increased – was that the scattered human groups of
Scipio's dream lacked the ability for reciprocal communication, something
which for Macrobius amounted to a violation of the human condition.[6]

   When in 1434 the first fleet of caravels sponsored by Prince Henry set out
with the intention of rounding Cape Bojador, which jutted out far into the
Atlantic from the Western Sahara and was then believed to mark the limits
of the navigable ocean, the image of the world they carried with them was
not very much different from Herodotus'. The European explorations of the
late fifteenth century, first of Africa then of Asia, however, soon loosened the
hold which the image of an encircling ocean and of scattered oceanic landmasses had had on the European geographical and anthropological
imagination. "Hence we can see", wrote the Portuguese cosmographer
Duarte Pacheco Pereira in 1508, "that the Ocean does not surround
the earth as the philosophers have declared, but rather the earth surrounds
the sea that lies in its hollow and centre."[7] The final discovery of a new
continent confirmed this image of a near continuous global landmass, and
the altered image of the space which humankind occupied led inexorably to

a changed conception of humankind in space. Human history could now be conceived as a narrative of human migration through space and time. As the English geographer Samuel Purchas explained in his collection of voyages of exploration of 1625, *Hakluytus Posthumus, or Purchas his Pilgrimes*, this "Pilgrimes" was not "a Booke of Travels in the World, but the World historified in a World of Voyages and Travels".[8]

For the new historians of oceanic navigation of the sixteenth and seventeenth centuries, for Purchas, for his predecessor Richard Hakluyt, for the earliest natural historian of America Gonzalo Fernández de Oviedo, for Gomes Eannes de Zurara and João de Barros, for Antonio de Herrera, for André Thevet, or Pierre François Charlevoix, the ocean was no longer a boundary, a frontier, but a highway, another kind of *via* which would eventually link together all the peoples of the world both known and still unknown. It was the means of bringing together all the scattered peoples Scipio had only been able to see in a dream. "The globe of the earth", as the Italian humanist Pietro Bembo makes Christopher Columbus declare "is of such a nature that to man has been given the capacity for going through all its parts."[9]

In fulfilling this role, mankind was not only expressing the capacity for *techne*, which was, of course, together with *logos* what marked it off from the brutes, it was also recovering something of the omniscience which had been lost by the Fall. In the preface to one of the earliest attempts to adjust the older spatial understanding of the world to accommodate the existence of America, the *Novus orbis regionum ac insularum veteribus incognitarum* of 1532, the Basle reformer Simon Grynaeus praised the new travelers for having recovered by their action precisely that dominium over the natural world once enjoyed by Adam.[10] For Grynaeus, the navigator together with the geographer, mathematician, and astronomer were God's instruments for the subjugation of nature to man's needs. These were men whose mission was comparable, both in its nobility and the distrust it aroused in the ignorant, to those – the Saints – who had similarly abandoned the settled and known world to seek the word of God. The new navigators, the desert fathers, even Christ and his disciples, could now be said to share something of the same identity.

Nearly a century later, the tirelessly punning Samuel Purchas also appropriated the legend of the expulsion from Eden as the source for the transformation of man's condition from the stationary to the migratory. For mankind, he wrote, "preferring the Creature to the Creator, and therefore is justly turned out of Paradise to wander, a Pilgrime over the world". This act of divine retribution had transformed for Purchas all human history – including the story of Christ's passion, which he called "the greatest of all peregrinations" from God to man and back again – into a narrative of human movement. This narrative, which at least as far as the modern world was concerned, had been initiated by Christ himself and by the Evangelists, who, since they also "planted the Church and settled on her foundations", were not only the first Christian travelers; they were also – and the association was crucial – the first colonists.[11]

All these narratives of modernity are, in broad outline, and in the moments of creation and transmission which they employ, familiar enough. Modern man had broken free from the limits which nature (or the gods or even God) had imposed on him by his capacity to transform the natural world, to transform wood into ships and flax into sails. In that curious collection of texts from the third-century CE, known as the *Corpus Hermeticum*, supposedly the writings of the magus Hermes Trismegistus whose wisdom was believed to predate even that of Moses, the Greek god Hermes is shown at work imprisoning the demiurges – the beings who had helped in the creation of the universe – in human bodies as a punishment for their attempt to rival the creativity of the gods. Even as he does so, the figure of Sarcasm (*Momos*) appears to congratulate him. "It is courageous thing you have done to have created man", he mocks,

> this being with curious eyes and a bragging tongue. For he will push his designing thoughts even to the limits of the earth. [These men] will extend their audacious busy hands even to the edge of the sea. They will cut down the forests, and will drive them [i.e., as ships] over the seas from bank to bank, all the way to those lands that are furthest away.[12]

By the late sixteenth century, the history of man's conquest of space, his final discovery – and subsequent appropriation – of all of "those lands that are furthest away", was conceived as having been marked by three moments in which a new technology could be said to have resulted in the discovery of America and the new sea route to India, and with them the final transformation of the human understanding of the world: the invention of gunpowder, the compass, and the printing press. The last two of these had made humans more mobile, and they made them better able to communicate with one another. The first had made the great European oceanic empires possible. The discoveries of the fifteenth and sixteenth centuries were believed to have enhanced the real potential to be derived from harnessing science to power. For they were, in ways that none of their predecessors had – or at least could be described as – discoveries of "new worlds". It should be stressed, however, that although Lopez de Gómara described the New World as "new" because of its differences from the old and somewhat incongruously because of its size, the term "new" generally implied only prior ignorance on the part of the discoverer. When argued Domingo de Soto in 1556, "we speak of a New World or a New Earth of islands and a continent which encompasses vast spaces", we use the term in the same ways as did the poet Lucan when he wrote the line, "Arabs you have come to a world unknown to you".[13] No one, that is, supposed that these places were literally "new". They were simply new to *us*. Most early modern Europeans – despite the accusations leveled at them by later historians – had always been conscious in this way of the antiquity of the autochthonous identity of the New Worlds which they were now discovering.

Newness for us, nevertheless, presented not only the image of a radically different past, one in which the knowledge of the ancients was not omniscient, it also offered the vision of an altered future. As the celestial guide in the Spanish humanist Juan de Maldonado's modernized version of the *Somnium Scipionis* of 1581 caustically observes, having "occupied a few of its beaches", the Spaniards "think they have found a New World". What lay beyond those beaches, and beyond America itself lay, as yet, in the future. Similarly there had always been an implicit possibility in the languages employed by the European powers to establish their rights over the discoveries that these applied not merely to known worlds but also over all possible future worlds. The pillars of Hercules stood at the entrance to the Atlantic and thus at the exit from the Mediterranean. They were, however, as the supposedly classical tag *ne plus ultra* indicated, not merely a self-imposed limit but also the measure of the possible. When in 1516 Charles V added Hercules' pillars (now transformed into neat Doric columns) to his coat of arms and transformed the line by rendering it as "plus ultra", he was not only celebrating the fact that his "Imperium" had passed beyond the limits of that of the emperor Augustus whose name he had assumed. He was also making a statement about the further possibilities that remained. The pillars now stood not on the boundaries of the known but at the entrance to the still-to-be known.[14] Indeed from the moment that the Portuguese Crown first sought papal approval for their attempts to colonize the coast of west Africa, all claims to sovereignty in the "undiscovered lands" were couched, inescapably, in the future tense.[15] Similarly, all the maps of America, Asia, and Africa made before the early eighteenth century – and those of Africa and the Pacific into the nineteenth – were projected over areas where the competing European powers claimed territorial sovereignty but about which, in reality, they knew next to nothing. The two earliest maps to attempt to depict the American mainland, the La Cosa and Cantino maps, make this point. In the first, produced for Castile in 1500, Castilian flags run all the way down the southern coast (there are a few English ones to the North, but no suggestion that Brazil fell well with the Portuguese area of jurisdiction established by the Treaty of Tordesillas). Most of the place names celebrate Spanish princes and the Italian navigators whom they employed. In the Cantino map of 1502 – produced for Manuel I of Portugal – the image is reversed. Here Portuguese flags not only claim most of Spanish America; they are also dotted along the coasts of Africa and various islands in what is still described as *Mare Oceanus*. The indeterminate future state of the world was further underscored by the existence of a Southern Continent – the "Unknown Southern Land", *Terra australis incognita*. No proof of the full extent of this was available until the eighteenth century. (In 1642 the Dutchman Abel Tasman had landed on Tasmania and the south island of

New Zealand and had circumnavigated Australia itself, but because he had failed to sight the eastern coast, he remained unaware of its full extent.) But the *Terra australis incognita* first appeared in Mercator's world map of 1569 and on all subsequent world maps. As with America before it, the Southern Continent provided future possibilities of mineral abundance and European domination. Persuaded by Victoria Ricci's very unusual projection of 1676, the Vatican in 1681 even created a *prefectura* for it.[16] So long, however, as it remained undiscovered, uncharted and unpossessed, the world, the *orbis terrarum*, remained in a perpetual state of becoming.

## II

As we have seen in Chapter 1, in the official Iberian accounts, the carving up of the newly discovered "new" world – and any further new worlds yet to be discovered – had been made possible, in the first instance, by means of a legal fiction: the claim that despite the huge diversity of peoples that existed in the world, of which the new geography bore irrefutable and abundant evidence, the *orbis terrarum* was, nevertheless, the sole property of either one man (the pope) or two (the pope and the emperor). Until the end of the sixteenth century this fiction had been largely respected by the two Iberian kingdoms, and the activities of the British and the French – for whom it was an absurdity – had been confined to North America and to fitful, and generally ineffectual, raids on Spanish shipping in the Caribbean. It was the emergence of the Dutch, with an extensive and powerful maritime fleet, which upset this precarious balance. The Dutch had taken their struggle with Spain – and after the union of the Iberian kingdoms in 1580, with Portugal – out into the Atlantic and then into the Indian Ocean. On the whole the Dutch East Indian Company (VOC) – in common with most early trading companies – avoided direct confrontation. Theirs was, they always insisted, a peaceful legitimate enterprise. Its political purpose was to make Holland wealthy and where possible to inflict economic rather than military damage on the Spanish-Portuguese empire. On the morning of February 25, 1603, however, a captain (later admiral) of the company, Jakob van Heermskerk, seized the Santa Catarina, a 400-ton Portuguese carrack in the entrance to the Singapore Straits and sailed it back to Holland.[17] The Portuguese protested and demanded the return of their cargo on the grounds that this had been an act of piracy. A number (most of them Mennonites) of the directors of the VOC agreed. Some refused to have any share in the prize; some sold their shares in protest; some even discussed the possibility of setting up a separate trading company under the protection of the king of France.[18] In the end, however, greed got the better of them, and the cargo, when finally put up for sale in Amsterdam, fetched nearly 3.5 million guilders, a sum equivalent to slightly just less than the entire annual revenue of the English government at the time.

Between 1604 and 1605 the twenty-one-year old Hugo Grotius (who was a cousin of Heermskerk) was asked to prepare a defence of the VOC's claims that the Santa Catarina had been taken as booty in a just war.[19] My work, he later wrote, "was conceived in the best patriotic spirit but it was written at an early age (*aetate juvenili*)".[20] He called it echoing – and the similarity in titles is not merely casual – Vitoria's *relectio* of 1539, *De Indis*, although now it was the East rather than the West Indies which were under consideration. The text, which has subsequently come to be known as *De iure pradeae* (*On the Right of Booty*) was never published. But in 1609, chapter 12 appeared anonymously under the title *Mare liberum* (*The Free Sea*). This was intended to be part of the Dutch armoury in the negotiations over the Treaty of Amsterdam of April 9, 1609, by which the Spanish hoped to secure a Dutch agreement to abandon what the Spanish considered to be their piratical activities in the East and West Indies. If it was, it proved to be ineffective. But it started a debate which ran on for nearly a century. The English and the Scots read the book as providing a possible attack on their fishing rights in the North Sea, the Spanish, understandably, as an assault on the foundations of their empire in the Americas, and the Venetians as a rebuttal of their claims to exclusive rights in the Adriatic.

Grotius' objective was to demonstrate that the Portuguese – although, because both Spain and Portugal were at the time united, he makes no clear distinction between them and the Spanish – could not claim dominium over the seas and therefore could not prevent the Dutch, or any other power from trading in the same oceans.[21] The way in which he expressed this objective was through the same initial concern with the laws of hospitality and the freedom of human movement across the surface of the globe which Vitoria had placed at the centre of "On the American Indians" to the degree that sections of the work read like an extended commentary on Question 3 Art. I of Vitoria's *relectio*. Like Vitoria, Grotius begins with a question: "Can any one nation have the right to prevent other nations which so desire, from selling to one another, from bartering with one another, actually from communicating with one another?"[22] The answer was, of course, no. Grotius' demonstration starts with the same Virgilian texts on the naturalness of hospitality and reciprocity and the need which all humans have for communication and international sociability which Vitoria had used.[23] "For even that Ocean" Grotius claimed, "wherewith God hath compassed the Earth is navigable on every side round about" so that "nature hath granted a passage from all nations unto all", which could be proved – if proof were required – by the fact that, Seneca "thinketh the greatest benefits of nature, that even by the wind she hath mingled nations scattered in regard of place and hath so divided all her goods into countries that mortal men must needs traffic among themselves". From this, he went on echoing Vitoria, "descendeth that most scared law of hospitality".[24]

Any attempt to interfere with this process must, therefore, constitute an offence against humanity. "Take away commerce", the first-century historian Lucius Annaeus Florus had warned, "and you break the Bond that ties Mankind together." "For no Body has a Right to hinder one Nation", Grotius wrote in his best-known work *On the Laws of War and Peace (De iure belli ac pacis)*, "from trading with another distant Nation; it being for the Interest of Society in general."[25] This vision of the oceans as having a privileged place in nature's (or God's) desire to facilitate communication between peoples survived well into the late eighteenth century. Even Immanuel Kant cites as one of the means for the realization of the future "cosmopolitan right", the existence of the seas as "arrangements of nature most favouring the commerce [of nations] by means of navigation".[26]

No wonder then, Grotius continued, citing what had become a standard roster of classical and humanist sources, that the Athenian degree prohibiting the Megarians from trading in any part of the Athenian Empire should have led to the Peloponnesian War, or that Agamemnon should have made war on the king of Mysia for attempting to limit the passage along the roads that led through his kingdom. The Italian humanist Andrea Alciati went so far as to argue that the chief reason for the Crusades had been that the "Saracens" had denied Christians access to the Holy Land, from which it clearly followed: "This right ... appertaineth to all nations, which the most famous lawyers enlarge so far that they deny any commonwealth or prince to be able wholly to forbid others to come unto their subjects and trade with them". Even if the Portuguese had been "lords of those countries wither the Hollanders go", and that was, as Grotius went on to explain, clearly not the case, "yet they should be wrong if they stopped the passage and trade of the Hollanders".[27] The question, at this stage was, as it had been – albeit in a largely different context – for Vitoria, the right of passage not occupation.

The Portuguese, however, were, as Grotius knew, unlike the other European imperial powers in laying claim to what were in effect not rights of property – although that was how they were expressed – but rights to use. For whereas the Spanish had claimed, by virtue of conquest, to exercise rights over both persons and lands – what Vitoria had defined as "private and public *dominium*" – the Portuguese claimed rights over commerce, and by implication over the seas. The *Ordenacões Manuelinas* of 1521 (a text which, however, incorporates a number of earlier decrees), for instance, prohibits the passage of "both natives and foreigners" in any ships other than the Portuguese to "the lands and seas of Guine [Africa] and India" and to "whatever other lands and seas of our conquests to trade, barter or make war therein without our permission and authority". Similarly, the historian João de Barros speaks of Manuel as "Lord of the conquest, navigation and commerce of Ethiopia, Arabia, Persia and India". European monarchs were, of course, fond of assuming titles over places to which they could only make the most improbable claims. These, however, had always only be territories.

Few if any had ever claimed sovereignty over "navigation and commerce". "Conquest", a term generally limited to the occupation of a land and its peoples, was routinely applied by the Portuguese to commerce, and consequently to the ocean. Barros is not claiming that Manuel is the legitimate ruler of most of Asia and the Middle East. He is claiming – as indeed was Manuel himself – that the Portuguese crown had "conquered", and may thus now exercise dominium, over the ocean and thus *commerce* between Europe and these places. Even the argument, widely employed by all the European powers, that they were bringing both the true religion and some kind of civil society to the "barbarians" beyond their shores was transferred by Barros from modes of existence to practices of exchange. The Portuguese, he argued, had acquired dominium in the Indian Ocean and its littoral – although he is suitably imprecise about just what this might entail – by imposing what he called "rules of prudence" (*regras de prudencia*) on areas which had previously been "governed and ruled by the force of greed which each person had [i.e., individual rather than collectively]". "We", he continued, "reduce and order them according to a system [*reduzimos e possemos em arte*] with universal and particular rules as have all sciences." Commerce, which by 1539 was already being described as a "science", became an instrument for "reducing" – a term which like conquest belongs properly to the language of war – a people to civility, what Barros understands by "rules of prudence" and a "system".

It was, Grotius argued, a language which was wholly inappropriate. If what the Portuguese were saying was that they had acquired the territories they occupied in Asia through conquest, then their claim was simply false. For leaving aside occasional conflicts, the Portuguese had never "conquered" anywhere, except Brazil, something in which they themselves frequently took pride, comparing their own peaceful trading practices with the destructive habits of the Spanish and the English. Ceylon, Java, and the Moluccas were all, in Grotius' view, legitimate states, having "their own kings, commonwealth, their law and their liberties" – that is to say, they constituted what the neo-Aristotelians described as "prefect communities".[28] In these lands, he wrote contemptuously, the Portuguese "pay tribute and obtain liberty of trade of the princes", which was sufficient evidence that they "have not so much as a title of dominion over those parts" and that consequently "they do not so much as dwell there but by entreaty".[29]

More importantly, however, you cannot speak of "conquering" or possessing the seas, not only because these were the common property of mankind – a point Grotius spelt out at greater length in *On the Laws of War and Peace* – but also because, and this was his key point, the seas are inexhaustible.[30] For "dominion properly signifieth that which so appertaineth unto one that after the same manner it cannot be another's".[31] No one, therefore, can claim to have dominium in "anything which although serving some one person, still suffices for the common use of all other persons".[32]

Furthermore the sea clearly belongs to that category of things "which cannot be occupied or were never occupied", and thus they "can be proper to none because all propriety hath his beginning from occupation".[33] To argue that you have conquered the seas was as ridiculous as claiming that you had conquered the air, "both because it cannot be possessed and also because it oweth a common use to men".[34] The same would, of course, apply to commerce itself because commerce, as a means of exchange, and communication, cannot, by definition, be subject to any possession or limitation, from which it followed that "on the land, which is given both to nations and every particular man in property, a quiet and harmless passage can justly be denied to no men of any nation, no more than drink out of a river".[35] And, he concluded, this right of free passage was not only a right in natural law and the law of nations, it had also been restated as part of Castilian civil law. (The implication here was that because Spain and Portugal were, at this time, a joint monarchy, the laws of Castile also applied to Portugal which was not in fact the case, as Grotius would have known full well.) The civil law of Castile had, of course, no standing outside Castile. By suggesting, however, that it contravened a principle of natural law, the Portuguese were also claiming that it was contrary to reason which would, of course, also make it invalid *within* Castile. (Samuel Pufendorf, as we have seen, made a similar objection to Vitoria's "right of natural partnership and communication".)[36]

Grotius then turned to what he identified as the four "titles" under which the Portuguese claimed to have "conquered" the commerce in Asia. They were (1) by Papal donation, (2), by having waged a just war, (3) by right of prior discovery, and (4) by "prescription or custom".[37] He dismissed the Papal Donation, and the grounds of which the Treaty of Tordesillas had been ratified, for the same reason as Vitoria had done – namely that the authority of the pope was widely recognized, even by Catholics, to be limited to spiritual matters. Furthermore, even if the pope had been "temporal lord of the whole world", he would still not be "lord of the sea" because the sea was something no human being, whatever the source of his authority, could own, and therefore, could not give away. Donation, wrote Grotius, "hath no force in things which are without the compass of merchandise, wherefore, seeing the sea or the right of sailing in it can be proper to no man, it follows that it could neither be given by the Pope, nor received of the Portugals." He made the further point, citing Vitoria once again, that even if the pope had possessed dominium over the entire globe, and its oceans, he could not have alienated any part of it to another prince, any more than the Emperor could "convert or alien at his pleasure the provinces of his empire to his own use".[38] Sovereignty, papal or otherwise, should not be confused with rights of property. As a purely civil treaty the Tordesillas agreement was clearly binding between Spain and Portugal. Since, however, the pope had no power, as James Otis sarcastically observed in 1764, to hand out "the kingdoms of the earth with as little ceremony as a man would leave a sheepcote", his decisions could not possibly be binding on third parties.[39] The argument that the donations had been grants made to evangelize and civilize the barbarians, – a common gloss placed on them by those, Bartolomé de las Casas among them, who wished to retain their moral force without committing themselves to their wider political implications – was similarly invalid because "forcing nations into a higher degree of civilisation against their will, the pretext once seized by the Greeks and by Alexander the Great, is considered by the theologians, especially those of Spain, to be unjust and impious".[40] In any case no matter what they might claim to be doing, "the Portuguese in most places do not further the extension of the faith, or indeed pay any attention to it at all, since they are alive only to the acquisition of wealth".

The supposition that the Portuguese had fought a just war, or wars, in Asia was similarly based on false premises. Such wars as they had made were clearly unjust because, as Vitoria had concluded of the America Indians, these "Indians of the East", as Grotius calls them, have "both publicly and privately authority over their own substance and possession which without just cause cannot be taken from them".[41]

This left the argument from discovery and from prescription, which, as we have seen, were closely linked. On the first of these both the Portuguese and the Spanish laid great stress. Although Vitoria dismissed it as providing "no support for the possession of these lands any more than it would if they had discovered us", it had, as he acknowledged, been "the only title alleged in the beginning", and despite Vitoria's dismissal, and the dismissal of most of the subsequent theorists of the "law of nations", it continued to be cited in official sources until well into the nineteenth century.[42] (Some version of it was used by Portuguese at the Berlin Conference of 1884, which divided up Africa between the competing European imperial powers, who complained that they were entitled to a far greater portion of the continent than they had been granted under the terms of the treaty because it was they who had been the first to discover the western coasts.[43]) Even if the Portuguese could have been said to have discovered – in Grotius' understanding of the term – certain parts of Africa, no such claim could be made about Asia. In the first place discovery could only provide a right of possession if what had been discovered was genuinely unknown and unoccupied – that is, if it were, res or terra nullius. Yet it was obvious that Asia had not been unoccupied when Vasco da Gama arrived there in 1498. Furthermore, as we have seen, Grotius stresses the now familiar point that "discovery" (*invenire*) is "not to see a thing with the eyes, but to lay hold of it with the hands."[44] On March 15, 1613, he went to England as a member of a Dutch delegation sent to work out an agreement between England and Holland over the East Indies. According to the Dutch account of this visit, James I is said to have remarked: "Where neither was in possession neither should impede the other's free commerce."[45] In order to constitute *rights*, both possession and sovereignty (*dominium iurisdictionis*) have to be exercised, a view that Grotius would certainly have shared. *Invenire* belonged to that category of actions, by which those things that Grotius described as "sometimes common, sometimes public" could be made into objects of property, in the same way that wild beast and birds can be acquired through hunting.[46]

It was also obvious that the Portuguese could not be said to have discovered Asia and Africa in the way that the Spanish might claim to have discovered America.[47] True, they might have sailed there before any other modern European power. India, however, had been widely known and visited in antiquity. Furthermore, all such arguments, if pressed to their logical conclusion, would exclude all European navigators from all but their own home waters. If the Portuguese were only claiming that they had opened new routes for Europeans, then, Grotius acknowledged, they deserved "the same thanks, praise and immortal glory wherewith all discoverers of great matters have been contented". This did not, however, allow them to make any claim to dominium on the basis of their achievements. Furthermore, their motives, like that of all the other European powers, but unlike those "discoverers of great matters" who had "endeavored not to benefit themselves but mankind", had been gain, so they were in no position to demand compensation in the form of exclusive rights for their efforts. They were, in any case, in Grotius' view, not so much virtuous as fortunate, the beneficiaries of an historical cycle; if Vasco da Gama had not been the first to find a sea route to India, then sooner rather than later, someone else would have done so. "For", he concluded, "the times were at hand wherein . . . the situation of seas and countries were daily more clearly known to us." Had not the Portuguese been the first to discover the sea route to Indian, then other nations, "no less inflamed with the desire of merchandise and foreign commodities", such as the Venetians, Bretons, English, and Dutch themselves would very soon have done so.[48]

The argument from prescription also would not work. The Roman law of prescription was – and remains – a powerful weapon in the internationalists' armoury. As we have seen in Chapter 4, it has been employed by all the European powers at one time or another and would seem to involve an initial claim to prior occupancy of precisely the kind the Portuguese most needed. As an existential legal argument, it was one which Grotius, as a good humanist, might have been expected to have endorsed. And in a sense he did. He insisted, however, that, as it was a truly existential argument, it could only be a matter of civil law and thus could not apply to contracts among "kings or among free peoples". It could not, in consequence, ever be a part of the law of nations. Neither, of course, could it be used to acquire possession in things – such as the sea – which cannot by their very nature become property.[49]

If, as Grotius now believed, he had demonstrated incontrovertibly that "both law and equity require that the trade of India should be free for us as for any other", it clearly followed that the Dutch were in a position to defend that right "whether we are at peace, truce or war with the Spaniard".[50] For "he that stop the passage and hinder the carrying out of merchandise may be resisted by way of fact, as they say, even without expecting any public authority".[51] The implication, of course, although Grotius nowhere alludes to it directly, was that the seizure of the Santa Catarina was an act of legitimate defence even if Heermskerk was indeed acting without "public authority" and, at that moment, Holland and the Spanish-Portuguese monarchy were not legally at war.

III

Grotius' treatise started a war of words, to which the Portuguese, French, English, Spanish, and Venetians all contributed. The earliest and most detailed attempt to refute its arguments, however, came, unsurprisingly, from the Portuguese. Grotius himself says that he had expected that "some Spaniard would write a reply to my little book, a thing which I hear was done at Salamanca". The reply to which he was alluding, although he never "happened to read that book", was written not by a Spaniard but by a Portuguese, Serafim de Freitas, Vespers Professor of Canon Law at the University of Valladolid.[52] In 1625 Freitas published a lengthy point-by-point refutation of *Mare liberum*, entitled *De iusto imperio lusitanorum asiatico*. Freitas' book has received far less attention, outside Spain and Portugal, than either *Mare Liberum* or the English jurist John Selden's *Mare Clausum* of 1636, an attempt to defend the English claims to the North Sea against Grotius, which employs arguments which are, in some way, very similar to Freitas'.[53] In part this is a matter of style. *De iusto imperio lusitanorum asiatico* is a very different kind of text from either *Mare Liberum* or *Mare Clausum*. Its point of departure is also a lengthy defence of the Papal Donation (as a canon lawyer, Freitas was bound to take a far stronger view of papal sovereignty than either Grotius himself or the civil lawyers and the theologians), which for anyone outside Spain and Portugal could have had no bearing on a dispute over claims to sovereignty under the law of nations. Furthermore Freitas' ingenious argument that the bulls of both Pope Nicholas V and Alexander VI had been granted to Portugal and Spain in recognition that they were the leaders of an anti-Islamic crusade in the East Indies would have implied that a just war could be made on the Muslims of Asia – who, unlike their fellow religionists in the Middle East, had had no part in the occupation of Christian territories – solely on grounds of belief, which for the neo-Thomists (although not Grotius) was untenable.[54] The better part of Feitas' argument, however, is one which like Grotius' own, like Vázquez's and Vitoria's, belongs to a recognizably modern discourse, one that is equally reluctant to accept any kind of universalist claims or arguments derived from military conquest as the grounds for dominium.

In a sense Freitas is doing what Barros had attempted, only in reverse – that is, to use the language of commerce to describe conquest, rather than the language of conquest to describe commerce.

Like Grotius, Freitas recognizes that the Portuguese claim hinges on the presumption that discovery can be the basis for dominium and that it is possible to exercise rights over the means for commerce and, finally, that commerce itself, if it is to be regarded as a mode of communication between peoples, must also be an instrument of civilization and treated as such. He begins by rejecting, although without ever mentioning it, Vitoria's "right of natural partnership and communication". In arguing that all peoples had a natural right of access to all others, Grotius had conflated two distinct forms of the natural law – the prescriptive and the permissive. "For all those species of things", he wrote,

> which do not belong to prescriptive [natural law] may change as circumstances change, thus freedom and servitude, the community of goods. ... Thus although navigation and commerce were carried out in the earliest times of the integrity of nature (*in primaevo naturae integrae*) it is not because of this that they belong to the precepts of the natural law.[55]

To endorse this argument, however, he first had to find an answer to Grotius' objection that the seas could not, by their nature, be subject to ownership. And since Grotius is fond of citing the poets as evidence, so, too, will he. (Freitas was no humanist, but he was perfectly able to meet Grotius on his own intellectual grounds.)[56] Virgil, he points out, had made Jupiter grant to the Romans lordship over the entire world, including the oceans. (*Aeneid* I, 286–7). Although the title *Dominus mundi*, which had been assumed by, or rather ascribed to, the Emperor Antoninus Pius in the second century might, as all the Spanish jurists had insisted, be merely a hyperbole to indicate the sheer size of the Roman empire, it nevertheless implied the logical possibility of a claim to property in the oceans.[57] (In fact, Antoninus, in reply to a complaint from one Eudaemon of Nicomedia that he had been robbed by the people of the Cyclades after being shipwrecked, had said, "I am lord of the world, but the law of the sea must be judged by the sea law of the Rhodians when our law does not conflict with it." And Justinian had similarly excluded the sea from his jurisdiction.)[58]

It was also the case that if it had now been established, as Duarte Pacheco Pereira had claimed, that the seas, in fact, lay *within* the land, then it followed that the seas could, logically at least, be possessed in the same way that lakes and rivers might.[59] Furthermore, Grotius had accepted that ships may be protected and pirates punished.[60] Although he had also insisted that this could only be achieved by a merely formal agreement between nations and could have no purchase on those who were not party to the contract, Freitas pointed out that any agreement of any kind which attempted to restrict the activities of vessels on the high seas implied some measure of dominium over the ocean.[61] This also provided Freitas with an answer to what was seemingly Grotius' most telling observation, namely, that the ocean was "so limitless that it cannot become a possession of anyone". This, Freitas was prepared to concede, was certainly true. The Portuguese, however, were not, in fact, claiming dominium over the Ocean as a body of water; they were claiming the right to control access to specific parts of it, in this case the Indian Ocean, in the same way that they – and the Dutch or any other nation – might claim rights of exclusion in those waters where their ships were threatened by pirates. The argument from size and inexhaustibility, he pointed out, could also be applied to land, particularly in places such as Asia and Africa, which are filled with immense deserts, yet it could be hardly concluded from this that the land – the *orbis terrarum* – was similarly indivisible. As for Grotius' supposition that the seas had to be free in the same way that all running water was because, like the air we breath, it was necessary for human survival, Freitas replied that the right to drink water was not the same thing as the "right to fish from it or trade in it"[62]. The Portuguese had no objection to the Dutch drinking from the Indian Ocean if they so wished. What they objected to was their trading in it, and in this way benefiting, as Freitas phrased it, from the "travails, sacrifices and the blood and lives of others"[63].

If, therefore, it was possible to claim some kind of dominium over the seas, then that claim could only be on the basis of historical fact. For although we may not, "by reason of its vastness, and our impotence, occupy all the seas, we can nevertheless partially protect, purge, dominate and impose our *imperium* over it so as to protect our things and to defend ourselves from enemies and pirates". In doing so, in demonstrating that they were able to exercise the kind of political authority implied here in the term *imperium*, the Portuguese had also established de facto – and hence on Freitas' understanding *de iure* – the rights they required to exclude other European powers.

It is in the context of these arguments, Freitas insisted, that the Portuguese claim to have discovered India and Africa must be understood. Grotius had denied, on the basis of the historical evidence, that the Portuguese could be said to have discovered somewhere already well-known in the ancient world and, furthermore, that even if they had, the mere fact of their having got there first did not constitute a discovery in the full sense of the term, and it certainly did not involve the acquisition of rights. Freitas' reply was that although it was obviously the case that parts of India had been known in antiquity, only parts had been, and except for Alexander's relatively brief stay in India, no European powers had established a sustained presence there before the Portuguese. It was then truly they who had "discovered other lands, other seas, other worlds, in the end even other stars" – *alia postremo Sydera*. (This last remark is a reference to the Southern Cross, which became something of a topos in Portuguese accounts of their navigational achievements.) Furthermore, argued Freitas, contrary to Grotius' assertion that discovery must involve occupation, *invenire* in fact means to "open up" as well as occupy, and this was the sense in which the Portuguese had always used the term.[64] This priority constituted for Freitas a legal claim, which granted the Portuguese king a right to acquisition.[65] Dominium, furthermore, does not require full possession. It is enough, he argued, "that the place be designated as such, and publicly so declared".[66] For Freitas this was the importance of the *padrões*. These were stone pillars which the Portuguese navigators carried with them and erected at strategic points on the coasts along which they sailed. They declared that the Portuguese had been there first and that these seaways, and the adjacent coasts, therefore belonged to the crown of Portugal. The Portuguese were not, of course, the only ones to indulge in such practices. Columbus had planted wooden crosses on the islands on the Caribbean which he visited, and even Antoine de Bougainville, despite being the leader of an expedition with no supposed colonization objectives, when he visited Tahiti in 1768, planted a wooden plaque, and a bottle containing the names of all the officers on his three ships, in the sands of Tahiti, which declared this and all Polynesia to be French territory.[67]

Freitas', point, however, was not that Vasco da Gama's *padrões* had given the Portuguese sovereignty in India but merely that by these acts of possession, they had secured historical priority for Portugal, over any other European power, as regards commerce.[68] They had also served to establish what he insists are legitimate Portuguese claims to both the Atlantic and the Indian Ocean by right of prescription, because although prescription is indeed a part of the civil law, it is also one, *pace* Grotius, which has been accepted by all nations "by the common consensus of mankind by the light of reason", and as such it constitutes a part of the law of nations.[69]

There is a further dimension to these claims. Discovery for Freitas, as for Grotius and for Soto – whom he quotes on the subject – did not mean literally coming across something which was altogether unknown. He knew perfectly well that both Asia and Africa had for long been inhabited, and inhabited by peoples of a very high degree of what he was prepared to recognize (despite his occasional use of the term "barbarian") as social and technological sophistication. His battle with Grotius had been only over whether these places had been known to the ancients. If, as he insisted, the answer was a (qualified) no, then this did not imply that they had had no prior existence before the Portuguese "encountered" them.

The true meaning of discovery lay elsewhere. By discovering the peoples of India, Freitas meant bringing them into the narrative of redemption and social and technological progress, which constitutes the history of the Christian world. By traveling to Asia, the Portuguese had thus been the first, as he phrased it, to "draw these [peoples] from the eternal darkness and ancient chaos into the light of day", something which, he claims, the Italian humanist Politian had recognized.⁷⁰ For Freitas, as indeed for Grotius, history was the Augustinian *operatio dei* in time. Those, then, who had had – whether through any fault of their own or not – no share in Christendom could also have no place on the evolving scale of being. Bartolomé de las Casas was making much the same point when he described the American Indians, before Christopher Columbus, the *Christum Ferrens* – the Christ Bearer – had arrived to lead them into history, as "these numberless peoples who had laid in oblivion throughout so many centuries". In Freitas' view, no less than in Las Casas', all Christians had an obligation to deliver the ignorant from their ignorance. This, after all, had been the implicit – and frequently explicit – injunction of all the papal bulls of donation to the kings of both Spain and Portugal. For some of the Spanish, this had implied the need for an armed presence, certainly for a settlement of Europeans able to instruct the Indians. It implied, that is, a license for colonization. Characteristically for Freitas, however, it is "navigation and commerce", not colonization, which are taken to be the instruments of evangelization.⁷¹ Grotius might protest that exporting civilization could be no ground for *dominium*, but as he had himself argued elsewhere, the basis of the law of nations as the secondary law of nature was, and could only be, the "customs of the most civilised peoples of the world".⁷² And if that was the case, then it must surely be acceptable to ensure that as many peoples of the world as possible had access to those customs.

By the time *De iusto imperio lusitanorum asiatico* appeared, Spanish and Portuguese views on the subject were beginning to change. To defend either the freedom of the seas or the right of restricted access could always, as the Dutch themselves were to discover as they tried to encroach on nominally English territories in North America, prove to be a double-edged sword. Similarly although Freitas' argument would ban Dutch ships from trading in the Indian Ocean, they could just as easily be used to ban Portuguese vessels from the China Sea and the North Atlantic.

Freitas' significance, however, lies elsewhere. His attempt to re-describe commerce as a good which might be possessed, or at least subject to some measure of political control, and his insistence that it was an instrument for civilization, although it belongs, as we have seen to an ancient discourse on the value of international communication, also places him in direct line of ascent to the nosier, more bellicose discussions over the rights to free trade in the eighteenth century. Like Grotius, like Selden – like Vitoria, Soto, and Vázquez who were the acknowledged predecessors of all three – he also contributed to that shift in the perception of empire which would ultimately lead to the Enlightenment hostility to all forms of overseas expansion, and the wish to replace all forms of territorial possession with commercial transaction. True, Freitas still employs the language of conquest to characterize commerce, but it is still commerce with which he is concerned, and in defending the Portuguese rights to the Indian Ocean, he is quite explicit about *not* endorsing any more conventional modes of conquest. In doing so, he was echoing the final remarks of Vitoria's "On the American Indians": "Look at the Portuguese, who carry on a great and profitable trade with similar sorts of peoples without conquering them."[73]

More widely still *De iusto imperio lusitanorum asiatico* can be read as a contribution to a discourse which, at least in the form it was to take in the following century, sought to bring about a radical change in social and political attitudes, one which would ultimately replace the values of the warrior aristocrat by those of the merchant. As the French physiocrat François Quesnay pointed out in 1776, it had been the Phoenicians in the ancient world, then the Portuguese, and now in his own day the British who had finally understood that only commerce could bring lasting benefit to mankind.[74] Hardly surprising perhaps then that it should have been Smith who had such (cautious) respect for Quesnay who saw in Columbus' and Vasco da Gama's epic voyage the true origins of the modern world. "The consequences", Smith reflected, had "already been very great. But in the short period between two and three centuries which have elapsed since these discoveries were made, it is impossible that the whole extent of their consequences have been seen".[75] He was none to sanguine as what the ultimate results might be. But one thing was certain, between them Columbus and Vasco da Gama had transformed forever not only the nature but also the political and moral significance of the understanding of maritime trade.

### Endnotes

1 *An Inquiry into the Nature and Causes of the Wealth of Nations*, 626 (IV. vii). Raynal's version reads: "There has never been any event as interesting for human kind in general, and for the peoples of Europe in particular, than the discovery of the New World and the passage to the Indies by way of the Cape of Good Hope." Guillaume-Thomas Raynal, *Histoire philosophique et politique des établissements et du commerce des Européens dans les deux Indes*, Anthony Strugnell et al. eds. (Paris: Centre International d'Études du XVIIIe siècle, 2010), I, 23.

2 Gómara had described the discovery of America as "The greatest thing since the creation of the world save for the incarnation and death of he who created it." Ernst Kapp, *Philosophische oder Vergleichende allgeine Erdkunde* (Braunschweig, 1845), II, 24–45. Carl Schmitt, *Land und Meer: Eine weltgeschichtliche Bertracchtung* (Leipzig: Reclam, 1942), 4, and *The Nomos of the Earth in the International Law of the Jus Publicum Europaeum*, 39, 69.

3 For a more extensive account, see my "La Découverte de l'Amérique et la transformation du temps et de l'espace en Europe", *Revue de synthèse*, 129 (2008), 1–16.

4 *Histories*, VII, 104. Herodotus' understanding of the divisions of the world is, however, both complex and sometimes contradictory. See Rosalind Thomas, *Herodotus in Context: Ethnography, Science and the Art of Persuasion* (Cambridge: Cambridge University Press, 2002), 80–6.

5 The *Somnium* takes up Book VI of *De re publica*, VI 19–20.

6 On Macrobius' vision, see John M. Headley, "The Sixteenth-Century Venetian Celebration of the Earth's Total Habitability: The Issue of the Fully Habitable World for Renaissance Europe", in *Journal of World History* 8 (1997), 1–27, at 6.

7 *Esmeraldo de situ orbis*, quoted in W. G. L. Randles, "Classical Models of World Geography and their Transformation Following the Discovery of America", in Wolfgang Haase and Meyer Rheinhold eds., *The Classical Tradition and the Americas* (Berlin; New York: W. de Gruyter, 1993), 5–76, at 63.

8 *Purchas His Pilgrimes* (London, 1625), IV, Dedicatory Letter.

9 Quoted in Headley, "The Sixteenth-Century Venetian Celebration of the Earth's Total Habitability", 16.

10 *Novus orbis regionum ac insularum veteribus incognitarum* (Basle, 1532),"Epistola nuncupatoria", ff. 92r.–93r.

11 *Purchas his Pilgrimes*, I, 49–50.

12 *Corpus Hermeticum*, A. J. Festugière and Arthur Darby Knock eds. (Paris: Société d'édition, "Les Belles Lettres, 1954), IV Fr. 23, 14–16.

13 *De iustitia et iure, libri decem* (Salamanca, 1556), IV ii (306). Gómara said of the Americas that, "no tanto se dicen nuevo por ser nuevamente hallado, cuanto por ser grandísimo y casi tan grande como el viejo, que contiene a Europa, África y Asia".

14 See Earl Rosenthal "*Plus ultra, non plus ultra*, and the Columnar Device of Emperor Charles V", *Journal of the Warburg and Courtauld Institutes* 34 (1971), 204–28. The device, which was not necessarily related to America – although it did clearly imply territorial expansion – was of Italian and Burgundian, rather than Castilian inspiration.

15 See pp. 41–2.

16 W. A. R. Richardson, "Mercator's Southern Continent; Its Origins, Influence and Gradual Decline", *Terrae Incognitae* 25 (1993), 67–98 at 95.

17 For details of the event, see Martine Julia van Ittersum, *Profit and Principle: Hugo Grotius, Natural Rights Theories and the Rise of Dutch Power in the East Indies (1595–1615)* (Leiden-Boston: Brill, 2006), 1–52, and Peter Borschberg, *Hugo Grotius, the Portuguese and Free Trade in the East Indies* (Singapore: National University of Singapore, 2011), 42–8.

18 Peter Borschberg, "The Seizure of the Sta. Catarina Revisited: The Portuguese Empire in Asia, VOC Politics and the Origins of the Dutch-Johor Alliance (1602–1616)", *Journal of Southeast Asia Studies* 33 (2002), 31–62.

19 David Armitage "Introduction" to Hugo Grotius, *The Free Sea*, xii. All future references to the English version of *Mare Liberum* are to this edition.

20 Quoted in C. H. Alexandrowicz, "Freitas *versus* Grotius", *British Yearbook of International Law* 35 (1959), 162–82, at 162.

21 On *dominium* see p.60 n.69.

22 Alexandrowicz was, of course, quite right to insist that both Grotius' and Freitas' texts referred to "problems arising out of actual State practice in South Asia and the Indian Ocean in the sixteenth and seventeenth centuries". It is nevertheless the case that their arguments are couched in terms of what was, in the end of fundamental concern to both namely the status of the Ocean, as a possible object of *dominium* in terms of the law of nations. Alexandrowicz, "Freitas *versus* Grotius", 163.

23 See pp. 53–4.

24 *The Free Sea*, 11–12.

25 *The Rights of War and Peace*, II, 439–44 (II. ii. xiii) The quotation from Florus is provided by Grotius. I have failed to locate the original.

26 "The Metaphysics of Morals", *Practical Philosophy*, 451, AK 6:352.

27 *The Free Sea*, 11–12.

28 Vitoria employed a similar, if more extensive, argument to demonstrate that before the arrival of the Spanish the American Indians "possessed as true dominion, both public and private, as any Christians" because "they have organized cities, proper marriages, magistrates and rulers, laws, industries and commerce". "On the American Indians", 1.6, *Vitoria: Political Writings*, 250. And see pp. 47–8.

29 *The Free Sea*, 13.

30 *The Rights of War and Peace* II, 459–74 (II, iii, vii–xv).

31 *The Free Sea*, 20.

32 Ibid.

33 Ibid., 24.

34 Ibid., 25.

35 Ibid., 37. And see Armitage, *Foundations of Modern International Thought*, 52–4.

36 See p. 55.

37 The first two of these repeat Vitoria's Question 2 articles 2 and 3; the first and the fourth are discussed under two separate headings: the first (Caps. 6 and 7) concerns navigation, the second (Caps. 10 and II) concern trading rights with "The Indians".

38 *The Free Sea*, 38.

39 "The Rights of the British Colonies Asserted and Proved" [Boston] in Bernard Bailyn ed., *Pamphlets of the American Revolution*, I: 1750–65 (Cambridge, MA: Harvard University Press, 1965), 438.

40 Citing Plutarch *Life of Alexander the Great* I, 5.

41 *The Free Sea*, 14.

42 "On the American Indians", 2. 3–2, *Vitoria: Political Writings*, 264–5.

43 Diogo de Sousa e Alvim, "A Disputa pelo Arquipélago do Pináculo (Senkaku/ Diaoyu) Uma Análise Jurídica" (February 27, 2011). Available at SSRN: http://ssrn.com/abstract=1772223.

44 *The Free Sea*, 13–14. The Latin, which makes no mention of "hands", reads, *Invenire enim non illud est oculis ursupare, sed apprehendere.*

45 Quoted in G. N. Clark, "Grotius' East India Mission to England", *Transactions of the Grotius Society* XX (1935), 64.

46 *The Free Sea*, 26.

47 *The Free Sea*, 14, n6. The manuscript of *De iure praedae* adds the comment: "For there is one reason for India and another for America." *Alia enim India, alia America ratio est.*

48 Ibid.

49 *The Free Sea*, 38.

50 Ibid., 57.

51 Ibid., 60.

52 "Defense of Chapter V of the *Mare Liberum*" [ca. 1615] in *The Free Sea*, 78, and in a letter to his brother dated earlier in April 1617. In February 1627, he

mentions Freitas by name, cited in Mónica Brito Vieira, "*Mare Liberum* vs. *Mare Clausum*: Grotius, Freitas, and Selden's Debate on Dominion over the Seas", *Journal of the History of Ideas* 63 (2003), 361–77, at 362.

53 On this see, Vieira, "*Mare Liberum* vs. *Mare Clausum*", 361–77. There is no evidence, however, that Selden had actually read Freitas. The Spanish jurist Juan de Solórzano Pereira whose *Política Indiana* of 1647 provides a long account of the history of the attempts to legitimate the Spanish occupation of the Americas, and who laid great stress on the Papal Bulls, speaks of Freitas as having satisfactorily disposed of all the "frivolous arguments ... of the author of *Mare liberum*". *Política Indiana*, Francisco Tomás y Valiente y Ana María Barrero eds. (Madrid: Biblioteca Castro, 1996), I, 115 (I, ix).

54 Alexandrowicz, " Freitas *versus* Grotius", 168–9.

55 *Do Justo império asiático dos Portugueses* (*De iusto imperio lusitanorum asiatico*) Miguel Pinto de Meneses trans, 2 vols. (Lisbon: Instituto de Alta Cultura, 1959, 2 vol.). All references are to vol. I (the Latin text), 5–9.

56 Ibid., 120–1.

57 Ibid., 123–4. The allusion is to *Digest* XIV, 2.9.

58 *Institutes*, II, 1.1.

59 Freitas, *De iusto imperio lusitanorum asiatico*, 130.

60 "Defense of Chapter V of the *Mare Liberum*" [ca. 1615] in *The Free Sea*, 128–9.

61 Freitas, *De iusto imperio lusitanorum asiatico*, 128.

62 Ibid., 147.

63 Ibid., 148.

64 Ibid., 127–8. Freitas here seems to be conflating the late Latin term "discoperio", which does indeed mean "open up" or "lay bare" with *invenio*.

65 See Alexandrowicz, " Freitas *versus* Grotius", 167.

66 Freitas, *De iusto imperio lusitanorum asiatico*, 227

67 See Friedrich August von der Heydte, "Discovery, Symbolic Annexation and Virtual Effectiveness in International Law," *American Journal of International Law* 29 (1935), 448–71, and Patricia Seed, *Ceremonies of Possession in Europe's Conquest of the New World, 1492–1640* (Cambridge University Press: Cambridge, 1995).

68 Freitas, *De iusto imperio Lusitanorum Asiatico*, 112–17.

69 Ibid., 182–3.

70 Ibid., 126, citing *Epistolae*, Bk. 10 *Epistola* 1a. He goes on to quote the opening lines of *Os Lusiadas*, which speaks of, "As armas e varões assinalados" who "Por mares nunca dantes navegados / Passaram ainda além da Taprobana [Ceylon]".

71 Ibid., 227. He speaks of *navigatio et commercium, in ordine ad bonum Indorum spirituale*.

72 See p. 211.

73 *Vitoria: Political Writings*, Conclusion 292.

74 "Remarques sur l'opinion de l'auteur de l'*Esprit des lois* concernant les colonies, Lib. IV. XXI. Chap. 17" in *François Quesnay et la physiocratie*, 2 vols. (Paris: Institut national d'études demographiques, 1958), II, 785, and see my *Lords of All the World*, 184.

75 Smith, *An Inquiry into the Nature and Causes of the Wealth of Nations*, II, 626 (IV, vii).

# 6

## *Cambiar su ser*

## Reform to Revolution in the Political Imaginary of the Ibero-American World

Para Luís Castro Leiva, *in memoriam*

### I

"In comparing South America with North America, we observe an astonishing contrast", wrote Georg Friedrich Hegel in 1830.

> In North America we witness a prosperous state of things; an increase of industry and population, civil order and freedom; the whole federation constitutes but a single state and has its political centres. In South America, on the contrary, the republics depend upon military force; their whole history is a continued revolution; federated states become disunited; other previously separated become united; and all these changes originate in military revolutions.

All of this, he believed, could be attributed to two things: the difference between a Catholic South and a Protestant North (from the latter of which, in Hegel's view, there "sprang the mutual confidence of individuals") and the politically more significant fact that "South America was conquered, but North America colonized". Colonization – the exportation to the Americas of European settlers – had created in the North a stable political base, so that

> Soon the whole attention of the inhabitants was given to labour, and the basis of their existence as a united body lay in the necessities that bind man to man, the desire of repose, the establishment of civil rights, security and freedom, and a community arising from an aggregation of individuals as atomic constituents; so that the state was merely something external for the protection of property.

This had provided the successor state with the cohesion it required to survive the traumas – physical, military, and psychological – of independence. It also required the colonizers to develop the true resources of the lands which they had occupied instead of relying on a defeated indigenous population to do the work for them. The Spanish, by contrast, had taken possession of "South America to govern it, and to become rich through occupying political offices and by exaction".[1] This had resulted in a brand of militarism which was, by nature, politically unstable, unruly, and ill suited to the kind of cooperative development which any fledgling state required.

Hegel's concern was with the kind of societies which were emerging in the early nineteenth century in the Americas, which he believed, like many Europeans, to be the "land of the future, where in the ages that lie before us, the burden of the World's History shall reveal itself".[2] The distinction, however, between lands of conquest and the kind of colonies which Hegel believed the English to have established in America – settlements in empty spaces, spaces with no history – had by the time he was writing already become a recognized explanation for the increasingly marked distinction between an unruly, unprofitable, and uncivil South and an ordered, prosperous, and politic North.

The term "conquest" belonged, as we have seen, to a distinctive political ideology. In view of the historical evidence, and the triumphal rhetoric which had accompanied the occupation of the Americas almost from the beginning, the conquest – at least of Mexico and Peru – could hardly be denied. These conquests had brought large indigenous populations under the control of what was known throughout most of the sixteenth and seventeenth centuries as the "Spanish" and sometimes between 1580 and 1648, when the kingdoms of the Iberian Peninsula were under one rule, as the "The Catholic" Monarchy. It was the largest, most extensive political unit the world had ever seen, which reached from Messina to Macao, and where, as the Spanish poet Bernardo de Balbuena nicely phrased it in 1604, "Spain is joined to China, and Italy to Japan".[3]

It was never, however, politically cohesive. There never was in name a Spanish *empire*. There was, of course, the Holy Roman Empire whose emperor was, for a while, also the king of the separate kingdoms of Spain. On occasions, the kings of Castile and of Aragon (and sometimes also the kings of Portugal) assumed universalist poses, styling themselves – or at least allowing themselves to be addressed as – "lords of Christendom" or, less modestly, and in imitation of the later Roman emperors, "lords of all the world". There was even a rumour in 1563, spread by the Venetian ambassador, that Philip II proposed to have himself made "Emperor of the Americas" to compensate for the fact that his father had failed to secure for him succession to the Holy Roman Empire; and both Philip III and Philip IV allowed themselves to be addressed in semi-official publications as "emperor".[4] None of them, however, took the initiative in any of this, and no Spanish monarch, other than Charles V, ever assumed the title *imperator*. (The last Byzantine emperor, Constantine IX Palaiologos, sold the imperial title *Basileus* to King Ferdinand of Aragon, although he never had the gall to use it and in 1494 sold it to Charles VIII of France.) Despite such projects as the Count Duke of Olivares' "Union of Arms" of 1624, no Spanish monarch, before Charles III in the eighteenth century, ever made any sustained attempt to mould the various, culturally heterogeneous realms of which the monarchy was composed into anything resembling, for instance, the single unitary state, the *etat unifié* of Louis XIV's imagination. The monarch himself acted as an agent of distribution and communal justice rather than undisputed political authority, and despite the centralizing efforts by successive Castilian rulers from Philip II to Charles III, constitutionally the monarchy more often resembled a federation of quasi-independent states rather than a single, legally undivided *imperium*. As the diplomat Diego Saavedra Fajardo observed in 1639, what Spanish jurists liked to refer to as "provinces" were, in fact, what in the other states of Europe were more properly designated "nations or kingdoms".[5] This was, of course, particularly true of the European dominions. Naples and Sicily remained sovereign kingdoms – as indeed did Aragon – Milan an independent Duchy, and the Netherlands a composite of counties and principalities. When in 1539 Francisco de Vitoria, in a lecture on the laws of war, wished to provide his audience with examples of what the Aristotelians called a "perfect community", defined as one "which is not part of another commonwealth (*respublica*) but has its own laws, its own independent policy, and its own magistrates", he chose as his examples "Castile, Aragon, and others of their like" (one of which was Venice).[6] Politically and linguistically, "Spain" in 1539 was still, to borrow Metternich's famous description of Italy in 1814, a "geographical expression". The Americas, although formally incorporated into the Crown of Castile in 1523, enjoyed a large measure of independent political authority, were invariably described, before the late eighteenth century, as the "Kingdoms of the Indies" (*Reinos de Indias*), and from 1680 had been governed by a separate code of laws.[7] Charles V even listed them separately among his many titles. The Habsburg monarchy was in effect, and in all but name, a federation.

With the accession of the Bourbons in 1700, some attempt was made to replace the old Habsburg system of conciliar government by something closer to a ministerial structure. In 1721 under Louis I – known significantly as "El liberal" – the Crown had created a ministry for the Navy and the Indies which took much of the power away from the ancient and reactionary Council of the Indies and the *Casa de la Contratación*, which had exercised exclusive control over trade with the Americas. Between 1754 and 1755 Ferdinand IV established five secretariats of State, Foreign Relations, Justice and Ecclesiastical Affairs, Treasury, the Marine and the Indies, and he abolished the *Consejo* and the *Casa* altogether.

It was, however, Charles III, in many respects the archetypal "enlightened despot", who did most to give the monarchy, from New Spain to the Philippines, some measure of administrative and political cohesion. He had inherited a monarchy which, as Andrés Muriel noted in his 1838 history of the reign, perhaps more than any other in Europe, "offered such plenitude of power together with absolute and peaceful domination".[8] It may not have been so "peaceful" nor as subservient as Muriel, looking back nostalgically from the far side of the Napoleonic Wars, had imagined. But it was certainly less fractious than it had been a century before. What it clearly still lacked, however, was cohesion. As king of Naples and Sicily from 1735 to 1759, and from his alliance with the reforming prime minster of the "Kingdoms of the Two Sicilies" Bernardo Tanucci, Charles had learned what was required to devise and implement a programme of reform, and by 1787 something very close to the modern state, as it was currently understood in the monarchies of Europe, in particular Bourbon France with which Spain maintained close political and familiar ties, had come into being. Most of the men who occupied the major posts in the new ministries which now administered the state were, in the broadest sense, "enlightened". They were widely read in a theoretical literature which was dominated either by Protestants, or those – like Voltaire, Diderot, and even Montesquieu – who, from Spain at least, looked like atheists, writers who were keen to restrict the Church's role in secular life and who had an extended notion both of the role of the state and of the place of reason in human agency. They constituted an entirely new aristocracy of service. Pedro Rodríguez Campomanes, for instance, Hellenist, jurist, and historian, who was minister of finance from 1762 until 1783 and governor of the Council of Castile from 1783 until 1792, was aptly described by Adam Smith's biographer, Dugald Stewart, as one of the authors (along with Smith himself, François Quesnay, Anne-Robert Turgot, and Cesare Beccaria) of those "most celebrated works" which had "aimed at the improvement of society, – not by delineating plans for new constitutions, but by enlightening the policy of actual legislators".[9] The conde de Floridablanca, first secretary of state, who had been born José Moñino, the son of a notary (and was himself a lawyer), had himself painted by Goya not on horseback, as any of his predecessors would have done, but surrounded by artists and scientists. Gaspar Melchor de Jovellanos, a canon lawyer by training and author of some of the most trenchant economic analyses of the monarchy, who became minister for justice in 1797, similarly chose to have himself painted, also by Goya, with his head resting on his hand, in the traditional pose not of the man of action, but of the philosopher and surrounded not by the symbols of power, but by books. These men were professionals, intellectuals, who, unlike the previous generation of government servants, had risen on their merit and wished to have this fact recorded for posterity. Beneath the ministers of state, Charles also appointed a large number of career civil servants, men who lived from fixed incomes rather than, as previous office holders had done, from the fees of office. We still know very little about these men. But in a world where the greatest threat to any administration was its inability to survive over time, the creation of a true *civil* service, one that was largely independent both of the person of the king and, more crucially, of the personal household of the minister, provided the continuity which every reforming state required. This is what Frederick the Great had understood, and what Diderot had urged upon Catherine the Great. And with this shift from a bureaucracy based either on venality or kin to one based on merit came a shift in the image of kingship. Charles III clearly had no ambition to emulate the stifled attempts by Peter Leopold Grand Duke of Tuscany between 1765 and 1792 to transform the Grand Duchy into a truly virtuous *respublica* or to limit his authority by means of a constitution and an independent code of law. But his attempts to reform Naples, if nothing else, had made him aware, to a degree which no previous Spanish monarch had been, that an absolute ruler had to be, above all, the chief executive of the state. It was his office – rather than the now old and threadbare notion of the divine origin of power – which conferred unquestioned sovereignty on him.

This shift in the way in which the institution of monarchy was regarded could also be seen elsewhere. On that long scale of monarchical obligations which ran from protection to welfare, the Spanish Crown had notoriously been more concerned with the former rather than the latter. By the mid-eighteenth century, however, economics, which barely fifty years earlier had still largely retained its original Greek meaning of "household management", had come to be seen as the instrument of "natural reason" in the sphere of collective human action. The "economic system", enthused José de Campillo y Cosío, secretary to the Navy and the Indies between 1741 and 1743, which until very recently had simply not existed at all, should now be looked on as the "the principal branch of political science" governed by "such certain rules" that those in authority could only ever go wrong by ignoring them.[10] And as this new discourse of economics came increasingly to dominate the political agenda, so the monarch was compelled to busy himself more and more with the welfare of his subjects. Of the six obligations of kingship Campillo provided in a 1741 pamphlet appropriately entitled "Spain Awake", three consisted of "giving heart to the Republic", "the rewards of merit", and the "time given to business".[11] Charles III saw himself, or at least was presented by his enthusiastic ministers, as being the embodiment of all these. As Jovellanos, addressing the members of the Royal Economic Society of Madrid in 1788, said of him,

> You my lords, you who work with such zeal towards the fulfillment of your paternal objectives, you will not be unaware what was the sprit which this nation was lacking: useful sciences, economic principles, and the general spirit of enlightenment – see here what Spain owes to the reign of Charles III. If you doubt that it is on these means that the happiness of a state depends, turn your eyes to those sad epochs during which Spain was given over to superstition and ignorance. How horrific and how sad a spectacle! Religion, which had been sent from Heaven to illuminate and console mankind, had been driven by self-interest to sadden and delude him. Anarchy set up in place of order, the head of state a tyrant or victim of the nobility ... the laws openly and or insolently broken, justice despised, the check of custom broken and every object of good and public order plunged into confusion and disorder. Where then lay the spirit to which all nations owe their prosperity?[12]

It was the creation of the means to revive this "spirit" (*espritu*), a word which is used again and again by all the self-consciously "enlightened" thinkers in Spain, which the great Venetian painter Giambattista Tiepolo was alluding to in the verses which he inscribed in the cartouche on the slim black pyramid, the symbol of the glory of princes, which dominates the fresco known as the *Triumph of Spain* on the ceiling of the Throne Room of the Royal Palace in Madrid: "The monuments that you raise, lofty and not knowing how to submit to time, give renown to you, Charles for your magnanimity."[13]

An archaic and corrupt administration, a general lack of understanding of their public duty by those in power and of a dedication to the common good, and all those other ills which Jovellanos described in such pained detail were not, however, the only real, or apparent, problems the Spanish monarchy had to face. At the core of the "Spanish problem" lay, and had lain for centuries, the Spanish "empire".

In common with most extended states, the Spanish monarchy had been continually expansionist from the moment it had ceased to be a single unitary territory. And, as many contemporaries believed, once any state had embarked on a policy of expansion, it had to continue to expand if it was to continue to survive. The problem with this was that exponential growth could only, in the end, lead to fragmentation and final collapse. "This is the danger of monarchies", wrote Saavedra Fajardo, "that in seeking repose, they become unsettled. Wishing to cease, they fall. In ceasing to work, they become ill."[14] By the mid-seventeenth century, to many such as Fajardo, this was the main reason the once great Catholic monarchy now seemed to be foundering: "The longer they last, the closer they are to their end."[15] It was the inevitable fate of large, overextended empires. "As many Empires", warned Charles Davenant, "have been ruined by too much enlarging their Dominions, and by grasping at too great an extent of territories, so our interests in America may decay, by aiming at more provinces and a greater tract of land than we can either cultivate or defend."[16] To many outsiders, however, the Spanish monarchy's real difficulties appeared to be less a result of its political fragmentation, or its inability to continue to absorb new territory, than its adherence to the ideological strains which had once provided it with its coherence: the close identification with the Catholic religion (if not always consistently with the Catholic Church) and the quest for military supremacy. Both had been on prominent display since 1492, that quasi-mythical year in which the conquest of Granada, the expulsion of the Jews, and Columbus' first voyage had, in much of the subsequent historiography, launched the future "Spanish Empire".

The discovery and conquest of the Americas had also resulted in the fortuitous discovery of massive mineral wealth. This, in particular from outside Spain, was looked on as not only a blessing but also a curse. Sir Josiah Child, president of the English East India Company, observed in 1665 that the Spanish, distracted by their "intense and singular Industry in their Mines of Gold and Silver", had never been in a position fully to understand the value of "Cultivating ... the Earth, and producing Commodities for the Growth thereof".[17] It had been this overdependence on staples, in particular precious metals, rather than overextension which had, in Child's view, been the principal cause of the famous "Decline of Spain", which he was himself witnessed. It was to become a widely shared explanation for the ever-deepening economic, and military, difficulties which afflicted the monarchy. Spain, reflected Montesquieu in 1725, had failed to grasp where the true wealth of states really lies. Instead of cultivating the land in America, which meant also improving the condition and welfare of the native inhabitants, successive Spanish rulers had concentrated only on the extraction of precious metals, which were merely "a fictional good or a sign". As a consequence they had abandoned "the sources of natural wealth for the wealth of signs", and, as he pointed out, the trouble with "signs" or "fictions" is that as their number increases and they come to represent fewer and fewer things, so their value diminishes: in other words, they are inflationary, and inflation was a very poorly understood process in the early eighteenth century.[18] He had, he wrote, often in the past "deplored the blindness of Francis I in having rejected Christopher Columbus who had turned to France to make her mistress of all the treasure of the Indies". Now on reflection, however, he had come to the conclusion that "one often achieves wise things by stupid means", and the current state of Spain "should be a consolation for us all".[19] Having now lost all its former territories in Europe and failed to develop the agriculture and industry on which the true wealth of every nation resides, it had become little more than a dependency of her own colonial settlements. "The Indies and Spain are two powers under the same sovereign", he wrote, "but the Indies is the main one and Spain is merely an accessory. The policy which seeks to make the accessory lead the main power is a hopeless one; the Indies will always draw Spain towards them."[20]

The solution to this predicament, suggested in different ways by Child and Montesquieu, was to transform the Spanish monarchy from one of conquest to one of commerce, from an ideologically "closed" society to an ideologically "open" one. Free trade and freedom from religious and other extra-economic considerations were the only ways in which a modern society could hope to flourish. In that way, concluded, Montesquieu, "in place of a great treasure [Spain] would have had a great people".[21] What this meant in effect was following what was widely believed to have been the path to success, which the English and the Dutch had adopted: the creation of empires based not on conquest but on supposedly peaceful settlement, and not on the extraction of raw materials but on trade. Modernity in the Atlantic world as within Europe itself meant replacing archaic warrior societies with ones based on peaceful exchange. In the modern world, which in the account that Adam Smith gives of it in *The Wealth of Nations* had been launched by the momentous voyages of Columbus and Vasco da Gama, trade would replace warfare.[22]

There were, at least by the beginning of the eighteenth century, many in Spain who had come to similar conclusions. One of them was the widely influential political economist Jerónimo de Uztaríz. Castile, he wrote in 1724, could only hope to emulate its enemies' astonishing success by adopting the "new maxims" – the mercantilist policies by which Louis XIV's controller-general of finances Jean-Baptiste Colbert had succeeded in transforming France from a nation of warriors into one of merchants[23] But adopting the "maxims" of your former enemies is, of course, no easy matter.[24] As the Spanish ambassador Alonso Cardenas is said to have told the Earl of Clarendon, in 1652, when the latter had argued that the insistence on religious conformity and the restriction of all overseas trade to Castile had been the ruin of Spain, "to ask a liberty from the Inquisition and free sailing in the West Indies, was to ask his master's two eyes".[25]

By the second half of the eighteenth century a number of powerful figures began to press for a reevaluation of the political and cultural objectives of the Spanish monarchy along the lines suggested by her French and British critics.[26] They also recognized that the need to reform the monarchy had become far more than the simple quest for an economically productive and political-compliant association of dominions. It had become, in effect, a crisis of identity. One of the most striking, and most influential, of these was José de Campillo y Cosío, secretary to the Navy and the Indies between 1741 and 1743, who in the 1740s drew up a project for the complete overhaul of the overseas empire, entitled *A New System of Economic Government for America*.[27]

Spanish America, argued Campillo, had been founded on, and was still run in the interests of, what had, by the mid-eighteenth century, been identified as the paramount national malaise, in a phrase echoed by every eighteenth-century Spanish reformer: "the spirit of conquest" – *el espiritú de la conquista*. As a consequence of this single-minded pursuit of military glory and mineral wealth, Spain now earned less from her American possessions than Britain and France did from the islands of Barbados and Martinique, respectively.[28] Campillo's observation was to become something of a commonplace, as was his unfavourable comparison with the histories of the overseas territories of Britain and France.

In Campillo's view, conquest had been both legitimate and, to a certain degree, profitable for the Spanish Crown during the sixteenth century. It had been in keeping both with the martial spirit of the times and with the immediate need to subjugate large numbers of Indians (something which neither the British nor the French had ever had to face).[29] But those times had passed very rapidly, and the following century which should have been a Golden Age had been instead "a century of disgrace and loss" as the Spaniards, rather than consolidating their hold over what they had already

gained and diversifying the colonial economy, had simply gone on conquering.[30] The conquistadores and their heirs, concerned only to perpetuate an
archaic society based on military valour, had failed to understand that the
true wealth of a society derived from political and social order, not from
pillage. The consequences had been dire. Look, said Campillo, at the Great
Khan (the ruler of China), with less able ministers than the King of Spain and
less territory, he nonetheless has a greater income, and, Campillo added
darkly, "nor are his vassals so oppressed".[31] The Americas had been laid
waste by their European conquerors. The greatest and most valuable part of
the state – its people – had been reduced to a fraction of its previous number
and what few Native Americans still remained had been rendered, through
tyrannical abuse, entirely unproductive. What had once been "a whole and
politic nation in the hands of the natives and in the darkness of barbarism"
had, under its European Christian rulers, become instead "so many great,
uncultivated, unpopulated, almost wholly annihilated provinces, which
might yet be the richest in the world".[32] It would have been far better, he
argued, if the Spaniards had followed the example of the French in Canada
and merely traded rather than slaughtered, at enormous cost to themselves,
peoples from whom they could have derived some economic benefit. Faced,
however, as Spain was with a land laid waste, she should now "follow
entirely different maxims" and with these transform the corrupt and indolent subjects of the Spanish crown "towards commerce and the cultivation of
those precious fruits [of the land], to create a just community, and by means
of good economic government, reduce the Indians to a civil life, by treating
them with kindness and sweetness, and thus encourage them to become
industrious, and by this means make them useful vassals, and Spaniards."
In other words, this would have the effect of making medieval subjects into
modern citizens and the still uncivil Indians into civilized beings – Spanish in
all but name – capable of taking their place in society alongside, and not
merely beneath, their Spanish masters. But, Campillo concluded ruefully,
"we are always standing with weapons in our hands".[33]

Campillo y Cosío's generally pessimistic view of the long-term effects of the
Spanish military ethos was echoed most powerfully by Campomanes. In
1762, at much the same time as Campillo y Cosío's *New System* began to
circulate in enlightened circles in Madrid, Campomanes published his *Reflections on Spanish Trade with the Indies,* in part a response to the criticisms of
the Spanish empire made by Josiah Child in his *A New Discourse on Trade –*
who, in Campomanes' opinion, had far more to offer "with great originality"
than any Spaniard on the subject – and to Montesquieu's remarks in *The
Spirit of the Laws.*[34] "All nations believe", he wrote, "that wealth, by means
of commerce, navigation and industry is the sole source of public happiness.
Today's wars are more concerned with gaining control over trade with the
colonies, than they are with dominium."[35] For centuries the Spanish Empire
had been nothing more than a conduit conveying gold and silver to all

the nations of Europe from which Spain itself had gained very little. And this he, too, attributed to the "spirit of conquest".[36] Throughout the political and economic crisis which, in one way or another, had devastated most of Europe during the seventeenth century, Spain, blinded by her stubborn premodern belief in the overwhelming need for military success, had resolutely failed to recognize "its true interests".[37] The English and the French, by contrast, who were "more refined" than the Spanish (he does not mention the Portuguese), had sought in the New World not "the foundation of a town or of a new empire" but instead "objects of commerce and, as such, [had] directed their attention to them".[38]

On this point Campomanes was entirely in agreement with both Child and Montesquieu. Like Campillo, he was also convinced that ultimately the Spanish problem could not be resolved by merely tinkering with existing structures. The Spanish monarchy had to change its very being; it had, in a phrase he used often, to *cambiar su ser*.[39] To do this it had to dedicate itself in ways it had never done before to what was known as "public happiness", a somewhat vague phrase which circulated widely in the various languages of political theory throughout Europe in the eighteenth century.[40] To bring widespread happiness to its subjects, the archaic Hispanic monarchy would have to be recast as, what it had sometimes claimed to be but in reality never had, not a single "composite state" but a metropolis with a number of colonies – in other words, as a true *empire*. To become a true empire, however, it would first have to be re-invented as something similar to the trans-Atlantic state which the British were then in the process of constructing in the North. The consequences for both Spain and Britain would, of course, in the end prove to be disastrous, but in 1762 Campomanes could not have foreseen that.

With this objective in mind, the *Reflections* set out to redescribe the old distinction between the Kingdoms of the Indies and the various dominions within Europe itself. Campomanes is one of the first to speak consistently of the American "colonies" and to treat them, not as a distinct although dependent part of Castile, but as communities comparable with the colonies which Britain, and to some degree France, had established in North America: quasi-independent communities whose benefits, and whose own internal development, depended on commerce and agriculture. The difference between the English and the Spanish colonies, however, was that the latter, like those of the Romans, Arabs, and Vikings which had preceded them, had been what Campomanes termed "military". The British, in contrast, had followed the example of the Greek and Phoenicians whose overseas settlements had been "mercantile and pacific".[41] And "from military colonies no country has ever derived any appreciable advantage because they have always been an instrument of oppression and arbitrary government". True, the Spanish colonies had had the effect of "reducing those barbarous nations and dispersing among them a state of civility and religious observation (*culto religioso*), without which they would have remained locked into barbarism and idolatry–their lands without any agriculture to check their ferocity", whereas the British had merely thrust the indigenes aside.[42] Laudable this might have been, it had, however, brought very little of any value to the mother country, nor, in the long run, had it resulted in the economic prosperity of the indigenous inhabitants themselves. They might now be Christians, but they were still a long way from being "civilized".

Having begun with the illusion that the Romans provided the only viable model for an expansive empire, the Castilian Crown, once it had conquered most of America, had then made "two capital errors", which the Romans would never have committed. The first had been to limit access to the American trade to Castilians. The Spanish Empire constituted a vast internal market, yet, in 1596, Philip II had even denied the Portuguese (who were at that time subjects of the Castilian Crown) any share in the American trade, and in 1634, Philip IV had prevented them for trading in the Philippines.[43] The same limitations had been applied to Flemings, Italians, and in some cases Aragonese. The second mistake had been to oblige all trade with the Indies to pass through the port of Seville. "Such has been the blindness and lack of economic principles which has deluded our politicians", he concluded in 1788, "for so long a span of years that illness become for them a second nature."[44]

Campomanes' project was, in broad outline, to transform the militaristic Spanish monarchy into something closer to the "Phoenician" British Empire. It would have opened up the American markets to all the subjects of the Castilian Crown and, crucially, deregulated the trade between them. The introduction of a free-trade zone, which would still be confined within the limits of the old Spanish *imperium*, was to be linked to a policy of educational restructuring. Spaniards – all Spaniards – in Campomanes' opinion, had to be trained to be modern economic beings. This was the claim behind his *Discourse on Popular Education* of 1775 – a text which reiterates many of the points made in the *Reflections* – and was taken up some years later by the political economist and one of Campomanes' correspondents, Gaspar Melchor de Jovellanos, in his widely influential *Inquiry into the Agrarian Law* of 1793. From such beginnings the ethos of the commercial society would come slowly to replace the older order of domination. And with the establishment of free trade between all its various far-flung regions, Campomanes was confident that Spain would finally be able to "change its being".

Like Campillo y Cosío and Jovellanos, Campomanes was calling initially for economic and structural, not political, change as a means of bringing about the new, modern commercial "being" of the Spanish monarchy. Yet it soon became apparent that the only political order which would make his new commercial order possible was not a revivified version of the ancient monarchy – the now rapidly dwindling concept of a trans-Atlantic community, of a *ius publicum*, embodied in the legal person of the king. Paradoxically the new modern "empire" could only be conceived as some kind of federation. This became increasingly obvious to both the Spanish and the French as the events of the 1770s moved inexorably toward war between the British Crown and its American colonies. In 1774, in a remarkably prescient reflection on what he saw as the inevitable progress of large imperial states to disintegration, Henry Home, Lord Kames, accurately predicted the inevitable outcome of the looming conflict with America. The American colonists, he wrote, "have the spirit of a free people and are enflamed with patriotism". Their "already rapid growth in population and in opulence" would ensure that in less than a century they would be "a match for the mother country". The outcome of the ensuing war – if the mother country were foolish enough to engage in one – would be inescapable. "Being thus delivered from a foreign yoke", he went on, "their first care will be a choice of a proper government; and it is not difficult to foresee what government will be chosen. A people animated with the new blessings of liberty and independence will not incline to kingly government . . . . We may pronounce with assurance that each colony will chuse for itself a republican government."[45] And if this were to be the outcome, then it would be far wiser for the "mother country" to grant its angry and dissatisfied daughters their independence before they took it for themselves. Two years later, Anne-Robert Turgot, *philosophe*, political economist, and then French minister of finance, reflecting of the possible fate of the Spanish colonies in the aftermath of the American War of Independence, came to very much the same conclusion. Colonies, he argued, had actually only ever been of real economic value to those who had free and independent commerce with them, which were generally not their political masters. "The revenue", he wrote, "which the government derives from its colonies is, therefore, worthless to the state considered as a political power." The states which had benefited most from the American colonies, both North and South, were the Low Countries, the Austrian lands, and Switzerland, the latter two of which had no overseas possession whatsoever. "One would be tempted to question", he wrote, "whether it would not be more advantageous for us [the Bourbon monarchy] to leave them to their own devices in complete liberty rather than wait for the events that will force us to take that course. . . . Wise and happy", he concluded, "would be the nation which would consent to see its colonies as allied provinces rather that subjected to the metropolis."[46]

Some kind of federal solution to the American colonial crisis – both North and South – was widely discussed in the 1770s as the conflict between Britain and its American colonies passed from being a imminent threat to an all-to-present reality. Writing in February 1778, when the outcome of the American Revolutionary War was still uncertain, Adam Smith, who in David Hume's opinion was "very zealous in American affairs", reflected that if the English were to win the war, the only possible outcome would be that any subsequent government would have to be a military one, and this would be unacceptable to the "ulcerated minds of the Americans", who "will for more than a century to come, be at all times ready to take up arms in order to overturn it". It would be massively costly to maintain, and Britain would gain from it "scarce anything but the disgrace of being supposed to oppress a people whom we have long talked of, not only as of our fellow subjects, but as of our bretheren and even as of our children". Far better would be a federal union which would link the Thirteen Colonies to Britain in much the same way as the union of 1707 had linked England to Scotland. "Unfortunately", he concluded, "the plan for a constitutional union with our colonies and of an American representation seems not to be agreeable to any considerable party of men in Great Britain."[47]

Five years later in 1782, when the war was all but over, William Petty, Earl of Shelburne (the man who would finally make peace with America), in a last desperate attempt to hang on to the colonies, came up with a not dissimilar proposal in which the Thirteen Colonies would be reconstituted as a species of consortium, each with its own legislature, but all ultimately subject to the Crown. Although the suggestion drew on the distinction between "internal" and "external" spheres of sovereignty which the colonists, Benjamin Franklin in particular, had previously accepted, it came too late to be of any practical use and was met with ironic derision.[48] "Surely", remarked Benjamin Franklin, "there was never a more preposterous chimera conceived in the brain of a minister." (In 1754, however, Franklin himself seems to have believed that just such a union would be "very acceptable to the colonies".)[49]

The man who saw most clearly that a federation of some kind was the only means by which the Spanish monarchy could preserve its hold over the Americas was Pedro Pablo Abarca de Bolea, Count of Aranda, one-time president of the Council of Castile, an acquaintance of Voltaire and the abbé Guillaume-Thomas Raynal, and a man who belonged to the same enlightened ministerial elite as Campomanes, Floridablanca, and Jovellanos. Aranda had spent much of the 1770s worrying about the possible fate of the Kingdoms of the Indies in the wake of a possible war between Britain and its colonies. In April 1775, he wrote to the First Minister, Pablo Jerónimo Grimaldi, warning him that should the British colonies become "united provinces", and he had little doubt that that was what they would eventually become,

> they might well assist the Spanish Americans to throw off the European yolk, supposing this to be as insufferable to the Spanish as it is to the English Americans, and even more so because of the travails they have had to endure from various governors who have sucked her blood, and because the burdens under which they live are infinitely more rigid than those of the English colonists, because in the end these partake, in great measure of the liberty of British laws.[50]

Immediately after the signing of the Peace of Paris at Versailles 1783, which formally recognized the independence of the United States, Aranda, who was then Spanish ambassador to France, prepared a secret memorandum, the *Presentation of the Count of Aranda to King Charles III on the Desirability of Creating Independent Kingdoms in America*, arguing for the possible dismemberment of the American colonial system. His worst fears had now been realized. "A day will come", he told Charles, all too presciently, "when this federal republic will grow and turn into a giant and a colossus, terrible for all those regions."[51] The only way to prevent the South following the North was to recast the Kingdoms of the Indies as semi-independent sovereign states. "Your Majesty", he wrote, "should dispossess himself of all his possession in both Americas", while preserving only the islands of Cuba and Puerto Rico as a basis for Spanish trade. All the rest, he suggested, should be transformed into three independent kingdoms ruled in loose federation by imported European princes seated on thrones in Mexico City, Bogotá, and Lima under, not a Spanish Monarch, but, as the Holy Roman Emperors had (supposedly) conceived the term, a Spanish Emperor.

Such a federation would, Aranda believed, yield more to the Spanish treasury in trade than the colonies now did in taxation. Once united, the three kingdoms would not only have no further incentive to seek complete separation from Spain but also be far more capable, and politically more inclined, to resist the new external threat now posed by the new United States. Federal states of the kind he was proposing were, he believed, likely in the long run to be far stronger, and economically more prosperous, than any other.

What made Aranda's project somewhat more plausible than Shelburne's had been was that it drew on the federalizing tendencies which had always existed within the older Habsburg *monarchia*. At the time, however, his vision of a new, independent but closely allied system of independent states fell on deaf ears. The Spanish ignored it; the Creoles rejected it. "We renounce", wrote Juan Pablo Viscardo in 1791, on behalf of his fellow "Spanish-Americans", "the ridiculous system of union and equality."[52] Thirty years later, however, it was revived by the Mexican historian Lucas Alamán, who had served as deputy for Guanajuato at the Cortes of 1821 and subsequently became secretary of state and minister of domestic and foreign relations of the now independent state of Mexico. Alamán described Aranda's *Presentation* as "prophetic" and argued that it had been because "these prudent councils were not heard in time" that the Creole population of the American colonies had been driven irreversibly toward independence from Spain.[53]

As Alamán had understood all too clearly with hindsight, Aranda's project was based on the assumption that the colonies could no longer remain a fully integrated part of the metropolis and that, if something radical was not attempted, the result could only be insurgency and the subsequent creation of new states – new nations – which might become not merely independent of the "mother country" but actively hostile to its interests.

II

After the first insurgency in Mexico in 1810, and the outbreak of war in what is now Venezuela two years later, the similarity between the position of the Spaniards then and the situation in which the English had found themselves in 1776 became starkly apparent. In keeping with the persistent adherence of both monarchs, to the "spirit of conquest" despite the writings of their advisors, and even of their more enlightened ministers, both had turned unthinkingly to war rather than reform and negotiation. In 1815, the French pamphleteer, former Napoleonic ambassador, and salaried champion of Simón Bolívar Dominique-Georges-Frédéric Dufour De Pradt called on the victors of the Napoleonic Wars to eradicate from Europe and its overseas dependencies forever the "military spirit". The monarchies of Europe, having laid down their "material arms" at the Congress of Vienna, should now also lay down what he described as "those weapons we might call moral – arms that are even more envenomed than the others: so that the language of war should be followed by the language of peace".[54]

Two years later, he warned Spain, which had failed to heed this message, that she "ought to ask of herself what it will be necessary to do when she can no longer *conqueror*, and no longer keep what she has conquered; whether it would not be as well to make friends of those whom she can no longer have for subjects".[55] As we know, however, the Spanish monarchs did not ask themselves such questions. Charles III and Charles IV (if not Ferdinand VII) had been able to imagine themselves as the rulers of a modern commercial empire. They could even accommodate themselves to a degree of local autonomy among the colonies and the possibility – actively pursued under Charles III – that Creoles and Castilians might have equal rights to public office in both the metropolis and the colonies. What they could not conceive, any more than George III, was the existence of fully autonomous regions within the territorial limits of the monarchy.

Their failure to do so led, of course, as it had done in the British case, to what was in effect a civil war and the final independence of the colonies. And, as in the North American case, this break resulted not only in the severance of authority between the former metropolis and the colonies but also, ultimately, to the creation of two distinctive political systems.

The Spanish-American colonies, however, were in a far more precarious condition than their northern neighbors. The Thirteen Colonies of British North America, although divided constitutionally, culturally (and religiously) were nonetheless ethnically homogenous. The indigenous populations might serve Thomas Jefferson as a model of "savage" courage and independence, but it was not one he wished to see replicated in the new United States. The example of the Iroquois Confederacy had prompted Benjamin Franklin to remark acidly that, if "Six Nations of ignorant savages should be capable of forming a scheme for such a union", then civilized, enlightened Englishmen "to whom it is more necessary and must be more advantageous, and who cannot be supposed to want an equal understanding of their interests" ought surely to be able to do the same.[56] But otherwise the American Indian existed only to be displaced. The Kingdoms of the Indies, however, had always formally been societies composed of Creoles, and Indians, and subsequently of Africans. The appeal to largely imaginary "Inca" and "Aztec" pasts, which had sustained so much so-called "criollo patriotism" throughout the late eighteenth century in Peru and Mexico and is still a potent component of modern Mexican national consciousness, would have been unthinkable in the North.

As Simón Bolívar – *El Liberator* – told his English correspondent in the most sustained of his political writings, the *Jamaica Letter* of September 1815, in a passage he repeated four years later in his address to the legislators of the new state of Venezuela, the Spanish Americans "hardly preserve a vestige of what was in other times, and, on the other hand, we are neither Indians nor Europeans, but a sort of middle species between the legitimate owners of this land and the Spanish usurpers".[57] Caught in this way between two cultures and separated by time, race, and, now, political aspiration from their European past, the Spanish Americans, "strangers to the world of politics, and estranged from anything which might in some measure exercise our intelligence", had, as Bolívar vividly phrased it, for 300 years, "passed down the centuries like blind men between colours".[58]

Bolívar was exaggerating, perhaps. But he was certainly right in his claim that the United States was, in many important respects, unlike anything to be found in the South.[59] As he told the future legislators of Venezuela, the English colonies had not only been largely self-governing for most of their existence, but also preserved their cultural and their ethnic purity. The Spanish Americans, by contrast, were "neither European nor American. ... It is impossible to know, with precision to which human family we belong. The greater part of the indigenes have been annihilated, the Europeans have mingled with Americans [i.e. Creoles] and Africans, and these have merged with the Indians and the Europeans." The only solution to such hybridity lay in its extinction, in what he called "a perfect political equality".[60] Henceforth, there would be no more Creoles no more Africans or Indians, no more of the proliferating range of mestizos and *castas* of which the old Kingdoms of the Indies had been made up. Now there would be only Venezuelans or Chileans, Mexicans or Peruvians. It is perhaps for this reason that no modern Spanish-America state has been properly multiracial or multicultural. Despite the celebration of Atahualpa and Montezuma, they certainly held out no more hope of self-determination for the Indians than their northern counterparts. With the exception of Cuba's celebration of Africaness, even modern Marxist groups have shown very little interest in the culture or political futures of non-Europeans – something which led some indigenous nationalist groups to reject socialism as fiercely as they have rejected their white rulers. The Guatemalan Maya, for instance, refused to associate with the Marxist-Leninist URNG – *Union Revolucionaria Nacional de Guatemala* – in the 1960s and 1970s because, in the words of one of their members, "the URNG was always colonial in its form (ladino rulers and Maya subordinates) in its content (the class struggle excludes, or should take precedence over the anti-colonial struggle) and its objective (there is to be no self-determination for the Maya people within the Ladino socialist state)".[61] The same held true for the much exploited hostility in Nicaragua in the 1980s between the Mesquito Indians and the Sandinistas. Even in Mexico – the state which continues to make the most extensive political use of the past of its aboriginal peoples – these peoples have always been subjected to a process of mythological sanitization. The great forebears of the Mexican nation are the "Aztecs" (themselves an eighteenth-century fiction). The modern population of Chiapas are merely "Indios".

At the moment of independence, furthermore, Creole identities were not necessarily linked to a sense of *political* separateness. They constituted, in the still useful distinction made by the German liberal historian Friedrich Meinecke in the early twentieth century, not "national-states" (*Statsnationen*), but "cultural-nations" (*Kulturnationen*).[62] And so long as these "cultural nations" remained part of a monarchy composed of a number of such nations under a single ruler, there clearly existed no call for political separateness. And what was true of, say, Mexico or Peru was equally true of Aragon or Navarre. Each colluded in the claim that they were autonomous regions voluntarily associated with a larger political entity which was, of course, not a nation either, nor even a federal government, but a symbolically embodied form: the monarchy itself. When, therefore, that monarchy was dissolved forcibly by Napoleon in 1808, and the monarch himself sent into exile, the traditional focus of loyalty in effect vanished. The Cortes of Cádiz, which convened in 1812, were charged with the task of creating a new and "liberal" – a term which the delegates at Cádiz were the first to use in its modern sense – constitution for the post-Napoleonic order. This sought to re-imagine the former integrity of the entire Hispanic world by declaring that the new Spanish nation was to include all "Spaniards", which was initially intended to mean all the residents – with the exception of African slaves and "pure" Indians – of the former kingdoms on both sides of the Atlantic and to grant all of them equal rights and equality of representation.[63] Napoleon's invasion of Spain, declared Benjamin Constant, might, like all his conquests, have been anachronistic and unjust, but it had served to "reawaken a generous people from their stupor".[64]

This initial awakening, however, proved to be a brief one. When Ferdinand VII returned in 1814, he dissolved the Cortes, repudiated most of the articles of the constitution, and, oblivious of what had taken place in the north three decades earlier, launched what was to become a prolonged, bloody, and ultimately futile attempt to reconquer America.

But even if the liberal constitution had survived, it is doubtful that it would have been workable, in the long run, for the entire Hispanic world. For the American Creoles, unlike their Peninsular counterparts, were unable, ultimately, to describe any future political order in terms of a tradition which could trace its origins back to the "Ancient Constitution" of Castile in which the king had supposedly ruled with the participation and consent of his subjects. There existed for them no plausible equivalent to Magna Carta, much less any events as recent as the Glorious Revolution of 1688 to which they could make some kind of legitimating appeal. They could not, as the leaders of the American Revolution had done, claim to be upholding values and political traditions which the metropolis itself had betrayed. The political experience of the Creole elite, as Bolívar said over and over again, had only ever been one, not of participation, but of exclusion. In the end they had no real option but to effect the transition from *Kulturnationen* to *Statsnationen*, and that required the creation of political societies *ex nihilo*. The North Americans by contrast had gone the other way. The provincial gentlemen who led the revolution were always, to use Jefferson's phrase, "British-Americans". In 1776, they had signed into being a new *Statsnationen*. It would take a long time, and a civil war, before they were able to create an enduring *Kulturnationen*.

Creating new states, however, was at best a precarious and protracted business. "The subversion of established principles, the mutation of customs, the overthrow of opinion", warned Bolívar in September 1814, "and the establishment of the goals of liberty in a land of slaves", even if it were within human reach, was impossible to achieve in the short run.[65] Without some obvious source of legitimacy, without some image, symbol, or ideology to compel the imagination of its future citizens, the new state was often doomed to disintegration once the always unsteady unity created by the initial revolutionary moment had passed. One solution to this problem – the solution which the United Provinces of the Netherlands had attempted in 1580 – was to look for political legitimacy through dynastic inheritance. The attempts to import European monarchs from the request in 1825 by the Argentine Manuel Belgrano, that the Infante Francisco de Paula, youngest son of Charles IV, be made independent sovereign of Rio de la Plata (which was denied), to the tragi-comic reign of Maximilian in Mexico in 1864–7 were, however, doomed to failure if only because a monarchy is always more than a monarch. None of these imported princelings, nor the new Bourbon monarchies which François -René, Vicomte de Chateaubriand proposed for South America at the Congress of Verona in 1822, could have survived in practice with only the support of an imagined aristocracy, "miserable", in Bolívar's words, "covered in poverty and ignorance", and with none of the social and cultural apparatus which had enabled the Europeans to command the loyalty of their subjects.[66] A reconstituted monarchism, however liberal, was, as most of the ideologues of the independence movement recognized, a cultural impossibility in societies whose integrity as communities had, by the first decades of the nineteenth century, come to be largely dependent on their separation from a monarchical regime. As De Pradt pointed out in 1817, "in the number of American constitutions which have come to my notice, there has not been one that included a single word referring to royalty. On the contrary all are marked by a strong die of republicanism and incline more to the institutions of the United States than to those of Europe."[67]

The American Revolution, by creating a republic in place of a monarchy, had, wrote De Pradt eight years later echoing Tom Paine, "set in motion the social reformation which would [henceforth] resonate throughout the universe". Whatever now became of the former Spanish colonies, they could not fail to follow that "social reformation".[68] Or as one historian of the emancipation of Peru Carlos Lissón bluntly phrased it in 1867, Peru "was independent because its sons became men, and republican because the Republic is the truth".[69] Emancipation from Spain, that is, had created among her former colonial subjects the desire to become citizens, and citizens in anything resembling Rousseau's sense of the term – which was also espoused by most of the political ideologues of the independence movements – could not be created under the enforced tutelage of monarchy.

The early emergence of such significant cultural and political divergences between the colonies and the mother country failed, however, to ensure any degree of political convergence between the colonies themselves (any more than they had in the North). By 1825, the *Uti possidetis* agreement of 1810, which had attempted to reaffirm the old Viceregal boundaries, had effectively collapsed, and the Kingdoms of the Indies had quickly dissolved into separate republics, each with a fierce sense of its own local identity and territorial boundaries. Once, that is, the monarch as a residual focus of loyalty had gone, the Spanish-American colonies had very little to hold them together beyond a common wish for independence and, at least in the first instance, a common commitment, as Du Pradt had seen, to a republican ideal. The fissiparous programmes for some larger structure of states, those of Francisco de Miranda's new "Inca Empire", which was to have embraced the former Viceroyalties of Peru and New Granada and subjected them to a state based on a curious conflation of the Roman Senate and the House of Commons – or Manuel Belgrano's, not dissimilar "Incan Monarchy" aptly named the "United Kingdom of the River Plate" of 1825 – all came to nothing, while, the grandest of them all, Bolívar's project for a union of "Gran Colombia", which was intended to reach from Venezuela to Chile, collapsed even before its creator's own death.[70]

The problem with the first two of these was that, despite Miranda and Belgrano's allusion to the Inca past, they were all conceived as essentially federal systems, and federalism, as Bolívar himself insisted, could not be made to work in the South as it had in the North because it relied on a system of representation; and in Bolívar's view, "our Moral Constitution did not yet possess the consistency necessary to receive the benefit of a fully representative government, Sublime enough that it could be adapted to a Republic of Saints".[71] The "federal system" demanded "virtues and political talents far superior to our own", while popular government, "far from being favourable to us will, I fear, be our ruin".[72]

A few years earlier the Neapolitan Vicenzo Cuoco had made much the same observation of the short-lived "Parthenopean Republic" of 1799 in Naples, which had been another attempt to transform a Bourbon monarchy into a form of representative republic. True republics, he wrote, could only be founded where there already existed, "the memory of some earlier better government like that Magna Carta which has been the compass of the English revolution".[73] No such memory existed in Naples, and none existed in Spanish America. In both cases the revolutionaries turned, not to "representation", but to "virtue', and they looked, not forward to modern commercial society, but back to the republics of the ancient world.

The marked differences in cultural origins between the British North and the Spanish South resulted in the creation of two very different kinds of republican projects, which have been conveniently labelled "ancient" and "modern" republicanism. The distinction was formulated most clearly by Benjamin Constant in his famous essay of 1819, "The Liberty of the Ancients Compared with That of the Moderns". Ancient republics, he pointed out, were necessarily small, militarized societies which involved all their citizens in the common project of government and defence. Their driving force, what Montesquieu had called their "principal", was "virtue". Such communities were composed, in Rousseau's highly influential redescription of the ancient model, not of men but of citizens, and the private life of the individual was subsumed entirely by the public life of the community, the *res-publica*. "What the ancients called liberty", wrote Constant, constituted in effect, "the complete subjection of the individual to the authority of the whole". The ancient citizen, as a citizen, decided on peace and war, but "as an individual, he is circumscribed, observed, and criticized in all his actions".[74]

Modern republics, by contrast, were large commercial societies whose citizens ruled through representation and whose private lives remained distinct from their public ones; indeed the public domain existed only to protect and enhance the private. They were constitutional and, in the familiar sense, they were liberal also. The liberty provided by the modern republic, and subsequently by liberal democratic society, created what, in Rousseau's terms, comes close to being a contradiction, namely, a "private citizen". In what its twentieth-century enemies called "the bourgeois liberal republic", in contrast, men were able to be men *and* citizens.[75] They had no need to be virtuous; they had only to be law-abiding. They had access, if only as voters, to a political life, which they had been denied under the monarchies of the ancien regime. They were thus permitted to become fully autonomous social beings; however, they were not wholly subject to the state of which they formed a part. The liberal state, in other words, provided its citizens not merely with *political* liberty but also with civil liberty. For most moderns the crucial defining features of republicanism were its reliance on representation and its dedication to commerce. This alone could ensure the citizen body the necessarily liberty from constraint – and in particular liberty from interference by the state – which they required to pursue their own private lives.

It would, of course, be an oversimplification to suggest that whereas the cultural and political traditions of the North had inclined Jefferson's "British-Americans" toward modern conceptions of the republic, Spanish Americans were exclusively drawn by the ancient models. It is broadly speaking true, however, to say that the Creoles had only ever pursued free-trade objectives for the immediate economic benefits they would obviously bring. They had little understanding of the European faith in commerce as a civilizing agency which had agitated Montesquieu and via Montesquieu, Campomanes and Jovellanos, and still less the ambition to extend its benefits to the whole of mankind. And they had no understanding of, nor particular sympathy for, the idea of representation. For although it is unlikely that, as Bolívar claimed, the *constitución moral* of the new states was not yet fit for representation, it was certainly true that representation implied, even in the restricted sense that term was used at the end of the eighteenth century, a broad franchise, which would inevitably have threatened the hegemony exercised by the Creole elite. Some kind of "ancient republicanism" by contrast seemed to offer the prospect of economic and social regeneration within a united community in which – since the ancient republic was oligarchical – the old élites could retain all their power and wealth. Only an essentially ancient republic could, in Bolívar's words, "regenerate the character and customs which tyranny and war have bequeathed to us", and only such a republic would be able to create in the rain forests "a Moral Power, taken from the depths of antiquity and from those forgotten laws which, at one time sustained virtue among the ancient Greeks and the Romans". Even that most cherished instrument of public compliance in the Ancient World, the Roman censors, was to be a feature of the new American Republic. Bolívar told the legislators at Angostura in a passage which, at least as far as the sentiments it expresses, could have been taken directly from Rousseau,

> [we shall] take from Athens the Areopagus and the guardians of customs and the Laws; from Rome take the censors and the domestic tribunals, and by making a holy union of all these moral institutions, we will revive in the world the idea of a people which is not content to be only free and strong, but also wishes to be virtuous. We will take from Sparta its austere establishments and by creating out of these three streams a fountain of virtue, we will give to our Republic a fourth force whose strength will be the childhood and the hearts of men: public spirit, good customs and Republican morality.[76]

And this democratic, ancient republic was, he told the Chilean general Bernardo O'Higgins in June 1822, in allusion to Rousseau's *Du Contrat social*, to be grounded on "the social pact which must make of this world one Republican nation".[77]

All of this might, as one anonymous and hostile observer noted in 1820, seem to be little more than the image of "a world which is, in some way fantastic, that can be made to justify the past and authorise the hopes of the future".[78] But its chimerical nature – which Bolívar himself both saw and rejected – was not its only defect. For it was precisely this "fountain of virtue", as Constant had himself recognized in an article in the *Courrier français* denouncing *El Liberator* as little more than a new, and diminished, Napoleon, which Bolívar consistently understood by the term "liberal". It was the liberty which could be extended only to those capable of practicing "republican virtue", and this, by definition, meant only those who were powerful enough to carry some force in political life. As Bolívar apparently told Charles Ricketts, the British consul in Lima, in 1826, his heart "beats in favour of liberty" but his head "leans towards aristocracy".[79] That aristocracy was still, of course, to be made up precisely of the *aristoi* – the best – but it would be an oligarchy none the less. Similarly the "public opinion" to which he, and so many other leaders of the independence movement, made continual reference, was not, as it was for all other liberal thinkers from Constant to Tocqueville and John Stuart Mill (and had been for Montesquieu), a force to be used to restrain the ambitions of those in power. It was instead the expression of a collective political will, a synonym for Rousseau's *volonté general*. The new Spanish-American republics, from Mexico to Argentina, were all in their often divergent ways attempts to create truly new societies in the new world. It was only paradoxical that the intellectual materials to which their most powerful advocates turned for inspiration were also ancient ones.

The former Kingdoms of the Indies had, thus, not merely seceded, they had taken on a political form, and espoused a political ideology, which were wholly unlike anything which had preceded them and anything which might have been imaginable within the older Hispanic world. Because the ideologues of the Spanish-American liberation movements had not, as the English Americans had, looked back to any imaginary past as a model for their own future, they were prevented from appropriating the kind of liberalizing institutions which had been behind the thinking of Jerónimo de Uztaríz, Campillo y Cosío, and Campomanes, if only because these had not, in the end, resulted in the kind of pan-Hispanic community Aranda had hoped for. Instead they had produced the ultimately disastrous Bourbon Reforms, an attempt to restructure the existing kingdoms along broadly French lines, which succeeded in cutting off the Spanish Creoles from much of the power the old system had offered them while providing them with nothing new in their place. And because of this, what they had all attempted in their own very different ways to create was a political culture which, ideologically at least, had far more in common with the French than the North American Revolution. As a form of modernity the Spanish-American experiments in republicanism were doomed, as surely as the French, to collapse, as they inevitably did, into some kind of despotic government.

### Endnotes

1  *The Philosophy of History*, J. Sibree trans. (New York: Dover Publications, 1956), 83–4.
2  Ibid., 86.
3  Serge Gruzinski, *Les Quatres parties du monde: Histoire d'une mondialisation* (Paris: Editions de la Martinière, 2004), 49.
4  See my *Lords of All the World*, 32.
5  *Empresas políticas: Idea de un príncipe político-cristiano*, A. Vaquero ed. (Madrid: Editorial nacional, 1976), 75–6.
6  "On the Law of War", 1. 2, *Political Writings*, 301.
7  The *Nueva Recopilación de leyes de los reynos de las Indias* compiled by the jurist Juan Solorzano y Pereira in the 1650s but only promulgated in 1680 after his death.
8  *Gobierno del señor rey Carlos III* [1838], Carlos Seco Serrano ed., *Biblioteca de autores españoles*, 115 (Madrid: Ediciones Atlas, 1959), 269.
9  "Account of the Life and Writings of Adam Smith" in Adam Smith, *Essays on Philosophical Subjects*, W. P. D. Wightman and J. C. Bryce eds. (Oxford: Oxford University Press, 1980), 311.
10 "España despierta" in *Lo que hay de mas y menos en España para que sea lo que debe ser y no lo que es* [1741], Antonio Elorza ed. (Madrid: Seminario de Historia Social y Económica de la Facultad de Filosofía y Letras de la Universidad de Madrid, 1969), 121.
11 Ibid., 68–9.
12 "Elogio de Carlos III, leído en la Real Socieded Económica de Madrid el día 8 de noviembre de 1788" in Jovellanos *Obras completas*, 10, 669.
13 For the iconography of the fresco, see my "La monarquía española en el siglo XVIII. A propósito de los frescos de Giambattista Tiepolo", *Reales Sitios. Revista del Patrimonio Nacional* 38 (2001), 2–9.
14 *Empresas políticas: Idea de un príncipe político-cristiano*, 604.
15 Ibid., 822.
16 "On the Plantation Trade", *The Political and Commercial Works of that Celebrated Writer, Charles D'Avenant LL.D.*, II, 26. Also see the observations in Peter Miller, *Defining the Common Good: Empire, Religion and Philosophy in Eighteenth-Century Britain* (Cambridge: Cambridge University Press, 1994), 155–9.
17 *A New Discourse on Trade* [1665] (Glasgow, 1751), 153.
18 *Considérations sur les richesses de l'Espagne*, in *Oeuvres complètes*, Roger Caillois ed. (Paris: Bibliothèque de la Pléiade, 1949–51), II, 10–11.
19 Ibid., 18.
20 Ibid., 14, and repeated in *De l'esprit des lois*, XXI, 22.
21 *De l'esprit des lois*, XXI, 22

22  *An Inquiry into the Nature and Causes of the Wealth of Nations*, II, 626–7.
23  *Theoríca y practica de comercio y de marina* (Madrid, 1724), 60–2. On Uztaríz, see Reyes Fernández Durán, *Gerónimo de Uztaríz (1670–1732). Una polítca económica para Felipe V* (Madrid: Minerva, 1999).
24  On the attractions and perils of emulation, see Gabriel B. Paquette, *Enlightenment, Governance and Reform in Spain and its Empire* (Houndsmills: Palgrave Macmillan, 2008), 29–55.
25  Quoted in David Armitage, "The Cromwellian Protectorate and the Languages of Empire", *Historical Journal* 35 (1992), 536.
26  For the background to this move, see J. H. Elliott, "Learning from the Enemy: Early-Modern Britain and Spain" in *Spain, Europe and the Wider World 1500–1800* (New Haven and London: Yale University Press, 2009), 25–51.
27  Although it was not printed until 1789, the *Nuevo sistema* circulated widely in administrative and court circles before that date. A version of the text, in most places word for word, also appeared as the second part of Bernardo Ward's *Proyecto económico en que se proponen varias providencias dirigidas a promover los intereses de España*, first published in Madrid in 1799. Ward's own contribution, which was confined to a discussion of metropolitan Spain, had been composed in 1762. For a discussion of the relationship between the two texts, see the introduction by Antonio Elorza to Campillo y Cosío, *Lo que hay de mas y menos en España para que sea lo que debe ser y no lo que es, España despierta* 11–16, and see J. Stein and Barbara H. Stein, *Silver Trade and War: Spain and America in the Making of Early-Modern Europe* (Baltimore: Johns Hopkins University Press, 2000), 204–15.
28  Campillo y Cosío, *Nuevo sistema de gobierno económico para la América*, (Madrid, 1789), 2–3.
29  Ibid., 14.
30  Ibid., 6–7.
31  Ibid., 2.
32  Ibid., 3.
33  *Nuevo sistema de gobierno económico para la América*,, 15–16.
34  *Reflexiones sobre el comercio español a Indias* [1762], Vicente Llombart Roas ed. (Madrid: Ministerio de Economía y Hacienda, 1988), 233, and see Elliott, "Learning from the Enemy: Early-Modern Britain and Spain", 48–9.
35  *Nuevo sistema de gobierno económico para la América*, 11–12.
36  *Discurso sobre la educación popular de los artesanos y su fomento* (Madrid, 1775), 410.
37  Ibid., 412.
38  *De l'esprit des lois*, XXI, 21.
39  *Reflexiones sobre el comercio español a Indias*, 23.
40  On this see Paquette, *Enlightenment, Governance and Reform in Spain and its Empire*, 56–62.
41  The comparison between the "Carthaginian constitution" of the British Empire and the Roman model supposedly adopted by the Spanish and the French was a familiar one in the eighteenth century. See pp. 195–6.
42  "Apuntaciones de lo que importa averiguar para resolver con acierto el gran problema de si conviene a la España, en el comercio de las Indias occidentales,

seguir el sistema antiguo o una libertad indefinida" in *Inéditos políticos* (Oviedo: Junta General del Principado de Asturias, 1999), 20–1.

43  Ibid., 9, and *Reflexiones sobre el comercio español a Indias*, 62.

44  Ibid., 11.       .

45  *Sketches of the History of Man*, James A. Harris ed. (Indianapolis: Liberty Fund, 2007), II, 395.

46  *Mémoires sur les colonies américaines, sur leurs relations politiques avec leurs métropoles, et sur la maniéré dont la France et l'Espagne on dû envisager les suites de l'indépendance des Etats unis de l'Amérique* [April 6, 1776] (Paris, 1791), 30–1.
    In the wake of a Family Pact of 1761, the two branches of the Bourbon dynasty pledged to defend each other in case of hostilities and kept a close on each other's actions. Consequently, Turgot speaks throughout of both the French and the Spanish Bourbon monarchies as "we".

47  "Smith's Thoughts on the State of the Contest with America", February 1778, in *The Correspondence of Adam Smith*, Ernest Campbell Mossner and Ian Simpson Ross eds. (Oxford: Oxford University Press, 1987), 381–4. Also see Duncan Bell, *The Idea of Greater Britain. Empire and the Future of World Order, 1860–1900* (Princeton: Princeton University Press, 2007), 68–70.

48  On "internal" and " external" spheres of sovereignty, see pp. 110–111.

49  See Eliga H. Gould, *The Persistence of Empire: British Political Culture in the Age of the American Revolution* (Chapel Hill: University of North Carolina Press, 2000), 166, and Elliott, *Empires of the Atlantic World. Britain and Spain in America*, 367.

50  Quoted in Luís M. Farías, *La América de Aranda* (Mexico: Fondo de Cultura Económica, 2003), 195.

51  "Exposición del conde de Aranda al rey Carlos III sobre el conveniencia de crear reinos independientes en América" in Muriel, *Gobierno del señor rey Carlos III* [*1838*], 399–401. And see Farías, *La América de Aranda*, 244–57.

52  *Carta derijida [sic] a los Españoles Americanos por uno de sus compatriotas* (London, 1801), 2

53  Quoted in Joshua Simon, *The Ideology of Creole Revolution: Ideas of American Independence in Comparative Perspective* (forthcoming). I am very grateful to Professor Simon for allowing me to consult his manuscript prior to publication.

54  *Du Congrès de Vienne* (Paris, 1815), I, xvi, II, 238, and see Mark Mazower, *Governing the World. The History of an Idea* (New York: Penguin Press, 2012), 22. Bolívar paid De Pradt a pension and once described him as "a sublime philosopher", playing Aristotle to his Alexander. Letter of 21 March 1826, *Obras completas*, Vicente Lecuna and Esther Barret de Nazaris eds. (Havana: Editorial Lex, 1950), II, 339.

55  *The Colonies and the Present American Revolutions* (London, 1817), 384.

56  Quoted in, *inter alia*, Francis Jennings, *Empire of Fortune: Crowns, Colonies, and Tribes in the Seven Years' War in America* (New York: W.W. Norton, 1988), 89. Benjamin's remark has led to the preposterous claim that the Iroquois Confederacy was, in fact, the *inspiration* behind the federal system of the United States. In 1987, in deference to this flight of historical fantasy, the U.S. Senate passed a resolution acknowledging the contribution of the Iroquois Confederacy

to the development of the U.S. Constitution and its contribution to the "enlightened, democratic principles of government".

57 "Contestación de un Américano meridional a un caballero de esta isla", known as the *Carta de Jamaica* September 1815, *Obras completas*, I, 165 and cf. the *Discurso de angostura*, III, 676–7. For a brief but suggestive reevaluation of Bolívar's political thought, see Roberto Breña, *El Imperio de las circumstancias. La independencias hispanoamericanas y la revolución liberal española* (Mexico: El Colegio de México, 2012), 61–94.

58 "Letter to the *Royal Gazette* of Kingston Jamaica", September [?] 1815, *Obras completas*, I, 176.

59 For Bolívar's complex, and changing, view of the United States, see David Bushnell, "The United States as Seen by Bolívar: Too Good a Neighbor" in David Bushnell and Lester D. Langley eds., *Simón Bolívar: Essays on the Life and Legacy of the Liberator* (Lanham: Rowman and Littlefield, 2008).

60 "Discurso de angostura", *Obras completas*, III, 682.

61 Cojti Cuxil, *Demetrio. El movimiento maya* (Guatemala: CHOLSAMJ, 1997), 34–5.

62 *Weltbürgertum und Nationalstaat: Studien zur Genesis des deutschen Nationalstaates* (Munich: R. Oldenbourg, 1922), 3–22.

63 *Constitución política de la monarquia española, promulgada en Cádiz a 19 marzo, 1812* (Cádiz, 1812), 23. See the essays in Antonio Annino and François Xavier Guerra eds., *Inventando la nación. Iberoamérica. Siglo XIX* (Mexico: Fondo de Cultura Económica, 2003). In an attempt to limit the number, and political influence, of the American delegates, the rights of those of mixed African and Indian descent – the *castas* – were progressively reduced in the drafting of the final document, until they had, in effect, been excluded altogether. On the place of America in the Cortes, see Roberto Breña, *El Primer liberalismo español y los procesos de emancipación de América* (Mexico: El Colegio de México, 2006), 119–74.

64 "Commentaire sur l'ouvrage de Filangieri" in Gaetano Filangieri, *Oeuvres* (Paris, 1822), VI, 71–2. Constant, however, was writing after the Liberal Revolution of 1820.

65 Quoted in Breña, *El Imperio de las circumstancias*, 68.

66 Letter to General O'Leary, September 13, 1829, *Obras completas*, III, 315.

67 *The Colonies and the Present American Revolutions*, xii–xiii.

68 *Congrés du Panama* (Paris, 1825), 85.

69 *La República en el Perú y la cuestión peruana* (Lima, 1867), 16.

70 On Miranda's *Monarquia incasica*, see my *Spanish Imperialism and the Political Imagination*, 130–2, and more generally, Jeremy Adelman, *Sovereignty and Revolution in the Iberian Atlantic* (Princeton: Princeton University Press, 2006), 261–3.

71 "Discurso de angostura" in *Obras completas*, III, 681.

72 Quoted in Breña, *El Imperio de las circumstancias*, 70.

73 *Saggio storico sulla rivoluzione di Napoli* (Milan, 1806), 117.

74 "The Liberty of the Ancients Compared with That of the Moderns", *Constant: Political Writings*, 312–3. This is probably the most important early source for the much debated distinction between "positive" and "negative" freedom, concepts which are something similar to, but certainly not identical with, Constant's

"ancient" and "modern" liberty. For the most recent, and most compelling account, see Eric Nelson, "Liberty: One Concept Too Many?", *Political Theory* 33 (2005), 58–78. And see Luís Castro Leiva and Anthony Pagden, "Civil Society and the Fate of the Republics of Latin America" in Sudipta Kaviraj and Sunil Khilnani eds., *Civil Society History and Possibilities* (Cambridge, Cambridge University Press, 2001), 179–203.

75 The phrase is that of the Chinese leader Deng Hsiao Ping. See John Dunn, "The Identity of the Bourgeois Liberal Republic" in Bianca Fontana ed., *The Invention of the Modern Republic* (Cambridge: Cambridge University Press, 1994), 206–25.

76 "Discurso de angostura", *Obras completas*, III, 692–3.

77 *Obras completas*, I, 619. In Cap VI of *Du Contrat Social*, Rousseau refers to the initial agreement which transforms a collection of individuals into "un corps moral et collectif" as a "pacte". *Du Contrat Social*, in *Oeuvres complètes*, édition publiée sous la direction de Bernard Gagnebin et Marcel Raymond (Paris: Bibliothèque de la Pléiade, 1964), III, 361. Bolívar was the proud owner of Napoleon's copy of *Du Contrat social*. On Bolívar's indebtedness to Rousseau, see Luís Castro Leiva, "Rousseau, acción y voluntad, los límites de la razón" in *Obras*, Carole Leal Curiel ed. (Caracas: Fundación Polar, 2005), I, 85–102.

78 *Reflexiones sobre el estado actual de la América, o cartas al Abate de Pradt* (Madrid, 1820), iv. The author is anonymous. Also see Luís Castro Leiva, *La Gran Colombia, una ilusión ilustrada* (Caracas: Monte Alva Editores, 1985).

79 Quoted in John Lynch, *Simón Bolívar: A Life* (New Haven and London: Yale University Press, 2006), 203.

# 7

## From the "Right of Nations" to the "Cosmopolitan Right"

### *Immanuel Kant's Law of Continuity and the Limits of Empire*

I

From Francisco de Vitoria until the Swiss jurist and diplomat Emer de Vattel, whose *Law of Nations or Principles of the Law of Nature, Applied to the Conduct and Affairs of Nations and Sovereigns* of 1757 became a textbook of the law of nations in the second half of the eighteenth century, every attempt to justify and regulate empire and colonization had been expressed in terms of the later Roman jurists' understanding of the "law of nations". This, as we have seen, was understood to be a secondary natural law, identifiable with what the eighteenth-century German philosopher and mathematician Christian Wolff described as that law which all nations "are bound to agree upon if following the leadership of nature they use right reason," which in practice could only amount to "what has been approved by the more civilized nations".[1] But Wolf's *The Law of Nations, Treated According to a Scientific Method* of 1750 was not only the longest attempt to provide an exhaustive definition of the law of nations but also one of the last. By the first decades of the nineteenth century the project had been largely abandoned, along with the entire conception of the "law of nature".[2] In its place came a new positive "international law" – a term coined by Jeremy Bentham, one of the fiercest opponents of the idea of natural law and natural rights in 1783. One of the key figures in this transition was Immanuel Kant.

Kant was famously dismissive of what he called the "sorry comforters" of mankind – Hugo Grotius, Samuel Pufendorf, Emer de Vattel – "and the like" – in effect, the entire tradition of thinking on the "law of nations", which had preceded him. For, in his view, their "code, couched philosophically or diplomatically", could never have any legal force in the state of nature in which all the nations of the world in his day still existed, because none of them were "subject to a common external constraint". The law of nations, in whatever form, had, as he rightly perceived, invariably been invoked as means to justify "offensive war". That war, furthermore, had generally been a war of conquest and occupation – a war in the pursuit of empire – and Kant was implacably hostile to all empire, or "universal monarchy" as he called it, which in his view could only ever lead to the "graveyard of freedom" and a "soulless despotism".[3] (ZeF 8:367)[4] Like his most brilliant and cantankerous pupil Johann Gottfried von Herder, with whom he agreed on very little else, Kant believed that nature would always find a way to frustrate what Herder bitingly described as the despot's dream of cramming "all the four quarters of the globe ... into the belly of a wooden horse".[5] In general, although his views changed, largely in keeping with his changing views on race, from the "earlier, pre-critical" period of the 1770s through to the early 1790s and the later period from the mid-1790s until his death in 1804, Kant saw empires as unnatural creations.[6] Humans had been separated by nature into distinct peoples, distinguished by languages and religious beliefs, things which for Kant, no less than for Herder – although they disagreed on much else – was nature's way "to prevent peoples from intermingling and to separate them" (ZeF 8:367). Any attempt to eliminate these and "all freedom would necessarily expire, and together with it, virtue, taste, and science (which follow upon freedom)". Finally the laws themselves would gradually lose their force, until the whole enterprise collapsed back into a collection of small, belligerent states, where it had originally been conceived. And then these "begin the same game all over again, so that war (that scourge of the human race)" continues unabated (Rel 6:35).

Every people possess in this way a linguistic and more broadly cultural and religious identity. But they also have a given place on earth. They constitute a "country [*Land*] or *territorium*" which is made up of fellow citizens who are subject to the same constitution "simply by birth", rather than through any legal act. As such every "country" is inescapably what Kant, despite his dislike for patriarchal conceptions of government, calls a "fatherland" (MdS 6:337).[7] The citizens of these "fatherlands" are those "human beings who constitute a people" (*Volk*), and they derive whatever legitimacy and social cohesion they possess by analogy with those born: "Of a common set of ancestors (*congenitti*) even if they in fact are not." They belong, that is, to a single lineage, although this is "legal and intellectual" rather than natural, whose common *mother* is the republic, understood as a constitution, rather than a particular patch of ground.[8] A people, then, is a conceptual and legal, rather than a biological, *gens* or *natio* (MdS 6:343).[9] (Kant's concept of citizenship is based strictly on *ius sanguinis*, despite his recognition that the *sanguis* in question is wholly metaphorical). A foreign country, by contrast, is described merely as one in which a person is not a citizen and, therefore, not a member of the *gens* or *natio*. However, when this foreign country "is a part of a larger realm" (*Landesherrschaft*) of the fatherland, it is what Kant calls "a province (in the sense in which the Romans used this word)". Because it is not an "integral part of the realm [*Reich*] (*imperii*)" or a *residence* [*Sitz*] of the citizens" but is instead "only a *possession* [*Besitzen*] a secondary house [*Unterhaus*]", it is compelled to "respect the land of the state that rules it as a *mother country (regio domina)*" (MdS 6:337). Those who live in such provinces, while bound to obey the "ruling state", do not, apparently, enjoy the rights of citizenship which they would have done had they been living in the mother country itself. This, at least, would seem to be the conclusion to be drawn from Kant's subsequent claim that a ruler may banish a recalcitrant subject either to a "province outside the [mother] country" where he "will not enjoy any of the rights of a citizen", or alternatively he may "exile him altogether (*ius exilii*) to send him out into the wide world" (MdS 6:338). On Kant's understanding then, a province is a subject state or community whose residents, although beholden to the *Reich*, are clearly not represented by it. They would seem to correspond to the status of the so-called Latin colonies under Roman rule whose residents were citizens of the colony, not of Rome, and who, although under Roman jurisdiction, were still largely self-governing.[10]

In all of this Kant never uses the term "colony". Later, however, he speaks of a colony as if it were identical with a province and defines it as "a people that indeed has its own constitution, its own legislation and its own land" (MdS 349).[11] This would make it, in most respects, indistinguishable from a *Land*, for which reason it is also described as a "daughter state" or one which is *ruled* by the "mother-state", which "has supreme executive authority (*oberste ausübende Gewalt*) over the colony or province". Unlike the province, however, the colony, on Kant's account, would appear to exercise a somewhat higher degree of independent executive autonomy, for it is said to *govern* itself "by its own parliament" or "possibly with a viceroy presiding over it (*civitas hybrida*)". Here all outsiders are "foreigners" even if they are also citizens of the "mother state". The examples he gives for this are "the relations of Athens to various islands" and "that Great Britain now has with regard to Ireland" (MdS 6:348–9).

There would, therefore, appear to be two distinct definitions of overseas settlements. Neither it should be said really corresponds, as Kant's use of Latin – if not consistently Roman – legal tags would imply, to Roman practice, since a Roman *provincia* was originally only the territory over which a magistrate exercised his authority (*imperium*), and the term was used to describe territories both within and beyond Italy, although it later came to be confined largely to those acquired overseas. It might include citizens and noncitizens, free cities, and even colonies within its borders. Although every province certainly "respected the state that ruled it" (MdS 6:337), it was clearly not a *possession*, either in the Roman sense of the term or in Kant's own. On the other hand neither of Kant's accounts looks much like a Roman *colonia* either. The best-known description of the status of the Roman, as distinct from the Greek, colonies (and the one probably familiar to Kant) is Livy's account of Emporiae in Spain, in which the Romans, unlike their Greek predecessors who had erected a wall between themselves and the native Spanish, are described as living together with the *indigenes* and granting them both, and the remaining Greeks, citizenship, so as to Romanize them.[12] Roman colonies, that is, were, and they were clearly recognized as being examples of the kind of attempts to incorporate noncitizens into a "universal monarchy" on which Rome prided herself and which Kant looked on as merely a form of tyranny.[13] Kant's description of the *Unterhaus* does, how-ever, correspond, very much mutatis mutandis, to certain kinds of early-modern European colonial rule. The Spanish Kingdoms of the Indies fits this description (as their Creole populations sometimes bitterly complained) as did the British presence in India (although not, however, in Ireland).

The second account of the province/colony has some affinities with the ancient Greek understanding of the *apoikia* (literally "from home") as a semi-independent community made up of persons displaced from, but who still depend upon, a metropolis, or "mother-city". However, and rather puzzlingly, Kant uses this second definition to characterize a people who are said to have "been degraded to a colony and its subjects to bondage" (MdS 6:348) through defeat in war, and the examples he provides certainly fit this description. In English law Ireland was, as was Virginia, a "land of conquest", and the Athenian *arche* was the result of an abuse of power by Athens over the cities of the Delian League.[14] In neither case, however, could the relationship of power also be said to be analogous to that between a mother and a daughter. There is a further complication with Kant's twofold account of the province/colony and its relationship with the motherland. For whereas in the first case what is clearly being described is a creole state, whose relationship to its original "fatherland" might therefore plausibly be cast in terms of familiar daughter-mother metaphors, the second is explicitly a land of conquest, and those who *govern* themselves "through its own parliament" are – like the Irish or the Melians – indigenes with no connec-tion in terms of lineage or ethnos to the mother state. What Kant's version of the mother/daughter analogy fits fairly accurately, however, is neither Ire-land nor Athens, but the Thirteen Colonies of British America, which Rich-ard Bland described in 1766, as "a distinct state, independent as to their *internal* government of the original kingdom, but united with her as to their external policy in the closest and most intimate LEAGUE AND AMITY, under the same allegiance, and enjoying the benefits of a reciprocal intercourse".[15]

In the course of the seventeenth and eighteenth centuries the "mother/daughter" analogy became something of a commonplace to characterize a largely benign and beneficial kind of colonial rule of supposedly Greek origin to be distinguished from a rapacious and destructive version of supposedly Roman origin, and this may well be what Kant had in mind. As Andrew Fletcher, eager to distinguish Britain from her Spanish and French rivals, argued in 1704, whereas Spain and France had true empires, with all the horrors which that had brought with it, and prided themselves on being modern Romans, the British colonies more closely resembled the

Greek cities of the Achaean League, to which Kant, of course, alluded frequently as the model for his future "league of peoples" (*Völkerbund*).[16]

Built into the mother/daughter analogy, however, was also, of course, the troubling – at least for the colonial power – implication that one day the "daughter" would grow up and acquire full independence. "Supposing, therefore", wrote Richard Price in 1776, "that the order of nature in establishing the relationship between parents and children ought to have been the rule of our conduct to the colonies, we should have been gradually relaxing our authority as they grew up." Instead, in the reckless pursuit of their own domestic interests, the British had behaved like "mad parents" and had "done the contrary", and, like mad parents, they were soon to lose both the love and respect of their offspring.[17] The same clearly applied to the implications of Kant's recognition that parental right extends only until "the time of his [the child's] emancipation (*emancipatio*) when they [the parents] renounce their parental right to direct him" (MAM 6:281). There would seem to be no reason to suppose, therefore, that the citizens of such daughter states should be any more deprived of their right to be represented by the mother state than its actual inhabitants. They should be, in effect, neither "colonies" – as the Romans understood them – nor "provinces", so much as municipalities. As several disgruntled British Americans pointed out in the 1760s, their status should be thought of not as a colonial one at all, but as analogous with that of the citizens of the kingdom of Hanover. "The people of England", wrote one "Britannus Americanus" in the *Boston Gazette* in the winter of 1765, "could have no more political connection with them or power and jurisdiction over them, than they now have with or over the people of Hanover who are also subjects of the same King."[18]

This, of course, had been one of the key legal issues at stake in the American Revolution. By taxing the colonists without their consent and claiming that they were being represented "virtually", and at the same time insisting that in any case the land on which they lived was held in "free and common socage" as of the manor of East Greenwich in Kent, the British Crown had, in effect, attempted to deny what it had hitherto accepted in practice (if not always consistently in law) that the Thirteen Colonies were, indeed "daughter states", self-governing and autonomous as far as their "internal affairs" were concerned.[19]

The real problem with the mother/daughter analogy was that it relied on the assumption that sovereignty would be divided between the mother and the daughter states: the daughter being entirely sovereign within her own borders while the mother exercised exclusive authority over all the external affairs of state. Although Kant was clearly aware of the need for some kind of division of sovereignty within the future "league of states", he was also certain that, as Arthur Ripstein has pointed out, the people of states which cannot be the "undisputed legislators" of their own affairs must consider themselves to be "passive in relation to their own independence".[20]

No matter how apparently contradictory Kant's description of overseas settlements might be, one thing is abundantly clear: both the first and second type of province/colony can only have been acquired initially through conquest. This, at least, is certainly implicit in the phrase, "the sense in which the Romans use this word". Both types, therefore, although this is only explicit in the case of the second, must lack the essential qualifications of a legitimate state. Both can only be, in effect, war booty. Kant's account of both only makes sense, therefore, in the light of his views on the legitimacy of war.

## II

Kant was no pacifist. True, in the world in which he lived he looked on war as the greatest of all human scourges – with the sole exception of "universal monarchy" (ZeF 8:363). But it had sometimes served mankind well in the past. It had been war which had forced humans to occupy the entire globe. Without it they would, like all other animals, still be huddling together on the small patch of land where they had first emerged. How else could one explain the presence of human settlements around the Arctic Ocean, Altay Mountains, or Patagonia (ZeF 8:363)? It had been warfare "as great an evil as it may be" which had motivated "the transition from the brutish state of nature into a state of civil society" (*bürgerliche Gesellschaft*) (ApH 7:330 and ZeF 8:364–5). At a later stage it had been war, all wars, which are only "so many attempts . . . . Not to be sure, in the aims of human beings, but yet in the aim of nature", which had compelled the more socialized human populations to establish relationships between states and create new ones (IaG 8: 24–5). Man is the only animal which "works so hard for the destruction of his own species" (KdU 5:430), and because of this it is war, and the fear of future war, which demands "even of the heads of states" to observe a certain *"respect for humanity"* (MAM 8:363).

War for Kant constitutes an extreme form of coercion, and coercion can be justified only if it is *"hindering a hindrance to freedom"*, for only then will it be "consistent with freedom in accordance with universal laws, that is, right" (MdS 6:231).[21] As with all previous accounts of the justice of warfare since Cicero, Kant therefore assumes that a just war can only ever be a defensive one when a state that "believes it has been wronged by the other state" seeks reparation for the evils it has suffered. War is, under such circumstances, the only means at its disposal since this "cannot be done in the state of nature by a *lawsuit*" (MdS 6:346). But precisely because there cannot, on Kant's understanding of interstate relations, exist any such thing as an international court, because "states considered in external relations to one another are (like lawless savages) by nature in a non-rightful condition" (MdS 6:344), and because *all* warfare must necessarily take place in a "lawless condition", the very concept of a "law" (*Gesetz*) – or right – of war would seem to be so inherently meaningless that "it is difficult even to form a concept of this or to think of law in this lawless state without contradicting oneself" (MdS 6:347).[22] The continuing trust that humans continue to place in the "codes", as he calls them, of the "Sorry Comforters" and their like is merely evidence that each human being possesses the "moral disposition" required to overcome the "evil principle within him" (ZeF 8:355). Encouraging though this might be, however, it did nothing to set limits on the condition of war which existed between states as they were currently constituted.

This outright dismissal of the law of nations as nothing more than a sign of good intentions is, however, curious since shortly after this outburst against his predecessors, Kant goes on to offer a threefold division of "public right" into *constitutional right, the right of nations*, and *cosmopolitan right* (ZeF 8:365). Although in the *Doctrine of Right* he claims that in German the second of these "is called not quite correctly *right of nations* [*Völkerrecht*] but should instead be called the 'right of states' [*Staatenrecht*] (*ius publicum civitatum*)", it is, in either version, indistinguishable from the *ius gentium* (MdS 6:343) and is explicitly described as such in *Towards Perpetual Peace* (ZeF 8:349). Just to make matters more perplexing still, in the description in the *Doctrine of Right* of the inevitability of the progress of humanity toward the "cosmopolitan right (*ius cosmopoliticum*)", this, too, is described as a "right of nations (*ius gentium*)" (MdS 6:311). Furthermore although "the right of nations" can clearly only exist in the present condition of lawlessness (that is before the creation of the "league of states", which will one day be the inevitable outcome of the triumph of the *ius cosmopoliticum*), in *Towards Perpetual Peace* Kant asserts unequivocally that it makes sense to speak of such a right "only under the presupposition of some sort of rightful condition" (ZeF 8:383). Presumably, because the possibility of any kind of international court is explicitly excluded, this could, at least in 1795 when *Towards Perpetual Peace* was written, only take the form of the kind of diplomatic solution favoured by Vattel. Treaties clearly do constitute what might count on Kant's understanding as a "rightful condition", but they do so only as long as the parties to them find it in their individual interests to observe them. For it had been precisely Kant's point that in the absence of any superior authority capable of enforcing oaths, the hallowed formula *pacta sunt servanda* could be based only on calculated self-interest.

It is here that the tension between what Kant calls "the right of nations" and "cosmopolitan right" begins to show. For unless we take all these different, and seemingly contradictory, descriptions to be merely manifestations of what one scholar has called the "terminological indecisiveness" of Kant's later writings, we must assume that what Kant understood by "the right of nations" was what – as we have seen – all of the writers in the natural-law tradition had called a natural law "in a secondary sense".[23] It was, in effect, a positive law framed in accordance with what all mankind could have been brought to agree upon, if it were possible to discover what its collective opinion might be. It was what Kant, referring to the idea of an "original contract", called "*only an idea* of reason" (GTP 8:297); and this broadly speaking is how all the "sorry comforters" had envisioned it.[24] They, however, had been able to extend it to all relations between states only because it had, in effect and particularly in the hands of Christian Wolff and Vattel, been given a strongly cosmopolitan and teleological component, a working toward what Wolff called the *civitas maxima* and Vattel a "universal republic".[25] Kant, however, wished to keep the *Völkerrecht* and the *ius cosmopoliticum* strictly separate not only as two distinct kinds of right but also as the manifestation of two distinct phases in human history. The "right of nations", or of states, was merely a set of ultimately ineffectual, possibly well-intended, attempts to regulate a situation which by its very definition could not be regulated. It had no ultimate objective, no *telos*. It belonged to the here and now, and it quite clearly will – indeed must – one day be abandoned. The *ius cosmopoliticum*, in contrast, belongs to a future stage of human history in which all states will have become "representative republics", and it will be possible to image a universal "league of states" that alone is capable of bringing about a condition of perpetual peace.

The sharp distinction between these two conceptions of right is especially evident in Kant's understanding of the "right to conditions of universal *hospitality*" (ZeF 8:357–8). This shares something in common with Francisco de Vitoria's "right of natural partnership and communication". But whereas for Vitoria, as we have seen, hospitality belongs with the *ius gentium* and, despite its reliance on the natural right "to visit and travel through any land", is therefore a positive law, for Kant it depends on the far from unproblematical assertion that all human beings have a "right of possession in common of the earth's surface" (ZeF 8:358)[26] and is the cornerstone of the *ius cosmopoliticum* – indeed in *Towards Perpetual Peace* the *ius cosmopoliticum* is famously said to be "limited to conditions of universal *hospitality*" (8:357–8). Stripped in this way of all the "cosmopolitan" components, with which the "sorry comforters" had provided the *ius gentium*, all that Kant's "right of nations" could possibly do, in effect, was to place limitations on the conditions and conduct of war. Only the *ius cosmopoliticum*, which would someday come to replace it, is directed toward *peace* or what the Academy of International Law at The Hague now defines as "general rules concerning the right of peace".[27]

Kant's "right of nations" rests on a series of rules and procedures, which follow, exactly as the "sorry comforters" had done, the conventional division between the *jus ad bellum* (the right to make war), the *ius in bello* (the law governing conduct during war), and – most crucially for Kant's views of colonization – the *ius post bellum*, that is, the laws which determine the behaviour, and the rights, of states after the war is over. For Kant, however, unlike any of his predecessors, the sole purpose of all these laws is to ensure that after the conclusion of any war "they always leave open the possibility of leaving the state of nature among states (in external relation to one another) and entering a rightful condition" (MdS 6:347). No state, that is, should be prevented by its involvement in any war from finally entering into the league of states which alone is able to bring about a condition of perpetual peace. In other words, although the *Völkerrecht* is strictly atemporal, it is also clearly understood to play a crucial, if only preventative, role in bringing about the future "universal *cosmopolitan condition*".[28]

War, as we have seen, can only be justified for Kant if it can be described as defensive. However, unlike most of the previous theorists in the natural law tradition from Vitoria to Grotius to Wolf and Vattel, Kant was fully prepared to accept what was called the argument from "just fear" as grounds for a just war.[29] For in Kant's view, in a condition of lawlessness it was perfectly reasonable for a state to act preemptively against any other state which, although it has not caused any "active injury", nevertheless posed a threat of war. Such threats includes either being the first to

> undertake preparations, upon which is based the right of prevention (*ius praeventionis*), or just the menacing increase in another state's power (by its acquisition of territory) (*potentia tremenda*). This is a wrong to the lesser power merely by the condition of the superior power ... before any deed on its part, and in the state of nature an attack by the lesser power is indeed legitimate. (MdS 6:346)

Most previous accounts of the laws of warfare had also assumed that a just war was a contest in which the justice of the victor's cause was demonstrated by his victory. It was, that is, believed to be exactly the kind of primitive substitute for the domestic law court as a means of resolving a dispute on the merits of the case involved which Kant describes – and condemns – it as being. For this reason, it also constituted a species of revenge for wrongs inflicted on the victor – by definition the righteous party – in which the victor was entitled to seek compensation for the sufferings he had supposedly endured.[30] Even the "sorry comforters", although they placed clear restrictions on what could, and could not, be claimed under the *ius post bellum* and were generally much more stringent than their predecessors had been about the justifications for war, were nevertheless, broadly in agreement. Kant, however, argues that not only cannot the merit of a case be decided by simple force, but that both sides are likely to believe that their cause is just, and that it is, therefore, they who are the offended party, whatever the actual outcome of the war. For this reason, "Right cannot be decided by war and the favourable outcome, *victory*" (ZeF 8:355). Any claim that the victor should be reimbursed for the cost of the war, furthermore, would have the effect of transforming the war "into a war of punishment and thereby would in turn offend his opponent". It is also the case that, "No war of independent states against each another can be a punitive war (*bellum punitivum*). For punishment occurs only in the relation of a superior (*imperantis*) to those subject to him (*subditum*), and states do not stand in that relation to each other" (MdS 6:347). Consequently the *ius post bellum* must be determined not, as had previously been assumed, "from any right he (the victor) pretends to have because of the wrongs his opponent is supposed to have done him; instead he lets this question drop and relies on his own force" (MdS 6:348). This is an outright rejection of the claim of the Roman jurists that the occupation of enemy territory in pursuit of a just war implied that the inhabitants of that territory, and their goods, both moveable and immovable, became the legitimate booty of the occupier. They, thereby, forfeited whatever political rights they had previously possessed, and their states became not colonies, in the Roman (or in the Greek) understanding of the term, but precisely provinces. Thereafter they had access to legal recourse, after 149 BCE under the *lex de rebus repetundis,* against any further depredations.[31]

Although Kant, like Pufendorf Wolf and Vattel, assumes that states are "moral persons", he also makes a clear distinction between the state itself in the person of its sovereign and the citizen body and, therefore, between the agent responsible for initiating any war and the people who have to fight it. Unlike all previous theorists of the just war, who treated states as indivisible persons, he insists that the blame for fighting a war must fall exclusively on the state and its sovereign, and not on the citizens. As a consequence, the citizens of defeated states cannot be deprived of either their freedom or their personal goods because "it was not the conquered people that waged the war; rather the state under whose rule they lived, waged the war *through the people*". For the same reason, although the victor may "extract supplies and contributions from a defeated enemy", he may not "plunder the people" and is obliged to provide "receipts ... for everything requisitioned". It also follows, of course, that the defeated state cannot be "degraded into a colony" (MdS 6:348). (This could not, however, apply to states with republican constitutions since here there can be no separation between the state and its citizens. Because it is the latter who must "give their free assent through their representatives, not only to waging of war in general, but also to each particular declaration of war", they would have to be held collectively responsible [MdS 6:345–6]. But then Kant's general assumption is that such republics will be the ultimate bearers of the *ius cosmopoliticum* precisely because they will never fight unjust wars.)

Like most theorists of the just war, Kant avoided claims made on behalf of third parties, unless these were specifically involved as "allies".[32] Any interference in the internal affairs of other states, no matter how awful their rulers might be, constituted a "violation of the right of a people dependent upon no other and only struggling with its internal illness" and was, therefore, *eo ipso* unjust (ZeF 8:346). In consequence, no conquest, or even intervention, would be legitimate under the terms of Vitoria's "defense of the innocent", much less in pursuit of any claim to be bringing civilization, in whatever form, to barbarian peoples. There would, however, seem to be one category of enemy whose behaviour posed a threat not simply to another state, but also, in some way, to the whole of human kind. This Kant calls the *"unjust enemy* in terms of the concept of the right of nations". It is defined, in accordance with the terms of the Categorical Imperative, as "an enemy whose publically expressed will (whether by words or deed) reveals a maxim by which, if it were made a general rule, any condition of peace among nations would be impossible, and instead a state of nature would be perpetuated" (MdS 6:349). Should such an enemy arise, then "all nations whose freedom is threatened by it . . . are called upon to unite against such misconduct in order to deprive the state of its power to do it". War against an unjust enemy should be pursued until it has been defeated no matter what the cost, short of resorting to precisely those means – the use of such things as assassins, snipers, poisoners, spies, and so on (Kant had an abhorrence of all forms of warfare which were not transparent) – which would render the belligerents "unfit to be citizens" once the war was over and would render the state itself "unfit to qualify, in accordance with the right of nations, as a person in the relation of states with one another" (MdS 6:347), which would consequently make "mutual trust impossible during a future peace" (ZeF 8:346).

This, at least in its potential scope, comes remarkably close to the claim made by Aberico Gentili, and which was taken up by most of the writers in the natural-law tradition: "It is the duty of man to protect men's interests and safety, this is due to any man from any other, for the very reason that they are all alike men; and because human nature, the common mother of the all, commends one to the other."[33] However, neither Gentili nor Kant were prepared to accept that even a war fought against an enemy such as this could confer on the victor – in this case the international community itself, or any state acting on its behalf – the traditional rights of conquest, appropriation, and colonization. Kant's account of the *ius post bellum* is unequivocal. It leaves the victor in a just war no grounds for the occupation of conquered territories or any but the most minimal compensation for damages suffered during the course of war, or even for any punishment of the aggressors as a *people*. Consequently, the victor has no right to "divide its territory among themselves and to make the state, as it were, disappear from the earth" since that would deprive the people of that state of their "original right to unite itself as commonwealth" (MdS 6:349). Any attempt, therefore, by one state to annex or colonize another which, "like a trunk", has "its own roots; and to annex it to another state as a graft is to do away with its existence as a moral person and to make a moral person into a thing"; whatever violation of natural right it might otherwise involve also violates the most basic "idea of the original contract, apart from which no right over a people can be thought" (ZeF 8:344).

For Kant, the state which had defeated an "unjust enemy" would not only not be in a position to acquire any rights to compensation, it would instead be under an obligation to bring about a condition which would allow the conquered people "to accept a new constitution that by its very nature is unfavorable to the inclination to wage war" (MdS 6:349–50). This may look remarkably like a charter for colonization under another name. In fact, however, Kant is adamant that victory does not allow the victor to impose his own rulers, or even native rulers of his own choosing, on the vanquished (a practice used widely by the British in Asia and Africa), since that, too, would be a violation of the right of all peoples to form themselves into a commonwealth. Kant assumes that people – unlike nonrepresentative rulers who are not "members of the state" but their proprietors – because they cannot be "shamed before … one another" and therefore have nothing to lose by reconciliation, if given the opportunity, cannot but chose a *"republican constitution"* which is the "sole constitution that can lead towards perpetual peace" (ZeF 8:350).

For much the same reason, although somewhat less precisely and a great deal more problematically, Kant also seems to have been prepared to accept that some kind of coercion might be justified in pursuit of what he describes as the "original right" which every state has to exit from the state of nature and to "establish a condition more closely approaching a rightful one" (MdS 6:344). So long as states remain, like isolated individuals, in the state of nature and consequently "independent from external laws", they constitute a standing threat to each other by their very existence, and thus if any one of them wishes to bring an end to this condition, it "can and ought to require the others to enter with it into a constitution, similar to a civil constitution in which each can be assured of its rights" (ZeF 8:355).[34] What is unclear is whether this demand could legitimately be backed up by some kind of military action, because it might be argued, although Kant himself does not, that any state which refused would, in effect, fall into the category of the "unjust enemy". Yet even if it did, the same rules governing the *ius post bellum* would obviously have to apply. The defeated state would be encouraged, assisted, or even coerced into creating what it would, in any ideal situation, clearly have chosen for itself: a representative republican constitution. Whatever else it might become it could certainly not be either a province or a "daughter" or a colony of the victorious state.

For the later Kant, at least, there would seem to be no legitimate grounds for the colonization under whatever pretext, or in whatever form, of any part of the territory of a defeated enemy no matter what the justice of the war fought against him, nor on whose behalf had that war been waged.[35]

## III

No province or colony, and consequently no empire, can, therefore, legitimately be created through war. There would, however, seem to exist at least two other kinds of settlement "from home" which, as they do not depend on acts of war, are legitimate. The first is by the settlement of what Kant calls "newly-discovered lands *(accolatus)*" (MdS 6:353).³⁶ Kant makes no direct allusion here to terrae nullius.³⁷ But it is clear from his insistence that any such occupation has to take place at a sufficient distance from "where that people resides that there is no encroachment or anyone's use of his land" that that was what he had in mind. True terrae nullius still belong in what he calls the "primitive community *(communio primaeva)*" (MdS 6:258) in which no property relations exist at all, so their acquisition can involve no interruption of the status quo ante.³⁸ The only thing that the settler had to do was to settle. For, unlike most of the writers on the natural law and the law of nations since Grotius, Kant rejects the so-called agriculturalist argument – the claim that "occupation" necessarily implies development or exploitation. All that colonization requires in this case is "taking control of it *(occupatio)*" (MdS 6:263). In reply to the question, "In order to acquire land is it necessary to develop it (build on it, cultivate it, drain it and so on)?", Kant gave an unqualified no. "Shepherds or hunters", he wrote, "who take up a lot of space", nevertheless have clear and inviolable rights over the "great open regions" they require for their livelihood (MdS 6:353), even if this contributes to the "lawless freedom" which prevents them from fulfilling their human duty to exit from the state of nature. Even when "our own will brings us into the neighborhood of a people that holds out no prospect of a civil union with it", we may not, because of this, legitimately, "found colonies by force if needs be in order to establish civil union with them and bring these men (savages) into a rightful condition (as with the American Indians and the Hottentots and the inhabitants of New Holland)". Kant, had no sentimental attachment to the "savage" as such and fully recognized that, had it not been for what he looked on as illicit occupation in the past, "great expanses of land in other parts of the world, now splendidly populated, would have otherwise remained uninhabited by civilized people" and might even "remain forever uninhabited so that the end of creation would have been frustrated".³⁹ In some of his earlier writings he had taken the view that the colonization of the uncivilized by the civilized, and even their enslavement, might be entirely for their benefit and that "our part of the world will probably someday give laws [*Gesetze geben*] to all the others" (IaG 8:29). By the mid-1790s, however, he appears to have become convinced that any claim that the advance of civilization could, in itself, justify occupation was "a veil of injustice (Jesuitism) which would sanction any means to good ends" (MdS 6:266).⁴⁰

Kant was also certain that what the English colonists in North America called "improvement" could not, in itself, constitute an act of possession but was, "nothing more than an external sign of taking possession, for which many other signs that cost less effort can be substituted" (MdS 6:265). "Taking first possession" has, therefore, a "rightful basis *(titulus possessionis)* which is original possession in common" and, as this is a "basic principle of natural right" (MdS 6:251), anyone who "expends his labor on land that was not already his has lost his pains and toil to he who was first" (MdS 6:269). The same applies to moveable goods since mankind's "common possession of the land of the entire earth (*communio fundi orginaria*)" (MdS 6:258) includes both the earth itself and the things on it. Even drift-wood without which the peoples of "the cold wastes around the Arctic Ocean" (ZeF B: 363) would hardly have been be able survive cannot be considered truly res nullius (MdS 6:270).[41]

In the original state of nature all human beings enjoyed a common possession of the earth (*ein gemeinsamer Besitz*) "because the spherical surface of the earth unites all the places on its surface; for if its surface were an unbounded plane, people could be so dispersed on it that they would not be able to come into community (*Gemeinschaft*) with one another" as nature had clearly intended them to do (MdS 6:262). This does not mean, however, that in this condition there existed what Kant calls an original "community (*communio*) of what is mine and yours" since that can come into being only by "an act that establishes an external right" (MdS 6:258), and this in turn would have to have been created through some kind of contract in which "everyone gave up private possessions, and by uniting his possessions with those of everyone else, transformed them into a collective possession". History, however, has preserved no record of any such contract, "for savages draw up no record of their submission to law" (MdS 6:339).[42] Although it would seem that individual possessions would require the existence of legal institutions – a *lex iustitiae distributiva* as Kant calls it – which can only exist in the civil condition, it is nevertheless our "duty to proceed in accordance with the principle of external acquisi-tion" even "before the establishment of the civil condition but with a view to it, that is, provisionally", because we all have an obligation qua human beings to exit from the state of nature as rapidly as we can, and the acquisition of personal property is the first step in that direction (MdS 6:267–8).[43]

It would seem to follow, therefore, that "herding or hunting peoples", although they may have a due right to occupy the lands on which they live and to live by whatever means they chose, "so long as they keep within their own boundaries", cannot exercise true property rights over them. They might, therefore, be said to have only the use rights – or possession (*posses-sio*) – in the lands they occupy but not true *dominium*. That, however, could never, in itself, constitute sufficient grounds for any more "developed" people to expropriate them. "Newly discovered" lands, furthermore, would have to be truly newly discovered in the sense of being entirely unknown to any one prior to the arrival of the new settlers. It was presumably into lands such as these that those who, in the beginning of human history, having reached the stage of "sociability and civil security", had extended themselves "everywhere from a single point, like a beehive sending out already-formed colonists" (MAM 8:119–20). In Kant's day it was possible that such lands might still be found; but they clearly did not exist on any of the four continents already known to Europeans.

The second means by which land might legitimately be acquired for settlement is through contract. Kant is clear, however, that this would be possible only between persons living in states and non-state individuals, for although a person living in a legally constituted state has the right to immigrate, all he is allowed to carry away with him are his moveable goods. He cannot sell any land he might have owned "and take with him the money he got from it", for although the "moral person" of the state is independent of the land on which it stands, it cannot exist without it (MdS 6:338). Non-state persons, not being bound by any civil constitution, are apparently able to dispose of their lands as they choose and to leave them with whatever they had received in exchange. Kant insists, however, that the laws of contract must still apply even if one of the parties is, in effect, living in a condition of lawlessness. For any contract to be valid, therefore, it has to be drawn up without "making use of our superiority without regard for their first possession" – something which Kant seems to have been aware had happened all too often in Africa and America (MdS 6:353). It is not entirely clear, however, what the settler would, in fact, be buying, for if savages only have the mere possession of their lands, then all they would seem to be able to sell would be something like a right of exclusive use. At best this comes down merely to the claim that in accordance with "the right of nations" all peoples, even savages, should be treated in accordance with due legal process.

Kant's defence of the rights and legal standing of nomadic or pastoral peoples should not, however, be taken to imply any particular respect or liking for them on his part or, indeed, any suggestion that theirs could for long remain a viable alternative to the agricultural-commercial state of civilization. Kant may, as Sankar Muthu has argued, have had scant appreciation of the species of "civilization" which the European states of his day were so eager to export to the "barbarian" peoples of the world.[44] He may sometimes have deplored the "glittering misery" of modern cities (MAM 8:120). But he was in no doubt that sooner or later savages would have to be brought into the historical process, which only properly begins with the creation of a civil constitution. In *Towards Perpetual Peace* hunting is described as the way of life "undoubtedly the most opposed to a civilized constitution", because "families, having to separate, soon become strangers to one another and subsequently, being dispersed in extensive forests, also hostile since each needs a great deal of space for acquiring its food and clothing" (ZeF 8:364). No people, he wrote, are more senselessly cruel than those "from the so-called state of nature", and he was horrified by all that he had read about "the scenes of unprovoked cruelty in the ritual murders of Tofoa, New Zealand, and the Navigator Islands [Samoa] and the never-ending cruelty ... in the wide wastes of northwestern America from which indeed no human being derives the least benefit" (Rel 6:33). Like most of his contemporaries, he also accepted that all humankind progressed, often despite itself, from the "lawless freedom of hunting fishing and pastoral life" to that of agriculture and thence to the urban existence associated with commerce (ZeF 8:364). All those, the peoples of Africa, Tonga, New Holland, America, and most famously Tahiti, who had failed to do so had chosen to detach themselves altogether from the process of amelioration, which is the natural condition of the species as a species. They are in a sense worthless as human beings, for such is man's "propensity to perfect himself" that it could be said, "the world would lose nothing if Tahiti were simply swallowed up" (R 15:785). Luckily for the Tahitians, however, as presumably for all the other primitive peoples of the world, they have now been visited by more "cultured nations" (*gesittetern Nationen*) who might – much as Kant despised their rapacious ways – have the unintended merit of returning them to the purpose for which nature had intended them (RezH 8:65).

But this is simply the ineluctable progress of human history. It certainly did not confer a *right* of any kind on the more advanced peoples of the world to help the less to hurry on up the scale of civilization. It certainly did not authorize the civilizers to benefit from the process. Any argument for occupation or settlement of the kind which European colonizers had employed in varying degrees – "the world's advantage", the fact that "these crude peoples will become civilized", or the idea that "one's own country will be cleaned of corrupt men and they, or their descendants will, it is hoped, become better in another part of the world" – although they might be grounded on "supposedly good intentions", could never, in Kant's view, "wash away the stain of injustice in the means used to attain them" (MdS 6:353).

Just what political status any settlement created on either vacant land or acquired through contract would have, however, is not at all clear. Since the settlers must have originally come from somewhere, and since their migration must have taken place in historical time, that somewhere can only have been a *Vaterland*. They are literally "from home", yet if the states which are subsequently created by those settlers are to be legitimate ones – which, by implication at least, they must surely be since "a subject (regarded also as a citizen)" of any state has "a right to emigrate for a state could not hold him back as its property" – they cannot belong to either of the types of province or colony Kant had described (MdS 6:337). Such states must, therefore, be truly independent foundations created ex nihilo, by means of a new "original contract". In time they will become true "fatherlands" in their own right, and their peoples a true *gens*. If that is indeed the case, then Kant would appear to be assuming an argument not unlike that used by Thomas Jefferson to describe the status of the Thirteen Colonies. In Jefferson's words, the rights of the "British-Americans" derived from the fact that our ancestors, before their emigration to America, were the free inhabitants of the British dominions in Europe, and possessed a right, which nature has given to all men, of departing from the country in which chance, not choice has placed them, of going in quest of new habitations, and of there establishing new societies, under such laws and regulations as to them shall seem most likely to promote public happiness.

In the same way that,

their Saxon ancestors had under this universal law, in like manner, left their native wilds and woods in the North of Europe, had possessed themselves of the island of Britain then less charged with inhabitants, and had established there that system of laws which has so long been the glory and protection of that country .... And it is thought that no circumstance has occurred to distinguish materially the British from the Saxon emigration.[45]

It would be unreasonable to suppose that if such subjects chose to settle on either terrae nullius or on lands acquired by contract, they would continue to be subject in any way to their mother country, any more than, to use Jefferson's analogy, the "Anglo-Saxons" who had settled in Britain were still legally subject to the original Saxon tribal leadership. And had it been true that, as Jefferson argues, there never had been "any claim of superiority or dependence asserted over them [the Thirteen Colonies] by that mother country from which they had migrated", then the British Crown would have had no more grounds for attempting to suppress what it claimed wrongly to be a rebellion than would the French or the Iroquois. (That it was, in fact, manifestly untrue does not, of course, alter the argument.)

But none of this could apply if – as was in fact the case in North America – the original act of colonization had been carried out under the aegis of the mother country. For, Kant, neither a creole people nor a colonized one, once it has been colonized, can claim any kind of right to self-determination, any more than the subjects of an un-colonized state groaning under an un-just sovereign. Kant strongly endorses resistance against any kind of authority which seeks to diminish the individual's right to self-determination. But that resistance may only take the form of what he famously called the *public use* of reason (WiA 8:37). Subjects may grumble. They may even go so far as to exercise the "freedom of the pen" – provided that "it is kept within the limits of a great esteem and love for the constitution" (GTP 8:304). They may not, however, offer any kind of *private* resistance. Even their public resistance may only be critical, not prescriptive, for they are prohibited from suggesting any alternative constitution, because no actual decision can be taken except by the sovereign himself.[46] "All resistance against the supreme legislative authority, all incitement in order to express through action the dissatisfaction of subjects, all protest that leads to rebellion is the highest and most punishable crime within a commonwealth because it destroys its foundations" (GTP 8:299). For in Kant's view, any insurrection against "a constitution that already exists", no matter how that constitution had come into being, nor how good or bad it might be, "overthrows all civil rightful relations therefore all right". It constitutes, that is, a violation of that "law of continuity *(lex continuo)*", which is precisely what separates civil society from the lawless condition of the state of nature. It is thus not a change of the civil constitution, "but a dissolution of it", and the "transition to a better constitution is not then a metamorphosis but a palingenesis which requires a new social contract on which the previous one (now annulled) has no effect" (MdS 6:340). Despite a passing remark that everyone is bound to obey whoever is in authority "in whatever does not conflict with inner morality" (MdS 6:371), Kant's citizens are not even, are as Hobbes' subjects, provided with the natural right to self-protection.[47] As Pufendorf, whom Kant follows quite closely on this issue, had phrased it, all subjects have an "obligation to obey whoever is in possession of the Crown ... [for] a state cannot survive without some kind of government and a good citizen who loves his country, should, on such occasions, give raise to no further troubles".[48] For Kant, furthermore, the people owes its very existence as a people "to the sovereign's legislation", so that any people who goes so far as to execute its monarch "must be regarded as a complete overturning of the principles of the relationship between the sovereign and his people" to the degree "that the state may be said to have committed suicide" (MdS 6:322).

Even those "uprisings by which Switzerland, the United Netherlands or Great Britain won its constitutions, now considered so fortunate" had been achieved by the people acting not "as a *commonwealth*, rather only as a mob", and the immediate outcome can only be "a state of anarchy ... with all the horrors it brings with it". Switzerland, the United Netherlands, and Great Britain had, in the end, turned out to be successful; had they not, however, "the reader of the history of those uprisings would see in the execution of their now so celebrated initiators nothing other than the deserved punishment of persons guilty of high treason" (GTP 8:301).[49]

Cleary what applied to an already existing state constitution applied also to the acquisition of new settlements. Any form of colonization inevitably involved the forcible interruption of someone else's legal continuity. For that reason, if for no other, it could never be legitimate. The sole exceptions to this rule are, of course, true *terrae nullius* – should such places be discovered to exist – and the acquisition of land by contract. In the first case the lands acquired still belong in what Kant calls the "primitive community *(communio primaeva)*" (MdS 6:258) in which no property relations exist at all; their acquisition can, therefore, involve no interruption of the status quo ante. In the second, "transfer by contract of what is mine takes place in accordance with the law of continuity *(lex continuo)* that is possession is not interrupted for a moment during this transaction" (MdS 6:274). Because of this both could be said to be in keeping with the idea of the original contract.

No matter what the conditions of its original creation, however, once a state has come into being de facto, under, or even in defiance of, "the right of nations", it then passes under the jurisdiction of "constitutional right" which, unlike the right of nations, "has binding force and thus objective (practical) reality" (GTP 8:306). This, although Kant never invokes it directly, is clearly an appeal to the law of prescription.

Given his overwhelming concern with the continuity of human legal institutions, all of Kant's injunctions on matters of "the right of nations" can only take the form of warnings against future acts of usurpation. Colonies cannot be formed under "the right of nations" – provisional and illusory – but neither can they be dissolved under the very precise terms of "the right of a state" once they exist. Although Kant does make claims in favour of some kind of restorative justice, he is unable to countenance any kind of right to self-determination, whether it be by creoles or by displaced native inhabitants, on the part of either form of his province/colony.[50] Both *Unterhäuser* and "daughter-states" are bound to obey their de facto rulers until such time as those rulers choose to leave of their own accord. Of course, all of this will be resolved when the wholly unsatisfactory "right of nations" gives way to the "cosmopolitan right", and with it, the "universal *cosmopolitan condition*". For Kant, of course, that existence was not merely the solution to a problem, it was the final end of human existence, "the end ... which nature has as its aim", and the "womb in which all original predispositions of the human species will be developed" (IaG 8:28).

Kant's discussion of colonies would seem to leave anyone who might hope to employ what would appear to be the ultimately emancipatory force of *ius cosmopoliticum* as a ground for opposing any form of colonial regime with severe problems of consistency. For although Kant is insistent that no kind of colonial regime, unless it has been established literally in terra nullius, can initially be a legitimate one, it is also clear that foundation is not all that matters and that his insistence on the need to preserve the legal continuity of the state at all costs empathically rules out any kind of struggle for independence. All that the colonized can do, like the subjects of all unjust but legitimate rulers, is to protest in the hope that the public assertion of their individual autonomy will contribute the final realization of the "league of peoples" (*Völkerbund*) in which all forms of involuntary subjugation would be unthinkable. But that is still a long way in the future.

### Endnotes

1 *Jus gentium methodo scientifica pertractatum* [*The Law of Nations, Treated According to a Scientific Method*], II, 17. On Wolff, see my *The Enlightenment and Why It Still Matters*. Grotius had, of course, used a similar formulation.

2 This was, in effect, the ninth volume of the *Jus naturae methodo scientifica pertractatum* [*The Law of Nature Treated According to a Scientific Method*], which appeared in eight volumes between 1740 and 1748.

3 On Kant's anti-imperialism, see Muthu, *Enlightenment against Empire*, 172– 20.

4 References to Kant's works are given, as is conventional, to the volume and page number of the Akademie edition. In general, I have followed the translations in the *Cambridge Edition of the Writings of Immanuel Kant* (Cambridge: Cambridge University Press, 1992).

I have used the following abbreviations:

ApH: *Anthropologie in pragmatischer Hinsicht* (1798), *Anthropology from a Pragmatic Point of View*

GTP: *Über den Gemeinspruch: Das mag in der Theorie richlig sein, taugt aber nicht für die Praxis* (1793), *On the Common Saying: "This may be true in theory, but does not hold in practice"*

IaG: *Idee zu einer allgemeinen Geschichte in weltbürgerlicher Absicht* (1784), *Idea for a Universal History with a Cosmopolitan Aim*

KdU: *Kritik der Urteilskraft* (1790), *Critique of the Power of Judgment*

MAM: *Mutmasschlicher Anfang der Menschengeschichte* (1786), *Conjectural Beginning of Human History*

MdS: *Metphysik der Sitten* (1797), *Metaphysics of Morals*

R: *Reflexionen aus dem Nachlass*

Rel: *Religion innerhalb der Grenzen der blossen Vernunft* (1793), *Religion within the Boundaries of Mere Reason*

RezH: *Rezensionen von J. G. Herders Ideen zur Philosophie der Geschichte der Menschheit* (1785), "Reviews of J. G. Herder's *Ideas for the Philosophy of the History of Humanity*"

WiA: *Beanwortung der Frage: Was ist Afklärung?* (1784), *An Answer to the Question: "What is Enlightenment?"*

ZeF: *Zum ewigen Frieden: Ein philosophischer Entwurf* (1795), *Toward Perpetual Peace, A Philosophical Project*

5 *Outlines of a Philosophy of the History of Man [Ideen zur Philosophie der Geschichte der Menscheit]*, T. Churchill trans. (London, 1800), 224.

6 Pauline Kleingeld, "Kant's Second Thoughts on Race", *Philosophical Quarterly* 57 (2007), 573–92; *Kant and Cosmopolitanism*, 111–117; and "Kant's Second Thoughts on Colonialism" in Katrin Flikschuh and Lea Ypi eds., *Kant and Colonialism: Historical and Critical Perspectives*, 43–67.

7 As with so many of Kant's Roman legal tags, this one is misleading. The *Digest* defines a *territorium* as simply "all the land included within the limits of any city. Some authorities hold that it is so called, [from terror] because the magistrates have a right to inspire fear within its boundaries, that is to say, the right to remove the people", which on Kant's use of the term would seem to be the one right that they would *not* have (*Digest* 50.I.8).

8 On Kant's distinction between the *gentes* as "natural communities" and "nations as states", see Otfried Höffe, *Kant's Cosmopolitan Theory of Law and Peace*, Alexandra Newton trans. (Cambridge: Cambridge University Press, 2006), 190–1.

9 True patriotism, he insisted, derived its name "from *patria* not from *pater*, for paternal government ... is the worst" (R 19:570).

10 I would like to thank Benjamin Straumann for this analogy.

11 "Eine *Colonia* oder Provinz ist ein Volk, das zwar seine eigene Verfassung, Gesetzgebung, Boden hat."

12 Livy 34.9.1. I would like to thank Clifford Ando for this reference and for all his help in sorting Roman from Greek colonial practices. See "The Roman City in the Roman Period" in Stéphane Benoist ed., *Rome, A City and Its Empire in Perspective: The Impact of the Roman World through, Fergus Millar's Research. Rome, une cité impériale en jeu: l'impact du monde romain selon Fergus Millar* (Leiden: Brill, 2012), 109–24.

13 See Sankar Muthu, *Enlightenment against Empire*, 155–62. Muthu calls this "state paternalism", although what Kant understood by "paternalism" was "a government established on the principle of benevolence towards the people, like that of a father towards his children – that is a paternalistic government . . . is the greatest despotism thinkable" (GTP 8:290). Roman government, in particular under the Principate, could certainly be described as "paternalistic" in this sense; however, it made no distinction between Roman citizens on grounds of ethnicity or place of birth.

14 On Virginia, see p. 105.

15 *An Enquiry into the Rights of the British Colonies*, 16. On Bland, see pp. oo.

16 "An Account of a Conversation Concerning the Regulation of Governments for the Common Good of Mankind", *The Political Works of Andrew Fletcher*, 436.

17 "Observations on the Nature of Civil Liberty, the Principles of Government and the Justice and Policy of the War with America" in *Political Writings*, 39. On Price, see pp. 1116, 123.

18 Quoted in Jack P. Greene, *Peripheries and Center. Constitutional Development in the Extended Polities of the British Empire and the United States 1607–1788* (Athens and London: University of Georgia Press, 1986), 94–5.

19 See pp. 110–111.

20 "Kant's Juridical Theory of Colonialism", Katrin Flikschuh and Lea Ypi eds., *Kant and Colonialism: Historical and Critical Perspectives*, 145–69.

21 "The best state never undertakes war except to keep faith or in defense of its safety." *De Republica* 3.34, and see Pierre Hassner, « Les concepts de guerre et de paix chez Kant », *Revue française de science politique* XI (1961), 642–70.

22 The translation of *ius gentium* as "law of nations", although conventional, is not unproblematical. *Ius* can mean both "right" and "law" and *gens* can mean a "nation" in something like the modern sense of the term, but also a "people". Kant generally makes a clear distinction between enacted law (*Gestez*) and right (*Recht*).

23 Simone Goyard-Fabre, *Kant et le problème du droit* (Paris: Vrin, 1975), and Brian Tierney, *The Idea of Natural Rights Natural Law, and Church Law, 1150–1625* (Atlanta, GA: Scholars Press, 1997), 74.

24 For an exhaustive analysis of the various ways in which the *ius gentium* was understood, see the discussion in Brett, *Changes of State: Nature and the Limits of the City in Early Modern Natural Law*, 75–89.

25 On this see, my *The Enlightenment and Why It Still Matters*.

26 Cf. MdS 6:267. On Vitoria and pre-Kantian conceptions of the obligation to offer hospitality, see pp. 53–6.

27 Quoted in Robert Kolb, *Réflexions de philosophie du droit international* (Brussell: Editions Bruylant, 2003), 24. And see Alexis Philonenko, « Kant et le problème de la paix » in *Essais sur la philosophie de la guerre* (Paris: Vrin, 1976), 32–5.

28 See Kleingeld, *Kant and Cosmopolitanism*, 76.

29 See Peter Haggenmacher, "Mutations du concept de guerre juste de Grotius à Kant", *Cahiers de philosophie politique et juridique* 10 (1986), 117–22.

30 See p. 48.

31 I would like to thank Benjamin Straumann for this observation.

32 See Barnes, "The Just War", *Cambridge History of Later Medieval Philosophy*, 775–8.

33 *De iure belli* 1.15, 111–12.

34 On Kant's very extensive conception of the possible grounds for war in pursuit of a final juridical world order, see Sharon B. Byrd and Joachim Hruschka, "From the State of Nature to the Juridical State of States", *Law and Philosophy* 27 (2008), 599–641.

35 For the earlier Kant, however, not only would conquest and subjugation seem to have been legitimate, for certain kinds of peoples – most notably Africans and American Indians – but so, too, would slavery. See Pauline Kleingeld, "Kant's Second Thoughts on Colonialism", Katrin Flikschuh and Lea Ypi eds., *Kant and Colonialism: Historical and Critical Perspectives*, 43–67.

36 *Accolatus* is, in fact, an obscure word of Biblical, pre-Jerome origin which was glossed as synonymous with *incola* and applied to persons who had residence but neither origin nor citizenship in a place. (I would like to thank Clifford Ando for this information.) What Kant understood by it in this context, or in the context of the *ius incolatus* at 6:353, in connection with the "right of a citizen of the earth to *attempt* to enter into community with all others", however, is anyone's guess.

37 On res and terra nullius, see pp. 77, 117–8. Kant discusses res nullius as if it were identical – which in Roman law it is – with terra nullius at MdS 6:265–6 and paraphrases Justinian's discussion of the acquisition of a river by the owner of its banks at MdS 6:271. Kant also accepts the possibility of colonization by invitation. The ruler of a state, although he clearly does not possess property rights in it, and cannot, therefore, alienate any part of it, nevertheless, "has the right to encourage *immigration* and settling by foreigners (colonists) even though his native subjects might look askance at this provided that their private ownership of land is not curtailed by it" (MdS 6:338). What Kant does not say, however, is whether these *Colonisten* would in fact be true colonizers, or merely immigrants, who would eventually acquire citizenship and thus become full members of the *nation*.

38 See Brian Tierney, "Kant on Property: The Problem of Permissive Law", *Journal of the History of Ideas* 62 (2001), 301–12.

39 See Muthu, *Enlightenment against Empire*, 88–9.

40 On the full meaning of Kant's claim in the "Idea for a Universal History with a Cosmopolitan Aim", see Pauline Kleingeld, "Kant's Second Thoughts on Colonialism", Katrin Flikschuh and Lea Ypi eds., *Kant and Colonialism: Historical and Critical Perspectives*, 43–67, at 43–5. And see Muthu, *Enlightenment against Empire*, 188.

41 On Kant's innate right to land, see Leslie Arthur Mulholland, *Kant's System of Rights* (New York: Columbia University Press, 1989), 218–20. Kant's comments on the dependence of the Inuit on driftwood for their boats, weapons, and huts are at ZeF 8:363.

42 Arthur Ripstein, *Force and Freedom Kant's Legal and Political Philosophy* (Cambridge, MA: Harvard University Press, 2009), 89–90, 155–6.

43  On Kant's three categories of *lex*, see Sharon B. Byrd and Joachim Hruschka, "Lex iusti, lex iuridica und lex iustitiae in Kants *Rechtslehre*", *Archiv für Rechts und Sozialphilosophie* 91 (2005), 484–500.

44  *Enlightenment against Empire*, 184–200.

45  *A Summary View of the Rights of British America*, 4. In fact, the British Crown had always maintained that the Thirteen Colonies, whatever the realities of their founding, were in law lands "conquest" and thus a part of the royal demesne. See pp. 105–112.

46  See Jeremy Waldron, "Kant's Theory of the State" in Pauline Kleingeld ed., *Towards Perpetual Peace and Other Writings on Politics, Peace and History* (New Haven and London: Yale University Press, 2006), 194–7. Waldron suggests that for Kant certain organizations which might call themselves states are in fact not in that they do not "amount to a legal system and administer what actually counts as law". In such cases their citizens would be under no obligation to obey their rulers. This, however, would require that the citizens pass an initial judgment on their rulers in precisely the way that Kant denies that they have the right to do.

47  On Kant's agreements and disagreements with Hobbes, see Tuck, *The Rights of War and Peace*, 207–25.

48  *De iure naturae et gentium libri octo*, VII. 8. para. 10.

49  The only exception to this would appear to be the French Revolution. On Kant's highly tendentious understanding of the events which led up to the declaration of the Republic in 1792, it had been Louis XVI himself who, by calling the Estates-General in an attempt to resolve a financial crisis, had voluntarily, if inadvertently, surrendered the "supreme authority" within the French state to the people, and "the consequence was that the monarch's sovereignty wholly disappeared (it was not merely suspended) and passed to the people." Once anything like this happens, a situation is created in which "the united people does not merely represent the sovereign: it is itself the sovereign" (MdS 6:341–2). In other words the Revolution had been no revolution at all, but only a legal transfer of power. For a further discussion of this point, see my *The Enlightenment and Why It Still Matters*, 366–8.

50  See Peter Niesen "Restorative Justice in International and Cosmopolitan Law" Katrin Flikschuh and Lea Ypi eds., *Kant and Colonialism: Historical and Critical Perspective*.

# 8

## "Savage Impulse-Civilized Calculation"

### Conquest, Commerce, and the Enlightenment Critique of Empire

I

Imperial expansion, wrote the great Austrian economist Joseph Schumpeter in 1918, as more than one European empire was coming to an ignominious end, was "the purely instinctual inclination towards war and conquest". This, he declared, confidently, had "no adequate object beyond itself. ... Hence the tendency of such expansion to transcend all bonds and tangible limits to the point of utter exhaustion."[1] The desire for expansion, conquest, and possession which had been the driving force behind every empire, from the Achaemenid to the British, had been, as he phrased it, entirely without "external objects". They had had no motive other than expansion itself; they had simply gone on and on until they had reached the natural limits of their resources or come up against a stronger power. But why this apparent blind rush into a seemingly shapeless future? "The explanation lies", Schumpeter replied, "in the vital needs of situations that moulded people and classes into warriors." If the members of the dominant warrior class wished "to avoid extinction", they had to continue to be warriors since transformation into something else was unavailable to them. "Imperialism", in Schumpeter's view, "is thus atavistic in character. It falls into that large group of surviving features from an earlier age .... In other words it is an element that stems from the living conditions not of the present but of the past." On this account imperialism was not the inescapable consequence of some profound, and eradicable, human aggressiveness, much less was it the expression either of class or economic interests – as the Marxists maintained – both of which could have been perpetuated, albeit in some other form, into the present. It was simply a phase in human history which would "tend to disappear as an element of habitual emotional reaction, because of the progressive rational-ization of life and mind". If this were so then, "cases of Imperialism should decline in intensity the later they occur in the history of a people and a culture". The best evidence that this had indeed been the case was, he believed, provided by the absolute monarchies of the eighteenth century which had, in his view, been "unmistakably 'more civilized' than their predecessors".[2]

In Schumpeter's account, the modern instrument which had finally shuffled imperialism off the world-historical stage was capitalism – for capitalism does have concrete objects outside itself: namely wealth and happiness. And while individuals are engaged in the pursuit of those goals they can have no interest in, or even time for, militarism. The age of war and conquest had been overtaken, gradually, haltingly to be sure, but ultimately irrevocably, by capitalism, and by capitalism's principle strength: free, and unhindered trade. "It may be stated as beyond controversy", Schumpeter concluded confidently, "that where free trade prevails no class has an interest in forcible expansion as such."[3]

In the closing months of the First World War, Schumpeter had good grounds for believing that, at long last, the pointless aggressivity of human-kind had been checked by a mastery of calculated self-interests. He should perhaps, however, have been rather more cautious since he, of all people, the author after all of a great *History of Economic Analysis*, could not have been unaware that for all the modernity of his convictions – and to be fair the subtlety of his arguments – he was in effect repeating a far older conviction and a predication which had proved to be wrong at least once in the past.

It was obviously false to claim that *all* empires had had as their objective nothing other than an inclination to war and conquest. If it really was the case that the monarchies of eighteenth-century Europe had become, in Schumpeter's assessment, "unmistakably 'more civilized' than their prede-cessors", this was because for most of them – including Spain – the idea of an empire based on Schumpeter's model of expansion had already come to be seen as a severely debilitating anachronism. By then warfare within Europe had, reflected Montesquieu in 1734, ceased to be capable of creating the kind of empire Schumpeter had in mind, the kind of empire the Romans had once had. Any such project in the mid-eighteenth century would, he concluded, have been "morally impossible". New military technologies had rendered the "power of all men, and consequently of all nations" more or less equal, and the scale of the kind of warfare now waged between the European powers required such massive reserves of manpower that they inevitably exhausted the resources of the states that employed them.[4] Out-side Europe, however, a different logic prevailed. There the inevitable fate of any conquering monarchy, Montesquieu had said, was "frightful luxury in the capital, poverty in the provinces at some distance from it, abundance at its furthest points". (In his view, the best modern example of this was China.)[5] The obvious outcome of such an imbalance was that, sooner or later, the former colonies would bankrupt the metropolis. For Montesquieu this is what had indeed had happened to Spain, which had become little more than an economic dependency of her overseas possessions. In 1776,

Adam Smith very much feared that something similar might befall Britain as a consequence of "the present unhappy war" if it did not shed its colonies in America.[6]

By the middle of the eighteenth century there was a general consensus among the enlightened elites of Europe that the existing European overseas empires had become rapacious machines designed for extracting wealth and with little regard for the welfare or the public good of either the colonist or, where these still existed, the indigenous populations. The result was that they had succeeded only in destroying the indigenes, arousing the enmity of the colonist, all of which, as Smith complained, with very little real benefit to the mother country. If they were to survive at all, they had to transform themselves into global polities which would be of benefit to all their inhabitants. The only way to achieve this end was to trade in conquest for commerce. "The present policy of Europe with respects to America", wrote Victor Riqueti, marquis de Mirabeau, in 1758 in his highly optimistic (and very popular) work of political economy *The Friend of Man*, constituted a "new and monstrous system" made up of a combination of three distinct and incompatible types of political association, or, as he called them "esprits": domination, settlement, and commerce. The present regime, he insisted, had to be abandoned in favour of a policy which encouraged settlement, privileged commerce, and abandoned conquest altogether.[7]

Mirabeau was not alone. Almost everyone who turned a dispassionate eye on the current state of the European empires came to much the same conclusion. "The rise and fall of empires is now no more," declared Diderot, in one of the more lyrical passages that he inserted into the abbé Guillaume Thomas Raynal's *Philosophical and Political History of the Settlements and Commerce of the Europeans in the Two Indies*.[8] Gone now were the malign tyrants and the antique warrior cults that had been the driving force behind the nations of antiquity. In this modern world, it would be impossible to find a man such as Alexander the Great before whom it could be said that "the earth fell silent":

> The fanaticism of religion and the spirit of conquest are no longer what they once were.... A war among commercial nations is a fire that destroys them all. The time is not far off when the sanctions of rulers will extend to the individual transactions between the subjects of different nations, and when bankruptcy, whose impact may be felt at such immense distances, will become affairs of state ... and the annals of all peoples will need to be written by commercial philosophers as they were once written by historical orators.[9]

Commerce had indeed become, in the words of the Dutch economic theorist Isaac de Pinto, the "craze of the century".[10] "Everything in the universe is commerce," wrote Mirabeau. "Because by commerce one must understand all the natural and indispensable relationships of the entire species, which are, and will always be, those between one man and another between one family, one society, one nation and another."[11] The history of commerce, as Montesquieu put it, was the history "of the communication of peoples".[12] The association of commerce with communication which, for Vitoria, had turned free passage into a natural right had, as we have seen in Chapter 5, been something of a commonplace since antiquity.

For men like Montesquieu, Mirabeau, Diderot, Pinto, and Smith, what in the eighteenth century was called "the commercial society", was conceived less as a mechanism for self-interested exchange than it was something resembling what we might call a political culture. Commerce, Montesquieu famously believed, "softens and polishes barbarous customs as we see every day". Commerce – the celebrated *doux commerce* – was the means by which nature had provided mankind with the necessary conditions for civilization.[13] It was far more than a simple means of exchange. It depended on cooperation and a certain degree of trust. Its principal agent was money which, in John Locke's account, had been introduced "by the tacit Agreement of man". Early men finding themselves in need of "enlarging" their possession "had agreed that *a little piece of yellow Metal*, which would keep without wasting or decay, should be worth a great piece of Flesh or a whole heap of Corn".[14] Money was a "sign" and thus a form of language, and like language, or the use of mathematical symbols, its creation could only be a collective enterprise. It spoke to coordination, and a degree of social harmony. Sometime in the fifth century BCE the Socratic philosopher Aristippus was shipwrecked on the coast of Rhodes. When he came ashore he saw geometrical figures – another form of language – drawn in the sand and cried out to his companions: "Let us be of good hope, for indeed I see the traces of men."[15] Centuries later Montesquieu picked up the story but turned these geometrical figures into money. "If you were alone," he wrote, "and happen to come by some accident to the land of an unknown people, and if you see a piece of money, you know that you have reached a civilized nation."[16]

Commerce not only had the power to transform human nature, to civilize mankind; it was a means for uniting nations in bonds of mutual dependence – and thus it was hoped to put a final end to warfare. "The world then" as the seventeenth-century Jansenist, French Pierre Nicole phrased it (in John Locke's translation), "is our city: & as inhabitants of it, we have intercourse with all man kinde, And doe receive from them advantages, or inconveniencys ... [all nations] are liked to us, on one side, or other; & all enter into that chain, which ties the whole race of men together by their mutuall wants".[17] And this bond, in Montesquieu's words, "produces in men a certain feeling for exact justice, opposed on the one hand to banditry and on the other to those moral virtues that make it so that one does not always discuss one's interests with rigidity and that one can neglect them for those of others".

It creates, in other words, a particular kind of society: one in which, unlike the ancient warrior societies whose members are constrained by unbending codes of conduct and whose principal goal is the quest for personal glory, the prime good is the welfare of each of its members; and because in such a society "all unions are based on mutual needs", everyone benefits to some degree without having actively to pursue the interest of others.[18] It was commerce which had transformed Europe itself, from a collection of squabbling monarchies into what Montesquieu believed was now, in effect, "one nation made up of many". France and Britain, he claimed, were now dependent on "the opulence of Poland and Muscovy" in much the same way that any one of the separate provinces of any single nation might be dependent on all the others.[19]

And what had occurred in Europe might perhaps one day be extended to the entire world. "Interest", declared the great Indianist, linguist, and jurist Sir William Jones – by which he meant economic interest – "was the magic wand which brought them [East and West] within one circle."[20] Even Kant, who was far less inclined to believe that commerce could have a transformative effect on the essential conflictual, human nature, believed:

> It is the *spirit of commerce*, which cannot co-exist with war and which sooner or later takes hold of every nation. In other words since the *power of money* may well be the most reliable of all powers (means) subordinate to that of the state, states find themselves compelled, (admittedly not through incentives of morality) to promote honorable peace and, whenever war threatens to break out anywhere in the world, to prevent through mediation.[21]

On balance modern economists have tended to agree.[22] Commerce also seemed to offer a means of reviving an older ecumenical image of "empire". For, in theory at least, commerce created a relationship between peoples which did not involve dependency of any kind and, most importantly, avoided any use of force. In the new commercialized societies the various peoples of the world would swap new technologies and basic scientific and cultural skills as readily as they would their foodstuffs. These would not be empires of conquest, nor of repression and destruction of the kind which the Spanish had perpetrated in America. They would, instead, be trading empires and, in the process, possibly also "empires of liberty". What final outcome for humanity would result from the discovery of America and the sea route to India those "great events" which had launched the modern commercial world and with it the modern commercial empires, reflected Smith, "no human wisdom can foresee". But "by uniting in some measure the most distant parts of the word by enabling them to relieve one another's wants, to increase one another's enjoyments and to encourage one another's industry, their general tendency would seem to be beneficial". True, the indigenous peoples of "both of the East and West Indies" had, as a consequence of their contact with the Europeans, only been "sunk and lost in ... dreadful misfortunes". But, he went on, in a remarkable passage, the time may yet come when the balance of power between the Europeans and "the inhabitants of all the different quarters of the globe" would change and so that the entire world might "arrive at that equality of courage and force which, by inspiring mutual fear can alone overawe the injustice of independent nations into some sort of respect for the rights of one another".[23] International trade might not only have the ultimate benefit of "softening" and immensely enriching the maritime nations but might also, in time, bring with it some degree of international justice to the entire globe.

Not all the older empires of conquest had been alike either in their objectives or in their outcomes. In some cases some conquest might have been the inescapable condition for the creation of lasting commercial relations. Montesquieu, influenced by the Greco-Roman moralist and biographer Plutarch's image of Alexander the Great as the instrument of Stoic universalism, took a very different view of his empire to, say, Diderot for whom all empires were unsustainable. Alexander, on Montesquieu's glowing account, had transformed the societies through which he passed yet preserved their customs so that he "wiped out all distinction between conquerors and the vanquished". In the process he had become not the leader of an empire but "the monarch of each nation and the first citizen of each town". But then Alexander's ultimate ambition had been, at least in Plutarch's imagination, to unite East and West, so that he would be remembered not as a conqueror at all but as "one sent by the gods to be the conciliator and arbitrator of the Universe". It was he who "using force of arms against those whom he failed to bring together by reason ... united peoples of the most varied origin and ordered ... all men to look on the *oikoumene* as their fatherland".[24] In Plutarch's account this union had been political and dynastic; on Montesquieu's it was ultimately commercial. By uniting "the Indies with the West by means of a maritime commerce", Alexander had, Montesquieu claimed, been responsible for bringing about a "great revolution in commerce", which had led to the creation, in Pierre Briant's words, of a "global political conception which united commerce communication and civilization".[25] In time all trace of the initial conquests would diminish and then disappear, and the world would be left with the Stoic philosopher Zeno of Citium's "dream or, as it were shadowy picture, of a well-ordered and philosophical community", of which, according to Plutarch, Alexander's empire had been the initial embodiment.[26] Alexander, then, had provided an example. Alas, few had chosen to follow it. The Romans, his most obvious heirs, had, in Montesquieu's view, only "conquered all in order to destroy all".[27] Modern empires, clearly, should follow the Macedonian, not the Roman model. Even if the perhaps overly optimistic confidence which Montesquieu had placed in the civilizing potential of commerce turned out to be illusory, it would still be true that the mere existence of transactions between peoples tended to benefit all those concerned. "I observe", insisted David Hume, who took a far more skeptical view of the political and moral benefits of trade than many of his contemporaries, that "where an open communication is preserved among nations, it is impossible but the domestic industry of every one must receive an enlargement from the improvements of the others."[28]

The conclusion to be drawn from this is that modern empires should become, in effect, trading companies operating in the interests of all their members. In 1756 Charles de Brosses, disciple of Buffon, friend of Diderot, president for life of the *parlement* of Burgundy, a powerful advocate for the already tentative French proposals for an exploration of the Pacific – and the man who gave the word "fetish" to the languages of Europe – published a widely read compilation of all the voyages hitherto undertaken into the "southern Seas": the *History of the Journeys to the Southern Lands*. The Pacific Ocean, he argued, was the last uncontaminated region of the world. Here, he enthused, one might create

> a future which is not at all like that which Christopher Columbus secured for our neighbours . . .. Their [the Spanish] example would instruct us. For we would avoid the two vices from which the Spaniards then suffered, avarice and cruelty. The former emptied their own country in pursuit of an illusory fortune, something which should never have been attempted. The latter, whose causes were national pride and superstition, has all but destroyed the human race in America. They massacred disdainfully, as if they were base and alien beasts, millions of Indians whom they could have made into men. They destroyed to the last man, hundreds of races, as though there was some profit to be had from uninhabited lands.

"Experience has shown", he continued, "that in these distant climates, one must trade not conqueror, that it is not a question of establishing imaginary kingdoms beyond the equator." Instead of these "imaginary kingdoms", the new French empire of the Pacific would create a network of trading stations, working for the mutual benefit of all those involved with them. Such an empire would draw the "savages" from "the woods" and "allow them to benefit from the advantages of human and social laws". The model for all future French empires should be, concluded De Brosses, not the Spaniards or the Romans – or even Plutarch's version of the Macedonian – but the Carthaginians, for they had created not dependencies or colonies but new nations. "What greater objective could a sovereign have", he concluded, "than that?"[29]

In the later years of the eighteenth century, the distinction between Rome and Carthage became a frequently used metaphor for distinguishing the old empires of conquest and plunder from the image of the new enlightened empires of commerce. For some of the French and Spanish critics of empire, the British, for all their obvious failings had come the closest to creating what the physiocrat François Quesnay in 1766 in a commentary on Montesquieu's *Spirit of the Laws* called a "Carthaginian constitution".[30]

Where not only the colonies but the provinces of the metropolis itself are subjected to the laws of commerce and carriage ... where the laws of maritime commerce pay no heed to the laws of politics ... where commerce in agricultural produce, the property in land, and even the state itself are regarded as accessories to the metropolis and the metropolis is made up of merchants.[31]

But, he went on, such a constitution "cannot serve as a model for monarchial empires in which politics and [personal] interests and are too strongly opposed to the interests of commerce an carriage". Britain, of course, was an exception to this rule only because, in Montesquieu's celebrated description, it was "the republic [that] hides under the form of monarchy".[32]

Not many, however, were prepared to accept the logic of Quesnay's claim that to create a true commercial empire along "Carthaginian" lines, France would first have to transform itself into republic in all but name. It would certainly, however, have to adjust its political priorities so that empire could be conceived, as De Brosses conceived it, as one intended to bring prosperity to, rather than domination over, the peoples it encountered.

It all sounds very ecumenical. Commerce, however, as all these writers conceived it, was always something more than mere trade. Indeed, in one crucial sense it was not trade at all, for it was obvious to all that what David Hume called the "Jealously of Trade", which constantly led "states that have made some advances in commerce ... to look on the progress of their neighbours with a suspicious eye", could all too easily be the occasion for another kind of conflict between peoples, and commerce another mode of warfare.[33] Or as Alexander Hamilton asked: "Has commerce hitherto done anything more than change the objects of war?" Were not commercial nations also – even "commercial republics, like ours" – governed by men quite as much given to "the impulse of rage, resentment, jealousy, avarice" as those who ruled over the older warrior monarchies? "Is not love of wealth", he went on, "as domineering and enterprising a passion as power of glory? Have there not been as many wars founded upon commercial motives since that has become the system of nations, as were before occasioned by the crudity of territory or dominion?" Experience, that "least fallible guide of human opinions", would seem to suggest that the answer was yes.[34]

There also existed another obstacle to the realization of this image of a world made into "one city" by the benign polishing and enriching effects of commerce. There was a widely held assumption that De Brosses' "Australians" (by which he meant the inhabitants of the South Pacific in general) were, he believed, so isolated "from the rest of the universe" and so "deprived of all the resources offered by proximity and understanding with other humans" that they must by waiting on their distant shores for their European benefactors to arrive and "polish" them.[35] The same also applied to the Africans, Asians, and what remained of the Americans. All the "numerous peoples" of these "vast countries", claimed the marquis de

Condorcet in 1794, who had for centuries slaved under tyrannical masters and corrupting habits, exactly as the Europeans themselves had once done, now waited patiently on their distant shores "to be civilized and to receive from us the means to be so, and find brothers among the Europeans to become their friends and disciples". The forward progress of these peoples, he was certain, would be more rapid and more assured than our own had been, "for they will receive from us what we were forced to discover". They will accept as simple truths "those certain methods which we have arrived at only after a long series of errors". Condorcet was no closet imperialist. He was, among many other things, an abolitionist and a champion of equal rights for women and for all peoples of all races. And his understanding of the European mission was based on what he saw as an obligation to export to the rest of the world the enlightenment which had finally liberated Europe itself from its own "sacred despots and stupid conquerors". His vision of the future French Empire was a globalized version of the project for a system of public education for France – and the first of its kind in the world – which he had presented to the National Assembly in 1792, which would contribute not only to the cultivation of the "physical, intellectual and moral faculties" of the French but also "to the general and gradual perfection of the human species the goal toward which every social institution ought to be directed".[36] It would ensure, he was certain, that there would arrive a day when mankind would be subject only to the power of reason and the "tyrants and slaves, the priests and their stupid or hypocritical instruments will exist only in the theater".[37]

But what if the basic assumption, which neither De Brosses nor Condorcet, nor any of the advocates of the "softening" power of commerce, and of the inevitable advent of civilization, ever seriously questioned that all the people of the world really did want to belong to one vast if also diverse, human community of the rational and the enlightened turned out to be wrong? What if these peoples did not want to be polished or introduced to the perhaps not always so self-evident "advantages of human and social laws"? As Sir William Jones cautioned Edmund Burke in 1784, "[a] system of *liberty*, if forced on a people invincibly attached to opposite *habits*, would be a system of cruel *tyranny*".[38] The possibility that peoples might need to be forced to be free, civil, and enlightened and the possible consequences of that was never an obvious part of the objective of the new commercial liberal empires.

## II

What finally brought the full force of this paradox to the empire builders themselves, and what finally shifted their conception of the kinds of empires they could hope to acquire, and build, overseas, was the attempt by a European to create a new empire of conquest within Europe itself, where at least since the end of the Thirty Years' War any such project, as

Montesquieu had seen, had been doomed to failure. Napoleon's empire was intended to be the empire of liberty, *par excellence*, marrying respect for local ways of life with a ruthlessly efficient legal and administrative machine all under the somewhat uncertain aegis of the "Rights of Man and Citizen". From his final exile on St. Helena, Napoleon told his amanuensis Emmanuel de Las Cases that his "great design" had been

> the agglomeration, the concentration of the same geographical peoples which revolutions and politics had broken down. I would have liked to make of each of these peoples one and a same national body . . .. Then perhaps it would have been possible to dream for the great European family, the application of the American Congress or of the Amphictyons of Greece.[39]

However much he might, as the allusion to the Greek leagues and the United States suggests, have aspired to be the founder of a kind of European Union *avant la lettre*, what Napoleon had in fact done was to wage prolonged and bloody war against peoples who, for the most part, did not see themselves in need of the kind of liberty and equality which the French Revolution, at least in its Napoleonic guise, claimed to offer. As Napoleon's mercurial foreign minister, the ever-cynical Charles Maurice de Talleyrand-Périgord, once warned him, expressing very much the same general truth as Jones: "taking freedom by open force to other peoples" was certain to "make that freedom hated".[40]

Napoleon had been the child of the Revolution and as Edmund Burke had observed, the Revolution, by destroying the old aristocratic order and replacing it with a group of fanatics who had grown rich on its spoils – by creating, in effect, a new conquering elite – had bypassed the commercial and necessarily civilizing stage of human development. The outcome had been Napoleon, and the Napoleonic empire which for all Napoleon claims to be reuniting the "family of Europe" was, in effect, as archaic as the empire of Charlemagne (who had had similar ambitions) had been.[41]

In 1813, when the end of Napoleon's rule seemed inevitable, the Swiss politician, political theorist, and man of letters Benjamin Constant, and one of Napoleon's fiercest critics, wrote a long pamphlet entitled *The Spirit of Conquest and Usurpation and Their Relationship to European Civilization.* Published in Hanover in January 1814, shortly after Napoleon's defeat at the battle of Leipzig, this was, in many respects, a re-working of part of Montesquieu's *Esprit de lois* for the coming post-Napoleonic world.[42] It was also the most forceful denunciation of conquest and the most compelling endorsement of commerce written during the nineteenth century.[43]

For Constant, the implications for the modern world of Napoleon's attempt to create in Europe a new *civitas* under a single law and a single government constituted a monstrous anachronism. War, Constant believed, was not in itself an evil, as many of his contemporaries who had lived through the carnage of the previous decades had come to think. At certain stages in human history, it had been a part of the human condition and, as such, had possessed a capacity for developing "the finest and grandest faculties" in humankind. This, however, had depended on "one indispensable condition: that war should be the natural outcome of the situation and national spirit of the people".[44] And at the beginning of the nineteenth century that time was long since past. Now conquest and usurpation – the objectives of any war which was not simply defensive – had become outmoded, and consequently highly dangerous, methods of achieving political objectives of any kind. The warrior communities of the ancient world which had created the first European (and all the Asiatic) empires, had been societies which were crucially small. Their customs were simple; they despised luxury and comfort and valued, above all else, generosity, hospitality, courage, and loyalty – loyalty to each other and loyalty to their leaders. "Each people incessantly attacked their neighbors or was attacked by them." Even "those who had no ambition to be conquerors, could still not lay down their weapons, lest they should themselves be conquered".[45] The modern world, as Constant saw it, however, was a very different place. Societies were now large and complex. No one knew anyone except his neighbors. Generosity, hospitality, courage, and loyalty were still looked on as virtues, but they had become purely private ones and now took second place to each individual's personal ambition to achieve a prosperous and untroubled life. The collective nightmare of the massed barbarians on their northern or eastern frontiers, which had haunted so many past generations of Europeans, was now no more. In modern societies, the "great mass of human beings" now had nothing to fear from the "hordes that are still barbarous". For them war is merely a burden, and "their uniform tendency is towards peace". The "sole aim of modern nations" was therefore, he believed, "repose and with repose, comfort and as the source of comfort, industry".[46] The only political goods which the moderns required were the peace and security which would allow them to pursue these essentially private goals unhindered. War, he added with nice irony, "has lost its charm as well as its utility. Man is no longer driven to it either by interest or by passion."[47]

What divided the ancient from the modern world in this way was once again, as it had been for Montesquieu, commerce. In Constant's view, however, commerce had replaced warfare not because it was benign or because it could "make men gentle". Like Thomas Hobbes, another survivor from a bitter civil conflict, Constant did not believe that human nature could be improved. It could only be reasoned with and manipulated. Humans were often blinded by fanaticism, religious belief, and other forms of irrationality. But the bulk of humankind, however vile its basic instincts, knew – or could be shown – how to recognize and act in its own self-interest. Constant, therefore, was less interested in the grand transforming power of *le doux commerce* than he was in the manipulative potential of the ethos of the *commerçant*. Commerce, *pace* Montesquieu, was inseparable from trade and trade and warfare "are only two different means to achieve the same end, that of possessing what is desired". What the invention of commerce had achieved, entirely despite itself, was a radical change in the *means* by which humans now calculated their interests. "Commerce", Constant wrote,

> is simply a tribute paid to the strength of the possessor by the aspirant to possession. It is an attempt to obtain by mutual agreement what one can no longer hope to obtain through violence .... War, then, comes before commerce. The former is all savage impulse, the latter civilized calculation. It is clear that the more the commercial spirit (*tendance*) dominates the weaker the martial spirit becomes.

Commerce, furthermore, even if it is not quite the universal civilizing agent Montesquieu and others supposed it to be, nevertheless "rests upon the good understanding of nations with each other; it can be sustained only by justice; it is founded upon equality; it thrives in peace".[48] Like Kant, whom he had read with care (and had had a celebrated exchange on the legitimacy of lying in extreme circumstances), Constant also imaged that commerce had had a generally globalizing effect.[49] It had, he claimed, "brought nations closer together and has given them virtually identical customs and habits". Monarchs, he added optimistically, "may still be enemies, but peoples are compatriots". This modem world, large, diverse, and plural, but also united in its interests and in its recognition of what was of value to the individual, could simply have no further interest in pursuing it objectives by any other means. In the Hegelian language to which Constant frequently reverted, commerce had become the expression of the "spirit of the age".[50] Had the war between Rome and Carthage been fought at the beginning of the nineteenth century instead of in the second and third centuries BC, it would have been Carthage who would have won, for "Carthage would have the hopes of the entire world on her side; the customs of today and the spirit of the times would be her allies."[51]

Empire did not, in Constant's view, derive from any desire to educate or civilize or otherwise liberate the benighted peoples of the world. It derived from a simple human quest for power, and from the most parochial, if also the most basic of human instincts, that "narrow and hostile spirit which men seek to dignify with the name of patriotism".[52] The true force behind Napoleon's seemingly globalizing ambitions was best summed up, not by the grandiloquent statements which Las Cases had attributed to him, but by something else he had said (significantly during the ill-fated conquest of Egypt in 1798): "Ce qui est bon pour les français est bon pour tout le monde."[53]

In Constant's new world of calculation, trade had taken over from empire, precisely because the "infinite and complex ramifications of commerce have placed the interests of [individual] societies beyond the frontiers of their own territories". Modernity, in other words, cannot be other than peaceful and global. Any modern government which today "wished to goad a European people to war and conquest would be committing a gross and disastrous anachronism. It would labor to impose upon that nation an impulse contrary to nature."[54]

And because any future attempt at imperial expansion would be an anachronism, its impact on its subject peoples would be far harder to endure than anything which had existed in the premodern world. For ancient empires had been essentially conglomerates, which had tolerated, had even welcomed, difference. Such, for instance, had been Alexander's empire. Alexander – whom Constant ranked alongside Attila the Hun and the insane Persian tyrant Cambyses – had left his subjects to pursue their own private lives unhindered, so long as they did not oppose him, not because as Montesquieu had imaged, he had anything so grand in mind as a Stoic union of East and West, but largely because those lives were unimportant both to them and to him. What mattered was the group not the individual. The modern empire, however, must exist in a world where the public had ceded much of its former space to the private – where it is the individual not the group which matters; it could, therefore, only secure its ends under the guise of a crippling uniformity. To survive it would have to pursue "the vanquished into the most intimate aspects of their existence. It mutilates them in order to reduce them to uniform proportions. In the past conquerors expected the deputies of conquered nations to appear on their knees before them. Today it is man's morale that they wish to prostrate."[55] For this reason any modern conqueror – and it was Napoleon Constant had in mind – would have to give to his Empire "an appearance of uniformity, upon which the proud eye of power may travel without meeting any unevenness that could offend or limit its view. The same code of law, the same measures, the same regulations, and if they could contrive it gradually, the same language, this is what is proclaimed to be the perfect form of social organization."[56] Inevitably such an empire inflicts far greater damage on its subjects than any that had existed in antiquity. "The vanity of civilization", he concluded, "is more tormenting than the pride of barbarity."[57]

The modern transition from warfare to commerce, by altering the ways in which goods were acquired, had also inevitably changed the very nature of the goods desired. In antiquity men had sought glory and despised luxury. Now, if anything, the positions were reversed. "Our century", wrote Constant, "which values everything according to its utility, and, as soon as one attempts to move out of this sphere opposes its irony to every real or feigned enthusiasm, could not content itself with a sterile glory, which we are no longer in the habit of preferring to other kinds."[58] In the ancient world, the tribal leader had only to point to the region of the world he wished to conquer and his warriors would follow him there. The objective was unimportant. Conquest of any kind, and for any ostensible reason, inevitably brought glory, and glory was the preeminent social good. In the modern world, calculating and concerned to protect its own interests, glory had generally become of only secondary importance. The only response a modern people would give to a leader who urged them to follow him and conquer the world would be "to reply with one voice: 'We have no wish to conquer the world'".[59] Men might still be coerced or paid to fight, but the modern conqueror could never be able to mobilize what for Constant was the source of lasting political power in the modern word: public opinion, without the support of which, as he had seen, no future, post-Revolutionary society could hope to survive for long. Representative government – if not yet "democracy" – could not be persuaded to act against its own interests. "The force that a people needs to keep all others in subjection", he wrote,

> is today, more than ever, a privilege that cannot last. The nation that aimed at such an empire would place itself in a more dangerous position than the weakest of tribes. It would become the object of universal horror. Every opinion, every desire, every hatred, would threaten it, and sooner or later those hatreds, those opinions, and those desires would explode and engulf it.[60]

In 1813, with Napoleon apparently on his way to becoming his own kind of anachronism, Constant could be confident that the very brevity and bloodiness of his ambition to transform Europe into a series of satellite kingdoms had indeed created the "universal horror", necessary to rend all such projects unrepeatable. In a sense, and despite Napoleon's brief return, he was right – at least until 1914, and at least within Europe.[61]

Beyond Europe, however, things were very different. Constant had seen that if a government succeeded through "sophisms and imposture" to "disturb the [nation's] reason, pervert its judgment and overturn its ideas", an entire people might be diverted from the true path of self-interest and be persuaded to fall prey, once again, to the delusions of "sterile glory".[62] What he had not foreseen, however, was that what would follow the final defeat of Napoleon would be the emergence of a nation quite unlike the community of rational self-interested, essentially utilitarian, beings he had imaged. The citizens of the new nation states which came into being after the Congress of Vienna turned out in the end to be animated as easily by the "narrow and hostile spirit" of patriotism as those of the ancient patria had been. They may not have been quite so willing as the ancients were to take on themselves the responsibility of conquering the world, but they were quite happy for others to do so for them.[63]

Nationalism transformed the nature of empire by making the acquisition of overseas possessions a source of national pride, and a potential instrument of national cohesion in times of crisis. In some sense, of course, it had always been that. The Roman general Scipio Africanus had famously evaded charges of corruption by appealing to the Roman people in the name of what he had achieved for their empire.[64] The English and French scramble for possessions in the Atlantic in the seventeenth century had been driven overwhelmingly by the desire not to be overtaken by Spain. Similarly in the world which emerged after the Congress of Vienna, "public opinion", far from turning an ironical eye on the imperialistic pretensions of its rulers, embraced them with enthusiasm – provided, that is, they were now conducted at a safe distance beyond their own frontiers.

The French invasion of Algeria in 1830 was undertaken precisely to reestablish the image of a France still tarnished by the defeat of Napoleon, and the hope – unfulfilled as it turned out – that a quick victory might allow the unpopular government of Charles X success at the polls, an act which Constant shortly before his death in December 1830 denounced as precisely the kind of "illusion and seduction" he had feared might be deployed by an unscrupulous government to turn a people away from the pursuit of their purely private pleasures.[65] Eleven years of unrelenting warfare later, when the French had failed to acquire more than a tenuous hold over large areas of the country, Alexis de Tocqueville was still in favour of the occupation, for to withdraw, he wrote in October 1841, would "in the eyes of the world be a certain declaration of the decadence [of France]". If France were ever to give up Algeria, he added, it certainly should not be at a time like the present when "she seems to be descending into the second rate, and appears to be resigned to seeing the direction of the affairs of Europe pass into other hands".[66] He was not alone in his assumption that it was the size and wealth – or sometimes merely the very existence – of possessions overseas which served to establish the status of a power within Europe. "As long as we rule in India", Lord Nathaniel Curzon is reported to have said in 1901, "we are the greatest power in the world. If we lose it, we shall drop straightaway to a third-rate power."[67]

The new imperialism turned out to be very different from the kind of "empire of liberty" for which the writers of the pre-Revolutionary generation had argued. None of what Edmund Burke had called the "sacred trust" of empire was involved here – only, in Joseph Conrad's famous description of it, "the taking away [of the earth] from those who have a different complexion or slightly flatter noses than ourselves".[68] In the eighteenth century empire, or at least the kind of enlightened "empires of liberty" envisaged by a broad spectrum of writers from Montesquieu to Burke, had become, in effect, a name for a particular kind of polity, and as John Pocock has argued, many in the eighteenth century looked on "empire" and "civil society" as "nearly if not fully interchangeable".[69] By the late nineteenth century, however, the word was being used to describe something very different, something more like a club to which only the most advanced industrial nations could belong. In the new nationalist calculus, the more of this earth you could take away, the greater you became. It was this that made Teddy Roosevelt so keen that the United States should acquire an overseas empire in the Caribbean and the Pacific, despite the generally hostile view of empire taken by most of the members of that grandly elusive entity, "the American people". It was for that reason that Meiji Japan between the 1850s and the 1910s attempted to re-invent itself as a European-style empire with a semi-scared emperor (something it had not previously had). It was also this which led the Ottoman Sultan, whose empire was now in disintegration, to reappropriate the title of "imperator" in a bid to be admitted to the Concert of Europe.[70]

It was, of course, the apparently imminent collapse of this imperial world which Schumpeter believed he was witnessing in 1918. Unlike his predecessors, however, Schumpeter seems to have been broadly right in his assumptions. He could not have foreseen the rise of the last (or at any rate the latest) attempts to build empires in Europe: Nazi Germany and Stalinist Russia. However, these, in part at least for the reasons which Schumpeter himself had given, were relatively short-lived and the circumstances which gave rise to one of them – the Soviet Union – makes it unlike any previous European land-based empires.

By 1945 the world of empires as it had been conceived within Europe since antiquity was on its last legs; two decades or so later it was no more. For even if we accept the view that the modern United States is some kind of empire, or that the European Union is, one thing remains constant: this post Cold-War "imperialism" is one guided by, and in the interests of, international trade. The modern "commercial society" may not be anything as just, unified, or ecumenical as the advocates of *doux commerce* from Montesquieu to Schumpeter had hoped, but it is certainly – at least among the trading nations themselves – a great deal more peaceful.

### Endnotes

1 *Imperialism and Social Classes [Zur Soziologie der Imperialismen]*, 6, 8, 99.
2 Ibid., 64–6.
3 Ibid., 75.
4 « Réflexions sur la monarchie universelle en Europe » in *Œuvres complètes*, Roger Caillois ed. (Paris : Bibliothèque de la Pléiade, 1951), II, 19.
5 *De l'esprit des lois* X, 9 and 14.
6 "Smith's Thoughts on the State of the Contest with America, February 1778", *The Correspondence of Adam Smith*, 382–3. On Montesquieu and Spain, see p. 153.
7 *L'Ami L'amides hommes, ou traité de la population*, III, 233–4.
8 On the contributions of Diderot, and others to the *History*, see Anoush Fraser Terjanian, *Commerce and Its Discontents in Eighteenth-Century French Political Thought* (Cambridge: Cambridge University Press, 2013), 16–22.
9 *Histoire des Deux Indes* in *Œuvres*, III, 689.
10 Quoted in Terjanian, *Commerce and Its Discontents in Eighteenth-Century French Political Thought*, 26.
11 *L'Ami des hommes, ou traité de la population*, III, 5.
12 *De l'esprit des lois*, XXI, 5.
13 The phrase "doux commerce", although frequently attributed to Montesquieu, is in fact Montaigne's and was later taken up by Albert Hirschman in his classic *The Passions and Interests: Political Arguments for Capitalism before Its Triumph* (Princeton: Princeton University Press, 1977), 61. Montesquieu himself did not claim that commerce was "sweet" but that it created customs or habits – *moeurs* – that were. On this, see Terjanian, *Commerce and Its Discontents in Eighteenth-Century French Political Thought*, 12–14.

14 *The Second Treatise of Government*, 311–12 (V, 36–7) and 319 (V, 47).

15 The story of Aristippus is told in the preface to the sixth book of the Roman architect Vitruvius' *De architectura*.

16 *De l'esprit des lois*, XVIII, 15.

17 "Treatise Concerning the Way of Preserving Peace" in *John Locke as Translator Three of the Essais of Pierre Nicole in French and English*, Jean S. Yolton ed. (Oxford: Voltaire Foundation, 2000), 117.

18 *De l'esprit des lois*, XX, 2.

19 "Réflexions sur la monarchie universelle en Europe," 34.

20 "A Grammar of the Persian Language" in *The Collected Works of Sir William Jones* [1807], facsimile edition, 13 vols. (New York: New York University Press, 1993), V, 165.

21 "Towards Perpetual Peace: A Philosophical Project", *Practical Philosophy*, 336–7 (AK 8:368).

22 See e.g., John E. Mueller, *Capitalism, Democracy, and Ralph's Pretty Good Grocery* (Princeton: Princeton University Press, 1999); G. Schneider and N. P. Gleditsch, "The Capitalist Peace: The Origins and Prospects of a Liberal Idea", *International Interactions* 36 (2010), 107–14; Bruce Russett and John R. Oneal, *Triangulating Peace: Democracy, Interdependence and International Organizations* (New York: Norton, 2001); and more generally Steven Pinker, *The Better Angels of Our Nature: Why Violence Has Declined* (New York: Viking, 2011).

23 *An Inquiry into the Nature and Causes of the Wealth of Nations*, 626 (IV. vii).

24 *On the Fortune of Alexander*, 329.

25 *De l'esprit des lois*, IV, 8. Pierre Briant, *Alexandre des lumières. Fragments d'histoire européenne* (Paris: Gallimard, 2012), 350.

26 *On the Fortune of Alexander*, 329. See p. 6.

27 *De l'esprit des lois*, X, 14.

28 "Of the Jealousy of Trade", *Essays, Moral, Political, and Literary*, 328.

29 *Histoire des navigations aux Terres australes* (Paris, 1756), I, 17–19.

30 For Britain's self-image as a maritime and thus essentially commercial empire, see Armitage, *Foundations of Modern International Thought*, 46–56.

31 "Remarques sur l'opinion de l'auteur de l' Espirt des lois concernant les colonies", in *François Quesnay et la physiocratie*, II, 785.

32 *De l'esprit de lois*, V, 19

33 "Of the Jealousy of Trade", 328, and see Istvan Hont, *Jealousy of Trade: International Competition and the Nation-State in Historical Perspective* (Cambridge, MA: Harvard University Press, 2005), 1–156.

34 *The Federalist Papers*, Isaac Kramnick ed. (New York and London: Penguin Books, 1987), Number VI, 106.

35 *Histoire des navigations aux Terres australes* I, 79.

36 « Rapport et projet de décret sur l'organisation générale de l'instruction publique » in *Œuvres complètes de Condorcet* (Paris, 1847–9), VII, 450.

37 *Esquisse d'un tableau historique des progrès de l'esprit humain* [1794], Alain Pons ed. (Paris: Flammarion, 1988), 269

38 "The Best Practicable System of Judicature for India", *The Collected Works of Sir William Jones*, I, cxxxiii.

39 Quoted in Bianca Fontana, "The Napoleonic Empire and the Europe of Nations" in *The Idea of Europe from Antiquity to the European Union*, Anthony Pagden ed. (Cambridge: Cambridge University Press, 2002), 123.

40 Quoted in David Lawday, *Napoleon's Master: A Life of Prince Talleyrand* (London: Jonathan Cape, 2006), 3

41 See J. G. A. Pocock, "The Political Economy of Burke's Analysis of the French Revolution" in *Virtue, Commerce and History* (Cambridge: Cambridge University Press, 1985), 193–212.

42 On Constant's admiration for, and indebtedness to, Montesquieu, see Biancamaria Fontana, *Benjamin Constant and the Post-Revolutionary Mind* (New Haven and London: Yale University Press, 1991), 26–7.

43 On Constant's somewhat ambivalent views on empire, see Jennifer Pitts, *A Turn to Empire: The Rise of Imperial Liberalism in Britain and France* (Princeton: Princeton University Press, 2005), 173–85, and "Constant's Thoughts on Slavery and Empire" in Helena Rosenblatt ed., *The Cambridge Companion to Constant* (Cambridge: Cambridge University Press, 2009), 115–45.

44 "The Spirit of Conquest and Usurpation and Their Relation to European Civilization", *Constant: Political Writings*, 51.

45 "The Liberty of the Ancients Compared with that of the Moderns", *Constant: Political Writings*, 312.

46 *The Spirit of Conquest and Usurpation and Their Relation to European Civilization*, 53–4.

47 Ibid., 55.

48 On Constant's often ambiguous and shifting views on commerce, see Stephen Holmes, *Benjamin Constant and the Making of Modern Liberalism* (New Haven and London: Yale University Press, 1984), 212–1. As Helena Rosenblatt and others have pointed out, in the later years of his life, as he became more concerned with the civilizing potential of religion, Constant became less confident in the virtues of utilitarianism. See Helena Rosenblatt, "Commerce et religion dans le libéralisme de Benjamin Constant, *Commentaire* 26 (3003), 415–26.

49 "Des réactions politiques" in L. Omacini and J.-D. Candaux eds., *Écrits de jeunesse (1774–1799)* (Tübingen: Max Niemeyer Verlag, 1998), 493, and see Robert J. Benton, "Political Expediency and Lying, Kant vs. Benjamin Constant", *Journal of the History of Ideas* 43 (1982), 135–44.

50 *The Spirit of Conquest and Usurpation and Their Relation to European Civilization*, 65.

51 Ibid. 53–4.

52 Ibid., 131–2.

53 Quoted in Clement de la Jonquière, *L'Expedition d'Égypte* (Paris, 1899–1907), I, 462.

54 *The Spirit of Conquest and Usurpation and their Relation to European Civilization*, 55.

55 Ibid., 77.

56 Ibid., 73.

57 Ibid., 72.

58 Ibid., 55.

59 Ibid., 64.

60 Ibid., 79. On the central role of public opinion in Constant's thought, see Fontana, *Benjamin Constant and the Post-Revolutionary Mind*, 81–97.

61 Joseph Schumpeter, *Imperialism and Social Classes*, Heinz Norden trans. (New York: Meridian Books, 1955), 7, 8.

62 *The Spirit of Conquest and Usurpation and Their Relation to European Civilization*, 63–4, and see Pitts, *A Turn to Empire*, 178.

63 On the conflicting arguments in Constant's "On the Spirit of Conquest and Usurpation", see Stephen Holmes, "The Liberal Uses of Bourbon Legitimism", *Journal of the History of Ideas* 43 (1982), 229–48.

64 The story is told by the first-century Roman miscellanist Aulus Gellius, *Noctes Atticae*, iv, 8.

65 See Pitts, *A Turn to Empire*, 184.

66 "Travail sur l'Algérie", *Tocqueville sur l'Algérie*, 96–7.

67 Quoted in Peter Clarke, *The Last Thousand Days of the British Empire: The Demise of a Superpower, 1944–47* (London and New York: Penguin Books, 2008).

68 Quoted in Bromwich, *On Empire, Liberty and Reform*, 15–16.

69 J. G. A. Pocock, *Barbarism and Religion* (Cambridge: Cambridge University Press, 1999), IV, 220.

70 Dariusz Kolodziejczyk, "Khan, Caliph, Tsar and Imperator: The Multiple Identities of the Ottoman Sultan" in Peter Fibiger Bang with Dariusz Kolodziejczyk eds., *Universal Empire: A Comparative Approach to Imperial Culture and Representation in Eurasian History* (Cambridge: Cambridge University Press, 2012), 189.

# 9

## Human Rights, Natural Rights, and Europe's Imperial Legacy

*You have theories enough concerning the rights of men; it may not be amiss to add a small degree of attention to their nature and disposition. It is with men in the concrete; it is with the common human life, and human actions, that you are to be concerned.*

Edmund Burke to Charles-Jean François Depont[1]

I

In 1947, the Saudi Arabian delegation to the committee responsible for drafting the Universal Declaration of Human Rights protested that the committee had "for the most part taken into consideration only the standards recognized by Western civilization" and that it was not the task of the delegation "to proclaim the superiority of one civilization over all others or to establish uniform standards for all the countries of the world".[2] (One might wonder what interpretation they had originally given to the word "universal".) Unsurprisingly their main objections were to Article 16, which guarantees women the freedom to choose their marriage partners, and to Article 18, which guarantees freedom of religion; but their opposition reflected a wider Islamic unease with the very conception of a "human" right.

In 1990, this rejection of what was viewed as an excessively Eurocentric conception of both the "human" and of "rights" led to the Cairo Declaration of Human Rights in Islam. This was subsequently joined by appeals on the part of Asian autocrats, and in particular Singapore's Lee Kuan Yew, for the recognition of the existence of a specific set of "Asian Values", which supposedly place the good of the community over those of individuals and thus dispenses with the need for any kind of rights whatsoever.[3] "Human rights" have also been denounced from within the Western academic establishment as overly dependent on a narrow, largely French, British, and American rights tradition.[4] Until very recently, and still in some

Utramontane quarters, the Catholic Church – if not individual Catholics – has also been a source of fierce opposition to what it saw as the triumph of lay individualism over the values of the Christian community.[5]

What all of these criticisms have in common is their clear recognition of – and objection to – the fact that rights, and human rights in particular, are cultural artefacts represented as universal, immutable values. As the Argentinian philosopher and jurist Eduardo Rabossi (followed by the American philosopher Richard Rorty) has argued, the post-Holocaust world has created what Rabossi called "a human rights culture" which is inescapably a product of a particular Western, and predominantly Roman, legal culture.[6] Outside this culture, and beyond the Western legal tradition, there simply is no autonomous conception of human rights – indeed no easily identifiable conception of rights of any kind. All those, like the ones in the Cairo Declaration, which claim to be, end up being reassertions of already extant legal prescriptions.[7] The concept of "right" (*al-haqq*) used in the Cairo Declaration is also interpreted – as one might expect, these are after all rights in Islam – in ways which are explicitly religious. Rights are characterized as gifts of God not inherent in the nature of the human person.[8] This may be obvious. But whereas those critics take this to be the self-evident refutation of the possibility of any kind of universal or natural human entitlement, the champions of rights, in particular of human rights, tend to pass over the specific origins of the concept in silence. Yet without some account of how the West came to conceive of the idea that human beings could be said to possess rights qua humans (and not solely as members of a particular group), it is hard to understand why human rights should now have become the single most important moral consideration in contemporary international relations.

The term "human right" is a very recent one. It does not seem to have appeared before the 1940s although "Rights of Man" had, of course, been in existence since 1789. (These, however, as we shall see, were not only not the same thing as "human rights"; in certain respects they were directly antithetical to them.) Recently the American historian Samuel Moyn has claimed that the concern with human rights, and the central role they now occupy in international relations, in fact dates from as recently as the 1970s. Before the U.S. president Jimmy Carter took up the issue in a relatively short-lived attempt to inject a degree of morality into U.S. foreign policy, human rights were widely looked on as a misguided distraction, a concern with inflated and impossible goals. Moyn has argued that most of struggles whose objectives have subsequently been expressed in terms of human rights, and in particular the struggles in the aftermath of the Second World War for independence on the part of the remaining colonized peoples of the world, had very little if anything to do with them. They were struggles for "self-determination", and the sole right which the liberators claimed on behalf of their peoples was the right to exercise sovereignty within their own newly created nation states.

Despite the fact that the statement, "All people shall have the right of self-determination", was finally, and after much deliberation, included in the 1948 Declaration, this was conceived not as a human, but as a state right.

Even if we accept Moyn's account, all that it tells us is when and where and for what contingent reasons the conception of human rights became an important element in international debates over political entitlements.[9] It does not tell us very much about the supposed content of those rights or – given that they were clearly not invented ex nihilo – their origin.[10] In general, human rights have been taken to be a simple extension of the earlier, essentially Thomist conception of "natural rights". On this account it could be argued that the term "natural", which carried with it an extensive baggage of neo-Thomist assumptions about innate ideas, had been jettisoned, and human, which had none, had come to take its place. The claim, however, that human beings could make certain claims on other humans because, and only because, of their identity as humans remained.

For whatever else human rights may be, they are self-evidently, and tautologically, dependent on an understanding of the human and the idea of rights; and both of these formed a central part of what has been called Aquinas' "ontologically divinised natural law".[11] If humans were the beneficiaries of certain kinds of rights denied to other living beings, this was, insisted the French Thomist philosopher Jacques Maritain in 1942, perhaps the most influential of the Catholic advocates of human rights during the Second World War, because "there are things owed to humans because they are human", because we are all "engaged in the universal order in the laws and regulations of the cosmos and in the immense family of created beings".[12] None of which, of course, is to deny the fact that the concept of human rights is the inescapable outcome of a Western conception of entitlements.

It was also the case, as the international lawyer Hersch Lauterpacht pointed out in 1942, that ever since antiquity there had existed a powerful claim that there must exist not merely a law which was above the law of the state but also one by which the ruler of the state acquired his (or her or its) own authority. For if, as is the assumption in all modern states, the right to rule derived untimely from the consent of the people (rather than from the intention of a divinity), then it followed that what he called "the natural rights of man" must be its inescapable expression. "The very notion of the social contract", he wrote, "implies, it will be noted, the existence of rights which the individual possess before organized society."[13] Otherwise there could have been no contract (nor Hobbesian covenant) in the first place, and, *pace* Hobbes, the individual does not, indeed cannot, surrender those rights on entering society. This, as we have seen, had been precisely the claim which Francisco de Vitoria had made about his "the right of natural partnership and communication".[14] Neither is the fact that individuals are rarely in a position to exercise their rights independently of the states to which they belong, grounds for denying their existence. "The position of the individual as a subject of international law", wrote Lauterpacht, "has often been obscured by the failure to observe the distinction between the recognition, in an international instrument, of rights enuring to the benefit of the individual and enforceability of these rights at his instance."[15]

Furthermore the distinction between the rights of states and the supra-state rights held by individuals cannot erase the fact that once we remove the idea that rights derive either directly from a God or – as the Christians had maintained – from a God-ordained natural order, then the only place in which any rights, whether collective or individual, can originate is the human person. All such rights must, in the end, become subjective. Human rights, therefore, clearly belong to individuals beyond and outside the authority of the state. In his famous article on natural rights, the English jurist, H.A.L. Hart argued that:

> there may be codes of conduct termed moral codes ... which do not employ the notion of *a* right, and there is nothing contradictory or otherwise absurd in a code or morality consisting wholly of prescriptions or in a code which prescribed only what should be done for the realization of happiness or some ideal of personal perfection.

As Hart pointed out, neither Plato nor Aristotle, nor indeed any other Greek author, uses a term which could be rendered as right, as distinct from "justice", and most Greek law and jurisprudence belong to the category of prescriptive codes about how to achieve the highest good. When Hart wrote his article in 1955 he added that such codes would be properly described as "imperfect".[16] Many modern commentators, in the wake of decades of discussions of cultural and moral pluralism, might shy away from even that. Yet the attempt to avoid the evident, culturally specific nature of the entire enterprise of defining rights has all too often resulted in surrender to the notion that the creation of one specific culture – particularly as that is also a powerful one with a long history of military aggression – must necessarily be invalid for all other cultures. Something which, if taken seriously, would deprive us of any means of establishing agreed modes of conduct between differing peoples. It is undeniable that, at present, the "international community" derives its values from a version of a liberal consensus which is, in essence, a secularized version of a Christian ethic, at least as it applies to the concept of rights.[17] But this does not necessarily invalidate its claim to be in the long-term interests of the majority of humankind. It might well be reasonable on some Kantian calculus to assume that all individuals in any possible community, even if they do not now possess, or recognize, such a conception as a human right, could nevertheless be brought to understand the meaning of the term. The history of human rights may serve to remind us that if we wish to assert any belief in the universal, we have to begin by declaring our willingness to assume, and to defend, at least some of the values of a highly specific way of life. The reluctance to accept that seriously weakens any argument against those for whom the values proclaimed by the modern liberal tradition are simply meaningless. (Or, indeed, against those, such as the young Karl Marx, who denounced "the rights of man" as the expression of the interests of a particular class, the "egotistical" bourgeoisie.[18])

The history of rights, of *iura*, and in particular of those rights which were to become human rights, is doubly embarrassing for their culturally sensitive defendants in that such rights were not only a creation of the Roman legal tradition; they were developed in the form we understand them today, in the context of *imperial*, legislative practices, and have remained closely associated with imperial expansion and its consequences until at least the late nineteenth century.[19] Some plausible account of the evolving relationship between rights and the development of the European empires might, perhaps, provide a better position from which to evaluate why we continue to believe that "our" values are necessarily conterminous with those of the human race as a whole, and whether we are justified in so doing.

II

The English word "right" is, of course, Germanic in origin, but it corresponds to the Latin term *ius*, which in Roman law was essentially a distribution of goods to each according to his right, *suum ciuque tribuere*.[20] It was also objective. That is, it was believed to be something discoverable. Disputants took oaths on the righteousness of their claims, one of which was upheld in a subsequent ordeal or by some other supernatural judgement. The verdict was a *ius*. This is why the term was, as Thomas Hobbes protested, "promiscuously used" throughout the middle ages and indeed well into the modern period as a synonym for law, *lex*.[21] Early Roman law lacked any notion of a right as we understand the word, fully separable from an enacted law. *Ius* covered both right and duty in that it defined something which was held to be binding. Neither did Roman law initially suppose the existence of a natural – that is, universal – category. Individuals could claim *iura* under the law. But no one had them by virtue of being human. The rulings of the *Corpus Iuris Civilis* were always those in civil law only and thus made no claims about a natural or universal order.

Later complications of the definition of *ius*, which initially arose out of the mid-thirteenth-century debates by the Franciscans over their right to hold property, and the equivalence between *dominium* and *ius*, introduced a distinction – which was to become crucial – between subjective and objective rights.[22] The latter are rights which exist only in objects themselves; that is, they form part the human positive law. Subjective rights – the category to which both natural and human rights belong – pertain to persons as subjects and as members, by definition, of the human community. This understanding of a right is summed up in the French jurist Michel Villey's celebrated, and all-embracing, account of a right as "a *quality* of the subject, one of his or her *faculties*, more precisely a license *(franchise)* a freedom, a possibility of acting *(une possibilité d'agir)*".²³ As such rights clearly were, and had been since at least the twelfth century, conceived of as a form of property *(dominium)*, as William of Ockham had argued, they therefore conferred on their possessor a power *(potestas)* – Villey's *possibilité d'agir*.²⁴ It is obvious that, on any such definition, a creature who could be said not to be in possession of his or her natural rights would have to be so seriously defective as not to be in any meaningful sense a sentient being. Many early-modern jurists were prepared to accept that even children who were generally deemed to possess, in Aristotle's formulation, an "immature" deliberative faculty could, nevertheless, have rights independently of their guardians. So, too, could the incurably insane, since, in Francisco de Vitoria's words, "a madman, too, can be the victim of an injustice *(iuria)*; therefore, he can have legal rights". Only the *insensati*, the truly nonhuman, were excluded.²⁵

Today, of course, the definition of human rights has been extended far beyond the limits which the Roman jurists and their heirs intended for natural rights. In part this has to do with the altered conception of the demands which individuals, in the name of their humanity, can legitimately make on the states to which they belong. The shift, however, from natural to human reflects a modern unease with the conception of an nature and, in particular since the death of the natural-law tradition in Kant, with the idea of the existence of guiding natural principles. The uncoupling of the human and nature has allowed us to speak of the right of a person not merely to property (an idea first introduced in France after the Revolution in 1789, by the *Déclaration des Droits de l'Homme*) but also to, say, "a standard of living adequate for the health and well-being of himself and of his family" or "the right to security in the event of unemployment, sickness, disability, widowhood, old age or other lack of livelihood in circumstances beyond his control" as demanded by Article 25 of the 1948 Declaration, both of which could plausibly be included under the heading of Villey's *possibilité d'agir*, but which, for the earlier jurists, would have implied that an uneducated or hungry person, or one without moveable goods, somehow ceased to be a person at all.²⁶

Furthermore, the modern concept of human rights is closely linked to a set of purely political claims made generally on behalf of underrepresented groups. This is how the *Déclaration des Droits de l'Homme* and the 1948 Declaration conceived them, and this generally is how they have been conceived in all subsequent human rights conventions and treaties. The concept of a natural right, however, although it was frequently deployed in explicitly political debates, was rarely, if ever, seen as a means of pressing a claim about the kind of life an individual might be expected to live, once their very limited claims under nature – their claim to a bare *possibilité d'agir* – had been realized. For all that, however, as with all such existential legal claims, this one also owes a great deal to its historical ancestry – and that ancestry is closely associated with the history of the European imperial system.[27]

Natural rights applied, of course, to all areas of human life. But they obviously only made any sense in terms of ways of understanding the natural law. In general, discussions over what these were, and what they implied, arose most acutely in relationship to war, as indeed have most modern formulations of human rights, since it is obvious that war is the most extreme condition under which, as the Roman jurists would have expressed it, a person might suffer injustice. It is also, of course, the condition which violates most flagrantly the frontiers between different peoples and thus between differing civil codes. A just war might only be waged defensively, which means in effect in defence of one's natural rights. Some of these, although hardly incontrovertible, were obvious enough and were generally limited to the survival and the necessities of existence: the right to life, liberty, freedom of movement, and so on. There were, however, other categories (all of which we have already encountered) which supposed that war may be made against both individuals and societies not on the basis of their behaviour toward potential belligerents but merely on the basis of the customs they practice among themselves. The activities, of such peoples, that is, constituted what Francisco Suárez characterized as an offence against, and thus a threat to, the "human republic" (*respublica humana*) which possessed, of itself, and independent of any particular sovereign authority, "the natural power and jurisdiction" to defend itself.[28]

Because, however, the law of nature had no obvious limits, any deviation from the more central normative rules by which civilized beings lived their lives could be construed not simply as different but as unnatural. Simply, the arguments came down to the claim that those who do not have cultures which perform as we assume cultures should perform can be dispossessed by those who do. And this, of course, implied that natural rights could only adequately be defined in terms of a concept of civilization. On this point, in their very different ways, the dominant and divergent conceptions of the natural law – the Thomist which held that it was, in Aquinas' formulation, the participation by rational beings in the divine law and relied on "innate ideas" – and the so-called modern theory associated with Hobbes and Grotius, which held that the "right" of nature could be reduced to an inalienable right of self-protection, would seem to converge.[29] For despite the latter's insistence that any peoples could be said to be observing the natural law if they lived in societies which provided the minimum necessary protection, it remained the case that very few societies could, in fact, provide this without also creating the kind of political order which, for the Thomists, had supplied the content of the law of nature. This is why Grotius claimed that all the peoples of the world had, in effect, to be guided by what he described as the customs of "the most civilised peoples of the world".[30] What definitions were given to "the most civilised peoples" depended, of course, on the working assumptions of whoever was making the definition. But it would seem obvious, to Grotius at least, that hunter-gatherers, or semi-nomadic peoples – peoples, that is, who did not live in what most Europeans, no matter what their religious attachments, would have accepted as a civil or political way of life – were necessarily excluded at least from any more rigorous definition of the term. Despite the attempt by both the Thomists and the modern natural-law theorists to detach the basic elements of the natural law, and thus natural right, from purely local political and social arrangements – from, that is, politics – politics always crept back in. Only the claim that there existed an omnipotent deity who had decreed that his creation possessed certain transcultural and immutable rights could ensure that those rights remained unaltered by the histories of the creature who possessed them. Neither the Thomist nor the modern natural-law theorists were prepared to take such an extremely voluntarist stance. As we shall see, precisely the same predicament faces modern human rights theorists.[31]

### III

The image of the world – the *orbis terrarum* – that gradually evolved between the sixteenth and eighteenth centuries was, broadly speaking, of a world civilization composed of differing societies, all of which, however, subscribed to certain natural rules and dispositions and pursued certain natural objectives, the terms by which natural rights would be understood. With Kant, however, the natural law tradition, and with it the notion of a natural right, comes to an end. By the first decade of the nineteenth century natural rights had indeed come to be seen as, in Jeremy Bentham's famous dismissal of them, "nonsense upon stilts" (although it is significant that Bentham's attack was directed against the shrinking *ius* naturalism of the *Déclaration des droits de l'homme et du citoyen* of 1789, rather than the early-modern natural-law traditions). The Kantian vision of a cosmopolitan world also sank beneath the rising tide of the new nationalism, much of which was driven onward by precisely the kind of imperial ambitions Kant himself hoped would finally be extinguished by the ever-increasing human inclination toward a cosmopolitan world order. The time seemed to have come to jettison the abstractions on which natural rights had been grounded, and as Edmund Burke demanded of his young French correspondent, to take a closer look not at humans as natural agents but at "men in the concrete" and at their share in a common human life.[32] In the background to both Kant and Burke, however, lies, of course, the French Revolution, and it is precisely the Revolution where the modern conception of human rights – "Rights of Man" – is generally held to begin.

The concept of natural rights implied what might be described as a negative association with the civil or human law, in that no law could be promulgated which was manifestly contrary to the natural law, and no person would be bound in conscience to observe such a law. No natural right, however, established any association with any political act or specific political order, although, of course, certain political acts – war being the most obvious – might follow from the violation of a right in nature.[33] The *Déclaration des droits de l'homme et du citoyen* of 1789 marks a departure from this way of thinking. As Norberto Bobbio has pointed out, the first three articles of the *Déclaration* repeat Rousseau's account of the creation of the social contract: the first refers to the condition of man in the state of nature, the second to the objectives of civil and political society, and the third to "the principle of legitimacy of power which resides in the nation".[34] Unlike the version provided in Rousseau's *Contrat social*, however, this is not intended to be a historical narrative because all the rights that each of these conditions might supposedly confer exist simultaneously. The Rights of Man are therefore still natural ones, in that they are "natural, inalienable and sacred to man" and that mankind is said to be "born and live free and equal in rights"; moreover, they must be supposed to continue to be so even after the formation of society.[35] These claims are, as Marx had seen, largely an initial denial that human identity is a necessarily and inescapably political one. Yet they are being made not merely on behalf of the whole of humanity but also in the name of a sovereign people, "constituted in a national assembly". Furthermore the basic rights which are said to be sacred and inviolable, although they follow closely the Hobbesian, Grotian conception of the natural law, are quite specifically civil and political ones[36]. They derive from the status of their holders as citizens, and all are held, and can only have any meaning, within the context not merely of civil society but also of a society constituted as a nation. As Lauterpacht pointed out, this "marked the radical innovation of the acknowledgment of the inherent right of man in the constitutional law of modern states". They are, that is (although this is was not how Lauterpacht saw them) the reversal of not only the Thomist but also the Grotian understanding of the *ius naturae* as that law which must necessarily have remained unaltered by the division of humankind into nations.[37] The inclusion of the right to property, which remains central to all subsequent Revolutionary legislation, and continues to be central to all modern human-rights thinking, effectively dissolves the entire early-modern distinction between the natural and the civil, since it was, of course, the distribution of Adam's inheritance among the several peoples of the world that had supposedly been the occasion of the social contract in the first place. The Revolution, as Tocqueville claimed, may have treated "humankind" independently of the social, legal, and normative worlds by which all people were necessarily constituted, and it might to him have seemed "driven more by the desire to regenerate human kind than to reform France". But the *Déclaration* had, nevertheless, built a very secure bridge between that kind of abstract reasoning which Tocqueville characterized as "religious" and the concrete, national, political ambitions which were to dominate the discussion of rights throughout the nineteenth century.[38]

The elision between the earlier conception of what was natural with a modern understanding of both the civil and the political becomes more emphatic in a number of drafts for various declarations of the "Rights of Man" which followed the creation of the Republic. In 1793, for instance, Condorcet drew up a project for what he called significantly a "Declaration of the Natural Civil and Political Rights of Men" (*Déclaration des droits naturels, civils et politiques des hommes*).[39] A year later, Jean-François Varlet, leader of the *enragé* party, drafted his "Declaration of the Rights of Men in the Social State" (*Déclaration des droits de l'homme en l'état sociale*) which, despite limiting such rights to humans in quite precise social conditions, nevertheless defined them as "drawn from nature which is always one and invariable" and "as ancient as the world ... holy, inalienable, imprescriptible".[40] Later the language changed further yet so that the Rights of Man, although still routinely described as originating in the nature of humankind, became specifically limited to those rights which the individual held as a citizen.[41] Phrases which qualified the natural origins of such rights – "right of peoples", "rights of man in society" – also become commonplace and are repeated in the declarations drafted for the Sister Republics of Liguria, Batavia (Holland), Rome, and Naples.[42] By 1848, although the Constitution of the Second [French] Republic speaks of "rights and duties anterior and superior to the positive laws", it does not describe these as natural; nor even does it describe them as rights of man but only as the "rights of citizens".[43]

With the intellectual discrediting of the very idea of natural and thus universal law, the belief in any possible natural right would seem to have fallen away completely. The rights of man were no longer those rights which could be held against society, or across differing societies. They were those which could only be held *in* society and, furthermore, only in a society of a particular kind: republican, democratic, and representative.

The rights of man – the *natural* rights of the 1789 declaration – had, to some degree, offered the possibility of freedom from colonial rule and was interpreted as such by both the French *colons* and subsequently by the Black population of Saint Dominque. By 1848, however, they had been transformed into a specific set of political entitlements, rights which could only be held by citizens of a particular state. As a consequence, they became increasingly useless as a notion in international or intercultural relations, in the absence of truly trans- or international agencies. For the liberals of the generation of John Stuart Mill and Tocqueville, one could only speak of rights within what had come to be called a civilization, by which was meant roughly the value system of the European peoples.[44] The distinction between nature and society, between the rights a person might hold as an individual, and those he or she might hold as member of a given community – which both the Thomists and the modern theorists of the natural law had fought to keep separate, albeit with limited degrees of success – had now collapsed altogether. Those who believed themselves to be civilized had a *duty* not to behave toward "backward" or barbarian peoples in a cruel and "inhuman" manner. But, there was no law in nature, no body of rights, to which the barbarian could appeal against any would-be aggressor. "To characterize any conduct whatever towards a barbarous people", wrote Mill, as a violation of the law of nations only shows that he who so speaks has never considered the subject. ... Barbarians do not have rights as a *nation.*" The relationship between civilized nations and barbarian peoples was a matter only for "the universal rules of morality between man and man", and this, although it should clearly act as powerful restraint on behaviour, could have no *legal* force whatsoever.[45]

IV

By the end of the Second World War, however, this view came increasingly into question. The idea of state sovereignty and state rights remained as powerful as ever, indeed it was as Moyn has argued, reenforced by the final success of the allies. But the atrocities which had been committed in its name had undermined any sustained belief in the existence of an all-embracing civilization. Furthermore, it was also evident that the former European empires, which since the late sixteenth century had provided the context in which all international relations and all discussion of international law and right had been conducted, were in the process of rapid disintegration. What was needed was a new consensus. The Universal Declaration of Human Rights of 1948 was clearly intended to provide this. In doing so, however, it had to shed the specifically political component on which the rights of man had come to be based. In its place came an appeal to an individual agency which could be sustained even against – in most cases, especially against – the political community to which the individual belonged. In this respect it constituted a turn away from the tradition which had begun with the *Déclaration des droits de l'homme* and, as Michael Ignatieff has pointed out, marked a "return by the European tradition to its natural law heritage".[46]

With the final defeat of Communism – the last major community in the West to offer a sustained ideological objection to the notion – human rights have become, in Pierre Manet's words, "the moral and political referent of the West".[47] In becoming so, they have always, perhaps inevitably, also become the platform for a new, shrunken conception of a civilization. For modern human rights theorists face much the same problem as did the early-modern theorists of natural rights. And they have, in a sense, found themselves repeating the same history from nature to culture followed by their early-modern predecessors. For unless, as some modern theologians have insisted, we accept the idea of a transcendent deity who has simply given us our rights as our property in the same way that He or She has provided us with hands and the capacity for speech, the very notion of a trans-local, transcultural human right only makes sense within the context of a conception of "humanity". Since humanity is, empirically, and for whatever historical reason, social, then this can, in effect, only make sense in the context of a given understanding of what a society should be.[48] For all early natural-rights theorists the realms in which it was possible to be human while not also being social had been historical, and purely conjectural. For all such theorists, furthermore, natural rights remained those which had survived the creation of civil society and could be used to trump the authority of the state when that seemed to be violating them. Even they, however, found themselves driven to relocate their understanding of the natural law within the broad context of a given conception of "civilization", a term which Mill defined as "the best characteristics of Man and Society; further advanced in the road to perfection, happier, nobler, wiser".[49] It therefore belonged within a specific, "Eurocentric" historical narrative, one, furthermore, which assumed human perfectibility and cultural and technological progress to be both interdependent and independent of any divine agency. Liberty, as Mill said, "has no application to any state of things anterior to the time when mankind have become capable of being improved by free and equal discussion".[50] In this condition, before any common agreement among peoples of varying cultural religious and social origins is at all possible, there can be no universal claims of any kind.

Modern theorists of human rights face much the same dilemma. What they lack is Mill's confidence in the universal progress of humankind toward commonly acceptable standards of behaviour. All accept to some degree the notion that human rights are the rights of human beings in society. None of the human rights languages in use today – indeed no talk of agency and of human personality – would make any sense in some modernized vision of the state of nature, even if we could make such a thing at all persuasive. It is society which is called on to observe basic human rights, and it is thus by implication only society which has the power to confer them. The difference is that now the sovereign nation state has been replaced by a broader political sphere generally called the "International Community". But even this has most of the same properties which the *Déclaration des droits de l'homme* conferred on the French people. Even John Rawls' "decent hierarchical peoples" – who clearly would not subscribe to many articles of the original *Déclaration* – observe at least some human rights. It is a necessary condition of their decency.[51] In doing so, we must suppose, that they, too, belong to the International Community. Those who do not, belong instead to "Outlaw" or "Rogue" states. Or, as John Stuart Mill would have said, they are "Barbarians".

To arrive, however, at some understanding of what the features of this new civilization might be, human rights advocates from 1848 until today have worked backwards. Whereas both the Thomists and their Hobbesian and Grotian opponents had begun with a notion of humanity from which they had deduced what their natural rights might be, the human rights charters begin with the notion of rights to arrive at the notion of what a person might be. "Might not this new phase in international rights", Norberto Bobbio has asked, "be called, in Kant's name, 'cosmopolitan right'?"[52] The answer would have to be a highly qualified yes. Certainly the principles which underpin the Universal Declaration of Human Rights, as the Saudis had rightly seen, are based squarely on Western notions of human agency. This conception, like Kant's understanding of the right to hospitality, depends on the perception of persons as communicating beings – beings, that is, who are able to conduct their relations with one another through reasoned argument. For this reason, the U.S. State Department's classification in its annual report of 1999 of human rights together with "money and the Internet" as the three universal languages of humankind is not such a crude advocacy of the virtues of late capitalism as it might at first seem.[53]

Human rights are also cosmopolitan in the Kantian sense, in that like the *ius cosmopoliticum*, their implementation, explicitly in Kant's case, implicitly in the case of most modern human rights claims, can only be properly realized in a specific political order. In Kant's case this was what he famously called a "representative republic". In the case of most human rights claims, it is democracy. For however much those like John Rawls might wish to insist that there can exist regimes which are "decent" enough to recognize human rights while at the same time refusing some mode of representative democracy, it remains the case that not only do no such regimes actually exist at present; today human rights talk and democracy are considered by most of the drafters of the new rights conventions to be inseparable.[54] Amy Gutman may be right in insisting that "human rights should not be conceived as guarantors of social justice, or for comprehensive conceptions of a good life", but it is hard to see how they could be formulated, or be given any real imaginative force, in the absence of *any* such conception, however minimally expressed.[55] Like Kant's concept of representation, it is hard to conceive a system of values, political or moral – a "civilization", in other words – which would at once both grant the need for most of the rights included in the Universal Declaration and at the same time deny political autonomy to its citizens. As Kant had seen, no world order of the kind which the *ius cosmopoliticum* or human rights represents could come into being on the basis of a legal system alone. Kant's objection to the international law arguments of his day was precisely that of many of those who are dubious about the possible efficacy of such legislation as the Universal Declaration: that they are, in the absence of any means of enforcement, mere words, covenants, to echo Hobbes, without swords.[56] Any attempt to impose a concept of human rights on a nondemocratic culture – that is to say, one which did not accept the basic principle of autonomy – could only ever fail in the long run. "Today", Norberto Bobbio has written, "the concept of democracy itself has become inseparable from that of the rights of man."[57]

The degree to which this is so can be measured from a document entitled *Our Global Neighbourhood*, published by the United Nations *Report of the Commission on Global Governance* in 1995. It was drafted by an international team and opens with a laudatory preface by Nelson Mandela. It is, therefore, not self-evidently the product of "Western exceptionalism". There now exists, it claims, a "global civic ethic" based on "a set of core values that can unite people of all cultural, political, religious, or philosophical backgrounds". Its authors set out to explain that although international law – the "law of nations" – had historically been "made in Europe by European jurists to serve European ends" and had been "based on Christian values and designed to advance Western expansion", it had, nevertheless, come up with the right answers because, despite its origins, it had been responsible for the creation of a universal conception of the person. And no other understanding of the law, backed as most of them were, by invoking the unsubstantiated desires of improbable deities, had achieved that. Therefore, they insisted, "no longer is it credible for a state to turn its back on international law, alleging a bias towards European values and influence". All that humankind now requires to bring about the elusive, but eternal, dream of "perpetual peace", is a "global citizenship" based on "a strong commitment to principles of equity and democracy grounded in civil society".[58] Like Kant, they may have been unduly optimistic, particularly at the time of writing when the war in Bosnia-Herzegovina was barely over. Like Kant, however, they also knew that only when this legal, political, and cultural order is in place will international law, and human rights which have now become its most powerful component, become at all effective. And like Kant, they knew that that will have to be a condition of future time.[59] "We have long since begun the transition from classical international law to what Kant saw as a 'cosmopolitan condition'", wrote Jürgen Habermas in 2004. "This is a fact", he went on, "moreover normatively speaking, I do not see any coherent alternative to such a development."[60] If this should, indeed, turn out to be in some measure and, to some degree, a prophecy fulfilled, then it will also be the final transvaluation of the old European imperial project.

## Endnotes

1 "Letter to Charles-Jean-François Depont" in *Further Reflections on the Revolution in France*, Daniel E. Ritchie ed. (Indianapolis: Liberty Fund, 1992), 13.
2 Quoted in Michael Ignatieff, *Human Rights as Politics and Idolatry*, Amy Gutman ed. (Princeton and Oxford: Princeton University Press, 2001) 59, and see Glen Johnson and Janusz Symonides, *The Universal Declaration of Human Rights: A History of Its Creation and Implementation, 1948–1998* (Paris: UNESCO, 1998).
3 Fareed Zakaria, "A Conversation with Lee Kuan Yew", *Foreign Affairs* 73 (1994), 109–26, and for a broader account of the "Asian Values" controversy, see Daniel A. Bell, *East Meets West: Human Rights and Democracy in East Asia* (Princeton: Princeton University Press, 2000).

4 See, for example, A. Pollis and P. Schwab eds. *Human Rights: Cultural and Ideological Perspectives* (New York: Praeger, 1979). These three sources of objection are all cited by Ignatieff, *Human Rights as Politics and Idolatry*, 58–95.

5 It was only during Vatican II in 1965 that the Church recognized religious freedom to be a right rather than a question of prudence. A document issued in 1975 by a Pontifical commission *Iustitia et Pax* and entitled "The Church and the Rights of Man" gave widespread recognition to the centrality of the notion of human rights and tried to appropriate it as closely as possible to the history of the Christianity. A Papal encyclical of 1991, *Centesimus annus*, drew up its own list of rights which, while recognizing the right of speech and free association and the right to live, nevertheless stressed the "right to grow up in a united family" and the right "to form freely a family". (This last seems to have been aimed at the Chinese limitation on the size of families and in generally at all forms of contraception.) Since then successive popes have made widespread use of the notion, predominantly against non-Christian societies.

6 Eduardo Rabossi "La teoría de los derechos humanos naturalizada", *Revista del Centrode Estudios Constitucionales* 5 (1990), 159–79, and Richard Rorty, "Human Rights,
Rationality and Sentimentality" in *Truth and Progress: Philosophical Papers* (Cambridge: Cambridge University Press, 1998), 167–87.

7 On the claim that human rights and the Shari'a are somehow compatible, see Heiner Bielefeldt, "'Western' Versus 'Islamic' Human Rights Conceptions?: A Critique of Cultural Essentialism in the Discussion on Human Rights", *Political Theory* 28 (2000), 90–121.

8 The preamble to the *Declaration* reads:
"Reaffirming the civilizing and historical role of the Islamic Ummah which Allah made as the best community and which gave humanity a universal and well-balanced civilization, in which harmony is established between hereunder and the hereafter, knowledge is combined with faith, and to fulfill the expectations from this community to guide all humanity which is confused because of different and conflicting beliefs and ideologies and to provide solutions for all chronic problems of this materialistic civilization." *Cairo Declaration on Human Rights in Islam*, Aug. 5, 1990, UN GAOR, World Conf. on Hum. Rts., 4th Sess., Agenda Item 5, U.N. Doc. A/CONF.157/PC/62/Add.18 (1993).

9 See Henry Klug, "Transnational human rights: exploring the Persistence and Globalization of Human Rights", *Annual Review of Law and Social Science* 1 (2005), 85–103. "More than 56% of the 185 member states of the United Nations made major amendments to their constitutions in the decade between 1989 and 1999, and of these at least 70% adopted completely new constitutions .... As a result, about half the member states of the United Nations had, by the beginning of the new millennium, incorporated bills of rights, fundamental rights, or some form of individual and/or collective rights into their constitutional orders."

10 *The Last Utopia Human Rights in History* (Cambridge, MA: Harvard University Press, 2010). For a further discussion of the relationship between the UDHR and the creation of new sovereign states – and of Israel in particular – see Roberto Farneti, *Effetto Israele: La sinistra, la destra e il conflitto Israelo-Palestinese* (Rome: Carocci, 2015).

11 The phrase is Walter Ullmann's, "Some Observations on the Medieval Evaluation of the 'homo naturalis' and the 'Christianus'" in *L'Homme et son destin d'après les penseurs du moyen âge: Actes du premier congrès international de philosophie médiévale* (Louvain-Paris, 1960), 145–51.

12 *Les droits de l'homme et la loi naturelle* (New York: Éditions de la maison française, 1942), 84–5.

13 "The Law of Nations, the Law of Nature and the Rights of Man", *Transactions of the Grotius Society* 29 (1943), 1–33.

14 See pp. 53–4.

15 *International Law and Human Rights* (London: Stevens and Sons, 1950), 27.

16 "Are There Any Natural Rights?", *Philosophical Review* LXIV (1955), 175–91.

17 Within the last twenty years the Catholic Church has taken up this historical account of the origin of human rights, in an attempt to ward off some of the more damaging implications of most human rights claims. See in particular, Leonard Swidler, "Diritti umani: una panoramica storica", *Concilium, Rivista internazionale di teologia* 26 (1990), 27–42. Individual Catholics have been often staunch, if cautious, defenders of the idea.

18 The most sustained and telling critique of Marx's position – even if it has now been somewhat overtaken by events – is Claude Lefort, "Droits de l'homme et politique", in *L'Invention démocratique* (Paris: Fayard, 1981), 45–83. For the hostility of the Left more generally to the idea of *individual*, rather than collective rights, see François Furet, *La Gauche et la révolution au milieu du XIXe siècle* (Paris: Hachette, 1986).

19 Cf. Richard Tuck, "It cannot be a coincidence … that the modern idea of natural rights arose in the period in which the European nations were engaged in their dramatic competition for domination of the world, and in which there were urgent questions about how both states and individuals adrift in a stateless world behave to one another and to newly encountered peoples." *The Rights of War and Peace*, 14.

20 For this, see the authoritative account in Michel Villey, *Philosophie du droit* (Paris: Dalloz, 1982), I, 65.

21 *Leviathan*, 1, 2, p. 200. For Hobbes, "*Right is Liberty*, namely the Liberty which the Civil Law leaves us."

22 On this, see the now classic study by Richard Tuck, *Natural Rights Theories* (Cambridge: Cambridge University Press, 1979), and Brett, *Liberty, Right and Nature*.

23 "[U]ne *qualité* du sujet, une de ses *facultés*, plus précisément une franchise, une liberté, une possibilité d'agir." "La genèse du droit subjectif chez Guillaume d'Ockham", *Archives de la philosophie du droit* 9 (1969), 97–127, and see the discussion in Brett, *Liberty, Right and Nature*, 4. This is very close to Ignatieff's claim that the Universal Declaration of Human Rights was "intended to restore agency". Ignatieff, *Human Rights as Politics and Idolatry*, 5.

24 Tuck, *Natural Rights Theories*, 7–9, 12–13. Brett, *Liberty, Right and Nature*, 10–48.

25 See "On the American Indians", 1.4, 20–23, *Vitoria: Political Writings*, 247–9. "Irrational creatures clearly cannot have any dominion for dominium is a right (*dominium est ius*)."

26 On these "basic rights", see Henry Shue, *Basic Rights: Substance, Affluence, and U.S. Foreign Policy* (Princeton: Princeton University Press, 1980), 23. The text of

the *Universal Declaration of Human Rights* is available online at http://www.
unorg/Overview/rigths.html.
27 Cf. Richard Tuck, *The Rights of War and Peace*, and "Rights and Pluralism" in
James Tully ed., *Philosophy in an Age of Pluralism: The Philosophy of Charles
Taylor in Question* (Cambridge: Cambridge University Press, 1994), 159–70,
and see Duncan Ivison, "The Nature of Rights and the History of Empire" in
David Armitage ed., *British Political Thought in History and Literature,
1500–1800* (Cambridge: Cambridge University Press, 2006), 191–211.
28 *Disputatio xii. De Bello*, 158–61. And see p. 92.
29 See Richard Tuck, "The 'Modern' Theory of Natural Law" in Anthony Pagden
ed., *The Languages of Political Theory in Early-Modern Europe* (Cambridge:
Cambridge University Press, 1987), 99–119.
30 Samuel Pufendorf later objected to this on the grounds that Grotius had thus
confused custom, which could only be the custom of one particular group, with
the natural law, which, if it was to be any use at all, had to be "of use for the
whole human race". It could thus be of no concern "whether Persians marry their
mothers or Egyptians their sisters". Quoted in Samuel Pufendorf, *On the Duty of
Man and Citizen According to Natural Law*, James Tully ed. (Cambridge: Cambridge University Press, 1991), xxvii–xxviii.
31 It is worth perhaps stressing the point made by Javier Muguerza that human rights
cannot derive from human nature because that nature – i.e., the biological condition of the human – is not capable of producing rights of any kind. It derives instead
from the "human condition", which is necessarily a sociohistorical category, "La
lucha por los derechos (Un ensayo de relectura libertaria de un viejo texto liberal)",
*Revista internacional de filosofía política* 15 (2000), 43–59, 53. Recently a number
of theologians on both sides of the Christian confessional divide have attempted to
appropriate the concept by insisting that without a grounding in some concept of
God, the concept of a human, as distinct from a civil, right makes no sense. See
Ignatieff, *Human Rights as Politics and Idolatry*, 82.
32 For Burke, of course, the natural law dictated only the need to respect the authority
of God and the civil law. The French declaration was, in his view, not only an
exercise of "enthusiasm" but also an attempt to sweep away the "prejudices" on
which the principles of the Roman law had been based. "If they [the English]", he
wrote, "find what they seek, and they seldom fail, they think it more wise to
continue the prejudice, with the reason involved, than to cast away the coat of
prejudice and leave nothing but the naked reason." *Reflections on the Revolution
in France*, J. G. A. Pocock ed. (Indianapolis: Liberty Fund, 1987), 76–7.
33 In this respect Ignatieff is right in saying that "Rights are inescapably political
because they tacitly imply a conflict between a rights holder and a rights 'with-
holder', some authority against which the rights holder can make justified
claims". *Human Rights as Politics and Idolatry*, 67.
34 *L'età dei diritti* (Torino: Einaudi, 1990), 103.
35 "Les droits naturels, inaliéables et sacrés de l'homme" (Preambule), "Les hommes
naissent et demeurent libres et égaux en droits" (Article 1), in Lucien Jaume ed.,
*Les Déclaration des droits de l'homme 1789–1793–1848–1946* (Paris: Flammarion, 1989), 12. Similar claims had, of course, also been made by the Bills of Rights
for Virginia, Maryland, and Massachusetts. But whereas American society is

conceived eudemonistical as for the "common benefit", "good of the whole", or "common good", the French perception of the social order, despite the evident influence of Rousseau on other parts of the constitution, is resolutely individualistic. "The purpose (*but*) of every political association is the preservation of the natural and imprescriptible rights of man." (Article 2)

36 "These rights are liberty, property, safety and the resistance to oppression." (Article 2)

37 Lauterpacht, however, lumped together with the "Rights of Man and Citizen", the "Declaration of Rights" of Virginia, Pennsylvania, Maryland, Delaware, New Jersey, and North and South Carolina, and the Declaration of Independence of 1776, the Declaration of Rights of Massachusetts of 1780, and the Bill of Rights of 1789. "The Law of Nations, the Law of Nature and the Rights of Man", 8.

38 *L'Ancien régime et la révolution*, Francoise Mélonio ed. (Paris: Flammarion, 1988), 107–8 (Bk. I cap. III).

39 Described by Jonathan Israel in *Revolutionary Ideas: An Intellectual History of the French Revolution from the Rights of Man to Robespierre* (Princeton: Princeton University Press, 2014), 342–73.

40 *Les Déclaration des droits de l'homme 1789–1793–1848–1946*, 240, 269. Article 1 of Condorcet's proposal reads: "Les droits naturels, civils et politiques des hommes, sont la liberté, l'égalité, la sûreté, la propriété, la garantie sociale, et la résistance à l'oppression."

On the drafting of the various *Déclarations* and the ideas which lay behind them, see Keith Michael Baker, "The Idea of a Declaration of Rights" in Dale Van Kley ed., *The French Idea of Freedom: The Old Regime and the Declaration of Rights of 1789* (Stanford: Stanford University Press, 1995), 154–96.

41 See, however, Olympe de Gourges' "Les droits de la femme of 1791" in *Les Déclaration des droits de l'homme 1789–1793–1848–1946*, 198–209, which claims that « la femme naît libre et demeure égale à l'homme en droits ». It had, however, to wait until 1946 until this principle was incorporated into the constitution of the French Fourth Republic.

42 As Pierre Manent has pointed out the fact that the declaration of 1789 spoke of "des droits de l'homme *et du citoyen*, on pourrait dire que les droits du citoyen l'avaient emporté sur ceux de l'homme". By the end of the nineteenth century, however, "on s'intéresa davantage à l'inscription *politique* des droits humains dans le cadre d'un état national qu'à l'affirmation générale des droits en tant que tels", *Cours familier de philosophie politique* (Paris: Fayard, 2001), 165.

43 *Les Déclaration des droits de l'homme 1789–1793–1848–1946*, 321–2.

44 Mill attributed two meanings to the word. "We are accustomed to call a country more civilized if we think it more improved; more eminent in the best characteristics of Man and Society; farther advanced in the road to perfection; happier, nobler, wiser …. In another sense it stands for the kind of improvement only, which distinguishes wealthy and powerful nation from savages and barbarians." John Stuart Mill, "Civilization," in *Collected Works of John Stuart Mill*, XVIII, 117, and see Pitts, *A Turn to Empire*, 141–4.

45 "A Few Words on Non-intervention" in *Collected Works of John Stuart Mill*, XXI, 119, and quoted in Pitts, *A Turn to Empire*, 141–4.

46 Ignatieff, *Human Rights as Politics and Idolatry*, 5.

47 *Cours familier de philosophie politique,* 163–4.
48 This is what Claude Lefort called the "triple paradox" of the *Déclaration des droits de l'homme.* The rights of man have been declared (*énoncés*) as the rights of *man* as an individual, yet it is man in society who is making the declaration. It was this paradox which had prompted Joseph de Maistre's famously acid comment that although he had met Italians, Russians, Spanish, English, and French and that "thanks to Montesquieu" knew that such creatures as Persians existed, he had never met "Man". "Droits de l'homme et politique", 64–7.
49 "Civilization", *Collected Works of John Stuart Mill,* XVIII, 119.
50 *On Liberty* in *On Liberty and Other Writings,* Stefan Collini ed. (Cambridge: Cambridge University Press, 1989), 14.
51 *The Law of Peoples* (Cambridge, MA: Harvard University Press, 1999), 78–81.
52 *L'età dei diritti,* 153.
53 Quoted in Ignatieff, *Human Rights as Politics and Idolatry,* 7.
54 John Rawls clearly believed it could. His fictional "decent" non-Liberal, non-democratic peoples are bound to accept some notion of human rights or surrender their claims to decency. It is a moot point whether any such peoples could possibly exist. Certainly his claim that a religious society could arrive at the creation of a constitutional democratic regime seems highly improbable. Even if his and Abdullahi Ahmed An-Na'im's vision of the Shari'a could be revised to permit freedom of religious choice and equality for women, the urge to revise the holy law in this way, and the languages in which it would have to be couched, could only come about from outside Islam. In which case it is hard to see how it could remain holy. A liberal democratic Islamic state is an oxymoron. For the only way to create such a state would be to separate the secular and the religious, something for which neither the Qur'an nor Islamic law makes any prevision. There are of course "liberal" societies which are Islamic in the sense that the majority of their populations are Muslims – Turkey, Morocco, Tunisia being perhaps the most obvious examples. But they are not Islamic in the sense of being governed by any version of the Shari'a. Rawls, *The Law of Peoples,* 151, drawing on Abd Allah Ahmed Na'im *Toward an Islamic Reformation: Civil Liberties, Human Rights, and International Law* (Syracuse: Syracuse University Press, 1990).
55 Introduction to Ignatieff, *Human Rights as Politics and Idolatry,* x.
56 See, for instance, the comments by Amy Gutman in Ignatieff, *Human Rights as Politics and Idolatry,* vii–x.
57 *L'età dei diritti,* 155.
58 *Our Global Neighbourhood: The Report of the Commission on Global Governance,* with an Introduction by Nelson Mandela (Oxford: Oxford University Press, 1995).
59 See Norberto Bobbio, "Kant e la Rivoluzione francese", *L'età dei diritti,* 142–54.
60 *The Divided West,* Ciaran Cronin trans. and ed. (Cambridge: Polity Press, 2008), 19.

# Bibliography

Abarca de Bolea, Pedro Pablo, conde de Aranda, "Exposición del conde de Aranda al rey Carlos III sobre el conveniencia de crear reinos independientes en América", in Andrés Muriel, *Gobierno del señor rey Carlos III [1838]*, Carlos Seco Serrano ed., Biblioteca de autores españoles (Madrid: Ediciones Atlas, 1959), 115.

Abercromby, James, "An Examination of the Acts of Parliament Relative to the Trade and the Government of Our American Colonies" (1752) and *"De Jure et Gubernatione Coloniarum, or An Inquiry in the Nature, and the Rights of Colonies, Ancient, and Modern"* (1774), Jack P. Greene, Charles F. Mullett, and Edward C. Papenfuse Jr. eds. (Philadelphia: American Philosophical Society, 1986).

Acosta, José de, *De promulgatione evangelii apud indo, sive De procuranda indorum salute libri sex* (Cologne, 1596).

  *Historia natural y moral de las Indias* [1590], Edmundo O'Gorman ed. (Mexico: Fondo de Cultura Económica, 1962).

Adams, John, *Works*, Charles Francis Adams ed. (Boston, 1850–6).

Adelman, Jeremy, *Sovereignty and Revolution in the Iberian Atlantic* (Princeton, Princeton University Press, 2006).

Albert, S., *Bellum Iustum* (Frankfurter Althistorische Studien 10). (Kallmunz 1980).

Alexandrowicz, C. H., "Freitas *versus* Grotius", *British Yearbook of International Law*, 35 (1959), 162–82.

Ando, Clifford, *Imperial Ideology and Provincial Loyalty in the Roman Empire* (Berkeley, Los Angeles, London: University of California Press, 2000).

  "The Roman City in the Roman Period", in Stéphane Benoist ed., *Rome, a City and Its Empire in Perspective: The Impact of the Roman World through, Fergus Millar's Research. Rome, une cité impériale en jeu: l'impact du monde romain selon Fergus Millar* (Leiden: Brill, 2012), 109–24.

Anghie, Antony, *Imperialism, Sovereignty and the Making of International Law* (Cambridge: Cambridge University Press, 2005).

Anidjar, Gil, "Lines of Blood: Limpieza de Sangre as Political Theology", in Mariacarla Gedebusch Bondia ed., *Blood in History and Blood Histories* (Florence: Edizioni del Galluzzo 2005), 119–36.

Annino, Antonio and François Xavier Guerra eds., *Inventando la nación. Iberoamér-ica. Siglo XIX* (Mexico: Fondo de Cultura Económica, 2003).

Anon., *Reflexiones sobre el estado actual de la América, o cartas al Abate de Pradt* (Madrid, 1820).

Aquinas, St. Thomas, *In decem libros ad Nicomachum exposition*, R. M. Spiazzi ed. (Rome-Turin: Marietti, 1964).

Aristides, Aelius, "The Roman Oration", in James H. Oliver, *The Ruling Power a Study of the Roman Empire in the Second Century after Christ through the Roman Oration of Aelius Aristides* (Transactions of the American Philosophical Society, New Series, 23) (Philadelphia: American Philosophical Society, 1953).

Armitage, David, "The Cromwellian Protectorate and the Languages of Empire", *Historical Journal*, 35 (1992), 531–55.

*The Ideological Origins of the British Empire* (Cambridge: Cambridge University Press, 2000).

"The Scottish Vision of Empire: Intellectual Origins of the Darien Venture," in John Robertson ed., *A Union for Empire: Political Thought and the British Union of 1707* (Cambridge: Cambridge University Press, 2006), 45–118.

*Foundations of Modern International Thought* (Cambridge: Cambridge University Press, 2013).

Bacon, Francis, *The Works of Francis Bacon*, James Spedding ed. (London, 1857–74).

Bailyn, Bernard ed., *Pamphlets of the American Revolution. I 1750–1765* (Cambridge, MA: Harvard University Press, 1965).

*The Ideological Origins of the American Revolution* (Cambridge, MA: Harvard University Press, 1967).

Baker, Keith Michael, "The Idea of a Declaration of Rights", in Dale Van Kley ed., *The French Idea of Freedom: The Old Regime and the Declaration of Rights of 1789* (Stanford: Stanford University Press, 1995), 154–96.

Balibar, Etienne and Immanuel Wallerstein, *Race, Nation, Class: Ambiguous Iden-tities* (London: Verso, 1991).

Banner, Stuart, *How the Indians Lost Their Land: Law and Power on the Frontier* (Cambridge, MA: Belknap Press, 2005).

Banton, Michael, *Racial Theories* (Cambridge: Cambridge University Press, 1987).

Barnes, Jonathan, "The Just War", in Norman Kretzmann, Anthony Kenny, and Jan Pinborg eds., *Cambridge History of Later Medieval Philosophy*, (Cambridge: Cambridge University Press, 1982), 775–8.

Barros, Joam de, *Asia de Joam de Barros dos feitos que os Portugueses fizeram no descobrimento e conquista dos mares et terras do Oriente* (Lisbon, 1781).

Bartlett, Robert, *The Making of Europe* (Harmondsworth: Penguin Books, 1994).

Bataillon, Marcel, "L'Unité du genre humain de P. Acosta à P. Clavigero", in *Mélanges à la mémoire de Jean Sarrailh* (Paris: Institut d'Études Hispaniques, 1966) I, 175–86.

Bell, Daniel A., *East Meets West: Human Rights and Democracy in East Asia* (Princeton: Princeton University Press, 2000).

Bell, Duncan, *The Idea of Greater Britain. Empire and the Future of World Order, 1860–1900* (Princeton: Princeton University Press, 2007).

"John Stuart Mill on Colonies", *Political Theory*, 38 (2010), 34–68.

Beltrán de Heredia, Vicente, "Coleción de dictámenes inéditos", *Ciencia tomista*, 43 (1931).

Benedict, Ruth, *Race and Racism* (London: G. Routledge, 1942).

Benhabib, Seyla, et al., *Another Cosmopolitanism* (Oxford: Oxford University Press, 2004).

Benton, Lauren and Benjamin Straumann, "Acquiring Empire by Law: From Roman Doctrine to Early-Modern European Practice", *Law and History Review*, 28:1 (2010), 1–38.

Benton, Robert J., "Political Expediency and Lying, Kant vs. Benjamin Constant", *Journal of the History of Ideas*, 43 (1982), 135–44.

Bernasconi, Robert, "Who Invented the Concept of Race? Kant's Role in the Enlightenment Construction of Race", in Robert Bernasconi ed., *Race* (Oxford: Blackwell, 2001), 11–36.

Bernier, François, "Nouvelle division de la Terre, par les différentes Espèces ou Races d'hommes qui l'habitent," *Journal des Scavans*, 12 (April 1684), 148–55.

Bielefeldt, Heiner, "'Western' versus 'Islamic' Human Rights Conceptions? A critique of cultural essentialism in the discussion on human rights", *Political Theory*, 28 (2000), 90–121.

Blackstone, Sir William, *Commentaries on the Laws of England*, Stanley Katz ed. (Chicago: University of Chicago Press, 1979).

Bland, Richard, *An Enquiry into the Rights of the British Colonies* (London, 1766).

Bobbio, Norberto, *L'età dei diritti* (Torino: Einaudi, 1990).

Bolívar, Simón, *Obras , completas* Vicente Lecuna and Esther Barret de Nazaris eds. (Havana: Editorial Lex, 1950).

Borello, Camillo, *De Regis catholici praestantia, eius regalibus, iuribus et praerogatiuis commentari* (Milan, 1611).

Borschberg, Peter, "The Seizure of the Sta. Catarina Revisited: The Portuguese Empire in Asia, VOC Politics and the Origins of the Dutch-Johor Alliance (1602–1616)", *Journal of Southeast Asia Studies*, 33 (2002), 31–62.

*Hugo Grotius, the Portuguese and Free Trade in the East Indies* (Singapore: National University of Singapore, 2011).

Boswell, James, *Boswell's Life of Johnson*, G. B. Hill ed. (Oxford: Oxford University Press, 1934).

Bougainville, Louis-Antoine de, *Voyage autour du monde par la frégate la Boudeuse et la flûte l'Étoile; en 1766, 1767, 1768 et 1769* [1771], Michel Bideaux and Sonia Faessel eds. (Paris: Presses de l'Université de Paris-Sorbonne, 2001).

Brading, David, *The First America: The Spanish Monarchy, Creole Patriots and the Liberal State, 1492–1867* (Cambridge: Cambridge University Press, 1991).

Bradley, Mark, ed., *Classics and Imperialism in the British Empire* (Oxford: Oxford University Press, 2010).

Breña, Roberto, *El Primer liberalismo español y los procesos de emancipación de América* (Mexico: El Colegio de México, 2006).

*El Imperio de las circumstancias: La independencias hispanoamericanas y la revolución liberal española* (Mexico: El Colegio de México, 2012).

Brett, Annabel, *Liberty, Right and Nature* (Cambridge: Cambridge University Press, 1997).

*Changes of State: Nature and the Limits of the City in Early-Modern Natural Law* (Princeton: Princeton University Press, 2011).

Briant, Pierre, *Alexandre des lumières: Fragments d'histoire européenne* (Paris: Gallimard, 2012).

Bromwich, David, ed. *On Empire, Liberty and Reform: Speeches and Letters of Edmund Burke* (New Haven and London: Yale University Press, 2000).

Brown, Peter, *The World of Late Antiquity* (New York and London: W.W. Norton and Company, 1989).

Bryce, James, *The American Commonwealth* [1888] (New York: Cosmo Classics, 2007).

Burbank, Jane and Fredrick Cooper, *Empires in World History: Power and the Politics of Difference* (Princeton: Princeton University Press, 2010).

Burke, Edmund, *A Letter to Edmund Burke, Esq., A Member of Parliament for the City of Bristol ... in Answer to his Printed Speech* (Gloucester, 1775).

*Writings and Speeches* (New York: J. F. Taylor, 1901).

*The Writings and Speeches of Edmund Burke*, P. J. Marshall ed. (Oxford: Clarendon Press, 1981).

*Reflections on the Revolution in France*, J. G. A. Pocock ed. (Indianapolis: Liberty Fund, 1987).

*Selected Works of Edmund Burke*, E. J. Payne ed. (Indianapolis: Liberty Fund, 1990).

*Further Reflections on the Revolution in France*, Daniel E. Ritchie ed. (Indianapolis: Liberty Fund, 1992).

Burke, Edmund and William Burke, *An Account of the European Settlements in America* (London, 1757).

Bushnell, David and Lester D. Langley eds., *Simón Bolívar: Essays on the Life and Legacy of the Liberator* (Lanham: Rowman and Littlefield, 2008).

Byrd, Sharon B. and Joachim Hruschka, "Lex iusti, lex iuridica und lex iustitiae in Kants *Rechtslehre*", *Archiv für Rechts und Sozialphilosophie* 91 (2005), 484–500.

"From the State of Nature to the Juridical State of States", *Law and Philosophy* 27 (2008), 599–641.

*Cairo Declaration on Human Rights in Islam*, Aug. 5, 1990, U.N. GAOR, World Conf. on Hum. Rts., 4th Sess., Agenda Item 5, U.N. Doc. A/CONF.157/PC/62/Add.18 (1993).

Campillo y Cosío, José de, *Nuevo sistema de gobierno económico para la América* (Madrid, 1789).

*Lo que hay de mas y menos en España para que sea lo que debe ser y no lo que es, España despierta* [1741], Antonio Elorza ed.(Madrid: Seminario de Historia Social y Económica de la Facultad de Filosofía y Letras de la Universidad de Madrid, 1969).

Campomanes, Pedro Rodríguez, conde de, *Discurso sobre la educación popular de los artesanos y su fomento* (Madrid, 1775).

Campomanes, Pedro Rodríguez, conde de, *Reflexiones sobre el comercio español a Indias* [1762], Vicente Llombart Roas ed. (Madrid: Ministerio de Economía y Hacienda, 1988).

*Inéditos políticos* (Oviedo: Junta General del Principado de Asturias, 1999).

Cano, Melchor, *De locis theologicis* (Salamanca, 1536).

Careil, Foucher de, *Nouvelles lettres et opuscules inédits de Leibniz* (Paris, 1857).

Castro Leiva, Luís, *La Gran Colombia, una ilusión ilustrada* (Caracas: Monte Alva Editores, 1985).

Castro Leiva, Luís and Anthony Pagden, "Civil Society and the Fate of the Republics of Latin America" in Sudipta Kaviraj and Sunil Khilnani eds., *Civil Society History and Possibilities* (Cambridge: Cambridge University Press, 2001), 179–203.

*Obras*, Carole Leal Curiel ed. (Caracas: Fundación Polar, 2005).

Chapman, Robert, *A Relation of the Second Voyage to Guiana* (London, 1596).

Cheyney, Edward P., "International Law under Queen Elizabeth", *English Historical Review* 20 (1905), 659–72.

Child, Josiah, *A New Discourse on Trade* [1665] (Glasgow, 1751).

Claeys, Gregory, *Imperial Sceptics: British Critics of Empire 1850–1920* (Cambridge: Cambridge University Press, 2010).

Clark, Bruce, *Native Liberty, Crown Sovereignty: The Existing Aboriginal Right of Self-government in Canada* (Montreal: McGill-Queen's University Press, 1990).

Clark, G. N., "Grotius' East India Mission to England", *Transactions of the Grotius Society* XX (1935), 45–84.

Clarke, Peter, *The Last Thousand Days of the British Empire: The Demise of a Superpower, 1944-47* (London and New York: Penguin Books, 2008).

Cohn, Bernard, "The Command of Language and the Language of Command", in Ranajit Guha ed., *Subaltern Studies* (Delhi, 1985), IV, 295–320.

Coke, Edward, *The Reports of Sir Edward Coke* (London, 1658).

*First Institute of the Laws of England* [1628] (Philadelphia, 1826-7).

Commission on Global Governance, *Our Global Neighbourhood: The Report of the Commission on Global Governance*, with an introduction by Nelson Mandela (Oxford: Oxford University Press, 1995).

Condorcet, Marie Jean Antoine Nicolas de Caritat, marquis de, *Œuvres complètes de Condorcet* (Paris, 1847–9).

*Esquisse d'un tableau historique des progrès de l'esprit humain* [1794], Alain Pons ed. (Paris: Flammarion, 1988).

Connor, Michael, *The Invention of Terra Nullius. Historical and Legal Fictions in the Foundation of Australia* (Sydney: Macleay Press, 2005).

Constant, Benjamin, "Commentaire sur l'ouvrage de Filangieri", in Gaetano Filangieri, *Oeuvres* (Paris, 1822).

*Constant: Political Writings*, Biancamaria Fontana trans. and ed. (Cambridge: Cambridge University Press, 1988).

*Écrits de jeunesse (1774–1799)*, L. Omacini and J.-D. Candaux eds. (Tübingen: Max Niemeyer Verlag, 1998).

*Constitución política de la monarquia española, promulgada en Cádiz a 19 marzo, 1812* (Cádiz, 1812).

Cortés, Hernán, *Letters from Mexico*, Anthony Pagden trans. and ed. (London and New Haven: Yale University Press, 1986).

Covarrubias, Diego de, *Opera omnia* (Geneva, 1697).

Cramb, J. A., *Reflections on the Origins and Destiny of Imperial Britain* (London: Macmillan, 1900).

Cuoco, Vicenzo, *Saggio storico sulla rivoluzione di Napoli* (Milan, 1806).

Curzon, Lord Nathaniel, *Speeches by Lord Curzon of Kedleston, Viceroy and Governor General of India* (Calcutta, 1900).

Cushman, Robert, *Reasons and Considerations Touching the Lawfullness of Removing out of England into Parts of America* (London, 1622).

Cuxil, Cojti, Demetrio. *El movimiento maya* (Guatemala: Cholsamj, 1997).

D'Amico, Juan Carlos, *Charles Quint maître du monde: entre mythe et réalité* (Caen: Presses universitaires de Caen, 2004).

Davenant, Charles, *The Political and Commercial Works of that Celebrated Writer, Charles D'Avenant LL.D.* (London, 1771).

De Brosses, Charles, *Histoire des navigations aux Terres australes* (Paris, 1756).

De Pradt, Dominque-Georges-Frédéric Dufour, *Du Congrès de Vienne* (Paris, 1815).

*The Colonies and the Present American Revolutions* (London, 1817).

*Congrés du Panama* (Paris, 1825).

Deckers, Daniel, *Gerechtigkeit und Recht. Eine historisch-kritische Untersuchung der Gerechtigkeitslehre des Francisco de Vitoria (1483–1546)* (Freiburg: Universitätsverlag Freiburg, 1991).

Dee, John, *The Limits of the British Empire*, Ken MacMillan (with Jennifer Abeles) eds. (Westport, CT, and London: Praeger, 2004).

Dewey, Clive, "The Influence of Sir Henry Maine on Agrarian Policy in India" in Alan Diamond ed., *The Victorian Achievement of Sir Henry Maine* (Cambridge: Cambridge University Press, 1991), 353–75.

Diderot, Denis, *Œuvres*, Laurent Versini ed. (Paris: Robert Laffont, 1994).

Donne, John, *A Sermon Preached to the Honourable Company of the Virginia Plantation 13 Nov. 1622* (London, 1623).

Duffy Burnett, Christina, and Burke Marshall eds. *Foreign in a Domestic Sense: American Expansion and the Constitution* (Durham: Duke University Press, 2001).

Dummer, Jeremiah, *A Defence of the New-England Charters* (London, 1721).

*Edits, ordonnances royaux, déclarations et arrêts du conseil d'état du Roi concernant le Canada* (Quebec, 1854–6).

Elliott, J. H., *The Old World and the New, 1492–1650* (Cambridge: Cambridge University Press, 1970).

*Empires of the Atlantic World. Britain and Spain in America 1492–1830* (New Haven and London: Yale University Press, 2006).

*Spain, Europe and the Wider World 1500–1800* (New Haven and London: Yale University Press, 2009).

Farías, Luís M., *La América de Aranda* (Mexico: Fondo de Cultura Económica, 2003).

Farneti, Roberto, *Effetto Israele: La sinistra, la destra e il conflitto Israelo-Palestinese* (Rome: Carocci, 2015).

Faure, Élie, *Mon périple* (Paris:Seghers, 1987).

Ferguson, Robert, *A Just and Modest Vindication of the Scots Design, for Having Established a Colony at Darien* (N.P., 1699).

Fernández de Oviedo, Gonzalo, *La Historia General de las Indias, primera parte* (Seville, 1535).

Fernández Durán, Reyes, *Gerónimo de Uztaríz (1670–1732). Una polítca económica para Felipe V* (Madrid: Minerva, 1999).

Fibiger Bang, Peter and Dariusz Kolodziejczyk eds., *Universal Empire: A Comparative Approach to Imperial Culture and Representation in Eurasian History* (Cambridge: Cambridge University Press, 2012).

Fitzmaurice, Andrew, *Humanism and America: An Intellectual History of English Colonization 1500–1625* (Cambridge: Cambridge University Press, 2003).

"The Genealogy of *Terra nullius*", *Australian Historical Studies* 38 (2007), 1–15.

Fletcher, Andrew, *The Political Works of Andrew Fletcher* (London, 1737).

Flikschuh, Katrin and Lea Ypi eds., *Kant and Colonialism: Historical and Critical Perspectives* (Oxford: Oxford University Press, 2014).

Fontana, Bianca, *Benjamin Constant and the Post-Revolutionary Mind* (New Haven and London: Yale University Press, 1991).

ed., *The Invention of the Modern Republic* (Cambridge: Cambridge University Press, 1994).

Fournel, Jean-Louis, *La Cité du soleil et les territoires des hommes: Le savoir du monde chez Campanella* (Paris: Albin Michel, 2012).

Fox Morcillo, Sebastian, *Brevis et perspicua totius ethicae, seu de moribus philosophiae descriptio* (Basle, 1566).

Franklin, Benjamin, *The Papers of Benjamin Franklin*, William B. Wilcox ed. (New Haven and London: Yale University Press, 1959–93).

Freitas, Serafim de, *Do Justo império asiático dos Portugueses (De iusto imperio lusitanorum asiatico)* trad. Miguel Pinto de Meneses (Lisbon: Instituto de Alta Cultura, 1959).

Frémeaux, Jacques, *Les Empires coloniaux dans le processus de mondialisation* (Paris: Maisonneuve & Larose, 2002).

Furet, François, *La Gauche et la révolution au milieu du XIXe siècle* (Paris: Hachette, 1986).

Furnivall, J. S., *Netherlands India: A Study of Plural Economy* (Cambridge: Cambridge University Press, 1939).

Garver, Eugene, "Aristotle's Natural Slaves: Incomplete *praxeis* and Incomplete Human Beings", *Journal of the History of Philosophy* 32 (1994), 175–96.

Gellner, Ernest, *Nations and Nationalism* (Oxford: Blackwell, 2006).

Gentili, Alberico, *Alberici Gentilis, De Iure Belli*, Thomas Erskine Holland ed. (Oxford: Clarendon Press, 1877).

*De iure belli*, John Rolfe trans. (Oxford: Clarendon Press, 1933).

*Hispanicae advocationis libri duo*, Frank Frost Abbott trans. (New York: Oceana Publications, 1964).

*De armis Romanis*, Benedict Kingsbury and Benjamin Straumann eds., David Lupher trans. (Oxford: Oxford University Press, 2011).

Ghosh, R. N., "John Stuart Mill on Colonies and Colonization" in *John Stuart Mill*, John Cunningham Wood ed. (London: Croom Helm, 1987), IV, 354–67.

Gibbon, Edmund, *Decline and Fall of the Roman Empire*, David Womersley ed. (London: Penguin, 1994).

Gibson, Charles, *The Spanish Tradition in America* (New York: Norton, 1968).

Gil, Juan and José Maria Maestre eds., *Humanismo latino y descrubrimiento* (Seville: Universidad de Sevilla and Universidad de Cadiz, 1992).

Gliozzi, Giuliano, *Adamo e il nuovo mondo* (Florence: La Nuova Italia, 1977).

*Differenze e uguaglianza nella cutura europea moderna* (Naples: Vivarium, 1993).

Gould, Eliga H., *The Persistence of Empire: British Political Culture in the Age of the American Revolution* (Chapel Hill, University of North Carolina Press, 2000).

Goyard-Fabre, Simone, *Kant et le problème du droit* (Paris: Vrin, 1975).

Greene, Jack P., *Peripheries and Center: Constitutional Development in the Extended Polities of the British Empire and the United States 1607–1788* (Athens and London: University of Georgia Press, 1986).

Grotius, Hugo, *De iure praedae commentarius (Commentary on the Law of Prize and Booty)*, G. L. Williams trans. (Oxford: Oxford University Press, 1950).

*The Free Sea [De Mare Libero]*, Richard Hakluyt trans., David Armitage ed. (Indianapolis: Liberty Fund, 2004).

*The Rights of War and Peace [De Jure Belli ac Pacis]*, Richard Tuck ed., from the edition by Jean Barbeyrac (Indianapolis: Liberty Fund, 2005).

Gruzinski, Serge, *Les Quatres parties du monde: Histoire d'une mondialisation*, (Paris: Editions de la Martinière, 2004).

Grynaeus, Simon, *Novus orbis regionum ac insularum veteribus incognitarum* (Basle, 1532).

Habermas, Jürgen, *The Divided West*, Ciaran Cronin trans. and ed. (Cambridge: Polity Press, 2008).

Haggenmacher, Peter, "Mutations du concept de guerre juste de Grotius à Kant", *Cahiers de philosophie politique et juridique* 10 (1986), 117–22.

Hakluyt, Richard, *The Original Writings and Correspondence of the Two Richard Hakluyts*, E. G. R. Taylor ed. (London: Hakluyt Society, 1935).

Halperín, Jean-Louis, *Entre nationalisme juridique et communauté du droit* (Paris: Presses Universitaires de France, 1999).

Hamilton, Alexander, James Madison, and John Jay, *The Federalist Papers*, Isaac Kramnick ed. (Harmondsworth: Penguin Books, 1987).

Hannaford, Ivan, *Race: The History of an Idea in the West* (Baltimore: Johns Hopkins University Press, 1996).

Hart, H. A. L., "Are There Any Natural Rights?", *Philosophical Review* LXIV (1955), 175–91.

Hassner, Pierre, "Les concepts de guerre et de paix chez Kant", *Revue française de science politique* XI (1961), 642–70.

Headley, John M., "The Sixteenth-Century Venetian Celebration of the Earth's Total Habitability: The Issue of the Fully Habitable World for Renaissance Europe", *Journal of World History* 8 (1997), 1–27.

Heath, Malcolm, "Aristotle on Natural Slavery", *Phronesis* 53 (2008), 243–70.

Hegel, Georg Friedrich, *The Philosophy of History*, J. Sibree trans. (New York: Dover Publications, 1956).

*Elements of the Philosophy of Right*, trans. H. B. Nisbet (Cambridge: Cambridge University Press, 1991).

Herder, Johann Gottfried von, *Outlines of a Philosophy of the History of Man [Ideen zur Philosophie der Geschichte der Menscheit]*, T. Churchill trans. (London, 1800).

Hermes Trismegistus, *Corpus Hermeticum*, A. J. Festugière and Arthur Darby Knock eds. (Paris: Société d'édition "Les Belles Lettres", 1954)

Hingley, Richard, *Roman Officers and English Gentlemen: The Imperial Origins of Roman Archaeology* (London and New York: Routledge: 2007).

Hirschman, Albert, *The Passions and Interests: Political Arguments for Capitalism before Its Triumph* (Princeton: Princeton University Press, 1977).

*Historical Collection of South Carolina; Embracing Many Rare and Valuable Pamphlets and Other Documents Relating to the State from Its First Discovery until Its Independence in the Year 1776* (New York, 1836).

Hobbes, Thomas, *Leviathan*, Richard Tuck ed. (Cambridge: Cambridge University Press, 1991).

Hobsbawn, Eric, *The Age of Empire, 1875–1914* (London: Abacus, 1987).

*On Empire: America, War and Global Supremacy* (New York and London: New Press, 2008).

Hobson, John Atkinson, *Imperialism: A Study* (London: James Nisbet, 1902).

Höffe, Otfried, *Kant's Cosmopolitan Theory of Law and Peace*, Alexandra Newton trans. (Cambridge: Cambridge University Press, 2006).

Holmes, Stephen, "The Liberal Uses of Bourbon Legitimism", *Journal of the History of Ideas* 43 (1982), 229–48.

*Benjamin Constant and the Making of Modern Liberalism* (New Haven and London: Yale University Press, 1984).

Home, Henry, Lord Kames, *Sketches of the History of Man*, James A. Harris ed. (Indianapolis: Liberty Fund 2007).

Hont, Istvan, *Jealousy of Trade: International Competition and the Nation-State in Historical Perspective* (Cambridge, MA.: Harvard University Press, 2005).

Howard, Michael, *Restraints on War* (Oxford: Oxford University Press, 1979).

Hume, David, *Essays, Moral, Political, and Literary* [1777], Eugene F. Miller ed. (Indianapolis: Liberty Fund, 1985).

Hyam, Ronald, *Britain's Imperial Century 1815–1914: A Study of Empire and Expansion* (London: B. T. Batsford, 1976).

Ignatieff, Michael, *Human Rights as Politics and Idolatry*, Amy Gutman ed. (Princeton and Oxford: Princeton University Press, 2001).

Isaac, Benjamin, *The Invention of Racism in Classical Antiquity* (Princeton; Princeton University Press, 2004).

Israel, Jonathan, *Revolutionary Ideas: An Intellectual History of the French Revolution from the Rights of Man to Robespierre* (Princeton: Princeton University Press, 2014).

Ivison, Duncan, "The Nature of Rights and the History of Empire" in *British Political Thought in History and Literature, 1500–1800*, David Armitage ed. (Cambridge: Cambridge University Press, 2006), 191–211.

James, Harold, *The Roman Predicament: How the Rules of International Order Create the Politics of Empire* (Princeton: Princeton University Press, 2008).

Jarcho, Saul, "Origin of the American Indian as Suggested by Fray Joseph de Acosta", *Isis* 59 (1959), 430–8.

Jaume, Lucien, ed., *Les Déclaration des droits de l'homme 1789- 1793–1848–1946* (Paris: Flammarion, 1989).

Jefferson, Thomas, *A Summary View of the Rights of British America* (London, 1774).

*Writings* (New York: Library of America, 1984).

Jennings, Francis, *Empire of Fortune: Crowns, Colonies, and Tribes in the Seven Years' War in America* (New York: W.W. Norton, 1988).

Jennings, R. Y., *The Acquisition of Territory in International Law* (Manchester: Manchester University Press, 1963).

Jèze, Gaston, *Étude théorique et pratique sur l'occupation* (Paris, 1896).

Johnson, Glen and Janusz Symonides, *The Universal Declaration of Human Rights: A History of its Creation and Implementation, 1948–1998* (Paris: UNESCO, 1998).

Johnson, Robert, *Nova Britannia, Offering Most Excellent Fruites by Planting in Virginia* (London, 1609).

Jones, William, *The Collected Works of Sir William Jones* [1807] facsimile edition (New York: New York University Press, 1993).

Jonquière, Clement de la, *L'Expedition d'Égypte* (Paris, 1899–1907).

Jovellanos, Gaspar Melchor de, *Obras completas*, Vicente Llombart and Rosa Joaquín Ocampo Suárez-Valdés eds. (Gijón: Instituto Feijoo de Estudios del Siglo XVIII, 2008).

Juricek, John Thomas, "English Claims in North America to 1660: A Study in Legal and Constitutional History", unpublished PhD thesis, University of Chicago, 1970.

Kant, Immanuel, *Lectures on Ethics*, Peter Heath trans. and ed., *The Cambridge Edition of the Works of Immanuel Kant* (Cambridge: Cambridge University Press, 1997).

*Practical Philosophy*, Mary Gregor trans. and ed., *The Cambridge Edition of the Works of Immanuel Kant* (Cambridge: Cambridge University Press, 1999).

*Anthropology. History, and Education*, Günter Zöller and Robert B. Louden eds., *The Cambridge Edition of the Works of Immanuel Kant* (Cambridge: Cambridge University Press, 2007).

Kapp, Ernst, *Philosophische oder Vergleichende allgeine Erdkunde* (Braunschweig, 1845).

Kaser, Max, *Ius gentium* (Cologne, Weimar, Vienna: Böhlau Verlag, 1993).

Keene, Edward, *Beyond the Anarchical Society: Grotius, Colonialism and Order in World Politics* (Cambridge: Cambridge University Press, 2002).

Kennedy, Paul, *The Rise and Fall of the Great Powers* (New York: Random House 1987).

Kennedy, W. P. M., ed., *Documents of the Canadian Constitution* (Toronto and New York: Oxford University Press, 1918).

Kidd, Colin, *The Forging of Races: Race and Scripture in the Protestant Atlantic World, 1600–2000* (Cambridge, 2006).

Kingsbury, Benedict "Confronting Difference: The Puzzling Durability of Gentili's Combination of Pragmatic Realism and Normative Judgment", *American Journal of International Law* 92:4 (1998), 713–23.

Kingsbury, Benedict, and Benjamin Straumann eds., *The Roman Foundations of the Law of Nations* (Oxford: Oxford University Press, 2010).

Kleingeld, Pauline, "Kant's Second Thoughts on Race", *Philosophical Quarterly* 57 (2007), 573–92.

*Kant and Cosmopolitanism: The Philosophical Ideal of World Citizenship* (Cambridge: Cambridge University Press, 2012).

Klug, Henry, "Transnational Human Rights: Exploring the Persistence and Globalization of Human Rights", *Annual Review of Law and Social Science* 1 (2005), 85–103.

Koebner, Richard, *Empire* (Cambridge: Cambridge University Press, 1961).

Koebner, Richard and H. Schmidt eds., *Imperialism: The Story and Significance of a Political Word, 1840–1960* (Cambridge: Cambridge University Press, 1964).

Koenigsberger, H. G., "Dominium regale or Dominium politicum et regale" in *Politicians and Virtuosi: Essays in Early-Modern History* (London: Hambledon Press, 1986).

Kolb, Robert, *Réflexions de philosophie du droit international* (Brussell: Editions Bruylant, 2003).

Korman, Sharon, *The Right of Conquest: The Acquisition of Territory by Force in International Law and Practice* (Oxford: Clarendon Press, 1996).

Koskenniemi, Martti, *From Apology to Utopia: The Structure of International Legal Argument* (Cambridge: Cambridge University Press, 1989).

*The Gentle Civilizer of Nations: The Rise and Fall of International Law 1870–1960* (Cambridge: Cambridge University Press, 2002).

"Ruling the World by Law(S): The View from around 1850" in Martti Koskenniemi and Bo Strath eds., *Europe 1815–1914: Creating Community and Ordering the World* (Helsinki: University of Helsinki, 2014), 16–32.

Kupperman, Karen Ordahl, *Settling with the Indians: The Meeting of English and Indian Cultures in America, 1580–1640* (Totowa, NJ: Rowman and Littlefield, 1980).

*America in European Consciousness 1493–1750* (Chapel Hill and London: University of North Carolina Press, 1995).

Las Casas, Bartolomé de, *Historia de las Indias*, Augustín Millares Carlo ed. (Mexico: Fondo de Cultura Económica, 1951).

Lauterpacht, Hersch, "The Law of Nations, the Law of Nature and the Rights of Man", *Transactions of the Grotius Society* 29 (1943), 1–33.

*International Law and Human Rights* (London: Stevens and Sons, 1950).

Lawday, David, *Napoleon's Master: A Life of Prince Talleyrand* (London: Jonathan Cape, 2006).

Lefort, Claude, "Droits de l'homme et politique" in *L'Invention démocratique* (Paris: Fayard, 1981), 45–83.

Leroy-Beaulieu, *De la colonization chez les peuples modernes* (Paris, 1874).

*De la colonization chez les peuples modernes* (Paris: Guillaumin, 1902, 5th edition).

Lissón, Carlos, *La República en el Perú y la cuestión peruana* (Lima, 1867).

Locke, John, *Locke's Two Treatises of Government*, Peter Laslett ed. (Cambridge: Cambridge University Press, 1960).

*John Locke: Political Essays*, Mark Goldie ed. (Cambridge: Cambridge University Press, 1997).

*John Locke as Translator Three of the Essais of Pierre Nicole in French and English*, Jean S. Yolton ed. (Oxford: Voltaire Foundation, 2000).

Lugard, Frederick John, *The Dual Mandate in British Tropical Africa* (London: Blackwood, 1923).

Lupher, David A., *Romans in a New World: Classical Models in Sixteenth-Century Spanish America* (Ann Arbor: University of Michigan Press, 2003).

Lynch, John, *Simón Bolívar: A Life* (New Haven and London: Yale University Press, 2006).

Mack Smith, Denis, *Mazzini* (New Haven and London: Yale University Press, 1994).

MacMillan, Ken, *Sovereignty and Possession in the English New World: The Legal Foundations of Empire, 1576–1640* (Cambridge: Cambridge University Press, 2006).

Maier, Charles, *Among Empires: American Ascendancy and Its Predecessors* (Cambridge: Harvard University Press, 2006).

Maine, Henry Sumner, *Ancient Law* (London, 1861).

*The Effects of Observation of India in Modern European Thought* (London: John Murray, 1875).

*International Law: A Series of Lectures Delivered before the University of Cambridge 1887* (London: John Murray, 1888).

Major, John, *In secundum librum Sententiarum* (Paris, 1519).

Malcolm, Noel, "Hobbes's Theory of International Relations" in *Aspects of Hobbes* (Oxford: Oxford University Press, 2002), 432–56.

Manent, Pierre, *Cours familier de philosophie politique* (Paris: Fayard, 2001).

Mantena, Karuna, *Alibis of Empire: Henry Maine and the Ends of Liberal Imperialism* (Princeton: Princeton University Press, 2010).

Marcoci, Giuseppe, *L'invenzione di un imperio: Politica e cultura nel mondo portoghese (1450–1600)* (Rome: Caroci editore, 2011).

Maritain, Jacques, *Les droits de l'homme et la loi naturelle* (New York: Éditions de la maison française, 1942).

Marshall, John, *The Life of George Washington: Commander in Chief of the American Forces during the War which Established the Independence of His Country, and First President of the United State* (to which is prefixed, an introduction containing a compendious view of the colonies planted by the English on the continent of North America) (London,1804–7).

Marshall, P. J., *The Impeachment of Warren Hastings* (Oxford: Oxford University Press, 1965).

Martínez, María Elena, *Genealogical Fictions: Limpieza de Sangre, Religion, and Gender in Colonial Mexico* (Stanford: Stanford University Press, 2008).

Mazower, Mark, *Governing the World: The History of an Idea* (New York: Penguin Press, 2012).

McCarthy, Thomas, *Race, Empire and the Idea of Human Development* (Cambridge: Cambridge University Press, 2009).

McConville, Brendan, *These Daring Disturbers of the Public Peace: The Struggle for Property and Power in Early New Jersey* (Ithaca: Cornell University Press, 1999).

Mcneil, Kent, "A Question of Title: Has the Common Law Been Misapplied to Dispossess the Aboriginals?", *Monash University Law Review* 16 (1990), 91–110.

Mede, Joseph, *The Works of the Pious and Profoundly-Learned Joseph Mede,* (corrected and enlarged according to the author's own manuscripts) (London, 1672).

Mehta, Uday Singh, *Liberalism and Empire: A Study in Nineteenth-Century British Liberal Thought* (Chicago: University of Chicago Press, 1999).

Meinecke, Friedrich, *Weltbürgertum und Nationalstaat: Studien zur Genesis des deutschen Nationalstaates* (Munich: R. Oldenbourg, 1922).

Miaja de la Muela, Adolfo, "El derecho *totius orbis* en el pensamiento de Francisco de Vitoria", *Revista española de derecho internacional* 18 (1965), 341, 348–52.

Mill, John Stuart, *Collected Works of John Stuart Mill*, J. M. Robson ed. (Toronto: University of Toronto Press, 1984).

*"On Liberty"* in *On Liberty and Other Writings*, Stefan Collini ed. (Cambridge: Cambridge University Press, 1989).

Miller, Peter, *Defining the Common Good: Empire, Religion and Philosophy in Eighteenth-century Britain* (Cambridge: Cambridge University Press, 1994).

Mirabeau, Victor de Riquetti, marquis de, *L'Ami des hommes, ou traité de la population* (The Hague, 1758).

Mommsen, Theodore, *Le Droit publique romain [Romisches Staatsrecht]*, P. F. Girard trans. (Paris, 1896).

Montesquieu, Charles de Secondat, baron de, *Oeuvres complètes*, Roger Caillois ed. (Paris: Bibliothèque de la Pléiade, 1949–51).

*Monumenta hericina* (Coimbra: Comissao Executiva das Comemorações do V Centenario da Morte do Infante D. Henrique, 1960–74).

Moyn, Samuel, *The Last Utopia Human Rights in History* (Cambridge, MA: Harvard University Press, 2010)

Mueller, John E., *Capitalism, Democracy, and Ralph's Pretty Good Grocery* (Princeton: Princeton University Press, 1999).

Muguerza, Javier, "La lucha por los derechos (Un ensayo de relectura libertaria de un viejo texto liberal)", *Revista internacional de filosofía política* 15 (2000), 43–59.

Mulholland, Leslie Arthur, *Kant's System of Rights* (New York: Columbia University Press, 1989).

Münkler, Herfried, *Empires*, Patrick Camiller trans. (Cambridge: Polity Press, 2007).

Muriel, Andrés, *Gobierno del señor rey Carlos III* [1838], Carlos Seco Serrano ed., *Biblioteca de autores españoles* (Madrid: Ediciones Atlas, 1959).

Muthu, Sankar, *Enlightenment against Empire* (Princeton and Oxford: Princeton University Press, 2003).

Na'im, Abd Allah Ahmed, *Toward an Islamic Reformation: Civil Liberties, Human Rights, and International Law* (Syracuse: Syracuse University Press, 1990).

Nardi, Bruno, "Pietro Pomponazzi e la teoria di Avicenna intorno alla generazione spontanea del uomo" in *Studi su Pietro Pompanazzi* (Florence: F. Le Monnier, 1965).

Nelson, Eric, "Liberty: One Concept Too Many?" *Political Theory* 33 (2005), 58–78.

Newcomb, Steven T., "The Evidence of Christian Nationalism in Federal Indian Law: The Doctrine of Discovery, *Johnson v. McIntosh* and Plenary Power", *New York Review of Law and Social Change* 20 (1993), 303–41.

Nicolet, Claude, *The World of the Citizen in Republican Rome*, P. S. Falla trans. (Berkeley and Los Angeles: California University Press, 1980).

Ninkovich, Frank, *The United States and Imperialism* (Malden: Blackwell Publishers, 2001).

Nussbaum, Arthur, *A Concise History of the Law of Nations* (New York: Macmillan, 1954).

Orford, Anne, *International Authority and the Responsibility to Protect* (Cambridge: Cambridge University Press, 2011).

Ortega Martínez, Francisco A., « Entre 'constitución' y 'colonia', el estatuto ambiguo de las Indias en la monarquía hispánica » in *Conceptos fundamentales de la cultura política de la Independencia* (Bogotá: Universidad Nacional de Colombia, 2012), 61–91.

Otis, James, "The Rights of the British Colonies Asserted and Proved" [Boston, 1764] in Bernard Bailyn ed., *Pamphlets of the American Revolution*. I: 1750–1765, (Cambridge, MA: Harvard University Press, 1965).

Pagden, Anthony, "The 'School of Salamanca' and the 'Affair of the Indies'", *History of Universities* 1 (1981), 71–112.

*The Fall of Natural Man: The American Indian and the Origins of Comparative Ethnology* (Cambridge: Cambridge University Press, 1986, Second revised and enlarged edition).

"Identity Formation in Spanish America" in Nicholas Canny and Anthony Pagden eds., *Colonial Identity in the Atlantic World, 1500–1800* (Princeton: Princeton University Press, 1987), 81–3.

*Spanish Imperialism and the Political Imagination: Studies in European and Spanish-American Social and Political Theory 1513–1830* (New Haven and London: Yale University Press, 1990).

*European Encounters with the New World from Renaissance to Romanticism* (New Haven and London: Yale University Press, 1993).

*Lords of All the World: Ideologies of Empire in Spain, Britain and France c.1500–c.1899* (New Haven and London: Yale University Press, 1995).

"Ley y sociabilidad en Giambattista Vico: hacia una historia crítica de las ciencias humanas", *Agora Papeles de Filosofía* 16:2 (1997), 59–80.

"The Struggle for Legitimacy and the Image of Empire in the Atlantic to c.1700" in Nicholas Canny ed., *The Oxford History of the British Empire*, I, *The Origins of Empire* (Oxford: Oxford University Press, 1998), 34–54.

"Stoicism, Cosmopolitanism and the Legacy of European Imperialism", *Constellations* 7 (2000), 3–22.

"La monarquía española en el siglo XVIII. A propósito de los frescos de Giambattista Tiepolo", *Reales Sitios. Revista del Patrimonio Nacional* 38 (2001), 2–9.

ed., *The Idea of Europe from Antiquity to the European Union* (Cambridge: Cambridge University Press, 2002).

"La Découverte de l'Amérique et la transformation du temps et de l'espace en Europe", *Revue de synthèse* 129 (2008), 1–16.

*The Enlightenment – and Why It Still Matters* (New York: Random House, 2013).

Palacios Rubios, Juan López de, *Insularum mari Oceani tractatus* in *De las islas del mar Océano por Juan López de Palacios Rubios*, Augustín Millares Carlo ed. (Mexico City: Fondo de Cultura Económica, 1954).

Panizza, Diego, *Alberico Gentili, giurista ideologico nell' Inghilterra elisabettiana* (Padua: la Garangola, 1981).

"Political Theory and Jurisprudence in Gentili's *De Iure Belli*: The Great Debate between 'Theological' and 'Humanist' Perspectives from Vitoria to Grotius", *International Law and Justice Working Papers* 15:5 (2005), available at http://www.iilj.org/publications/2005-15.

Paquette, Gabriel B., *Enlightenment, Governance and Reform in Spain and its Empire* (Houndsmills: Palgrave Macmillan, 2008), 29–55.

Paterson, William, *The Writings of William Paterson, Founder of the Bank of England*, S. Bannister ed. (London, 1858).

Pereña, Luciano, *Misión de España en América* (Madrid: Consejo Superior de Investigaciones Scientíficas, 1956).

Philonenko, Alexis, « Kant et le problème de la paix » in *Essais sur la philosophie de la guerre* (Paris: Vrin, 1976), 32–5.

Pinker, Steven, *The Better Angels of Our Nature: Why Violence Has Declined* (New York: Viking, 2011)

Pitts, Jennifer, *A Turn to Empire: The Rise of Imperial Liberalism in Britain and France* (Princeton: Princeton University Press, 2005).

"Constant's Thoughts on Slavery and Empire" in Helena Rosenblatt ed., *The Cambridge Companion to Constant* (Cambridge: Cambridge University Press, 2009), 115–45.

"Empire and Legal Universalism in the Eighteenth Century", *American Historical Review* 117 (2012), 92–121.

Pocock, J. G. A., *Virtue, Commerce and History* (Cambridge: Cambridge University Press, 1985).

"A Discourse on Sovereignty: Observations on the Work in Progress" in Nicholas Phillipson and Quentin Skinner eds., *Political Discourse in Early-Modern Britain* (Cambridge: Cambridge University Press, 1993), 377–428.

*Barbarism and Religion* (Cambridge: Cambridge University Press, 1999).

Pollis, A. and P. Schwab eds., *Human Rights: Cultural and Ideological Perspectives* (New York: Praeger, 1979).

Popkin, Richard, *Isaac La Peyrère (1596–1676): His Life, Work and Influence* (Leiden and New York: Brill, 1987).

Price, Richard, *Political Writings*, D. O. Thomas ed. (Cambridge: Cambridge University Press, 1991).

Prien, Hans-Jürgen, "Las Bulas Alejandrinas de 1493" in Bernd Schröter and Karin Schüller eds., *Tordesillas y sus consequencias: La política de las grandes potencias europeas respecto a América Latina (1494–1898)* (Frankfurt: Vervuet Iberoamericana, 1995), 12–28.

Pufendorf, Samuel, *De iure naturae et gentium libri octo*, C. H. Oldfather and W. A. Oldfather trans. (Oxford: Clarendon Press, 1934).

*On the Duty of Man and Citizen According to Natural Law*, James Tully ed. (Cambridge: Cambridge University Press, 1991).

Purchas, Samuel, *Purchas his Pilgrimes* (London, 1625).

Quesnay, François, *François Quesnay et la physiocratie* (Paris: Institut national d'études demographiques, 1958).

*Rapport fait à l'Assemblée Nationale, sur les colonies, au nom des Comitées de Constitution, de Marine, d'Agriculture, de Commerce et des Colonies, le 23 Septembre, 1791* [Paris].

Rabossi, Eduardo, "La teoría de los derechos humanos naturalizada" *Revista del Centro de Estudios Constitucionales* 5 (1990), 159–79.

Randles, W. G. L., "Classical Models of World Geography and Their Transformation following the Discovery of America" in Wolfgang Haase and Meyer Rheinhold eds., *The Classical Tradition and the Americas* (Berlin and New York: W. de Gruyter, 1993), 5–76.

Raustiala, Kal, *Does the Constitution Follow the Flag? The Evolution of Territoriality in American Law* (Oxford: Oxford University Press, 2009).

Rawls, John, *The Law of Peoples* (Cambridge, MA: Harvard University Press, 1999).

Raynal, Guillaume-Thomas, *Histoire philosophique et politique des établissements et du commerce des Européens dans les deux Indes*, Anthony Strugnell et al. eds. (Paris: Centre International d'Études du XVIIIe siècle, 2010).

Recchia, Stefano and Nadia Urbinati eds., *A Cosmopolitanism of Nations: Giuseppe Mazzini's Writings on Democracy, Nation Building and International Relations* (Princeton: Princeton University Press, 2009).

*Recopilación de leyes de los reynos de las Indias* (Madrid, 1791).

*Records of the Governor and Company of the Massachusetts Bay*, Nathaniel Shurtleff ed. (Boston: William White, 1853–4)

Richardson, W. A. R., "Mercator's Southern Continent; Its Origins, Influence and Gradual Decline", *Terrae Incognitae* 25 (1993), 67–98.

Ripstein, Arthur, *Force and Freedom Kant's Legal and Political Philosophy* (Cambridge, MA: Harvard University Press, 2009).

Rorty, Richard, *Truth and Progress: Philosophical Papers* (Cambridge: Cambridge University Press, 1998).

Rosenblatt, Helena, "Commerce et religion dans le libéralisme de Benjamin Constant, *Commentaire* 26 (2003), 415–26.

Rosenthal, Earl, "*Plus ultra, non plus ultra*, and the Columnar Device of Emperor Charles V", *Journal of the Warburg and Courtauld Institutes* 34 (1971), 204–28.

Rousseau, Jean-Jacques, *Oeuvres complètes*, édition publiée sous la direction de Bernard Gagnebin et Marcel Raymond (Paris: Bibliothèque de la Pléiade, 1964).

Rubies, Joan-Pau, "Hugo Grotius' Dissertation on the Origins of the American Peoples, and the Use of Comparative Method", *Journal of the History of Ideas* 52 (1991), 221–44.

Russell, Frederick H., *The Just War in the Middle Ages* (Cambridge: Cambridge University Press, 1975).

Russett, Bruce and John R. Oneal, *Triangulating Peace: Democracy, Interdependence and International Organizations* (New York: Norton, 2001).

Saavedra Fajardo, Diego, *Empresas políticas: Idea de un príncipe político-cristiano*, A. Vaquero ed. (Madrid: Editorial Nacional, 1976).

Sahagún, Bernardino de, *Historia de las cosas de la Nueva España* (Mexico City: Fondo de Cultura Económica, 1938).

Sahlins, Marshall, *Islands of History* (Chicago: Chicago University Press, 1985).

Schiavone, Aldo, *Ius: L'invenzione del diritto in Occidente* (Turin: Einaudi, 2005).

*Storia e destino* (Turin: Einaudi, 2007).

Schmidt, Benjamin, *Innocence Abroad: The Dutch Imagination and the New World, 1570–1670* (Cambridge: Cambridge University Press, 2001).

Schmitt, Carl, *Land und Meer: Eine weltgeschichtliche Bertracchtung* (Leipzig: Reclam, 1942).

*The Nomos of the Earth in the International Law of the Jus Publicum Europaeum*, G. L. Umen trans. and ed. (New York: Telos Press, 2003).

Schneider. G. and N. P. Gleditsch, "The Capitalist Peace: The Origins and Prospects of a Liberal Idea, *International Interactions* 36 (2010), 107–14

Schofield, Malcolm, "Ideology and Philosophy in Aristotle's Theory of Slavery" in *Saving the City: Philosopher Kings and Other Classical Paradigms* (London: Routledge, 1999), 115–40.

Schumpeter, Joseph, *Imperialism and Social Classes [Zur Soziologie der Imperialismen]*, Heinz Norden trans. (New York: Meridian Books, 1955).

Scott, James Brown, *The Spanish Origin of International Law: Lectures on Francisco de Vitoria (1480–1546) and Francisco Suárez (1548–1617)* (Washington, DC: School of Foreign Service, Georgetown University, [1928]).

Seed, Patricia, *Ceremonies of Possession in Europe's Conquest of the New World, 1492–1640* (Cambridge: Cambridge University Press, 1995).

Seeley, John Robert, *The Expansion of England: Two Courses of Lectures* (London: Macmillan, 1883).

Sepúlveda, Juan Gines de, *Democratus secundus, sive de justis causis belli apud Indos*, in *Democrates Segundo, o justas causas de la Guerra contra los indios*, Angel Losada trans. and ed. (Madrid: Consejo Superior de Investigaciones Científicas, 1951).

Sherwin-White, A. N., *The Roman Citizenship* (Oxford: Oxford University Press, 1973).

Shklar, Judith, "Subversive Genealogies" in *Political Thought and Political Thinkers*, Stanley Hoffman ed. (Chicago: Chicago University Press, 1998), 132–60.

Shue, Henry, *Basic Rights: Substance, Affluence, and U.S. Foreign Policy* (Princeton: Princeton University Press, 1980).

Sicroff, Albert A., *Les controverses des status de "pureté de sang" en Espagne du XIVe au XVIIe siècles* (Paris: Didier, 1960).

Simms, Brendan and D. J. B. Trim eds., *Humanitarian Intervention: A History* (Cambridge: Cambridge University Press, 2011).

Sissa, Giulia, "La Génération automatique" in Barbara Cassin and Jean-Louis Labarrière eds., *L'Animal dans l'antiquité* (Paris: Vrin, 1997).

Smiley, T. S., *Principles and Methods of Colonial Administration, Colson Papers* (London: Butterworth Scientific Publications, 1950).

Smith, Adam, *An Inquiry into the Nature and Causes of the Wealth of Nations*, W. B. Todd ed. (Oxford: Clarendon Press, 1976).

*Essays on Philosophical Subjects* W. P. D. Wightman and J. C. Bryce eds. (Oxford: Oxford University Press, 1980).

*The Correspondence of Adam Smith*, Ernest Campbell Mossner and Ian Simpson Ross eds. (Oxford: Oxford University Press, 1987).

Smith, Joseph Henry, *Appeals to the Privy Council from the American Plantations* (New York: Columbia University Press, 1950).

Solórzano Pereira, Juan de, *Política Indiana*, Francisco Tomás y Valiente y Ana María Barrero eds. (Madrid: Biblioteca Castro, 1996).

Soto, Domingo de, *De iustitia et iure, libri decem* (Salamanca, 1556).

*De legibus. Comentarios al tratado de la ley*, Francisco Puy and Luís Núñez trans. and ed. (Granada: Universidad de Granada, 1965).

Sousa e Alvim, Diogo de, "A Disputa pelo Arquipélago do Pináculo (Senkaku/Diaoyu) Uma Análise Jurídica" (February 27, 2011), available at http://ssrn.com/abstract=1772223.

Stein, J. and Barbara H. Stein, *Silver Trade and War: Spain and America in the Making of Early-Modern Europe* (Baltimore: Johns Hopkins University Press, 2000).

Stein, Peter, "The Development of the Notion of Naturalis Ratio" in A. Watson ed., *Daube Noster: Essays in Legal History for David Daube* (Edinburgh: Edinburgh University Press, 1974), 305–16.

Story, Joseph, *Commentaries on the Constitution of the United States* (Boston, 1891).

Strachey, William, *The Historie of Travell into Virginia Britania*, Louis B. Wright and Virginia Freund eds. (London: Hakluyt Society, 1953).

Straumann, Benjamin, "The Right to Punish as a Just Use of War in Hugo Grotius' Natural Law", *Studies in the History of Ethics* 2 (2006), 1–20.

Stuurman, Siep, "François Bernier and the Invention of Racial Classification", *History Workshop Journal* 50 (2000), 1–21.

Suárez, Francisco, *Opus de triplici virtute theologica: Fide spe et charitate* (Paris, 1611).

    *Disputatio xii. De Bello* [from *Opus de triplice virtute theologica, fide spe et charitate* Paris, 1621] in Luciano Pereña Vicente, *Teoria de la guerra en Francisco Suárez* (Madrid, 1954), II.

    *Tractatus de legibus ac Deo Legislatore* [1612], Luciano Pereña ed. (Madrid: CSIC, 1971).

Swidler, Leonard, "Diritti umani: una panoramica storica" in *Concilium, Rivista internazionale di teologia* 26 (1990), 27–42.

Tanner, Marie, *The Last Descendant of Aeneas: The Habsburgs and the Mythic Image of the Emperor* (New Haven and London: Yale University Press, 1993).

Terjanian, Anoush Fraser, *Commerce and Its Discontents in Eighteenth-Century French Political Thought* (Cambridge: Cambridge University Press, 2013).

Thomas, Rosalind, *Herodotus in Context: Ethnography, Science and the Art of Persuasion* (Cambridge: Cambridge University Press, 2002).

Thomasius, Christian, *Fundamenta juris naturae et gentium ex sensu communi deducta* (Halle, 1718).

*The Three Charters of the Virginia Company of London with Seven Related Documents*, with an introduction by Samuel M. Bemiss (Williamsburg: Jamestown 350th Anniversary Historical Booklets, 1957).

Tierney, Brian, *The Crisis of Church and State 1050–1300* (Toronto: Toronto University Press, 1988).

    *The Idea of Natural Rights Natural Law, and Church Law, 1150–1625* (Atlanta, GA: Scholars Press, 1997).

    "Kant on Property: The Problem of Permissive Law", *Journal of the History of Ideas* 62 (2001), 301–12.

Tocqueville, Alexis de, *L'Ancien régime et la révolution*, François Mélonio (Paris: Flammarion, 1988).

    *Tocqueville sur l'Algérie*, Seloua Luste Boulbina ed. (Paris: Flamarion, 2003).

Todorov, Tzvetan, *Le Nouveau désordre mondial: Réflexions d'un Européen* (Paris: Robert Laffont, 2003).

Trudel, Marcel, *The Beginnings of New France, 1524–1663*, Patricia Claxton trans. (Toronto: Toronto University Press, 1973).

Tuck, Richard, *Natural Rights Theories* (Cambridge: Cambridge University Press, 1979).

    "The 'Modern' Theory of Natural Law" in Anthony Pagden ed., *The Languages of Political Theory in Early-Modern Europe* (Cambridge: Cambridge University Press, 1987), 99–119.

"Rights and Pluralism" in James Tully ed., *Philosophy in an Age of Pluralism: The Philosophy of Charles Taylor in Question* (Cambridge: Cambridge University Press, 1994), 159–70.

*The Rights of War and Peace: Political Thought and the International Order from Grotius to Kant* (Oxford: Oxford University Press, 1999).

"Alliances with Infidels in the European Imperial Expansion" in Sankar Muthu ed., *Empire and Modern Political Thought* (Cambridge: Cambridge University Press, 2012), 61–83.

Tucker, Robert W. and David C. Hendrickson, *Empire of Liberty: The Statecraft of Thomas Jefferson* (Oxford: Oxford University Press, 1990).

Tully, James, *An Approach to Political Philosophy: Locke in Contexts* (Cambridge: Cambridge University Press, 1993).

"Aboriginal Property and Western Theory: Recovering a Middle Ground", *Social Philosophy and Policy* 11 (1994), 153–80.

Tuori, Kaius, "Alberico Gentili and the Criticism of Expansion in the Roman Empire: The Invader's Remorse," *Journal of the History of International Law* 11 (2009), 205–19.

Turgot, Anne-Robert-Jacques, baron de Laune, *Mémoires sur les colonies américaines, sur leurs relations politiques avec leurs métropoles, et sur la maniéré dont la France et l'Espagne on dû envisager les suites de l'indépendance des Etats unis de l'Amérique* [6 April, 1776], (Paris, 1791).

Twiss, Travers, *Two Introductory Lectures on the Science of International Law* (London: Longmans, 1856).

Ullmann, Walter, "Some Observations on the Medieval Evaluation of the 'homo naturalis' and the 'Christianus'" in *L'Homme et son destin d'après les penseurs du moyen âge: Actes du premier congrès international de philosophie médiévale* (Louvain-Paris, 1960), 145–51.

Uztaríz, Gerónimo de, *Theoríca y practica de comercio y de marina* (Madrid, 1724).

Valls, Andrew, "A Lousy Empirical Scientist": Reconsidering Hume's Racism" in Andrew Valls ed., *Race and Racism in Modern Philosophy* (Cornell: Cornell University Press, 2005), 127–49.

Van Ittersum, Martine Julia, *Profit and Principle: Hugo Grotius, Natural Rights Theories and the Rise of Dutch Power in the East Indies (1595–1615)* (Leiden-Boston: Brill, 2006).

Vattel, Emer de, *Le Droit des gens, et les devoirs des citoyens, ou principe de la loi naturelle* (Nimes, 1793).

*The Law of Nations or, Principles of the Law of Nature*, Béla Kapossy and Richard Whatmore eds. (Indianapolis: Liberty Fund, 2008).

Vázquez de Menchaca, Fernando, *Controversiarum illustrium aliarumque usu frequentium, libri tres* [1563], Fidel Rodriguez Alcalde ed. (Valladolid,1931–5).

Vico, Giambattista, *Opere*, F. Nicolini ed. (Bari: Laterza, 1911–41).

Vieira, Mónica Brito, "*Mare Liberum* vs. *Mare Clausum*: Grotius, Freitas, and Selden's Debate on Dominion over the Seas", *Journal of the History of Ideas* 63 (2003), 361–77.

Villey, Michel, "La genèse du droit subjectif chez Guillaume d'Ockham" in *Archives de la philosophie du droit*, 9 (1969), 97–127.

*Philosophie du droit* (Paris: Dalloz, 1982).

Viscardo, Juan Pablo, *Carta derijida [sic] a los Españoles Americanos por uno de sus compatriotas* (London, 1801).

Vitoria, Francisco de, *De Justitia*, Vicente Beltrán de Heredia ed. (Salamanca, 1932). *Comentarios a la Secunda Secundae de Santo Tomás*, Vicente Beltrán de Heredia ed. (Salamanca: Biblioteca de teólogos españoles, 1934).

*Vitoria: Political Writings*, Anthony Pagden and Jeremy Lawrance trans. and eds. (Cambridge: Cambridge University Press, 1991).

Von der Heydte, Friedrich August, "Discovery, Symbolic Annexation and Virtual Effectiveness in International Law," *American Journal of International Law* 29 (1935), 448–71.

Wagner, Andreas, "Francisco de Vitoria and Alberico Gentili on the Legal Character of the Global Commonwealth", *Oxford Journal of Legal Studies* 31:3 (2011), 565–82.

Waldron, Jeremy, "Kant's Theory of the State" in Pauline Kleingeld ed., *Towards Perpetual Peace and Other Writings on Politics, Peace and History*, (New Haven and London: Yale University Press, 2006), 194–7.

Ward, Robert, *An Enquiry into the Foundations of the Laws of Nations in Europe from the Time of the Greeks and Romans to the Age of Grotius* (London, 1795).

Williams, Bernard, *Shame and Necessity*. (Berkeley, Los Angeles, and Oxford: California University Press, 1993), 110–16.

Williams, Gwyn A., *Madoc: The Legend of the Welsh Discovery of America* (London: Methuen, 1979).

Wolff, Christian, *Jus gentium methodo scientifica pertractatum* (Oxford: Clarendon Press, 1934).

Wood, Gordon, *The Creation of the American Republic 1776–1787* (New York and London: W.W. Norton, 1972).

Wright, Quincy, "The Goa Incident", *American Journal of International Law* 56 (1962), 626–37.

Yirush, Craig, *Settlers, Liberty and Empire: The Roots of Early American Political Theory 1675–1775* (Cambridge: Cambridge University Press, 2011).

Young, Arthur, *Political Essays Concerning the Present State of the British Empire* (London, 1772).

Zakaria, Fareed, "A Conversation with Lee Kuan Yew", *Foreign Affairs* 73 (1994), 109–26.

Zielonka, Jan, *Europe as Empire: The Nature of the Enlarged European Union* (Oxford: Oxford University Press, 2006).

# Index

Printed in the United States
By Bookmasters